D1020772

Sensitivity to Nonverbal Communication

Sensitivity to Nonverbal Communication

THE PONS TEST

ROBERT ROSENTHAL   JUDITH A. HALL   M. ROBIN DiMATTEO
PETER L. ROGERS   DANE ARCHER

THE JOHNS HOPKINS UNIVERSITY PRESS
Baltimore and London

BF
637
C45
S43

Copyright © 1979 by The Johns Hopkins University Press

All rights reserved. No part of this book may be
reproduced or transmitted in any form or by any means,
electronic or mechanical, including photocopying,
recording, xerography, or any information storage and
retrieval system, without permission in writing
from the publisher.

Manufactured in the United States of America

The Johns Hopkins University Press, Baltimore, Maryland 21218
The Johns Hopkins Press Ltd., London

Library of Congress Catalog Card Number 78-17322
ISBN 0-8018-2159-2

Library of Congress Cataloging in Publication data
will be found on the last printed page of this book.

For Mari M. Tavitian

51429

91192

Contents

Figures

Tables

Preface

This book tells the results of a program of research on nonverbal communication that was begun in 1971 and is still in progress. The purpose of our research program was to learn about the ability to understand or decode nonverbal cues transmitted by facial expressions, body movements, and tones of voice. Earlier research on the effects of teacher expectations on pupils' intellectual development and on the effects of experimenter expectations on subjects' responses in behavioral research had shown that our understanding of these self-fulfilling prophecies might depend on our ability to measure sensitivity to nonverbal cues. But no multichannel instrument was available to permit the measurement of individual differences in sensitivity to these cues.

One part of our research program, then, was to develop an instrument for the simultaneous assessment of such channels of nonverbal communication as facial expressions, body (and arm) movements, facial and body cues combined, and tones of voice as measured in two very different ways. The three visual channels could each be combined with the two auditory channels to yield six audiovisual channels. The nonverbal decoding ability of any person or group could be described in terms of the profile of scores on the five "pure" channels and the six "mixed" channels. Because of the profile nature of the assessment, we called the test the Profile of Nonverbal Sensitivity, or the PONS test.

This book is addressed to social and behavioral scientists, their students, and those whose applied work can profit from a better understanding of interpersonal relationships, such as practitioners in education, medicine, counseling, and management. It is not intended to be the central text for any course unless that course deals primarily with the measurement of sensitivity to nonverbal communication. This book is intended, however, to be a supplementary text in courses in departments of psychology, sociology, anthropology, communication, and speech.

One way in which this book differs from most other empirically oriented works in the behavioral and social sciences is in its strong emphasis on effect sizes. Only rarely have we been content here to specify that a relationship was statistically significant. Whenever we could, we have tried to make it clear how large an effect was. Sometimes in the social and behavioral sciences one gets a good idea of the effect sizes from the "raw" data, but more often a standard index is required to allow a judgment of the size of any effect or relationship. Usually we employ correlational indices or standard deviation units as our measures of effect size (Cohen 1969). We believe that all social and behavioral scientists should give an estimate of effect size for every result reported. Also, for readers unfamiliar with the various statistical tests and indices employed, we have always tried to describe findings verbally so that the results will be clear.

The research on which this book is based was supported by awards by the National Science Foundation, the John Simon Guggenheim Memorial Foundation, the Australian American Educational Foundation, and by the Milton Fund of Harvard University grant to the first author and the Biomedical Research Support Grant of The Johns Hopkins University to the second author.

Many people have helped us in the collection of data for this book and in other important ways. We have tried to be conscientious in thanking these gracious collaborators, and many are acknowledged in the text itself when their contribution is described. But we may well have failed to be exhaustive, and we apologize to those whose names have inadvertently been omitted from the list we thank so gratefully: John Adair, Ray Adams, Mary Fran Archer, Elizabeth Ashburn, Mick Bennett, William Berkowitz, Ron Bernheim, Edward Blacker, Deena Bloch, Chris Brand, Tanis Bryan, Ross Buck, Jim Burruss, John Carroll, E. Casas, Tony Castelnovo, Patricia Clarity, Robert Clark, Alex Clarke, Leo Cohen, Anne Conway, Geoff Coyne, Beverly Crane, Charles Dailey, Mrs. Carl Davis, Dan Davis, Ray Debus, Bella DePaulo, Angeline DiMatteo, Barbara Domangue, Mervyn Dunkley, David Efron, Barry Ekman, Ralph Exline, Lauri Fidell, Martha Finn, Chantal Fisch, Karen Fischer, John Fitzpatrick, Susan Frank, Malcolm Gordon, Janice Gorn, Paul Guild, Madeleine Hall, Brian Hansford, Jeremy Harbison, Ruth Harrison, Terry Haubenhofer, Roberta Rosenthal Hawkins, Rae Hensley, Nancy Hirschberg, Chuck Hill, the Hope House of Boston, Lenore Jacobson, Ron Johnson, James Jones, Max Kelley, Wes Kilham, Judy Kleinfeld, George Klemp, Elaine Koivumaki, Vic Koivumaki, Dennis Krebs, Jim Lester, Helmut Lück, Jack Lyle, Russell Mack, Leon Mann, Jack Manual, Sarah Matthews, John Mayfield, Alex McAndrew, David McClelland, Bob McCoid, Mordechai Mordechai, Steve Morse, Roy Nash, Jim O'Neil, Lee Owens, Trude Parzen, Dan Perschonok, Gordon Persinger, William Person, Frankie Phillips, Ruth Pinnas, Bill Pitty, The Proposition, Boyd Purdom, Charles Reavis, John Reynolds, Ken Rogers, Suzi Rogers, Marylu Clayton Rosenthal, Ann Ruben, Zick Rubin, Ross St. George, Klaus Scherer, Claire Schmais, Eileen Schrecongost, Jerrold Shapiro, Gloria Shoemaker, Ian Smith, Dottie Stafford, Alfred Stanton, Ray Stroobant, Angelo Taranta, Mari

Tavitian, William Taylor, Richard Thompson, Ray Tongue, Eric Wanner, Alf Webster, Tom Williams, Myron Wish, Laurence Wylie, Innes Yates, Paul Yelsma, and Miron Zuckerman. For his careful reading and his valuable suggestions for the improvement of the entire manuscript, we are particularly grateful to Donald W. Fiske. Finally, we would like to thank Wendy Harris of The Johns Hopkins University Press for her good judgment and skill in editing our long manuscript.

The typing of the book in its various incarnations was superbly rendered by Mari M. Tavitian, who served not so much as typist but as midwife to the book. It is for these things and for all she has done for all of us that we dedicate this book to her.

Harvard University	ROBERT ROSENTHAL
The Johns Hopkins University	JUDITH A. HALL*
University of California, Riverside	M. ROBIN DiMATTEO
Harvard University	PETER L. ROGERS
University of California, Santa Cruz	DANE ARCHER

*Formerly Judith H. Koivumaki

Sensitivity to Nonverbal Communication

1 | Introduction

Although nonverbal communication plays a central role in human behavior, it remains far from well understood. We have just begun to learn about the ways in which our nonverbal behavior affects other people, about differences among people in their abilities to understand and convey nonverbal messages, and about the ways in which such differences matter to people's lives.

There are several reasons why our knowledge about nonverbal behavior is so incomplete. One explanation has to do with the strong verbal orientation of our society. For example, schools in our culture teach children that communication is equivalent to the successful use of words. There are other, more subtle reasons for our lack of formal knowledge in the area of nonverbal behavior. Different types of nonverbal communication are so embedded in our daily lives that we use the nonverbal messages without being aware of them. When we form an opinion of what someone is like, for example, the opinion is probably based in part upon a complex analysis of nonverbal information. When we conclude that someone we have just met is angry or jealous or anxious to leave, we may have reached this conclusion as much by listening to the person's tone of voice and by observing how agitated the person's movements were, or by forming an impression of the warmth of his or her facial expression, as by interpreting what was actually said.

Even though we use nonverbal cues every time we meet or talk with someone, we are generally unable to describe the cues we employ. Instead, if asked why we reached an opinion about someone, we are likely to say that it was just a "feeling," or that there was "something" about the way the person acted. And yet, we are intuitively aware that we perceive (often accurately) an enormous number of nonverbal messages. This "tacit knowledge" (Polanyi 1962) paradox of being able to use nonverbal cues that we cannot describe was what the anthropologist Edward Sapir had in mind when he said that people could understand gestures because of "an elaborate and secret code that is written nowhere, known by none, and understood by all" (1949).

These factors have limited the discussion of the role of nonverbal behavior

1

in everyday life and also produced a relative neglect of this area in social science research. The scientific study of nonverbal communication has, in addition, met substantial methodological barriers. Unlike attitudes or other types of verbal behavior, nonverbal communication has in the past been very difficult to record, code, analyze, and reproduce. The development and diffusion of film and videotape technology have produced a recent and marked increase of investigation in this area.

Research on nonverbal communication has also been complicated by the wide range of behaviors that are, at least in some way, nonverbal. Nonverbal behavior includes (at least) facial expressions, head nods, eye movements, body movements, hand gestures, postures, and tones of voice. These different levels of nonverbal communication are often operationally called "channels." Many different channels are often involved in even the simplest communication. If we see someone admonishing a child, for example, we may simultaneously detect displeasure in the voice, a disapproving facial expression, a warning hand gesture, and so on. There are exceptions, of course, to simultaneous channel involvement, as in telephone conversations, when we have only auditory cues (tones of voice, speech hesitations, accent, and so on). In face-to-face interactions, however, we are generally presented with a virtual symphony of different nonverbal cues. The complexity and redundancy of much of this nonverbal communication complicate research by making it difficult to study exactly what is being done nonverbally, which cues are most important, and variations in people's skills in sending and judging nonverbal messages.

Most research that has been done in the nonverbal area falls into two major categories outlined in a classic paper by Duncan (1969). These are the "structural" and the "external variable" approaches.

Structuralists view nonverbal communication as roughly analogous to verbal communication. Researchers of this type (for example, Birdwhistell [1970]; Scheflen [1972, 1974]) seek to uncover the internal rules and units of nonverbal communication much as a linguist would do in the study of a verbal language. This approach is largely descriptive, relying on observational rather than experimental data. Its major thrust is that nonverbal language is learned early and is culturally determined, and that a great deal of what transpires between individuals and groups is predetermined, even rituallike, in its regularity.

The external variable approach involves looking for systematic relationships (both within and between persons) between nonverbal behavior and psychological states, or between nonverbal behavior and the perception of meaning (see Exline [1972]; Ekman, Friesen, and Ellsworth [1972]). Researchers using this approach might ask what meanings are conveyed by various facial expressions, how variations in nonverbal behavior (such as eye contact or interpersonal distance) can affect interpersonal relationships, and whether the meanings attributed to different nonverbal behaviors are the same in different cultures. Of course, these particular questions are merely illustrative of the kinds of relational questions dealt with in this social psychological tradition.

In a third and more recent approach to the study of nonverbal communication, researchers focus primarily on individual differences in nonverbal behavior and secondarily on regularities across people or groups. This is a more personality-oriented approach, since it looks at aspects of nonverbal behavior—skill or style—that are considered to be somewhat enduring characteristics of a person. The research reported in this book falls into this category, for it deals with individual differences in people's skill at judging the meanings of nonverbal expressions. In subsequent chapters, we will be presenting results of a seven-year program of research on the judging of nonverbal cues conveyed by the face, body, and voice tone channels. This research has been centered on a film test we developed called the Profile of Nonverbal Sensitivity, or PONS.

The study of the decoding of nonverbal cues is not new. Many efforts have been made in the past to assess the accuracy of judgments of nonverbal cues defined both broadly and narrowly. Research on social intelligence (Walker and Foley 1973), empathy (Campbell, Kagan, and Krathwohl 1971), judging personality (Cline 1964), and person perception (Tagiuri 1969) all involve the decoding of nonverbal cues to varying degrees. Such decoding is often mixed to an unknown extent with other skills and behaviors, such as ability to judge contextual or situational cues, knowledge of personal dispositions, wisdom in choosing one's social responses, and various motivational states. Decoding strictly nonverbal cues also has a long history of study, and in fact is one of the oldest traditions in social psychology (e.g., Allport 1924). We hope that our research adds something new in its emphasis on individual differences and in its systematic attempt to develop and validate an instrument for assessing these individual differences.

We feel an important obstacle in investigating nonverbal communication has been the absence of standardized measures of individual accuracy in interpreting and conveying nonverbal cues in various channels. Obviously, well-validated measures of decoding and encoding skills would make it much easier to study individual differences in nonverbal skills, individual differences in the use of various channels of communication, sex differences in nonverbal abilities, nonverbal abilities in special groups and occupations, cross-cultural differences, and so on. Researchers interested in these kinds of questions have had to make up their own measuring instruments, often on an ad hoc basis and often without having time and resources to devote to establishing their validity. The absence of standard measures has also, of course, made it hard to study the correlates of these skills. Without such measures, it is difficult to learn whether people with developed nonverbal skills differ from other people and if so, in what ways. It would be important to know, for example, whether those who are better at sending or receiving nonverbal cues are more successful, better liked, more intelligent, better leaders, more artistic, and so on.

Actually, the PONS test grew not only out of our interest in individual differences per se but also out of a desire to understand the variables that may moderate interpersonal outcomes of many sorts. The immediate context of this interest was research on the effect of teachers' expectations on the performance of their pupils and the effect of experimenters' expectations on the behavior of their research subjects (Rosenthal 1966, 1967, 1971, 1976; Rosenthal and Jacobson 1968). This research has shown that one's expectations for the behavior of other people can unintentionally influence those other people to change their behavior in the direction of those expectations, that is, that expectations can become a self-fulfilling prophecy.

Although the processes by which these expectations operate are not well understood, there is some reason to think that the effect is mediated by various types of nonverbal communication (Adair and Epstein 1968; Duncan and Rosenthal 1968; Rosenthal 1969; Rosenthal and Fode 1963; Troffer and Tart 1964; Zoble and Lehman 1969). A teacher might communicate high expectations for a given pupil, for example, in the tone of voice used when speaking to him or her in class. Unless the pupil is sensitive to the nonverbal qualities of the teacher's voice, the unintended message may go unnoticed. But if the pupil is sensitive to paralanguage, he or she may be influenced to change his or her performance in the direction of the teacher's expectation (Conn, Edwards, Rosenthal, and Crowne 1968; Rosenthal 1971, 1974).

Teachers undoubtedly vary, like other people, in the clarity of their nonverbal encoding in different nonverbal channels. Pupils also vary, like other people, in their decoding ability or sensitivity to nonverbal communication in different nonverbal channels. Variations in these nonverbal abilities might determine the outcome of an interaction between two people. It might be, for example, that teachers whose best encoding channel is vocal would be most effective with pupils whose best decoding channel is auditory. Similarly, teachers who are most expressive in the facial channel might be most effective with pupils who are best at decoding faces. Teachers might be less effective, of course, if their best encoding channel did not correspond to a pupil's best decoding channel.

Ultimately, then, what we would want would be a series of accurate measurements for each person describing his or her relative ability to send and to receive in each of a variety of channels of nonverbal communication. It seems reasonable to suppose that if we had this information for two or more people we would be better able to predict the outcome of their interaction regardless of whether the focus of the analysis were on the mediation of interpersonal expectations or on some other interpersonal transaction.

Our model envisages people moving through their "social spaces" carrying two vectors or profiles of scores. One of these vectors describes the person's differential clarity in sending messages over various channels of nonverbal communication. The other vector describes the person's differential sensitivity to messages sent over various channels of nonverbal communication. Diagrammatically for any given dyad:

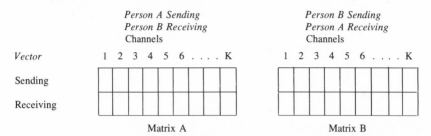

Within each of the two matrices the scores on sending channels of the sender can be correlated with the scores on receiving channels of the receiver. A higher correlation reflects a greater potential for more accurate communication between the dyad members, since the receiver is then better at receiving the channels that are the more accurately encoded channels of the sender. The mean (arithmetic, geometric, or harmonic) of the correlations between matrix A and matrix B reflects how well the dyad members "understand" or decode each other's communications. That mean correlation need not reflect how well the dyad members like each other, however, only that A and B should more quickly understand each other's intended and unintended messages, including how they feel about one another. Although a high mean correlation of channel scores may be an indication of a high degree of efficiency in dyadic communication, excellent communication could also take place between people who show little profile similarity but who may be *uniformly* good senders and receivers of nonverbal cues.

The original idea for the PONS test grew out of this framework. We believed that our predictions about the outcome of an interaction between two people, whether in an expectancy situation or some other setting, would be improved if we had information about the decoding and encoding abilities of the participants. A well-validated measure of encoding has not yet been developed, partly because of methodological difficulties. The PONS test as a measure of decoding is therefore only a first step in our ability to test the hypotheses presented above. As background to a review of earlier research and a discussion of the advantages and limitations of the PONS design, we will provide a brief description of the test and how it works. In Chapter 2, the development and format of the PONS test are reported in detail.

The PONS test is about forty-five minutes long and consists of 220 two-second segments of an encoder's nonverbal behavior. These segments or items are presented in what we call channels; for example, one item will show only the person's face on the screen, a second item will show only the person's body from the neck down, a third item will not have any visual content but only the emotional tone of the person's voice, and so on.

The PONS test isolates eleven nonverbal channels. Three of these are "pure" visual channels: (1) the *face*; (2) the *body* from the neck to the knees; and (3) the *entire figure* (face and body down to the knees). An additional two channels are "pure" auditory channels that use two very different techniques to disguise the words spoken, but preserve other aspects of "paralanguage," such as tone of voice, pitch, and affect: (4) *randomized spliced voice,* a random scrambling of the speaker's taped voice; and (5) *content-filtered voice,* an electronic treatment that removes the high frequencies that help identify specific words. These two auditory channels make it impossible to tell exactly *what* a peson is saying, but still make it possible for some decoders to tell the *way* it is said—friendly, hostile, soft, loud, etc. In addition to these five pure channels, the PONS film contains an additional six channels. These extra channels are the paired combinations of a single visual channel with a single auditory channel: (6) *face + randomized spliced voice;* (7) *face + content-filtered voice;* (8) *body + randomized spliced voice;* (9) *body + content-filtered voice;* (10) *figure + randomized spliced voice;* and (11) *figure + content-filtered voice.*

Some photographic examples of the PONS channels may be helpful. In figure 1.1, the three visual channels are illustrated with still photographs. Two photographs show the encoder's face only, two show the encoder's body, and two show the encoder's entire figure. Naturally, these still photographs do not indicate the movement contained in the two-second-long PONS sequences, each of which contains forty-eight individual frames. Unfortunately, it is also impossible to provide examples of the two PONS auditory channels.

The eleven individual PONS channels were created by simultaneously recording the encoder with three videotape cameras. One camera focused on the encoder's face, the second focused on the encoder's body between the neck and the knees, and the third focused on the encoder's entire figure down to about the knees. At the same time that the three cameras were videotaping the encoder, sound recordings were made that were later modified to form the two auditory channels.

The encoder in the PONS test is shown expressing 20 different affective or emotional situations. These scenes cover a wide range of affects, ranging from relatively subtle emotions (e.g., "expressing motherly love") to more dramatic affects (e.g., "threatening someone"). Each of the 20 scenes appears eleven times in the PONS film, once in each of the eleven PONS channels. This creates a total of 220 scenes, which occur in a random order in the film.

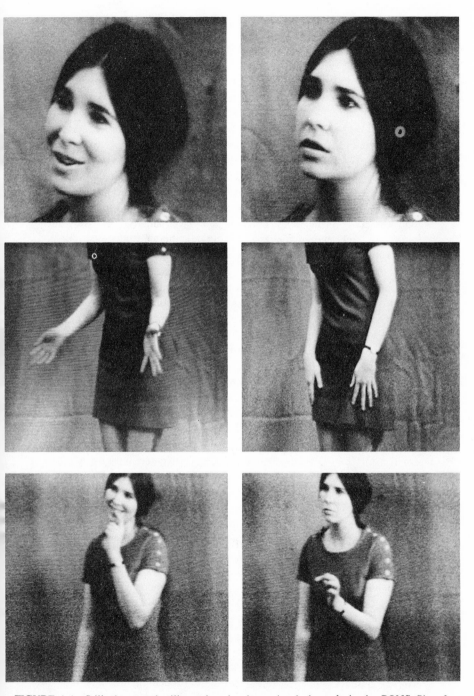

FIGURE 1.1. Still photographs illustrating the three visual channels in the PONS film: face, body, and figure

A person being tested with the PONS watches and/or hears each item and then tries to identify or decode it. This is done using a multiple-choice format on a four-page answer sheet. The viewer chooses from two alternate descriptions, one of which is correct, of the item just seen and/or heard. For a given item, for example, the test taker is asked to choose between two descriptions of what the person in the item is doing—e.g., (A) nagging a child, or (B) expressing jealous anger.

One important feature of the test is its division of the same nonverbal behavior into different channels. The channels make it possible to assess the accuracy of a person on different nonverbal channels, as well as their general decoding ability on the entire PONS test. This enables us to compare individuals (or entire groups) not only on their total accuracy but also on the "profile" of their accuracy on the eleven PONS channels. For example, three people with the same PONS total score could have quite different decoding abilities: one person might be most accurate in reading faces, the second person might be poor at reading faces but very good at decoding bodies, and the third person might be a poor judge of visual behavior but a very accurate judge of voices.

It is because of this channel feature, which makes it possible to assess the profile of a person's decoding accuracy on eleven different channels, that we named the test the Profile of Nonverbal Sensitivity. In addition, it should be noted that the word "sensitivity" in the name of the film is used only in the dictionary sense of a person's "reception of sense impressions" and not that he or she is necessarily "sensitive" in any other sense (that is, artistic, warm, easily offended, etc.).

Subsequent chapters in this book report results of a seven-year program of research using the PONS test and our attempts to integrate this research into what is already known about sensitivity to nonverbal cues. Our first responsibility as test developers has been to determine whether our measuring instrument is a valid indicator of the construct "sensitivity to nonverbal cues." In the process of studying the characteristics of our test, we feel we have learned a great deal about nonverbal sensitivity in addition to learning about our test. We hope that future researchers, using the PONS as well as other and better nonverbal instruments, will continue to explore more deeply the many areas that we have been able to treat only superficially.

Our studies have attempted to address some new and some classic questions, including:

1. Are women more accurate decoders than men?
2. Are members of certain professions (e.g., actors, psychologists) exceptionally good at decoding emotions?
3. Are parents better nonverbal decoders as a result of interaction with their prelanguage children?
4. Are members of different cultures able to interpret the same nonverbal behavior with equal accuracy?

5. Is nonverbal decoding correlated with general intelligence or other cognitive skills?
6. Are people accurate judges of their own nonverbal sensitivity?
7. Does nonverbal sensitivity decrease or increase with age?
8. Are people handicapped in vision or in hearing more sensitive, as a result, in other sensory channels?
9. Are there personality correlates of individual differences in sensitivity?
10. Can nonverbal sensitivity be trained or increased?
11. Are psychiatric patient populations unusually sensitive or insensitive in some nonverbal channels?
12. Can people decode emotions accurately from extremely fleeting nonverbal cues?
13. Does sensitivity predict success—for instance, are better decoders more popular or more effective in their work?

Based on our research with the PONS test, we have tried to present answers to these and other questions. These answers are sometimes strong and unequivocal, sometimes weak and tentative. In subsequent chapters our findings concerning each of these questions, as well as many others, will be presented. It is our hope that the results of this research with the PONS film will contribute to the development of knowledge and theory about the interpretation of nonverbal communication and that it will serve as an introduction to a specific instrument that may prove to be of value to other investigators.

BRIEF OVERVIEW OF DECODING RESEARCH

The PONS research is not the first effort to study the decoding of emotions conveyed via nonverbal cues. The scientific study of decoding probably began with Charles Darwin. Most of Darwin's 1872 book, *The Expression of Emotions in Man and Animals,* was devoted to his conclusions about the nature and origins of emotional expressions, and particularly about the muscular movements that accompany facial expressions. In addition, however, Darwin also reported the results of some more or less systematic efforts to see whether or not facial expressions could be reliably interpreted.

He used photographs published in 1862 by a French anatomist named Duchenne that showed the face of a man being stimulated by "galvanism" (electricity); the man's face is visibly distorted. Darwin showed the photographs to several people he knew, and asked them to identify the emotion on the man's face.

Since Darwin's informal decoding study, many writers have been interested in the expression of emotion (e.g., Tomkins 1962) and many researchers have studied the kinds of information that can be inferred from photographs and other samples of nonverbal expression (e.g., Izard 1971). Fairly detailed reviews of research on the decoding of various types of nonverbal stimuli are

contained in works by Argyle (1975); Cook (1971); Davitz (1964); Ekman
(1973); Ekman, Friesen, and Ellsworth (1972); Knapp (1972); and Tagiuri
(1969). There are also a number of anthologies that include research reports
on decoding and other aspects of nonverbal behavior, and these include two
collections edited by Hinde (1972) and Weitz (1974).

In view of the availability of these reviews and collections, we will only
provide very brief summaries of the current state of decoding research, focus-
ing on types of methods and instruments and not attempting an exhaustive
review of substantive findings. (Reviews of particular topical areas can be
found in various chapters of this book.) In addition, our review here will be
confined to studies of the decoding of emotions or personal states from nonverbal sources, since that has been the focus of the PONS research program.
Much decoding research, including some reviewed or reprinted in the vol-
umes cited above, has been concerned with the judging of other kinds of
information—for example, personality variables, whether a person is lying, a
person's age and social class, and so on. Our brief review considers decoding
studies of emotion in the face, the body, and the voice, and also discusses
some general characteristics of decoding research.

FACE. A great many researchers have continued Darwin's interest in the
face and, as a result, the face has been the most studied of all nonverbal
channels. Until recently, decoding studies of the face have mainly used still
photographs and, in a few cases, drawings. Studies have varied widely in the
sources from which their photographs were taken. Some studies have used
posed facial expressions and some have used spontaneous or experimentally
induced facial expressions.

The procedure followed in most decoding studies has been to show the
photographs of facial expressions to a group of judges. The judges are asked
to identify the emotion in the photographs, using a multiple-choice format,
free description, or some set of rating scales. The criterion of accuracy in
these judgment studies has depended upon the source of the photographs used.
In studies using posed emotions, of course, the criterion of accuracy has been
whatever emotion the encoder intended to communicate. In studies with experimentally induced emotions, the criterion of accuracy has been inferred a
priori from the situation that produced the facial expression.

The reactions of judges in these decoding studies are then analyzed to see
whether the judges have been able to identify the facial expressions accurately, whether some emotions are more difficult to recognize than others, and
so on. In some of these research designs, there are a number of difficult
methodological problems inherent in trying to decide whether judges have
succeeded better than chance. In addition, if the judges are asked to indicate
their choices using a multiple-choice format, their accuracy level will obviously be affected by how similar or different the alternative items are (Knapp
1972, p. 122; chapters 3 and 12 below).

The earliest decoding studies continued Darwin's interest in whether a wide range of facial expressions could, in fact, be recognized (Hastorf, Schneider, and Polefka 1970). One of these was done by Feleky (1914), who was herself photographed while portraying a wide range of emotions. She showed these photographs to judges, who were asked to label the expressions by choosing from a list of emotions. Feleky found considerable variation among emotions; some seemed to be recognized consistently (e.g., surprise), while others seemed to elicit inconsistent responses (e.g., hate). In a reanalysis of these data, however, Woodworth (1938) found that the mistakes made by Feleky's judges involved synonymous or similar emotions. For example, anger and determination tended to be confused, as did fear and suffering. This research produced an interest in whether there were underlying dimensions of emotions that affected how easily different emotions could be distinguished. Different dimensional systems of describing emotions in this sense have been suggested by Schlosberg (1954) and by Osgood (1966).

Perhaps the best-known contemporary decoding studies using posed facial expressions have been those of Paul Ekman and his colleagues (Ekman, Friesen, and Ellsworth 1972; Ekman 1973). Ekman and his colleagues have considered a wide range of questions about the expression of emotions in the face. These have included studies of the number and range of possible facial expressions, of the specific facial muscles accompanying the expression of different emotions, of the degree to which posed photographs can be decoded by judges from different cultures (see chapter 9 below), and of the interpretability of facial cues in psychiatric and clinical settings. This research has even produced a practical manual to assist readers in recognizing emotions from facial expressions (Ekman and Friesen 1975).

Studies using spontaneous emotions are less common than studies using posed emotions, undoubtedly because posed photographs are easier to obtain. Most of the studies using induced emotions have tried to produce "real" emotions by various experimental techniques. For example, Dunlap (1927) used a range of manipulations, many of them raising ethical questions among contemporary social researchers, to elicit and photograph strong emotions. For example, a pistol was fired behind the heads of unsuspecting subjects to produce a startled look and hypnotized subjects were told that members of their family had been killed in a wreck to produce an expression of intense grief. Somewhat less extreme manipulations were used to induce emotions by Landis (1924), who photographed subjects in various activities. These included looking at pictures of nudes, receiving electric shocks (the technique used by Duchenne to produce the pictures Darwin used), and decapitating a live rat. Photographs of spontaneous emotional expressions have also been used from "real," nonlaboratory settings. For example, Munn (1940) reported a study on judging facial expressions using pictures taken from photographic news magazines.

Almost all decoding studies have used still photographs. This is unfortunate, since there is evidence that films and videotapes produce much higher levels of decoding accuracy (Knapp 1972, p. 125; Gitter, Kozel, and Mostofsky 1972). Some of the disadvantages of using still photographs include: (1) the inability of judges to see how long an expression lasts; (2) possible confusion between permanent facial features (e.g., a "permanent frown") and temporary emotional expressions; and (3) the absence of the successions or blends of different emotions as they occur in real life. All of these factors argue strongly for the use of filmed or videotaped emotions in preference to still photographs.

Like decoding studies using photographs, studies using films or videotapes have used posed or spontaneous expressions, or both. Some studies have used both still and moving stimuli. For example, Gitter, Kozel, and Mostofsky (1972) compared decoding accuracy for still versus moving faces, in two posed conditions: still photographs and ten-second segments of 16 mm film. Perhaps not surprisingly, the filmed expressions produced significantly higher decoding accuracy than the still photographs. Earlier workers, too, had found higher decoding accuracy for film than for still photographs (e.g., Frijda 1953).

Film studies of unposed emotions have either recorded the reactions of subjects to specific stimuli (e.g., filming the faces of people reacting to slides) or else filmed people in interviews or in spontaneous interaction. An example of the first design is a study by Buck et al. (1972), in which subjects were covertly videotaped as they watched different types of slides—scenic pictures, disgusting pictures, etc. The researchers then assessed the decodability of these tapes by playing them to judges who were asked to guess which types of slides had produced the facial expressions.

At this time, the relationship between the accuracy of decoding posed and spontaneous emotions or situations remains somewhat unclear. At least one researcher (Tagiuri 1969) reported that decoding levels are more accurate with posed photographs than with photographs of spontaneous or "real" emotion; and Zuckerman, Hall, DeFrank, and Rosenthal (1976) found decoding of posed videotaped affects to be more accurate than decoding of spontaneous videotaped affects (using the same senders in both conditions). They found, however, that accuracy of decoding spontaneous sending (videotapes of faces) was highly correlated with accuracy of decoding posed sending ($r = .58$, $p <$ .001), suggesting that although there may be a difference in the overall accuracy obtained in the two modes, judges performing well in one mode are quite likely to perform well in the other mode.

Differences in accuracy of decoding between posed and spontaneous emotions may have to do with cultural "display rules," which influence people to try to conceal certain expressions (Ekman and Friesen 1969a). For example, some of the subjects who were asked to decapitate a rat in the study by Landis (1924) apparently smiled, perhaps because they were trying to conceal the stress or disgust that the experience probably caused. Compared to posed sending, therefore, spontaneous facial sending may be more likely to contain unexpected expressions or curious blends of different emotions.

BODY. The decodability of the body's emotional expressions has not been researched as thoroughly as that of the face. Some reviews of work in this area are given by Cook (1971), Knapp (1972), and Harrison (1974). Most research on the body has been concerned with one or more of the following discrete behaviors: (1) *hand and arm gestures,* (2) *body positions* and *posture* (as recorded, for example, by still photographs), and (3) *body movements* (as recorded by film and videotape).

Some research on hand and arm gestures has concerned these behaviors as communicating specific ideas or intents (e.g., the "OK" gesture) or as accompanying conversation. In terms of one classifying system, that of Ekman and Friesen (1969*b*), most research on gestures has focused on their use as emblems, illustrators, regulators, and adaptors of conversation.

On the basis of their results, some researchers have concluded that body position is a much poorer guide to an encoder's emotion than his or her facial expression. Ekman (1965) concluded from a study in which photographs of the head, body, and head plus body were judged that the face communicates the specific emotion being experienced, while body positions are likely to communicate the intensity of the feeling. In another study, Dittmann, Parloff, and Boomer (1965) used a film of a woman during an interview. The film was shown to judges in two conditions: with only the woman's face showing, and with only the woman's body showing. The researchers found that the judges decoded the presence of negative emotions from the body less accurately than from the face.

Other researchers have speculated about the kinds of affective information that can be decoded from the body. For example, Ekman and Friesen (1969*a*) studied ratings of filmed facial and body expressions in interviews with psychiatric patients. Using independent sources of information, the researchers identified cases where the patients were trying to conceal their true emotions. Ekman and Friesen found that the ratings of body movement were better clues to deceptive behavior than were ratings of facial behavior. This finding led Ekman and Friesen to conclude that the *least* effective encoding channels (feet and legs) are the *best* channels to use when looking for "leakage"—nonverbal cues to deception.

VOICE. Research on decoding emotion from the voice has faced one difficult problem not encountered by researchers of the face or body. This has been the need to disentangle the nonverbal and verbal elements of speech. In a judgment study, for example, it would be a rare judge who could not correctly identify the emotion in a speaker's voice if the speaker's words were known—e.g., "I hate you" said in any angry voice. A review of this issue in voice research is given by Kramer (1963).

Researchers have developed a number of strategies to solve this problem. These strategies have been of three general types: (1) the use of *standard content* readings, (2) the use of a *foreign language* unknown to the decoders, and (3) the use of special techniques to create *content-free* speech.

The standard content approach involves having encoders express different emotions on each reading of the same verbal material. For example, Davitz and Davitz (1959) had encoders read meaningless content (parts of the alphabet) ten times while expressing a different emotion on each reading. Davitz and Davitz found that decoders in a judgment task were able to identify these emotions at far better than the chance level.

A standard content approach closer to language involves having encoders read the same sentence or passage several times, expressing different emotions on each reading. For example, in a standard content study by Beier and Zautra (1972), encoders used different emotions while reading this phrase: "There is no answer. You have asked me that question a thousand times and my reply has always been the same. It will always be the same." Senders in Zuckerman et al. (1975) recited the sentence: "I have to leave now."

The standard content approach was used in an extensive program of research by Davitz (1964). Davitz found that emotions could be judged at above chance levels of accuracy using standard content speech, that emotions varied in the ease with which they could be decoded, and that decoders varied considerably in their ability to decode standard content speech.

A number of researchers have criticized the standard content approach. These criticisms have raised questions about whether this approach produces naturalistic emotions or whether encoders are merely using exaggerated vocal stereotypes (Kramer 1963; Knapp 1972, p. 159). An alternate approach involves the use of a foreign language unknown to potential decoders. This solution was indicated by Kramer (1964) in a judgment study that used emotions expressed in Japanese. Kramer found that English-speaking American judges were able to decode the Japanese emotions at better than the chance level. It should be noted that this approach rests on the assumption that emotions conveyed in speech originating in one culture can be recognized in another; in this study, at least, they were.

The third strategy of eliminating verbal clues from speech involves the use of special techniques to produce content-free speech. At least two techniques have been developed to remove or to mask the words present in speech, while preserving paralanguage. One of these techniques uses a low-pass filter to remove the high frequencies of speech, without which individual words cannot be recognized (Rogers, Scherer, and Rosenthal 1971). The resulting filtered speech sounds very much like conversation heard through a wall. Soskin and Kauffman (1961) compared ratings of emotional content in normal tape recordings with ratings of the emotional content in the same recordings after they had been content-filtered with a low-pass filter. The authors found significant agreement between the ratings of the two sets. Similar results were found by Scherer, Koivumaki, and Rosenthal (1972), who compared semantic differential ratings of normal, filtered, and randomized spliced speech.

The content-filtered approach has been used in a number of decoding studies. Starkweather (1956) found that clinical psychologists were able to decode emotions reliably from content-filtered recordings of the 1954 Army-McCarthy hearings. In Milmoe et al. (1967), judges' ratings of doctors' content-filtered voices postdicted the doctors' success at referring alcoholic patients into treatment. In another study, ratings of mothers' content-filtered voices postdicted aspects of their babies' behavior (Milmoe et al. 1968).

Although the evidence suggests that the content-filtered approach is successful in removing verbal cues from speech, some researchers have been concerned about the possible loss of important nonverbal information as well (Ochai and Fukumura 1957; Kramer 1963). The accuracy with which content-filtered speech can be judged, however, suggests that any nonverbal information that is filtered out, although it may be important, is at least not indispensable to the kinds of judgment required in a decoding study.

The second special technique developed to produce content-free speech is very different from the content-filtered technique. Called randomized splicing, this second technique preserves all the frequencies of speech (unlike the filtering technique), but scrambles the order of speech segments instead. This technique, developed by Scherer (1971), can mask verbal content and can be accomplished without sophisticated equipment. Randomized splicing involves cutting an audiotape into small segments of equal length and then reassembling them in a random order. In the resulting tape, aspects of paralanguage are preserved, but words become unrecognizable. Naturally, any nonverbal information that relies upon the natural sequence of speech (e.g., hesitations) is lost in the randomized splicing technique.

GENERAL CHARACTERISTICS OF DECODING RESEARCH

As this brief review indicates, researchers have studied the decoding of emotions using a wide range of nonverbal behaviors. Most of the studies cited here used a judgment format in which samples of nonverbal behavior (photographs, tape recordings, etc.) were played to judges who were asked to identify the emotions expressed in the nonverbal samples. Most of these studies have investigated specific hypotheses, often about whether or not a specific form of nonverbal behavior was meaningful—that is, could be decoded for emotional content. As a result, almost all decoding studies have been limited to a single channel—facial photographs, or audio tapes, or pictures of posture, etc.

Very few studies have simultaneously investigated more than one nonverbal channel, and the few studies that have done so have generally been interested in simply comparing the relative decodability of two channels. For example, Ekman's study (1965) with still photographs of both facial and body expressions contrasted the decodability of these two types of photograph. A number of researchers have used two channels to create contradictions like a positive verbal content said with negative paralanguage (e.g., Mehrabian 1972) to see which channel has primacy in a judgment task. As far as we have been able to tell, however, researchers have not used several nonverbal channels to create a standard test of decoder ability in different channels.

Other limitations or constraints of decoding research have been discussed elsewhere (Brunswik 1956; Frijda 1969; Cook 1971, pp. 81–83; Knapp 1972, pp. 122–27, 160–62). Some of these concerns have been: (1) that some researchers have used professional actors, whose expressions may be in some way idiomatic; (2) that most studies of visual nonverbal behavior have used only still photographs, which are much less naturalistic than films or videotapes; (3) that many studies of vocal paralanguage have used the standard content approach, which may elicit highly stereotyped and nonnaturalistic expressions from encoders; (4) that the criterion of accuracy of judgments is always a difficult problem in decoding studies (cf. Cook 1971, p. 82) and is generally either the *subjective* criterion of what emotion an encoder intended to express, or is an *ascribed* criterion of whatever emotion the researcher decides the encoder was experiencing, or is the modal judgment made by a group of judges; (5) that there seems to be an unfortunate trade-off between internal validity and external validity in decoding research: the greater the sophistication and control of the research design (isolation of behavior from its context, the use of channels, etc.), the less the resulting nonverbal behavior resembles natural emotional expression; and finally, (6) that the range of emotions used in most decoding studies has been extremely constricted and that the emotions that have been used have often been studied in an exaggerated or even grotesque form.

This last concern, about the range and quality of the emotional expressions studied in decoding tasks, is as much a matter of judgment as it is a scientific question. There does seem to have been a tendency to study only dramatic expressions (hate, joy), with a resulting neglect of the more mundane emotions that people are likely to encounter in everyday life (Cook 1971, p. 85). Dramatic or greatly exaggerated expressions may also have been used extensively because they are likely, out of all possible emotions, to be decoded most easily and reliably. Some researchers have, in fact, used a high degree of interjudge agreement as a way to select a few emotional expressions out of many.

While this is an ideal procedure to sample expressions that will be unmistakable, it also has an obvious tendency to eliminate subtle and mundane emotions in favor of those that are dramatic or exaggerated (not to speak of the danger of reducing variance in decoding scores). Some researchers have published the photographs used in their studies, allowing the reader to form his or her own opinion of the range and subtlety of expressions used. Films, videotapes, and audiotapes are, of course, not publishable in research reports, and readers are therefore generally unable to form subjective opinions about the subtlety and naturalism of these nonverbal samples.

These considerations about concrete details of decoding studies have important implications for generalizations about the interpretability of emotional expressions. Conclusions about what emotions can be recognized, or what channels can be decoded, etc., may be circumscribed by the specific features of the studies upon which these generalizations are based. There is a tendency in summarizing research to make statements such as "Anger can be recognized from the face," rather than a statement closer to the actual research findings: "Using still photographs of the face, judges were able to identify anger at an above-chance level of accuracy."

Despite the range of decoding research designs, and despite the problematic characteristics of some of these designs, some generalizations about the interpretability of emotions from nonverbal behavior seem justified. If the specific nonverbal samples and specific procedures of the decoding literature are kept in mind, the following generalizations seem warranted: (1) some emotions can be accurately decoded from samples of nonverbal behavior in the face, body, and voice; (2) these nonverbal channels probably differ in their decodability, probably with the face easier to decode than the body; (3) emotions differ in decodability, with some emotions relatively unmistakable and others relatively indistinguishable from similar emotions; and (4) people definitely differ in their ability to decode emotions from nonverbal behavior, with good decoders tending to perform uniformly better than poor decoders (Zuckerman et al. 1975).

LIMITATIONS AND ADVANTAGES OF OUR APPROACH

Although the PONS test overcomes at least some of the serious problems in previous decoding research, the test is not without its own limitations. In making the PONS test, there were some trade-offs—perhaps inevitable—between experimental control and ecological validity. While trying to make the PONS a reliable measure of decoding in separate channels, we also tried to make its content representative of real-life behavior. It is probably impossible to achieve both fully. For example, the price we would have paid for filming behavior occurring in natural settings would be uncertainty over the proper label for the emotion and perhaps even for the psychological context; uneven control over technical quality; probably giving up the idea of filming and audiotaping all the relevant behavior occurring in different channels simultaneously; and so on.

Because of our choice of method, there are a number of ways in which the nonverbal behavior in the PONS film differs from nonverbal behavior in everyday life, and also ways in which the judging is quite different from the kind of judging that people do every day. These differences are intentional design features of the PONS, not unwitting conceptual oversights.

CHANNEL ISOLATION. In everyday life, we generally have multiple channels available for interpretation at the same time. In interacting with someone, we can try to decode all of their channels of communication simultaneously. There are some circumstances, of course, under which the channels available for interpretation are limited, such as talking on the telephone. In most face-to-face interaction, however, we have available to us all the nonverbal cues that the PONS film isolates into separate channels. In everyday life, it might be the case that we use a hierarchy of channels, starting with the channel easiest to decode. For example, in trying to judge someone's emotions, we might tend to prefer the face, and only use other channels when the face is for some reason unavailable. The PONS film, however, isolates nonverbal behavior into different channels and therefore restricts the nonverbal cues available to the decoder in a manner unlike everyday life, at least for some of its eleven channels. For other "channels" that are actually combinations of "purer" channels, the stimulus becomes more like everyday life (e.g., face + body + tone).

ABSENCE OF VERBAL INFORMATION. In everyday life, most nonverbal behavior occurs in conjunction with verbal behavior. When we try to decode a person's emotion in a face-to-face situation, we may be using both these levels of information in reaching an interpretation. It could be that nonverbal cues acquire meaning principally in terms of their reinforcement (or contradiction) of what the person is saying, rather than as a completely independent source of information.

The nonverbal behavior in the PONS film occurs in pure form, that is, the encoder's verbal behavior has been entirely eliminated. This was intentional, of course, since the PONS was designed to be a measure of nonverbal sensitivity alone.

SOME NONVERBAL CUES NOT EXAMINED. The PONS film measures eleven channels of nonverbal behavior, and these channels contain behavior encoded by the face, body, and voice. There are, however, other types of nonverbal information that the film does not operationalize. For example, Argyle (1972) provides an inventory of ten different headings of nonverbal communication; and Cook (1971) lists fifteen classifications.

Some of the cues on these lists only have meaning when two or more people interact (proximity, body contact, eye contact, conversational head nods, etc.), and others are embedded in channels already in the PONS film (posture, physique, hair style, clothes, etc.). Finally, there are even more types of nonverbal clues—in addition to those listed by Argyle and by Cook—that are not in the PONS film (olfaction, flushed skin color, sweating, etc.). In choosing channels for inclusion in the PONS film, we selected those that seemed most indispensable to the decoding of emotions.

DECODING ONLY. The PONS film provides extensive information about an individual's decoding abilities, but provides no information about the encoding abilities or expressiveness of the person. In face-to-face interaction, a person is both an encoder and a decoder at the same time, and both these abilities are likely to be important determinants of the outcome of the interaction. The obstacles involved in creating a standardized test of encoding abilities are at least formidable; at any rate, the PONS is a measure of decoding only.

POSED CRITERION. The criterion of accuracy for each item in the PONS test is in part the situation or feeling that the encoder intended to portray. In everyday life, of course, we are more likely to be decoding spontaneous or unposed emotions. The PONS encoder's portrayals were also rated and selected for authenticity, as described later in chapter 2. This procedure was followed to ensure that her emotional expressions were not ineffectual, melodramatic, or stereotyped.

The problem of a criterion in researching emotion, however, is complex. A number of researchers have discussed the relative merits of different types of criteria in decoding research (Frijda 1969; Cook 1971; Knapp 1972; Ekman et al. 1972; Ekman 1973a). For example, Cook (1971, p. 83) lists five alternate ways of establishing a criterion: (1) face validity—what the encoder intended to send; (2) researcher opinion—the way the researcher labels the emotion; (3) ratings—a panel of judges rates the portrayals; (4) self-description—the encoder evaluates his or her own feelings; and (5) objective or biographical data—independent measures of what the encoder was actually feeling as in the observation of reactions to experimental or naturally occurring stimuli.

In selecting the portrayals for inclusion in the PONS film, we used a total of four of these methods: face validity (what our encoder meant to send), researcher opinion (we evaluated the effectiveness of each portrayal), ratings (a panel of judges rated each portrayal), and self-description (the encoder evaluated her own feelings).

These four methods were the only appropriate procedures, given the design of the PONS film. We did not want to use experimental manipulations to induce real emotions, since only a very restricted range of real emotions could have been ethically produced in this manner. As a result, the PONS encoder was not spontaneously experiencing hate, mourning, jealousy, and the other emotions in the film. Since the encoder was portraying—but perhaps not "really" experiencing—the emotions in the film, Cook's other criterion procedure was inappropriate. It would not have made sense to obtain objective data like physiological measures because the encoder was not spontaneously experiencing the emotions she portrayed. In summary, the criterion of accuracy in the PONS film is a combination of the emotion the encoder intended to send and the emotion the researchers, the encoder, and various judges decided she had in fact sent.

On a priori grounds, but not on empirical grounds, we might prefer spontaneous over posed stimuli because it is ultimately the decoding of everyday nonverbal cues about which we want to make inferences. However, it would be an error of logic, though a common one, to assume that because our ultimate interest is in spontaneous nonverbal cues, a better index of accuracy could be constructed from the use of such stimuli. Surface similarities between models and things modeled are no guarantee of predictive utility. A model's utility lies in our knowing the relationship between the properties of the model and the thing modeled. At the present time we do not know whether "real-life" stimuli would, for our purposes of assessing individual differences, be better or worse or not different from the posed stimuli we have employed for the PONS. What is known, however, that is useful to our understanding of our measure of decoding accuracy, is that those people who are good at decoding posed stimuli are also good at decoding spontaneous stimuli ($r(58) = .58$, $p < .001$) (Zuckerman, Hall, DeFrank, and Rosenthal 1976).[1]

Although methods have been employed to elicit identifiable "spontaneous" nonverbal cues by surreptitiously recording subjects' faces while they watch emotionally laden stimuli (e.g., Buck et al. 1972), it is questionable whether such cues are any more like "real-life" interpersonal communication than are the posed cues used in the PONS. Interpersonal communication probably consists of a mixture of cues that are unknowingly conveyed and cues that are conveyed quite deliberately. To some extent people may be capable of choosing their nonverbal behavior as consciously as they are capable of choosing their words. The posed cues embodied in the PONS may not, therefore, be as unrepresentative of "real" interpersonal nonverbal communication as one might think at first.

ONE ENCODER. The PONS film contains the nonverbal behavior and expressions of only a single encoder. In everyday life, of course, we are sur-

---

1. It is also the case that people who "send" accurately in the posed mode were also good at sending in the spontaneous mode in two studies ($r = .35$, Buck 1975; $r = .46$, Zuckerman, Hall, DeFrank, and Rosenthal 1976).

rounded by large numbers of encoders who probably vary in their expressiveness. However, the available literature on nonverbal communication, discussed earlier, suggests that good decoders are likely to be more accurate than poor decoders across different encoders. In addition, the various validity studies reported later in this book effectively discount the possibility that the PONS encoder is extremely idiosyncratic in her encoding behavior. It does seem justified, therefore, to generalize from the decoding measured by the PONS test to decoding ability in general, though we could not know at the outset that this would be the case. It is only because of the network of validational findings that we can conclude that the PONS was not, in fact, disadvantaged by the use of a single encoder. In principle, of course, it might well have been.[2]

ONE SEX. One consequence of employing only one encoder was that only one sex could be represented. It was important to ascertain the degree to which this fact could affect our results, particularly results having to do with sex differences in decoding. For example, women might be superior to men in decoding a woman sender but not a man sender. A review of decoding studies employing nonverbal judging tasks other than the PONS showed clearly that the sex of the encoder made no difference either in the number of studies showing female advantage or in the magnitude of the effect (see chapter 7 below and Hall (1978a). The literature suggests, therefore, that we suffered no overall loss of generality from employing only one sex.

CONTEXT-FREE. The emotional situations in the PONS film are presented without a context. In real life, we are often able to interpret emotions in light of several types of contextual information: (1) the situational antecedents of the emotion or situation at hand (is the person smiling to conceal nervousness or because a loved one is near?); (2) our past history with the encoder (is the person exceptionally angry or is this level of agitation an enduring characteristic of this person?); and (3) our knowledge about the onset and duration of an emotion (is the person exploding into sudden rage or is the emotion a smouldering anger?).

The PONS items are, of course, presented without context, so that we may know better what information is being judged. This kind of decoding is not without a naturalistic counterpart. We are frequently in situations where we

2. Further analysis of a set of 59 encoders sending 4 scenes in each of 3 modes (spontaneous, talking, and posed) (Zuckerman, Hall, DeFrank, and Rosenthal 1976) showed that the median of the 12 internal consistencies (coefficient alpha) of .87 was essentially the same as the internal consistency of the PONS (.86) when alpha was based on 220 items in both cases. Thus, agreement among different senders is very similar to agreement among different items sent by the single sender of the PONS. In short, the single sender of the PONS evoked no more homogeneous responses to the 220 scenes than would have been evoked by a set of 220 different senders each sending a single scene.

form an opinion, on the basis of minimal exposure, about the emotion a perfect stranger is experiencing.

RECOGNITION VERSUS INTERPRETATION. The PONS test measures whether a decoder can recognize emotions that the encoder is making no effort to disguise. In everyday life, we sometimes need to interpret a person's emotions whether or not they are manifest. That is, we sometimes need to go beyond a recognition of the manifest "performance" of an emotion to try to see whether this performance in fact conceals greater complexities of emotion "inside" the person. For example, is a defeated athlete's hearty congratulation of the winner genuinely good-natured, or does it conceal bitter disappointment—and how do we tell the difference?

The PONS test is more a measure of the decoder's ability to recognize the manifest level of emotion than it is a measure of the decoder's ability to draw complex interpretations about the true state of the encoder. Interpretations of this kind are probably based on a weighing of many different levels and intensities of cues (which may be in concert or in conflict), and are clearly beyond the scope of the PONS test. As the validity studies reported later indicate, however, the PONS test does tap decoding abilities that are related to a person's life in the "real" world.

THE PONS TEST

For a number of different reasons, the PONS test makes possible a wide range of studies that could not have been done using previous measures of decoding. The complexity of the PONS test makes it possible to study how accurate different individuals are in decoding different scenes in different nonverbal channels.

Unlike the nonverbal expressions of emotion sampled in previous decoding research, the PONS test presents (1) nonverbal behavior in eleven different channels, including visual and auditory channels; (2) movement in both face and body channels, unlike earlier studies using still photographs; and (3) a wide range of emotional expression, ranging from commonplace and subtle expressions to more dramatic emotions, with more emphasis on the identification of situations and emotional contexts than on identifying specific emotions.

Because of these design characteristics, the PONS test makes possible a complex research program directed at describing the distribution of this type of nonverbal sensitivity in the population, identifying correlates of this sensitivity in a variety of settings, and investigating whether this sensitivity is increased by or otherwise related to a variety of personal experiences.

2 | Design and Development of the PONS Test

The Profile of Nonverbal Sensitivity (PONS) is a forty-five-minute black and white 16-mm film and soundtrack composed of 220 numbered auditory and visual segments. These segments are a randomized presentation of twenty short scenes portrayed by a young woman, each scene represented in eleven "channels" of nonverbal communication. The test taker's assignment is to view the film and for each segment to circle the label that correctly describes the scene enacted in the segment. He or she makes this choice from two alternative labels printed on an answer sheet containing 220 such pairs of descriptions. Each segment is followed by a pause long enough for the decision to be made and recorded.

This chapter will be devoted to describing the 220-item, or "full" PONS test. Several short forms of the PONS test have been developed, as well as several short forms based on the PONS format but employing different portrayers. All of these short tests will be described in chapter 6 and in other chapters of this book.

THE CHANNELS

The eleven channels represented in the PONS are made up of various kinds of auditory and visual information "sent" by the portrayer. These channels can be thought of as falling into two types. The first five channels are "pure" channels: (1) face alone, no voice; (2) body from neck to knees, no voice; (3) face and body down to thighs (called "face + body," or "figure"), no voice; (4) electronically content-filtered voice, no picture (called CF); and (5) randomized spliced voice, no picture (called RS). The remaining six channels are "mixed" channels, made by combining the pure channels:

23

(6) face plus randomized spliced voice; (7) face plus electronically filtered voice; (8) body plus randomized spliced voice; (9) body plus electronically filtered voice; (10) figure plus randomized spliced voice; and (11) figure plus electronically filtered voice. Table 2.1 displays the eleven channels.

The nonverbal channels used in the PONS, represented as they are in pure and combined channels, have reasonable analogues in real life, even though no one ever talks in filtered speech and we rarely see *only* someone's face or body. But there are times when all channels are not accessible to the receiver—listening to someone on the telephone, watching someone at a distance, watching someone's hands when a wall or piece of furniture obscures the face. Thus, in isolating the channels for purposes of studying discrete skills, ecological validity was not entirely lost.

In scoring and data analysis, the channels are often combined into larger groupings, called "marginals," or "pooled channels" (see table 2.1), partly because the individual channels have lower reliability (due to the relatively few items in each channel) and partly because the marginals have greater content validity. For example, instead of thinking of "face" as existing in three separate channels (face plus electronically filtered speech, face plus randomized spliced speech, and face alone), we can combine these three channels into a larger category, which could still be called "face." This makes the channel more meaningful in real-life terms; it is easy to think of one's skill at reading "face," but it is not so easy to see what it means to be differentially good at reading face combined with one kind of voice and face combined with another kind of voice.

VOICE CONTENT MASKING. Until relatively recently, researchers interested in eliminating the verbal meanings conveyed in utterances had to use a method known as "standard content" (see chapter 1). In this method, the speaker would recite either standard, meaningless material, such as the alphabet or numbers, or some standard, meaningful, but affectively neutral or ambiguous material, usually a word, a phrase, or a sentence or two. In each of these cases, the speaker would recite the material, varying the mood or voice tone to suit the emotion being "sent." The listener can understand the words, but the words do not help to identify the emotion.

Several masking techniques have been developed that seem like an improvement over the standard content method. In these new methods, the speaker is free to use whatever words are appropriate for the emotion or situation, since the words are made unintelligible afterward by altering the voice recording in various ways. The advantage of this approach is in increasing the spontaneity and authenticity of the original portrayals. It also allows for the masking of voices recorded unobtrusively—a clear advantage over the standard content method.

Both of the masking methods used in the PONS test have been used in

TABLE 2.1. The Channels of the PONS Test

	Video				
Audio	No Cues	Face Cues	Body Cues	Figure Cues (Face + Body)	Marginals
No cues	a	20[b]	20	20	video 60
RS[c] cues	20	20	20	20	RS 80
CF[d] cues	20	20	20	20	CF 80
Marginals	tone 40	face 60	body 60	figure 60	total 220
		face 120		body 120	

[a]Empty cell in design. In statistical analyses, this cell is frequently filled in with a chance-level score for each person in order to allow for a fully crossed repeated measures analysis.

[b]Numbers refer to the number of test items falling in each cell and marginal. For example, tone 40 has forty items (sum of RS 20 and CF 20).

[c]RS = randomized spliced voice

[d]CF = electronically content-filtered voice

previous research (see chapter 1). For example, both randomized splicing and electronic content-filtering were used and compared in Scherer, Koivumaki, and Rosenthal (1972).

The randomized splicing technique (Scherer 1971) requires the audio tape to be physically cut into small pieces, reordered randomly, and reassembled. The length of the pieces depends on the speed of tape transport; in the PONS the tape speed was 7½ inches per second and the pieces were 2 inches long. When the spliced tape is played back, the voice sounds natural in many ways, but of course the words cannot be understood because they are scrambled. In the PONS test, twenty random orders for the cut-up pieces were devised, one for each of the twenty scenes. Appendix 2A contains a detailed description of the randomizing scheme used.

The electronic filter used in making the PONS was modeled on the one reported in Rogers, Scherer, and Rosenthal (1971). It removes selected bands of frequencies and clips the audio signal so that the voice sounds muffled and slightly distorted. By carefully adjusting the various controls, the intonation, rhythm, tempo, and loudness of the voice can be kept the same, while speech intelligibility is lost. For the PONS, the controls were first set to attenuate all frequencies above 650 Hertz. Other control adjustments were then made to reduce speech intelligibility further. The settings for frequency attenuation and distortion were chosen by consensus of the authors after they listened to an assortment of possible settings, on a subjective criterion of overall intelligibility. It was assumed that if the authors, who were thoroughly familiar both with the actual words and with the speaker's real voice, could not catch the words, then fresh listeners certainly would not be able to.

The decision to use two kinds of speech filtering where one kind might have sufficed was based on the findings of Scherer, Koivumaki, and Rosenthal

(1972), which suggested that these two techniques systematically affect the voice in different ways. The randomized splicing seems to make the voice seem more pleasant, peaceful, and nice than ordinary speech, as rated by judges in the study cited above.[1] The electronic filter seems to make the voice sound more easy, calm, and steady. The randomized splicing retains the acoustic properties of the voice while altering the correct sequence of the communication, whereas the electronic filtering does just the reverse: it noticeably changes some acoustic properties of the voice but keeps the sequence intact. In a sense, then, the two methods are complementary.

Subjects' performance on the PONS has shown that, at least for the female voice used, electronic content-filtering removes more nonverbal cues than randomized splicing does, since most people score slightly lower on electronically content-filtered (CF) speech than on randomized spliced (RS) speech. In addition, the mode of content masking interacts with the location of the scenes in a two-dimensional emotional space (positivity and dominance); in other words, some kinds of scenes are easier to identify in one type of masking, and other kinds of scenes are easier to identify in the other type of masking, for our sender (see chapter 3).

PORTRAYAL OF THE SCENES

The portrayals in the PONS test were done by a member of our research group. She is Caucasian, from the northeastern United States, and was twenty-four years old when the test was made. After it had been decided not to use a professional actress (for reasons given below), our portrayer was selected for convenience and because her continued participation in the group assured the possibility of gathering additional information on her if the need arose. She was not chosen on the basis of knowledge of her nonverbal sending skill or other nonverbal characteristics, about which little was known.

Thirty-five scenes were videotaped, of which twenty-one were written in advance, not by the portrayer,[2] and the remainder were added during rehearsal, at the suggestion of the portrayer and the other members of the research group. At no time was a script rigidly adhered to, but rather the exact wording often changed with each repetition of the scene. This flexibility of wording was intended to enhance the genuineness of the feelings expressed, which was hoped to reflect the natural style of the portrayer and not be artificial, memorized, or self-conscious. Naturalistic expression was the focus, not the specific words.

Whether truly authentic expression was achieved might, of course, be

1. All judges in this study were females.
2. Credit goes to Roberta R. Hawkins for writing these twenty-one scenes.

questioned, since the portrayals did take place before three video cameras and several observers and were done "on command." Though authenticity ratings were made and used to select the final set of portrayals, we cannot evaluate how much the portrayals actually departed from the portrayer's "real" repertory of sending behaviors. Some recent research suggests that sending accuracy scores in posed and spontaneous modes are substantially correlated (Zuckerman, Hall, DeFrank, and Rosenthal 1976); this does not mean, however, that senders employ exactly the same behaviors to convey their messages in the two modes.

We decided that the method of using a relaxed person enacting preselected scenes was preferable to using an actress (who might use stylized code, or who might emphasize certain channels depending on whether her experience was on stage, on radio, or in television and motion pictures), and also preferable to trying to find a person in the midst of experiencing "real" emotions inside or outside the laboratory—the candid camera approach. The difficulties of the candid camera approach are many; they include problems of technical consistency, finding sufficient variety of emotions and situations, concealing recording instruments, and, of course, invading privacy. Even if these problems could somehow be overcome, there would still remain the problem of identifying the emotions being felt or expressed; in the portrayal method, at least, little doubt could be had about what emotional expressions were being attempted.

The thirty-five videotaped scenes were chosen on the basis of certain broad criteria. The first interest was to represent a wide variety of situations and emotions, both strong and mild, positive and negative. In addition, a special attempt was made to find interactive situations. Since the purpose of the test was to measure ability to understand cues sent by another person, it made sense to concentrate on cues sent in interaction. The kinds of cues we emit while alone (reading a book, thinking about our experiences) may be qualitatively different from those emitted intentionally or unintentionally in interaction with another person.[3] Also, ideas for scenes were discarded if the scene might not be meaningful in other cultures. There is some evidence that at least one of the scenes did not meet this criterion fully: in Northern Ireland, a test taker reported that as a Catholic she found the divorce scene confusing.

Several other limitations on the possible scenes emerged during rehearsal.

3. Researchers are sensitive to possible differences in sending in "posed" versus "spontaneous" modes. Most research on sending and/or receiving nonverbal cues, including the PONS research, falls under the posed category. Some researchers (Buck et al. 1972; Zuckerman, Hall, DeFrank, and Rosenthal 1976) do employ a cue-eliciting paradigm in which senders are not aware that their faces are being videotaped while they view emotionally laden slides or videotaped scenes. However, the apparent advantage of this "spontaneous" sending may be somewhat offset by the fact that the expressions so elicited are also private—not engendered in an interpersonal context and therefore possibly quite different from expressions used "spontaneously" in interaction.

51429

For one thing, all scenes had to have a female speaker, which ruled out many possible scenes; scenes requiring the speaker to be vastly different in age from the portrayer had to be avoided; and scenes requiring "giveaway" gestures had to be either avoided or altered. One such alteration occurred in the scenes involving interaction with a child. If the portrayer cast her eyes down as though talking to a child, the test taker would quickly know that the right answer for that scene must have something to do with a child. To eliminate this cue, these scenes were enacted with the portrayer keeping her eyes straight ahead. Finally, scenes were discarded that were so alien to the portrayer's own experience that she felt unable to enact them.

THE VIDEOTAPING

The videotaping session took place in the departmental social psychology laboratory, a room with neutral sound characteristics (heavy carpeting, acoustical tile ceiling). The backdrop for the portrayer was a blue-gray blanket draped over a frame. This was placed twelve feet from three video cameras, which were arranged so that the camera angles did not vary more than a few degrees with respect to each other. The fluorescent lighting level in the room was high, so as to provide good picture detail. Additional lighting was provided by three seventy-five-watt floodlights mounted on a wing stand and placed to the right of the camera grouping. The incandescents improved the contrast of the video and highlighted the features of the portrayer.

In order to enhance her feeling of interaction—which seemed necessary if the cues she sent were to be those normally used in interaction rather than in monologue—the portrayer addressed a man (one of the authors) who stood as close to her as possible without being on camera (about five feet) and who gesticulated where appropriate and mouthed silent responses. This semblance of interaction gave the portrayer a face on which to focus her attention and made her feel much more at ease than when she had tried addressing an empty wall or a person standing farther away and/or acting unresponsive. This is mentioned not only for methodological interest but also because the relationship—young woman addressing young man—may have affected the nature of the nonverbal communication in subtle ways that are impossible to examine without doing research employing more pairs of senders and receivers.

Particular attention was given to the selection and adjustment of video camera lenses and to the positioning of the cameras so as to provide the three video modes of face, body, and figure (face plus body). These adjustments were made just prior to the shooting and were not changed for the remainder of the session. Several takes or versions were recorded of each of the thirty-five scenes.

In order to obtain the high-quality recordings necessary for the production of a good final master tape, considerable attention was given to the selection and use of components in the audio-video system. The audio components were assembled as a separate subsystem, with the major units installed in a specially designed portable console. This console was used several times during the project, the interconnections being altered to suit the particular production phase under way at the time. Appendix 2B contains a detailed description of the components and their functions.

FINAL SELECTION OF THE SCENES

Choosing the "best" scenes for inclusion in the final version of the PONS was done by eight raters, who as a group viewed the figure (face plus body) takes of all the scenes, in their full length (averaging 5.5 seconds) and without any kind of content filtering of the voice. Four of the raters were Judith A. Hall (the portrayer), Peter L. Rogers (the technical director), Dane Archer (who played the off-camera interactant in the scenes), and Robert Rosenthal (principal investigator). The other four raters were their spouses, all of whom were familiar with the project and had at least some prior acquaintance with the portrayer.

For every scene each rater (1) ordered the several takes according to his or her overall preference, (2) gave the best-chosen take a score of 0 to 100 on the basis of how well the scene conveyed the intended emotion or situation, and (3) rated the best-chosen take on a scale from 1 to 7 for each of three dimensions (positive affect, dominance, and intensity).[4]

For the thirty-five first-choice takes, the correlation of positivity ratings with dominance ratings was −.05. Intensity ratings were correlated .35 with dominance ($p < .05$, two-tailed), and −.50 with positivity ($p < .005$, two-tailed). Intensity ratings were subsequently ignored for being significantly related to the other two rating dimensions.

The final "best" take for each scene was the one having the lowest sum of the ranks given by the eight raters (a scene with more first choices would have a lower sum of ranks than a scene with more second and third choices). The scenes were then categorized on the positivity and dominance dimensions: high positive, low positive, high dominant, and low dominant. Finally, from

4. One or more of these dimensions has been found useful for describing affects in general by many researchers through the years (Argyle 1975; Bain 1875; Bales 1970; Heller, Myers, and Vikan Kline 1963; Leary 1957; Osgood, Suci, and Tannenbaum 1957; Rosenberg and Sedlak 1972; Schlosberg 1954; Schutz 1958; Stratton 1928; Wish, Deutsch, and Kaplan 1976; Wundt 1912), and they have also been found useful for describing nonverbally communicated affects in particular by many workers (Abelson and Sermat 1962; Argyle 1975; Dawes and Kramer 1966; Frijda and Philipszoon 1963; Mehrabian 1970; Osgood 1966; Scherer 1974; Sweeney, Tinling, and Schmale 1970; Williams and Tolch 1965).

TABLE 2.2. Twenty Scenes Arranged in Four Affect Quadrants

	Dominance	
Positivity	Submissive	Dominant
Positive	helping a customer ordering food in a restaurant expressing gratitude expressing deep affection trying to seduce someone	talking about one's wedding leaving on a trip expressing motherly love admiring nature talking to a lost child
Negative	talking about the death of a friend talking about one's divorce returning faulty item to a store asking foregiveness saying a prayer	criticizing someone for being late nagging a child expressing strong dislike threatening someone expressing jealous anger

each of the quadrants formed by the intersection of the positivity and dominance dimensions, five scenes were selected; in general, these were the five having the highest score on the 0–100 rating for success in conveying the intended emotion or situation (some scenes were also excluded due to technical flaws). Table 2.2 shows the final selection of scenes and their positions in the four quadrants formed by the positivity and dominance dimensions, and appendix 2C contains the transcripts of all twenty scenes. For these twenty scenes, the correlation of positivity ratings with dominance ratings was $-.38$ ($p = .10$, two-tailed), and the reliability [(MS scenes $=$ MS scenes $\times$ judges) / MS scenes] of ratings of positivity and of dominance were .97 and .92, respectively.

THE DATA ANALYTIC MODEL

The eleven channels and four quadrants can be conceptualized in terms of an analysis of variance model so that each person assessed provides five replications (scenes) in each cell of a $2 \times 2 \times 11$ (positive-negative $\times$ dominant-submissive $\times$ channels). An even more useful model is based on the assumption of a hypothetical twelfth channel called "no video–no audio." The expected accuracy rate for this channel is 50 percent, but adding it to the model permits a more powerful and more compact analytic model: $2 \times 2 \times 2 \times 2 \times 3$, or

A. Positive versus negative
B. Dominant versus submissive
C. Face shown versus face not shown
D. Body shown versus body not shown
E. No audio versus randomized spliced versus content-filtered

For each person or for any homogeneous group of persons, this model permits an evaluation of accuracy in nonverbal communication as a function of these five orthogonal factors and the two-, three-, four-, and five-way interactions among them. In addition, individuals and groups can be compared with one another on the relative importance to each person or to each group of all five factors taken singly or in interaction.

For some purposes a sixth factor of order or learning is added. Thus, within each combination of channel and scene type there are five scenes that can be arranged for analysis into the order in which they are shown in the PONS test. This order or learning factor with its five levels is fully crossed with the five factors listed above. The one-degree-of-freedom (df) contrast for linear trend is an overall index of improvement over time in PONS performance. Individuals and groups can, therefore, be compared for their degree of learning as well as their level of performance. In addition, the interaction of the one-df learning contrast with other one-df contrasts provides interesting information on such questions as which channels show greater learning, which content quadrants show greater learning, and various combinations of these questions.

It should be noted that our data analytic model does not make frequent use of all eleven channels or of all forty-four combinations of channels and affect quadrants. While the model employs all this information, it employs it in a more efficient and reliable manner by subdividing parts of the eleven-channel profile into larger subsections than channels based only upon twenty scenes each. Thus, all scenes employing the face can be compared to all scenes not employing the face, all scenes employing the body can be compared to all scenes not employing the body, all scenes employing audio information can be compared to all scenes not employing audio information, etc. This series of comparisons, or contrasts, is appreciably more reliable and powerful than the simultaneous examination of all eleven channels.

STABILITY OF SCENE CLASSIFICATION

Through the assistance of Ralph Gundlach we were able to check our classification of the final twenty scenes as to their degree of positivity and dominance. As part of his intensive analysis of the scenes of the face, body, and figure channels of the full PONS, he obtained ratings for each of the sixty scenes on its degree of positivity and its degree of dominance. Scenes were rated by groups of four to thirty English college students. We employed for our analysis the median rating given by the judges to each of the scenes.

For each of the three channels the scenes we had classified as more positive were rated as more positive by the English judges, with the degree of agreement corresponding to a correlation (η) of .79 ($F(1,16) = 26.68$). When the mean ratings of all twenty scenes by the English judges were correlated with the mean ratings of all twenty scenes by the original eight judges, the resulting

$r = .88$ ($F(1,18) = 62.35$). In addition, for each of the three channels, the scenes we had classified as more dominant were rated as more dominant by the English judges with the degree of agreement corresponding to a correlation of .67 ($F(1,16) = 13.24$). When the mean ratings of all twenty scenes by the English judges were correlated with the mean ratings of all twenty scenes by the original eight judges, the resulting $r = .63$ ($F(1,18) = 12.01$). For the English judges, the correlation over the twenty scenes of ratings of positivity and ratings of dominance was $-.18$.

The very substantial correlations between ratings of scenes made by the original judges and the English judges would probably have been higher still but for some important differences in the precise stimulus scenes employed by the original group of eight judges and the present group of thirty English college students. The original group had made their ratings on the unedited video tapes containing five-second-long scene exposures in the figure channel accompanied by synchronous unfiltered speech. The later group of English judges rated items that actually appeared in the PONS test (see below)—two seconds long and unaccompanied by any audio information. In view of these differences, the obtained reliabilities of classification were reassuring.

We also wanted to examine the agreement among the three channel versions of each of the twenty scenes in the degree to which they were rated as either positive or dominant. We employed the index of reliability (MS scenes $-$ MS scenes $\times$ channels)/MS scenes, and found the reliabilities to be .80 and .85 for ratings of positivity and dominance, respectively. The three different versions of each of the twenty scenes (face, body, figure), therefore, were judged as very similar in their degrees of positivity and dominance.

For both the positivity and dominance variables, we performed a three-way analysis of variance on the median judges' ratings with the two between-scenes factors of positivity (negative/positive) and dominance (submissive/dominant), and one within-scenes factor of channel (face/body/figure). For the analysis of dominance ratings, no effects were large (or significant) except for the effect of dominance described earlier ($\eta = .67$). For the analysis of positivity ratings, however, there were large (and significant at $p < .001$) effects of channel ($\eta = .60$) and channel $\times$ positivity ($\eta = .74$) in addition to the effect of positivity described earlier ($\eta = .79$). The effect of channels was due to the higher rating of positivity given to the face than to the body, with the mixed channel (figure) falling in between. The channel $\times$ positivity interaction was due to the much greater accuracy of differentiation of positive from negative scenes that occurred when the face was present in the scene compared to when it was absent. Faces, then, or at least the face employed in the PONS, appear to be judged more positively than bodies and, not surprisingly, the face was able to register a greater range of positivity than was the body.

THE VIDEO TAPE PONS TEST

A composite master video tape was made (see appendix 2D for the method) containing the 220 auditory and visual segments in random order (see below), interspersed with numbers and reminder beeps to introduce the segments and pauses for answers to be recorded. This tape was projected informally for a test group for the purpose of discovering how easy or hard the test was. Subjects did much better than expected, scoring over 90 percent. For psychometric reasons it was desirable to have an average level of accuracy that was nearly midway between chance (50 percent) and perfect performance. In several informal sessions, the lengths of the scenes were shortened from the original average of 5.5 seconds to 2 seconds, at which length overall accuracy was between 75 percent and 80 percent, a figure that remained fairly stable throughout subsequent testing. An exposure time of 2 seconds was chosen as a result of these early trials.

THE FILM PONS TEST

Although video tape was satisfactory for pretesting and for local use, it would not serve in a large-scale testing program because of the difficulty of obtaining compatible video playback facilities and limitations on the size of the group that could be tested at one showing. In addition, the timing and technical precision of the numbers, beeps, segments, and pauses could not be held to close tolerances because of problems inherent in the medium. Therefore, a kinescope copy was made of the composite master video tape. The kinescope process transferred video and audio information from the video tape to 16-mm motion picture negative and magnetic audio track. This negative and the magnetic track were edited as described below. After editing, the magnetic track was made into an optical soundtrack, which was transferred onto the film when final prints were made from the negative. Although the kinescope product is not of as high quality as a film made with a movie camera, it has all the other advantages of film—compatability with all 16-mm sound projectors, the capacity to be shown to considerably larger groups of people at one sitting, and the capacity to be edited easily and precisely.

Perhaps the most important result of this ability to time segments exactly—aside from producing a more consistent and professional-looking film—was that now the two-second stimulus from each scene could be chosen from a prearranged location within the scene. This was felt to be an important control for the possibility that early, middle, or late cues have special characteristics that should be controlled for in the selection of the stimulus. It was decided to take the earliest two-second segment that was accompanied by continuous or near-continuous audio. The editing rule went as follows: (1) Using the audio track as a guide, the first two seconds of audio that had sound precisely in the middle were chosen. (2) If the video that accompanied these two seconds had no video "noise" or picture "tearing" in the frames, then those two seconds were edited into the film; if the accompanying video was technically flawed, the process was begun again with the audio track, so that the first two seconds that did meet all criteria could be located. If the segment in question required no video (that is, it was destined to be an audio-only item in the final product), only step 1 was performed; if the segment required no audio (a video-only item), the first two seconds of technically good video were chosen. The net result of this editing process was 220 two-second stimuli, each selected from the early part of the communication and each having at least a central portion of audio when necessary.

The film PONS was assembled in the same random order of presentation as the video tape PONS. New credits and numbers were professionally photographed for this version; the rating pauses, pauses between each number and its corresponding audiovisual segment, and video pauses (required for audio-only segments) were made by inserting blank pieces of film of specified lengths in the appropriate places during the editing of the negative. The final format of the film PONS is as follows: credits, simultaneous item number and beep (two seconds), pause (two seconds), PONS segment (two seconds), rating pause (five seconds, except for first five items, where more time is allowed), item number, and so on.

THE ANSWER SHEET

DESCRIPTION. For each of the 220 items, the answer sheet shows the correct response alternative paired with an incorrect alternative. The alternatives are the brief descriptions listed in table 2.2. Appendix 2E gives the correct answer and channel of each of the 220 items.

The position of the correct alternative—whether it was in the "A" or "B" position—was decided randomly, with the constraint that half the correct answers would be in the "A" position and half in the "B" position. The choice of the incorrect alternative for each pair of choices was also made randomly, by randomly picking one of the nineteen scenes that were not the correct answer. A few adjustments were made after randomization to bring into better balance scenes that were overrepresented and underrepresented as incorrect alternatives. Before adjustment, the least often represented scene occurred 5 times and the most often represented scene occurred 16 times; after adjustment, the range was 8–14.

CHECKING THE RANDOMIZATION. The order of presentation of the 220 segments was randomly determined, with the constraint that no two scenes could appear consecutively. A check on the randomization of the items was performed. Each item was coded with a sequence number showing the order of its occurrence in the test (1–220), and this sequence number was correlated with a series of dummy-coded (1,0) variables indicating whether the item did or did not represent (1) a given quadrant in the correct response alternative, (2) a given quadrant in the incorrect response alternative, or (3) a given channel. Any correlation deviating substantially from zero in either the positive or negative direction would indicate that items showing a given channel or quadrant tended to occur too frequently either later or earlier in the test, while a correlation of zero would indicate that items showing that channel or quadrant were evenly distributed throughout the sequence.

The correlations thus computed between sequence and the four quadrants of the correct response alternative ranged from $-.09$ to $.07$ ($df = 218$). The correlations for the four quadrants of the incorrect response alternative ranged from $-.09$ to $.10$. The correlations for channels ranged from $-.11$ to $.13$, with a median of $-.003$. The largest of these, $.13$ for body + RS, was the only significant correlation ($p < .05$), and indicated that items showing body + RS tended to occur slightly more frequently later in the test.

Suggestions from our colleagues Reid Hastie and David Kenny led us to examine our answer sheet to determine whether our particular pairings of correct and incorrect alternatives might have an effect on the scores of subjects strongly inclined to perceive or guess all scenes as positive, or negative, or dominant, or submissive, or any of the four combinations of positivity and dominance. Such systematically biased responding might lead to higher-than-chance accuracy if there were a bias in the answer sheet.

Suppose, for example, that a subject always chooses the submissive alternative. Of our 220 items, 110 were classified as submissive. If 70 of those were paired with dominant incorrect alternatives, our biased subject would get all 70 of these correct. Of the remaining 40 items, since the incorrect alternative is also a submissive scene, guessing "submissive" would lead to a correct response only 20 times out of the 40. Thus, our subject earns 70 + 20, or 90 items correct out of 110 possible without any "true" accuracy at all. The high score is entirely due to biased guessing of all scenes as submissive. Of the 110 items that were classified as dominant, our biased subject would miss all items that have been paired with submissive incorrect alternatives, since he or she would always choose the latter. Of those actually dominant items that are paired with dominant incorrect alternatives, we assume that our biased subject would get half of them correct by random choice (e.g., 40 of 80 such items). These 40 correct items are added to the 90 already earned to yield 130 out of 220, or 59 percent correct, instead of the 50 percent correct we would expect if our subject couldn't really decode nonverbal cues. It seemed unlikely that our procedure for designing the answer sheet would permit so large a bias, but we thought there might be some bias because we were not able to balance the occurrence of incorrect alternatives perfectly.

We calculated the number of times each of the four types of incorrect response alternatives occurs with each of the four types of correct response alternatives, and found no significant association of incorrect with correct response alternatives ($\chi^2(9) = 8.94$, $p = .44$). The net bias resulting from any extreme guessing strategy was computed by adding (a) the number of items in which the correct favored alternative is paired with a different incorrect alternative (N_{+-}), and (b) one-half the number of items in which both alternatives are favored (N_{++}), and (c) one-half the number of items in which neither of the alternatives is favored (N_{--}). From this sum we subtracted the number of correct choices expected by chance in the absence of bias (110). Put algebraically, net bias = $(N_{+-}) + (N_{++}/2) + (N_{--}/2) = 110$.

Table 2.3 shows the maximum bias possible due to the pattern of pairings of correct and incorrect alternatives for each of eight possible types of bias, from always choosing positive alternatives (bias 1) to always choosing alternatives that are both negative and submissive (bias 8). The biases have been converted to percentages for this table by dividing the raw bias score by 220 and multiplying by 100. Table 2.3 shows that none of the eight maximum possible biases is large, with a range from -2.3 to $+2.3$ percentage points. Thus, no matter how extreme the bias of any individual or of any group, the expected value under the hypothesis of random guessing is not much affected.

An additional approach to the question of bias is possible by considering the intercorrelations among parts of the PONS. If it were the case, for example,

TABLE 2.3. Maximum Bias Possible for Subjects Giving All Responses of One Type

Type of Bias	Accuracy[a]	Bias
Positive	47.7%	−2.3%
Negative	52.3	2.3
Dominant	48.6	−1.4
Submissive	51.4	1.4
Positive-dominant	48.0	−2.0
Positive-submissive	49.8	−0.2
Negative-dominant	50.7	0.7
Negative-submissive	51.6	1.6
Median	50.2	0.2[b]
Mean	50.0	0.0
σ	1.8	1.8

[a]Expected value in the absence of bias = 50.0
[b]The median, mean, and σ for absolute rather than algebraic values of bias are 1.4, 1.5, and 0.7, respectively.

that a very large number of negative items would be correctly answered simply because of a bias to choose negative alternatives, we might expect to obtain a large negative correlation between accuracy in positive versus negative items. In fact, however, this correlation is positive and very large ($r = .60$, $N = 480$ S's of high school norm group). Similarly, the correlation between accuracy in dominant versus submissive items is positive and very large ($r = .65$, $N = 480$ S's of high school norm group). Even the correlations between accuracy in the various quadrants were positive and large, ranging from .54 to .32 with the median $r = .46$. On the basis of these correlations, as well as on the basis of the analysis of table 2.3, then, there appeared to be little evidence for appreciable bias in the answer sheet.

PROCEDURE FOR ADMINISTERING THE PONS TEST

The PONS film requires a 16-mm sound projector and screen, used in a dim room. Lighting should be adjusted so that test takers can both view the film with sufficient contrast and also read their answer sheets. Test takers read the alternatives printed on their answer sheets and record their answers during the pauses that are incorporated into the film. The electronically generated "beep" introducing each segment serves the function of reminding test takers that a segment is due for their attention, and this is particularly important for segments that offer information in the video mode only. Group size has varied from 1 to over 120 people, with the upper limit set only by the size of the room and the size of the screen. Appendix 2F contains the complete text of the instructions read by the administrator immediately before starting the film.[5]

SCORING

Appendix 2G gives a full account of the scoring procedure and the various scores that can be generated for each test taker. In the analyses reported in this book, "credited" scores were employed; these scores include a chance-level credit for test items left unanswered. Since most test takers leave very few

5. In an experiment conducted by Ann Weber and James Simmons at The Johns Hopkins University, high school students took the sixty-item still photo PONS (see chapter 6) under one of two experimental conditions. In a control condition, subjects were administered the standard instructions. In the experimental condition, subjects were administered standard instructions plus a mild recommendation that reading over the response alternatives before each item has been found to be helpful. There was a nonsignificant tendency for control group subjects to score higher than experimental subjects (75% versus 73%), $F(1,126) = 3.34$, $p < .10$, effect size = $.32\sigma$). This suggests that subjects choose a strategy that is optimal for them when not instructed to employ a single specific strategy.

items unanswered, there is no effective difference between uncredited and credited scores in most samples.

ACOUSTIC CORRELATES OF PONS DIMENSIONS OF AFFECT

As a step in making the PONS film, each of the twenty scenes was judged to fall into one of four quadrants of affect formed by the crossing of the positivity dimension and the dominance dimension. Those judgments had been made initially by eight raters who watched the unedited video tapes while hearing the original unfiltered speech that accompanied each scene. We were also interested in whether the scenes assigned to each quadrant by the judges might be distinguishable from those in other quadrants on the basis of some of the purely physical characteristics of the voice, namely, the frequency level and amplitude level of the audio portion in each audio modality (original audio, content-filtered audio, and randomized spliced audio). In order to accomplish this, Peter Rogers constructed an instrument called the "audio analyzer."

THE AUDIO ANALYZER. The details of the audio analyzer are given in appendix 2H. Here it is enough to note that the instrument distributes data related to pitch and loudness to one or more of five counters or dials so that for any audio sample a five-point profile of sound frequencies and a five-point profile of peak amplitudes is produced. The five frequency levels and the five amplitude sensitivity levels corresponding to the five counters or dials of the audio analyzer are shown here:

Frequency (Hertz)   30, 250, 500, 900, 1800
Sensitivity (Volts)   0.2, 0.4, 0.6, 0.8, 1.0

The audio stimuli to be analyzed were the original full-length scenes before they were reduced to the two-second lengths of the final PONS test. These full-length scenes varied somewhat in length from about five to seven seconds, so that the readings from the five counters were a function of duration as well as of frequency or amplitude. The data for each of the five counters were, therefore, expressed as a proportion of the total reading of all five counters for any given stimulus to be analyzed.

In the initial testing of the audio analyzer, all twenty unfiltered scenes were analyzed three times for frequency and three times for amplitude in order to permit the calculation of the reliability of the five-point profiles created for each of the scenes. The estimate employed was the mean square for the counter × scenes within quadrants interaction minus the mean square for the counter × scenes within quadrants × replications interaction, all divided by the mean square for the counter × scenes within quadrants interaction, or

TABLE 2.4. Significant Differences in Relative Occurrence of Five Levels of Frequency and Amplitude As a Function of Scene Dominance and Modality

Source	df	Frequency		Amplitude	
		F [a]	η	F [a]	η
Level of counter	4,64	222.64	.97	156.91	.95
Level × dominance	4,64	19.05	.74	13.87	.68
Level × modality	8,128	66.12	.90	34.57	.83
Level × dominance × modality	8,128	3.94	.44	5.24	.50

[a]All $p < .001$.

(CS − CSR)/CS. Reliability for profiles of frequency was .986, and for profiles of amplitude reliability it was .991.[6]

For both frequency and amplitude the readings of the audio analyzer were made the subject of a four-way analysis of variance comprised of two levels of positivity (positive and negative), two levels of dominance (dominant and submissive), three levels of modality (unfiltered voice, content-filtered, and randomized spliced), and five levels of counter. Scenes were the unit of analysis and so the first two factors were *between* unit sources of variation, while the last two factors were *within* unit sources of variation. In the analyses of variance for both frequency and amplitude, the same four terms reached $p < .05$; in both cases p for each was $< .001$, and the effect sizes in terms of η were large for all four significant results. Table 2.4 shows df, F, and η for all four significant effects for frequency and amplitude.

FREQUENCY. Figure 2.1 shows the proportion of readings occurring at each of the five levels of frequency for dominant and submissive scenes in the unfiltered voice, the content-filtered voice, and the randomized spliced voice. Figure 2.1 illustrates the nature of the significant effects for frequency shown in table 2.4. Thus, the huge effect of level of counter is simply due to the quadratic trend associated with low counter readings at both the lower and the higher frequencies. The level × dominance interaction is due primarily to the relative increase in high frequencies for dominant as compared to submissive scenes. The level × modality interaction is due primarily to the tendency for the original voice to be overrepresented at both the highest and lowest fre-

6. The basis for this estimate of reliability derives from the analysis of variance of the counter × scene × replication data matrix. We have no interest in the main effects of counter, scene, or replication, or in the interaction of replication × counter or replication × scenes. Our interest is primarily in the counter × scene interaction (CS), which tells us the extent to which there is variation in the patterning of counter readings as we go from scene to scene. We are also interested, however, in CSR, which represents the error term for CS. Thus, the quantity (CS − CSR)/CS gives an indication of the magnitude of the CS effect relative to its expected value.

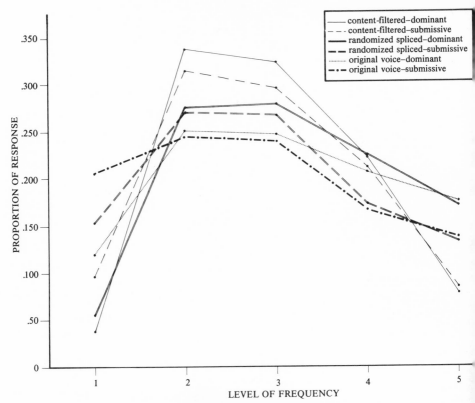

FIGURE 2.1. Relative occurrence of five levels of frequency for dominant and submissive scenes in three modalities

quencies while content-filtered speech is underrepresented at the extremes. Randomized spliced speech does not show these quadratic components of the interaction but tends instead to be overrepresented at the highest level of frequency. The level × dominance × modality interaction is due primarily to the tendency for the dominant scenes to register at higher frequencies for unfiltered and randomized spliced speech but at lower frequencies for content-filtered speech compared to the submissive scenes.

AMPLITUDE. Figure 2.2 shows the results for amplitude in analogous form to figure 2.1. The very large effect of level of counter shown for amplitude in table 2.4 is due to the strong downward linear trend, showing merely that higher amplitude readings are rarer than lower amplitude readings. This is of no substantive interest, since the audio analyzer records amplitude in a cumulative manner so that every "loud" stimulus also activates all less "loud" counters. The level × dominance interaction is mainly due to the relative increase in high amplitudes for dominant as compared to submissive scenes. The level × modality interaction is due primarily to the tendency for the content-filtered voice to be overrepresented at the higher amplitudes while the unfiltered voice is underrepresented at the higher amplitudes compared to the randomized spliced voice. The level × dominance × modality interaction is due primarily to the tendency for the dominant scenes to register at the higher amplitudes too often in the randomized spliced voice and too seldom in the content-filtered voice relative to the unfiltered voice.

PROFILE RELIABILITY. Earlier we reported the reliability of the profile of frequency and amplitude generated by the audio analyzer and found both to be approximately .99, showing that successive analyses yielded nearly identical results. But given high machine reliability, we also wanted to know the profile reliability of frequency and amplitude across the four types of scenes. Such reliability addresses the question of whether the profile differences between

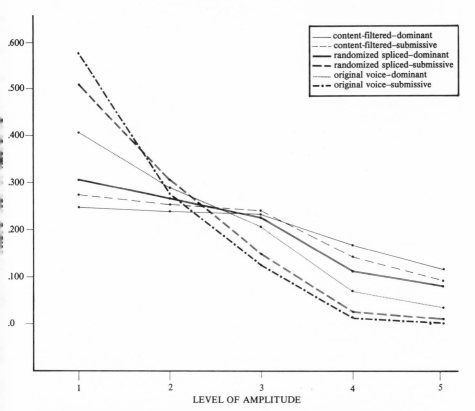

FIGURE 2.2. Relative occurrence of five levels of amplitude for dominant and submissive scenes in three modalities

quadrants (or dimensions) are substantially greater than the profile differences among scenes within quadrants.

As a computational example, consider the twenty five-point profiles generated for the twenty scenes, of which five are nested in each of the four quadrants. Profile reliability is here defined as the interaction of counters $\times$ quadrants minus the interaction of counters $\times$ scenes within quadrants, all divided by counters $\times$ quadrants, or $(CQ - CS)/CQ$. The first column of table 2.5 shows these reliabilities for various modalities for both frequency and amplitude.[7] The following three columns show the reliabilities for the positive versus negative quadrants, dominant versus submissive quadrants, and the interacting or diagonal quadrants (positive dominant plus negative submissive versus negative dominant plus positive submissive). This table shows there is substantial profile reliability or distinctiveness among the four quadrants for both frequency and amplitude. Most of this marked differentiating ability of the profiles appears to be due to the strong profile differences between the dominant and submissive scenes rather than to differences between positive and negative scenes or to the differences in profiles associated with the interaction of the dominance dimension with the positivity dimension. These results are consistent with the results of table 2.4, figure 2.1, and figure 2.2, as they should be.

A question closely related to but not identical with the question of profile reliability is the question of the reliability across quadrants (or dimensions) of the general level of frequency or amplitude. To compute an estimate of general level of frequency or amplitude for each scene, each of the counter readings was multiplied by the counter number (1, 2, 3, 4, or 5), and the readings thus weighted were added. For example, readings of 0, .1, .2, .3, and .4 in each of the five counters would yield a weighted sum of $(0)(1) +$ $(.1)(2) + (.2)(3) + (.3)(4) + (.4)(5) = 4.0$. The same readings in reverse order would yield a weighted sum of only 2.0. In table 2.5, the last rows in the sections on frequency and amplitude each provide estimates of the reliability across quadrants and dimensions of the general level of frequency and amplitude. These reliabilities, which are related to the linear trend component of the five-point profile, tend to be of the same order of magnitude as the analogous profile reliabilities, or perhaps a little higher.

Altogether six such weighted levels were computed, one each of frequency and amplitude for the original unfiltered voice, the randomized spliced voice, and the content-filtered voice. The intercorrelations among these six variables showed that frequency and amplitude were significantly and highly correlated for unfiltered speech ($r = .94$), for randomized spliced speech ($r = .86$), and for content-filtered speech ($r = .54$). Content-filtered frequency and

7. The basis for this estimate of reliability is similar to that described in note 6, except that in the earlier application the error term was generated by crossing, while in this application the error term is generated by nesting.

TABLE 2.5. Reliabilities of Profiles of Frequencies and Amplitudes across Quadrants

	Quadrants (df = 12,64)	Positive-Negative (df = 4,64)	Dominant-Submissive (df = 4,64)	Positive × Dominant (df = 4,64)
Frequency				
Original voice profile	.77	0	.91	.34
Randomized spliced profile	.89	0	.96	.26
Content-filtered profile	.59	0	.85	0
Total profile	.85	0	.95	0
Total mean frequency[a]	.95[b]	0[c]	.95[c]	.13[c]
Amplitude				
Original voice profile	.77	.32	.90	.51
Randomized spliced profile	.77	0	.91	.39
Content-filtered profile	.37	.17	.74	0
Total profile	.82	0	.93	.46
Total mean amplitude[a]	.94[b]	0[c]	.93[c]	.34[c]

[a] Reliability of mean of all three modalities scored for overall frequency and amplitude by summing over all five counters with each counter reading weighted by its counter number, i.e., 1, 2, 3, 4, or 5.
[b] $df = 3,16$
[c] $df = 1,16$

amplitude showed the lowest correlations with the remaining variables. On the whole, however, our indices of frequency and amplitude showed very considerable overlap.

CONTROL FOR USE OF LANGUAGE. When substantial reliability of differences among the mean profiles of the four quadrants was obtained, we wonder whether we were actually assessing the reliability of affects expressed by the PONS sender or whether her particular choice of language to accompany the scenes of each quadrant might have been responsible for the reliability of profiles over quadrants. Thus, perhaps quadrants may have shown discriminable profiles because of the particular choice and pattern of phonemes employed in each scene rather than because of the affect that was intended to be communicated in that scene. As a control for this possibility, the original PONS sender made a new tape in which she expressed one standard content phrase in each of the four affect quadrants of the PONS. Although this tape showed a higher average frequency than the original unfiltered voice of the PONS ($F(1,16) = 8.64, \eta = .59$), the shapes of the profiles were essentially the same for the original and control tapes in going from quadrant to quadrant, with no F as large as 1.5 for either frequency or amplitude. The agreement between the profiles of the original and the control tape in going across the four quadrants is expressed by a correlation of .87 for frequency and .84 for amplitude. These results show quite clearly that the profiles of frequency and amplitude differentiating the various affect quadrants are associated with the specific types of affect as expressed by our sender rather than with the words she uttered under the various affect conditions.

It would be useful briefly to recapitulate the principal findings of the analysis of the acoustic correlates of the PONS dimensions of affect. The audio analyzer was constructed to permit the convenient assessment of the profiles of frequency and amplitude of the audio portions of the PONS. The reliability of the audio analyzer in measuring the profiles of both frequency and amplitude was .99.

The analysis of frequency showed that dominant scenes contained higher frequencies on the average than submissive scenes, and that this difference was greater for the original unaltered voice and the randomized spliced voice than for the content-filtered voice. In addition, relative to the original voice, the randomized spliced voice showed higher frequencies, while the content-filtered voice showed too few very low or very high frequencies.

The analysis of amplitude showed that dominant scenes had higher amplitude on the average than submissive scenes, and that this difference was greatest for the randomized spliced voice and smallest for the content-filtered voice. In addition, relative to the randomized spliced voice, the content-filtered voice showed higher amplitude, while the original voice showed lower amplitude.

The analysis of the reliability of the profiles of frequency and amplitude across the affect quadrants of the PONS showed that the very substantial reliabilities obtained were due primarily to the ability of the profiles to differentiate dominant from submissive scenes. In addition, for the present measures of frequency and amplitude, the average level of frequency was found to be substantially correlated with the average level of amplitude.

Finally, a control tape was produced that allowed us to determine that the profiles of frequency and amplitude differentiating the PONS affect quadrants were associated with the specific affects expressed by our sender rather than with the particular words she used to express the various affects.

Appendix 2A

RANDOMIZED SPLICING

For the PONS, twenty sequences of random numbers between one and fifty were devised, each of which was used to reassemble the cut-up audio tape of one scene. When the tapes were cut, most of them fell into fewer than twenty-five pieces, and this meant merely that the higher numbers in the randomized sequences were not assigned a piece of tape.

To make these twenty sequences, the numbers one through fifty were first randomized, using a table of random numbers, and then they were divided into deciles containing five numbers each. Ten new sequences were easily created from these numbers, by simply transferring the topmost decile on the list to the bottom of the list ten times, creating ten new arrangements of the deciles. The order of the five numbers within each decile remained the same. Another ten sequences were made by taking the original randomized order of one to fifty, *reversing* it, and then proceeding with the division into deciles, the same as before. Again, the order of the five numbers within each decile remained the same, but each group of five numbers occurred in a different order from the first set of deciles. Combining the first ten sequences (derived from the original randomization) and the second ten sequences (derived from the reversal of the original randomization) produced twenty sequences, one for each of the scenes to be randomized spliced.

When the twenty scenes were played back to naive judges, it became apparent that, in cases where two splice cuts had fallen at the beginning and end of a word, the word was sometimes still understandable. To correct this, a rule was followed whereby the segment in question was cut in the middle, and one of the two adjacent segments was also cut in the middle. The segment thus removed was reinserted randomly somewhere else in the tape. By this method, half of the word that had been understandable remained in its first location, and half the word was moved to a new location. This procedure was followed as many times as necessary until all giveaway words were judged to be effectively scrambled.

Appendix 2B

THE AUDIO-VIDEO SYSTEM

The audio and video equipment and accessories used to record the original master tapes and during subsequent editing sessions were obtained from the Center for the Behavioral Sciences at Harvard University. Certain specialized devices, such as the audio analyzer (see "Acoustic Correlates of PONS Dimensions of Affect," chapter 2), were designed and constructed in the electronics shop of Harvard's Department of Psychology and Social Relations.

All video recording was carried out on Ampex professional video recorders (two model 7500, one model 6000). One-inch video tape was used (Memorex #79P-ON-7084-W3 for original masters; Scotch #360-1-3000-R97-B for edited copies). During the recording session in the laboratory, two Sony video cameras (model CVC-2100A) were mounted on tripods. One camera was connected to each Ampex 7500 recorder. A Shibaden video camera (model HV-14) was similarly mounted and was connected to the Ampex 6000 recorder. The controls on all cameras and recorders were adjusted for the best picture. These settings were maintained throughout the recording session. The two Ampex 7500 recorders were later used during editing sessions (see appendix 2D). One Ampex 7500 recorder was used to play the master video tapes during the selection of the scenes (see "Final Selection of the Scenes," chapter 2) and for the presentation of the video tape PONS (see "The Video Tape PONS Test," chapter 2). A Setchell-Carlson monitor/receiver (model 2100-SD) was used for all video monitoring and playback.

Several good quality microphones were tested in the departmental social psychology laboratory to determine their acoustical response and sensitivity. A Wollensak dynamic microphone (model A-0454) was selected as the primary microphone. This was connected to one channel of a Switchcraft audio mixer (model 308TR). An Electrovoice levalier microphone (model 649B) was fed to a second channel of the mixer to allow the technician to identify each selection verbally prior to a take (see "The Videotaping," chapter 2). The mixer output was then sent to a Dynakit monophonic preamplifier (model PAM-1) in a specially designed audio console. The output of the preamplifier was routed to a Sony audio tape deck (model 666-D), which recorded a master audio tape later used in the randomized splicing procedure (see appendix 2A). In addition to feeding the Sony audio tape deck, the preamplifier was connected within the audio console to a Dynakit forty-watt monophonic power amplifier (model Mark IV) by way of a master level control. This amplifier provided the necessary power to drive a Heathkit monitor speaker system (model AS-81) or an audio output line. The selection of either the monitor speaker or the audio output line was determined by the setting of a console selector switch. The audio output line was split three ways in a distribution box and each branch line was connected directly to the audio line input of each Ampex video recorder. The audio signals thus recorded were later used to produce the synchronized, electronically filtered audio portions of the composite master video tape (see appendix 2D). An audio level meter and a set of Superex earphones (model SW-2) were also wired to the output of the power amplifier to indicate to the technician both the relative loudness of the signals and the quality of the audio being recorded. A Mallory solid state oscillator/transducer (model SC-628) was also mounted in the audio console, together with a small direct-current power supply. The transducer produced a very penetrating tone when a remote push button was pressed by the technician. This "beep" was used to signal the portrayer during the recording session (see "The Videotaping," chapter 2), and as an aid in "cuing" the master video tapes during the subsequent editing sessions (see appendix 2D).

Appendix 2C

TRANSCRIPT OF TWENTY SCENES (BEFORE EDITING)

Positive-Submissive

1. "Oh, I'm sorry, we don't have that anymore. But I have something else that is very similar, and I think you might like it. Would you like to look?" (helping a customer)
2. "I'd like a Danish pastry please, and a cup of tea with cream, and a glass of milk, I guess. Thanks." (ordering food in a restaurant)
3. "Oh, thank you! I thought I'd lost that. I just can't thank you enough." (expressing gratitude)
4. "I love you. I think I'll always love you. I just want to do things with you and be with you." (expressing deep affection)
5. "Hey, don't go. I think we'll have a good time tonight if you stay." (trying to seduce someone)

Positive-Dominant

6. "I'm so excited! The wedding's next month, and we have all these flowers, and my dress, and all these invitations—it's just wonderful!" (talking about one's wedding)
7. "I'm sure I have everything I need. Now if I forget anything I'll call you. And I'll write you all the time." (leaving on a trip)
8. "Are you sure you're warm enough, dear? Why don't you put on a sweater? That's good. Have a good time." (expressing motherly love)
9. "Have you ever seen such a beautiful day? Did you know the flowers are out already down by the river?" (admiring nature)
10. "Oh, don't cry. Where do you live? Everything will be okay. Just tell me, what's your daddy's name?" (talking to a lost child)

Negative-Submissive

11. "I just can't believe it—he had so much to live for and he was so young. It's just terrible." (talking about the death of a friend)
12. "Well, I'm sorry it had to happen, but we just couldn't get along and I think we're better off now. I'm just glad it's over with." (talking about one's divorce)
13. "I'm terribly sorry, but this clock I bought just doesn't work, at least it doesn't seem to. Could I exchange it?" (returning faulty item to a store)

14. "I'm sorry I said that. It sounded awful. I know how you must have felt. I'm so sorry." (asking forgiveness)
15. "Dear Lord, please guide us in our time of misery and help us to make the right decisions." (saying a prayer)

Negative-Dominant

16. "Where have you been? I've been waiting here for two hours. I just don't have all afternoon." (criticizing someone for being late)
17. "How many times have I told you not to leave things all over the house? It just makes it a mess." (nagging a child)
18. "I hate you! I just don't want anything to do with you—everything you do hurts me." (expressing strong dislike)
19. "Look, I've told you before, don't push me on that or I'll get you." (threatening someone)
20. "You took my husband! You took my husband and he was all I had. Give him back to me." (expressing jealous anger)

Appendix 2D

THE COMPOSITE MASTER VIDEO TAPE

In making the composite master video tape, two Ampex video recorders (model 7500) were used. These were designated as the "playback Ampex" and the "recording Ampex" respectively. Two Sony video cameras (model CVC-2100A) were employed. The first camera provided a "dead air" video signal for the rating pauses between segments by being operated in the "stand-by" mode. The second camera was mounted on a short tripod and was focused on white, magnetically attractive identification numbers. These were mounted on a steel sheet with a flat black finish. The numbers were changed prior to the recording of each new segment, and ran from 1 to 220. A Setchell-Carlson monitor/receiver (model 2100-SD) was connected to the recording Ampex to provide visual and auditory monitoring of the recording process.

In addition to the specially designed audio console and the Sony audio tape deck used during the making of the original master tapes (see appendix 2B), several other electronic components were used in setting up the editing system. One advantage in using professional equipment like the Ampex 7500 video recorder is that it can be operated from a remote location through the use of externally mounted controls. In order to take advantage of this feature, a specially designed control unit was built. This device made it possible for the technician to operate both Ampex video recorders, the Sony audio tape deck (after some modification), and other auxiliary equipment from a single, remote location.

The source materials used in producing the composite master video tape were the three master video tapes (face, body, and figure) containing the original audio and video recorded in the laboratory, and the randomized spliced audio tape that was made from a copy of the original master audio tape (see appendix 2A). Those segments that were to include electronically filtered audio were recorded on the composite master video tape by passing the original audio from the master video tapes through the electronic voice content filter (Rogers, Scherer, and Rosenthal 1971) during the editing process (see description below).

One reason for paying close attention to detail in setting up the rather complex array of equipment was to ensure that the composite master video tape would be produced with a fairly high degree of consistency and accuracy. The basic editing procedure consisted of the following operational steps, some of which were varied depending on the kind of auditory and/or visual material required for the segment being recorded:

1. Using the randomized sequence of segments previously established (see "The Answer Sheet," chapter 2), the appropriate master video tape was loaded on the playback Ampex. This tape was run ahead at high speed in order to locate the correct scene and take. The verbal identifications recorded during the laboratory taping session made this possible (see appendix 2B). If the sequence sheet called for randomized spliced audio for that segment, the randomized spliced audio tape was run ahead (or back) to the same scene and take on the Sony audio tape deck. Both tapes were then "cued" to the same starting points using the prerecorded "beep" signal. In other words, each scene and take was located and cued on the playback Ampex and/or the audio tape deck so that it could be copied by the recording Ampex in the correct channel and sequence. For segments not requiring randomized spliced audio, it was necessary only to select and cue the proper scene and take on the playback Ampex.

2. The segment identification number was then positioned so as to appear in the center of the monitor screen. (The control unit could be operated in a "preview" mode to allow the technician to monitor all video and audio sources prior to the actual recording of a segment.)

3. Depending on the particular segment being recorded, the control unit was then prepared so that the technician could start and stop the various devices in the proper sequence to produce the desired results.

4. Small adjustments were made to the recorders, electronic filter, and other equipment as deemed necessary. The technician then operated the appropriate switches on the control unit, and the following operations ensued:

    a. The recording Ampex was started and allowed to run for four seconds while recording the "dead air" video signal from the first video camera.

    b. A control was operated after the four-second interval, switching the video input signal from the first video camera to the second, which was set to pick up the segment identification number. Simultaneously, a 500-millisecond pulse generator, built into the control unit, was triggered. The generator turned on an audio gate, which passed a new "beep" signal from an external audio oscillator to the recording Ampex. This new signal, occurring simultaneously with the appearance of the identification number on the screen, would serve as an auditory reminder for subjects to prepare for the oncoming segment. The playback Ampex was also started at this same instant.

    c. By carefully cuing the selected master video tape on the playback Ampex during step 1 above, the original "beep" recorded on this tape in the laboratory was reproduced approximately two seconds after the machine was started. (This signal was not fed to the recording Ampex, but was monitored by the technician through earphones.) Immediately following this signal, another control was operated, switching out the second video camera and connecting the video output from the playback Ampex directly to the recording Ampex. This latter control could be operated in two different modes, depending on the auditory information required for a given segment. In the first mode, the audio signals from the master video tape, after being fed through the electronic filter and audio console, were routed through an audio gate to the recording Ampex. In the second mode, the Sony audio tape deck was started at the same instant as the playback Ampex, and the audio signals from the randomized spliced audio tape were gated to the recording Ampex after passing through the audio console.

    d. The visual and/or auditory information was then recorded in full (about 5.5 seconds) and was faded out during a one-second interval.

    e. All recorders were stopped and operational steps 1 through 4 were repeated for the next segment.

For those segments representing the "pure" channels, i.e., requiring audio only or video only, selected playback controls and other interconnections were changed prior to step 4, above, to meet the necessary conditions.

The technically oriented reader might question the advisability of using the audio track recorded on the master video tapes as source for electronically filtered audio, because of the somewhat inferior quality of the signal when compared with that on the original audio tape as recorded by the Sony audio tape deck. Although the randomized spliced audio track could not, by its very nature, be synchronized with the video information when combined in a given segment, the electronically filtered audio did require synchronization with the video, particularly when it was paired with face. Due to the extreme difficulty of synchronizing the video and audio tracks from two individual machines when making a composite recording, the audio tracks from the original master video tapes had to be used whenever electronically filtered audio was called for.

Appendix 2E

SCORING KEY FOR FULL PONS TEST

TABLE 2.6. Scoring Key for Full PONS Test

Test Segment	Channel	Alternative & Quadrant	Test Segment	Channel	Alternative & Quadrant
1	CF	A. expressing jealous anger ND _B._ talking to a lost child PD	3	RS	A. talking about the death of a friend NS _B._ taking to a lost child PD
2	FA + RS	A. talking to a lost child PD _B._ admiring nature PD	4	CF	_A._ leaving on a trip PD B. saying a prayer NS

Table 2.6. *Continued.*

Test Segment	Channel	Alternative & Quadrant	Test Segment	Channel	Alternative & Quadrant
5	FA	A. criticizing someone for being late ND _B._ expressing gratitude PS	19	FA + CF	_A._ asking forgiveness NS B. leaving on a trip PD
6	FIG + RS	_A._ helping a customer PS B. expressing gratitude PS	20	FIG	A. expressing gratitude PS _B._ leaving on a trip PD
7	RS	A. criticizing someone for being late ND _B._ leaving on a trip PD	21	FIG + CF	A. leaving on a trip PD _B._ returning faulty item to a store NS
8	BO	A. talking about one's wedding PD _B._ expressing gratitude PS	22	FA + RS	A. returning faulty item to a store NS _B._ talking about one's divorce NS
9	FA + CF	_A._ helping a customer PS B. talking about one's divorce NS	23	RS	_A._ expressing jealous anger ND B. talking about one's divorce NS
10	BO + CF	A. talking about the death of a friend NS _B._ trying to seduce someone PS	24	FA + CF	A. talking about the death of a friend NS _B._ threatening someone ND
11	CF	A. talking to a lost child PD _B._ helping a customer PS	25	BO + CF	_A._ expressing deep affection PS B. saying a prayer NS
12	BO + CF	_A._ admiring nature PD B. expressing motherly love PD	26	FIG	A. expressing deep affection PS _B._ trying to seduce someone PS
13	FIG	A. expressing deep affection PS _B._ nagging a child ND	27	BO + CF	_A._ nagging a child ND B. expressing motherly love PD
14	BO	A. expressing motherly love PD _B._ asking forgiveness NS	28	BO + CF	_A._ leaving on a trip PD B. ordering food in a restaurant PS
15	FA	_A._ admiring nature PD B. helping a customer PS	29	FIG	_A._ helping a customer PS B. expressing jealous anger ND
16	BO	A. admiring nature PD _B._ saying a prayer NS	30	BO	_A._ criticizing someone for being late ND B. expressing gratitude PS
17	FIG + RS	_A._ nagging a child ND B. admiring nature PD	31	RS	_A._ threatening someone ND B. talking about one's wedding PD
18	FA	A. nagging a child ND _B._ criticizing someone for being late ND	32	FA + CF	A. admiring nature PD _B._ expressing strong dislike ND

Table 2.6. *Continued.*

Test Segment	Channel	Alternative & Quadrant	Test Segment	Channel	Alternative & Quadrant
33	RS	<u>A.</u> ordering food in a restaurant PS B. criticizing someone for being late ND	46	FA + CF	A. asking forgiveness NS <u>B.</u> saying a prayer NS
34	FA + CF	A. leaving on a trip PD <u>B.</u> talking about one's wedding PD	47	RS	<u>A.</u> expressing motherly love PD B. helping a customer PS
35	FIG + CF	<u>A.</u> talking to a lost child PD B. expressing strong dislike ND	48	FIG + CF	<u>A.</u> admiring nature PD B. expressing strong dislike ND
36	FIG + RS	<u>A.</u> trying to seduce someone PS B. expressing jealous anger ND	49	FA + CF	A. expressing motherly love PD <u>B.</u> leaving on a trip PD
37	FA	<u>A.</u> expressing strong dislike ND B. expressing deep affection PS	50	BO + RS	<u>A.</u> talking about one's divorce NS B. ordering food in a restaurant PS
38	FA + RS	A. leaving on a trip PD <u>B.</u> threatening someone ND	51	FA	<u>A.</u> asking forgiveness NS B. nagging a child ND
39	BO + RS	<u>A.</u> expressing deep affection PS B. talking about the death of a friend NS	52	FA	A. admiring nature PD <u>B.</u> expressing motherly love PD
40	BO + CF	A. talking to a lost child PD <u>B.</u> criticizing someone for being late ND	53	FA + RS	<u>A.</u> returning faulty item to a store NS B. criticizing someone for being late ND
41	BO + CF	<u>A.</u> ordering food in a restaurant PS B. expressing gratitude PS	54	FA + RS	<u>A.</u> talking about one's wedding PD B. expressing deep affection PS
42	BO	<u>A.</u> expressing motherly love PD B. threatening someone ND	55	RS	<u>A.</u> expressing strong dislike ND B. ordering food in a restaurant PS
43	BO	<u>A.</u> expressing strong dislike ND B. ordering food in a restaurant PS	56	FIG	<u>A.</u> admiring nature PD B. ordering food in a restaurant PS
44	FIG	A. expressing motherly love PD <u>B.</u> talking to a lost child PD	57	FA	<u>A.</u> returning faulty item to a store NS B. helping a customer PS
45	FA	<u>A.</u> expressing deep affection PS B. nagging a child ND	58	FIG + RS	<u>A.</u> expressing strong dislike ND B. expressing gratitude PS

Table 2.6. *Continued.*

Test Segment	Channel	Alternative & Quadrant	Test Segment	Channel	Alternative & Quadrant
59	FA + CF	_A._ expressing deep affection PS B. expressing gratitude PS	72	FA + CF	_A._ nagging a child ND B. talking to a lost child PD
60	BO	A. saying a prayer NS _B._ threatening someone ND	73	CF	A. talking to a lost child PD _B._ criticizing someone for being late ND
61	CF	A. saying a prayer NS _B._ ordering food in a restaurant PS	74	FA	A. talking about one's divorce NS _B._ trying to seduce someone PS
62	CF	A. admiring nature PD _B._ asking forgiveness NS	75	FIG + RS	_A._ expressing jealous anger ND B. helping a customer PS
63	FA + RS	_A._ talking to a lost child PD B. expressing gratitude PS	76	BO + CF	_A._ talking about one's divorce NS B. expressing deep affection PS
64	BO + CF	A. talking about one's wedding PD _B._ saying a prayer NS	77	FIG	_A._ expressing gratitude PS B. talking to a lost child PD
65	FIG + CF	A. talking to a lost child PD _B._ threatening someone ND	78	BO + RS	A. expressing deep affection PS _B._ asking forgiveness NS
66	CF	A. expressing motherly love PD _B._ nagging a child ND	79	BO + RS	_A._ threatening someone ND B. nagging a child ND
67	FA + CF	A. expressing motherly love PD _B._ returning faulty item to a store NS	80	FIG	_A._ talking about the death of a friend NS B. trying to seduce someone PS
68	FIG + CF	A. expressing gratitude PS _B._ expressing strong dislike ND	81	RS	A. talking about one's wedding PD _B._ talking about one's divorce NS
69	FIG + CF	A. expressing strong dislike ND _B._ talking about one's wedding PD	82	FIG	A. trying to seduce someone PS _B._ criticizing someone for being late ND
70	BO	_A._ helping a customer PS B. asking forgiveness NS	83	FA + RS	_A._ helping a customer PS B. admiring nature PD
71	FIG + RS	_A._ threatening someone ND B. expressing motherly love PD			

Table 2.6. *Continued.*

Test Segment	Channel	Alternative & Quadrant	Test Segment	Channel	Alternative & Quadrant
84	BO + CF	<u>A.</u> returning faulty item to a store NS B. nagging a child ND	97	FIG + CF	A. expressing jealous anger ND <u>B.</u> asking forgiveness NS
85	FIG + CF	<u>A.</u> nagging a child ND B. leaving on a trip PD	98	FA + CF	A. expressing motherly love PD <u>B.</u> criticizing someone for being late ND
86	FIG	<u>A.</u> talking about one's wedding PD B. admiring nature PD	99	BO + CF	<u>A.</u> talking about one's wedding PD B. talking about the death of a friend NS
87	FIG + CF	<u>A.</u> criticizing someone for being late ND B. expressing deep affection PS	100	BO + CF	<u>A.</u> expressing strong dislike ND B. asking forgiveness NS
88	RS	A. admiring nature PD <u>B.</u> returning faulty item to a store NS	101	BO + RS	A. saying a prayer NS <u>B.</u> helping a customer PS
89	FIG + RS	<u>A.</u> asking forgiveness NS B. expressing strong dislike ND	102	BO + RS	<u>A.</u> nagging a child ND B. leaving on a trip PD
90	BO + CF	<u>A.</u> expressing motherly love PD B. helping a customer PS	103	FA	<u>A.</u> talking about one's divorce NS B. asking forgiveness NS
91	RS	<u>A.</u> asking forgiveness NS B. leaving on a trip PD	104	FA + RS	A. ordering food in a restaurant PS <u>B.</u> expressing jealous anger ND
92	FIG + CF	A. criticizing someone for being late ND <u>B.</u> helping a customer PS	105	RS	A. criticizing someone for being late ND <u>B.</u> talking about the death of a friend NS
93	RS	<u>A.</u> talking about one's wedding PD B. threatening someone ND	106	BO + RS	A. talking about the death of a friend NS <u>B.</u> ordering food in a restaurant PS
94	RS	A. expressing motherly love PD <u>B.</u> nagging a child ND	107	FA	A. leaving on a trip PD <u>B.</u> nagging a child ND
95	CF	<u>A.</u> expressing motherly love PD B. expressing gratitude PS	108	FIG + RS	<u>A.</u> saying a prayer NS B. talking about one's divorce NS
96	CF	<u>A.</u> talking about one's divorce NS B. trying to seduce someone PS	109	BO + RS	<u>A.</u> expressing strong dislike ND B. trying to seduce someone PS

Table 2.6. *Continued.*

Test Segment	Channel	Alternative & Quadrant	Test Segment	Channel	Alternative & Quadrant
110	BO + CF	A. ordering food in a restaurant PS *B.* asking forgiveness NS	123	FA	A. nagging a child ND *B.* talking to a lost child PD
111	FIG + RS	A. talking about one's wedding PD *B.* leaving on a trip PD	124	FA + CF	A. returning faulty item to a store NS *B.* expressing motherly love PD
112	RS	A. expressing deep affection PS *B.* admiring nature PD	125	FA + CF	*A.* talking about one's divorce NS B. admiring nature PD
113	FIG	*A.* expressing jealous anger ND B. criticizing someone for being late ND	126	BO + RS	A. expressing deep affection PS *B.* talking about the death of a friend NS
114	FIG	A. talking about one's divorce NS *B.* threatening someone ND	127	FIG + RS	A. talking about one's divorce NS *B.* admiring nature PD
115	FIG + RS	A. expressing strong dislike ND *B.* returning faulty item to a store NS	128	FIG + CF	*A.* expressing deep affection PS B. admiring nature PD
116	FA	*A.* ordering food in a restaurant PS B. threatening someone ND	129	BO + CF	*A.* talking to a lost child PD B. admiring nature PD
117	FA + CF	*A.* talking to a lost child PD B. criticizing someone for being late ND	130	FA + RS	A. returning faulty item to a store NS *B.* talking about the death of a friend NS
118	FA + RS	A. admiring nature PD *B.* nagging a child ND	131	FIG	A. talking about one's wedding PD *B.* returning faulty item to a store NS
119	FA	A. expressing strong dislike ND *B.* helping a customer PS	132	CF	*A.* admiring nature PD B. leaving on a trip PD
120	FIG + RS	*A.* talking about one's wedding PD B. ordering food in a restaurant PS	133	FA + RS	*A.* asking forgiveness NS B. helping a customer PS
121	FIG + CF	*A.* expressing gratitude PS B. expressing motherly love PD	134	FA + CF	A. expressing strong dislike ND *B.* ordering food in a restaurant PS
122	BO	A. leaving on a trip PD *B.* expressing deep affection PS	135	FA	A. returning faulty item to a store NS *B.* talking about the death of a friend NS
			136	FIG + CF	A. expressing deep affection PS *B.* saying a prayer NS

Table 2.6. *Continued.*

Test Segment	Channel	Alternative & Quadrant	Test Segment	Channel	Alternative & Quadrant
137	FIG + RS	A. saying a prayer NS *B.* criticizing someone for being late ND	150	FA + RS	A. talking about the death of a friend NS *B.* expressing motherly love PD
138	FA	*A.* talking about one's wedding PD B. talking about one's divorce NS	151	CF	A. expressing gratitude PS *B.* expressing strong dislike ND
139	CF	*A.* expressing gratitude PS B. expressing motherly love PD	152	RS	*A.* expressing deep affection PS B. returning faulty item to a store NS
140	FA	*A.* expressing jealous anger ND B. threatening someone ND	153	CF	A. expressing gratitude PS *B.* threatening someone ND
141	FIG + CF	A. asking forgiveness NS *B.* expressing motherly love PD	154	FIG + CF	*A.* leaving on a trip PD B. talking to a lost child PD
142	FA + CF	*A.* admiring nature PD B. ordering food in a restaurant PS	155	BO	A. talking about the death of a friend NS *B.* expressing jealous anger ND
143	BO + RS	*A.* expressing motherly love PD B. expressing jealous anger ND	156	BO + RS	A. helping a customer PS *B.* expressing gratitude PS
144	CF	*A.* expressing jealous anger ND B. helping a customer PS	157	FIG	A. asking forgiveness NS *B.* saying a prayer NS
145	CF	A. ordering food in a restaurant PS *B.* returning faulty item to a store NS	158	RS	*A.* trying to seduce someone PS B. expressing gratitude PS
146	BO	A. talking about one's divorce NS *B.* leaving on a trip PD	159	FA + CF	*A.* expressing jealous anger ND B. saying a prayer NS
147	CF	A. nagging a child ND *B.* saying a prayer NS	160	RS	A. criticizing someone for being late ND *B.* helping a customer PS
148	BO + RS	*A.* trying to seduce someone PS B. criticizing someone for being late ND	161	FIG + RS	A. expressing strong dislike ND *B.* expressing deep affection PS
149	BO	A. expressing deep affection PS *B.* admiring nature PD			

Table 2.6. *Continued.*

Test Segment	Channel	Alternative & Quadrant	Test Segment	Channel	Alternative & Quadrant
162	FA + CF	A. expressing deep affection PS *B.* talking about the death of a friend NS	174	BO + RS	A. expressing gratitude PS *B.* returning faulty item to a store NS
163	FA + RS	A. returning faulty item to a store NS *B.* leaving on a trip PD	175	BO + RS	A. expressing motherly love PD *B.* criticizing someone for being late ND
164	FA + RS	*A.* expressing gratitude PS B. expressing jealous anger ND	176	BO	*A.* ordering food in a restaurant PS B. expressing jealous anger ND
165	FA + RS	A. talking about one's wedding PD *B.* trying to seduce someone PS	177	FIG + RS	*A.* expressing gratitude PS B. returning faulty item to a store NS
166	FIG + CF	A. talking to a lost child PD *B.* expressing jealous anger ND	178	FIG	*A.* expressing strong dislike ND B. talking about one's divorce NS
167	CF	A. talking to a lost child PD *B.* talking about the death of a friend NS	179	FIG + RS	*A.* talking about one's divorce NS B. talking about the death of a friend NS
168	FIG	A. talking about one's divorce NS *B.* asking forgiveness NS	180	FIG + CF	*A.* ordering food in a restaurant PS B. returning faulty item to a store NS
169	BO + CF	A. trying to seduce someone PS *B.* threatening someone ND	181	BO	A. expressing motherly love PD *B.* talking to a lost child PD
170	BO + CF	A. expressing gratitude PS *B.* expressing jealous anger ND	182	FA + CF	*A.* trying to seduce someone PS B. talking about one's wedding PD
171	CF	*A.* talking about one's wedding PD B. criticizing someone for being late ND	183	BO + RS	*A.* leaving on a trip PD B. trying to seduce someone PS
172	BO	*A.* returning faulty item to a store NS B. expressing strong dislike ND	184	BO + CF	*A.* talking about the death of a friend NS B. asking forgiveness NS
173	FA + CF	*A.* expressing gratitude PS B. talking to a lost child PD	185	BO	*A.* trying to seduce someone PS B. talking to a lost child PD

Table 2.6. *Continued.*

Test Segment	Channel	Alternative & Quadrant	Test Segment	Channel	Alternative & Quadrant
186	FIG + RS	*A.* expressing motherly love PD B. ordering food in a restaurant PS	199	FA + RS	A. trying to seduce someone PS *B.* expressing deep affection PS
187	BO + RS	*A.* saying a prayer NS B. expressing jealous anger ND	200	FA + RS	A. threatening someone ND *B.* expressing strong dislike ND
188	FIG + CF	A. trying to seduce someone PS *B.* talking about the death of a friend NS	201	BO	A. talking about one's wedding PD *B.* talking about the death of a friend NS
189	FIG + RS	*A.* ordering food in a restaurant PS B. talking about the death of a friend NS	202	FIG	*A.* talking about one's divorce NS B. talking about one's wedding PD
190	CF	A. helping a customer PS *B.* trying to seduce someone PS	203	FA	*A.* threatening someone ND B. expressing strong dislike ND
191	FIG	*A.* expressing motherly love PD B. criticizing someone for being late ND	204	BO + RS	*A.* admiring nature PD B. criticizing someone for being late ND
192	FA	*A.* saying a prayer NS B. nagging a child ND	205	FIG	*A.* ordering food in a restaurant PS B. nagging a child ND
193	CF	A. talking to a lost child PD *B.* expressing deep affection PS	206	BO + CF	*A.* expressing gratitude PS B. threatening someone ND
194	BO	*A.* talking about one's divorce NS B. returning faulty item to a store NS	207	FA + RS	A. talking about one's wedding PD *B.* saying a prayer NS
195	BO + CF	A. threatening someone ND *B.* helping a customer PS	208	FIG + RS	A. admiring nature PD *B.* talking about the death of a friend NS
196	FA + RS	*A.* criticizing someone for being late ND B. talking about one's divorce NS	209	FIG + CF	*A.* trying to seduce someone PS B. saying a prayer NS
197	BO	A. expressing jealous anger ND *B.* nagging a child ND	210	FIG + CF	*A.* talking about one's divorce NS B. threatening someone ND
198	BO + RS	A. talking about one's wedding PD *B.* expressing jealous anger ND	211	FIG	*A.* expressing deep affection PS B. trying to seduce someone PS

Table 2.6. *Continued.*

Test Segment	Channel	Alternative & Quadrant	Test Segment	Channel	Alternative & Quadrant
212	BO	A. saying a prayer NS *B.* talking about one's wedding PD	217	FA + RS	A. leaving on a trip PD *B.* ordering food in a restaurant PS
213	FA	*A.* leaving on a trip PD B. trying to seduce someone PS	218	BO + RS	A. expressing strong dis-like ND *B.* talking to a lost child PD
214	FIG + RS	A. saying a prayer NS *B.* talking to a lost child PD	219	RS	A. expressing jealous anger ND *B.* saying a prayer NS
215	BO + RS	A. admiring nature PD *B.* talking about one's wedding PD	220	RS	A. asking forgiveness NS *B.* expressing gratitude PS
216	RS	A. expressing jealous anger ND *B.* criticizing someone for being late ND			

NOTE: Italic type indicates correct answer. FA = face; BO = body; FIG = figure (face + body); RS = randomized spliced speech; CF = content-filtered speech; PS = positive-submissive; PD = positive-dominant; NS = negative-submissive; ND = negative-dominant.

Appendix 2F

INSTRUCTIONS READ BY TEST ADMINISTRATOR

The film and sound track you are about to witness was designed so that we may learn how well people can match facial expressions, body movements, and tones of voice to the actual situation in which the expressions, movements, and tones originally occurred.

You will see and hear a series of audio and video segments, and for each one you are to judge which of two real-life situations is represented by the segment you have just seen or heard. After each segment you will have a short period of time in which to record your judgment.

Some of the visual segments will have no sound track. Some of the visual segments will have a sound track, but you will not be able to understand the words. Instead, you will hear speech that has been changed in various ways, so that you will be able to judge *only the tone of voice* in which something was said. Some of the segments will be made up of only these speech-altered portions of the sound track, and for these there will be no film to watch at all. In fact, the very first segment is like this.

Each segment you will see and/or hear has been numbered on the screen, and this number corresponds to a number on your answer sheet. Your answer sheet lists two brief descriptions of everyday life situations for each segment. One of these descriptions correctly describes the actual situation you will see and/or hear, while the other description does *not* describe the situation accurately. For each numbered segment, please circle the letter *A* or *B* next to the situation you believe to correspond to the segment you have just seen and/or heard.

When you see a number appear on the screen, please find the corresponding number on your answer sheet and place your finger just in front of the number, to keep your place. Watch and/or listen to the segment that follows the number, and as soon as the segment ends circle the letter *A* or *B* corresponding to the situation you believe the segment to have been based upon. Then look to the screen again promptly to find the next number flashed on the screen.

Many of the choices will be difficult, but you should choose one of the descriptions even though you may feel quite uncertain about the correct answer. Choose the more likely description for each segment even if you feel you might be guessing. Your guesses may be much more accurate than you would imagine. In fact, we request that you do not change any answers once you have made a choice. For every segment, then, do the best you can to judge accurately the situations upon which each segment is based. Your answer sheet contains a sample answer, which you should look at now.

All ready to start? Now we will begin.

Appendix 2G

SCORING THE PONS TEST

The "A's" and "B's" circled on the answer sheets are coded as "0's" and "1's." The first important step in the scoring program translates these 0's and 1's into new 0's and 1's representing incorrectness and correctness rather than A and B. Once this is done, the overall score and subscores are computed by adding up the number of correct answers in the various channels, scenes, and affect quadrants. For each test taker, output data cards are computer punched. These cards contain the following information, in "uncredited" or "credited" form. "Crediting" means that the test taker receives one-half point for each item left unanswered—in other words, he or she is given the points that would have been obtained if the test taker had guessed at those items instead of leaving them blank.

In this book, these scores were used:

1. 220 scored items (0 for each wrong answer, 1 for each right answer, 0.5 for each omitted item).
2. 11 channel scores, computed by adding up the number of points earned for the items in each channel; these scores can range from 0 to 20.
3. A count of omitted items for each channel.
4. 20 scene scores, computed by adding up the number of points earned for each scene; this score can range from 0 to 11.
5. A count of omitted items for each scene.
6. 4 affect quadrant scores, computed by adding the scores for the five scenes in each quadrant; these scores can range from 0 to 55.
7. A count of blanks for each affect quadrant.
8. Quadrant marginal scores (all positive, all negative, all submissive, and all dominant).

9. Overall score, computed by adding up the total number of points earned.
10. Channel marginal scores (tone 40, RS 80, CF 80, face 60, body 60, figure 60, video 60, face 120, and body 120).

Appendix 2H

THE AUDIO ANALYZER

Earlier Work in Speech Analysis

Two specific ways of measuring speech spectra (the various audio frequencies contained in human speech) have been used in the past (Miller 1951): (1) the spectrum was measured over periods of time short enough that the differences in spectrum for the different speech sounds could be detected, and (2) the spectrum was measured over a long period of time, with all sounds represented together in a single average spectrum. Early sound spectrograms (actual recordings of speech spectra that could be studied visually) were produced by a device developed by the Bell Telephone Laboratories and were used in the study of short-term speech spectra (Potter, Kopp, and Green 1947). The apparatus combined time, frequency, and amplitude (loudness) in a single record. Acoustic analysis of these spectrograms showed that different frequency regions were emphasized in the different vowels, and that the vowels radiated the most power while the consonants were relatively weak. Other early research (Rudmose et al. 1948) emphasized the fact that, with respect to the long-term measurement of speech spectra, differences among the speech sounds and short-term variations are both lost in this kind of analysis. In addition, it was discovered that most speech energy was contained in the frequency range below 1000 Hertz but that the presence of speech pressure could be detected up to frequencies of 8000 Hertz or more.

In early studies of the frequency distribution of conversational speech power (Sivian 1926), it was noted that the distribution shifted as a speaker changed from a low (confidential) talk level to a normal (conversational) level and to a high (declamatory) level. The total change in power from low to high was twenty-four decibels. In general, power was transferred from the frequency range below 500 Hertz to the range between 500 and 4000 Hertz as the talking level was raised.

In studying the relationships among fundamental frequency, vocal sound pressure, and rate of speaking (Black 1961), it was found that increments in vocal effort were accompanied by an increase in fundamental frequency, the latter shifting upward increasingly with successive steps in sound pressure. Within a thirty-decibel range, the voice rose in excess of an octave in pitch.

In recent examination of the contributions of fundamental frequency and of amplitude to the transmission of the emotional content of normal human speech, complex hardware was utilized to isolate the frequency and amplitude information contained in original tape recordings made of persons speaking in several emotional modes (Liberman and Michaels 1962). The researchers concluded that there was no single acoustic correlate of the emotional modes used in their experiment. Phonetic content, gross changes in fundamental frequency, the fine structure of the fundamental frequency ("perturbations"), and the speech envelope amplitude all contributed to the transmission of the emotional information contained in human speech.

In a more recent study of transient voice changes associated with emotional stimuli (Alpert, Kurtzberg, and Friedhoff 1963), it was found that the major intensity shifts that accompany emotional stimuli occurred in the lower portion of the speech spectrum.

These published results led us to believe that we would most probably obtain very different sets of data from the audio analyzer for those PONS scenes that were portrayed with very different kinds of emotional affect. Subsequently, we made some fairly general predictions concerning the data that would be produced by an audio analysis of the PONS scenes. (1) The vocal affect in each scene would, indeed, have a direct bearing on frequency and loudness, i.e., we would obtain different frequency and loudness distributions for the different scenes. These differences would be maximized when the data for those scenes belonging to the same PONS quadrants were added together and the quadrants themselves compared. (2) Those scenes that contained the largest audio signals (were the loudest) would show a significant upward shift in their frequency distributions.

Design Considerations

Since we wanted to be certain that our own device for speech analysis would respond equally well to major shifts in overall frequency (long-term variations) and to specific levels of energy contained in certain speech sounds, such as vowels (short-term variations), several design requirements were established. (1) The response of the device to an audio signal would have to be nearly instantaneous, limited only by the operating speed of the components used. (2) The frequency response of the device would have to cover the entire audio range of human hearing (20 to 20,000 Hertz) and be reasonably flat in the speech frequency range. (3) Some means of controlling the length of time the device acted upon the audio signals fed into it would have to be included. Clearly, a single output representation such as the spectrogram would be difficult to evaluate and would be subject to many sources of error, the most obvious of which would be on the part of the person interpreting the recording. Some form of digital readout device, such as a counter, would be much more convenient and the data could be read off directly. Multiple counters would be required, since we were interested in different bands of frequencies and several degrees of loudness. A single counter would respond to all of the information collectively. The next task, therefore, was to determine how many output channels to employ and what each of them was to represent.

One technique for analyzing speech uses both multiple output channels and bandpass filters (Miller 1951). A number of audio filters are selected that resonate to different bands of frequencies. The first filter might respond to all audio signals from 20 to 500 Hertz, the next from 500 to 1000 Hertz, the third from 1000 to 1500 Hertz, etc. The output of each filter drives some kind of metering device that registers the amount of energy in the frequency range of each filter. If constructed in a similar fashion, our device would then have a number of bandpass filters and an equal number of output registers or counters. Two design considerations were of prime importance at this point: (1) What bands of frequencies should the filters respond to, or pass?, and (2) How many filter/output sections would we need for good resolution?

Significant early contributions to the study of human speech have been made by researchers in the field of psychophysics (Stevens, Egan, and Miller 1947). It was found that by selecting filter cutoff frequencies (those frequencies along the frequency scale beyond which specific filters did not respond or pass) that were located at equal intervals along the mel scale of subjective pitch, a speech sample could be divided into frequency bands that stimulated equally wide regions on the basilar membrane. Consequently, a set of nominal cutoff frequencies for the filters could be determined that were spaced along the frequency scale at points that appeared to the ear to be equidistant in pitch. Examples of these cutoff frequencies are in Hertz: 160, 394, 670, 1000, 1420, 1900, 2450, 3120, 4000, 5100, 6600, 9000, 14000.

If we were to model our device after these findings, it would be necessary to construct a total of twelve or thirteen filters coupled to an equal number of output registers. This would involve a large expenditure of time and resources and we felt that, for our purposes, such a high degree of resolution might not be necessary. Further study of prior investigations in the area of speech analysis revealed some reassuring facts. The contributions made by different frequency bands to the intelligibility of speech is proportional to the width of the band in mels (Stevens, Egan, and Miller 1947). This relation holds only for the range of frequencies important for the transmission of speech: from about 250 to 7000 Hertz. Within this range, approximately equal contributions are made to intelligibility by frequencies contained in each of the bands. It seemed, then, that we could safely limit the number of filters employed to those that would pass frequencies between 250 and 7000 Hertz. It also seemed appropriate to reduce the number still further by extending the bandwidth of each filter so as to include a broader range of frequencies. While this would reduce the degree of resolution of our device, the data obtained would still be a reasonable representation of the audio samples, provided that the entire speech frequency range of from 250 to 7000 Hertz was covered.

To gain support for our decision to reduce the number of filter/output sections by broadening the bandwidth of each filter, recent work in the area of shortwave communications was reviewed. In one report (Wicklund 1974), it was stressed that an audio frequency range of 330 to about 3000 Hertz provided good quality voice communication. A much narrower band of 500 to 2000 Hertz was also acceptable, but the voice tone was degraded somewhat. If wider bandwidths were used, noise and adjacent signals made the voice more difficult to understand.

We did not anticipate having to deal with the noise or interference problems normally associated with shortwave reception, since our audio signals were of very good quality to begin with, having been recorded on tape in a quiet laboratory room. We felt justified, therefore, in broadening the bandwidth of each filter to a considerable extent, using the 330 to 3000 Hertz audio frequency band the communications experts deemed necessary for good reception as the minimum range of frequencies. By increasing this very limited band substantially, we should be more than adequately representing, in the form of our output data, the critical speech frequencies contained in our audio samples.

The decision concerning the number of filter/output registers and the specific frequency bands each would represent was based, then, on several diverse sets of information. The final choices represented a kind of dual compromise. By reducing the total number of filters, we lost some resolution but gained simplicity and lowered the cost. By broadening the bandwidth of each filter we again lost resolution, particularly with regard to short-term type analyses, but we extended the overall frequency range to include all of the speech frequencies. The loss of accuracy and resolution for short-term analyses was not too detrimental, since our samples were to be analyzed using the long-term technique. We decided to use five filter/output registers with a total frequency range of from 30 to approximately 10,000 Hertz. It was felt that these five registers would also provide adequate resolution when collecting loudness data on an audio sample.

Since we wished to obtain one set of data for the frequency distribution and a second set of data for the loudness of an audio sample, our device would have to respond to speech frequencies at one time and to loudness or intensity at another. The latter condition would be met by including a selector switch that routed the audio signals around the filter circuits directly to the output stages. These stages would be designed to operate when a given signal threshold value was exceeded. In the loudness mode, each of the five stages would receive a different amount of audio signal depending on the settings of five audio level controls. The controls would be preset to cover a total range of from 0.2 to 1.0 volts. Thus, an output counter would be activated whenever the audio signals were greater than the threshold level for that stage. In this way, very soft passages in the audio samples would activate only the first one or two output register, while very loud passages would activate all, including the fifth, or "least sensitive" register. In actual operation, a stream of pulses was gated to each counter via a relay that was activated by a circuit receiving the audio signals. There were five separate relay driver circuits, one for each counter. A pulse rate of 10 Hertz was used. Its accuracy and stability were high, due to the use of the 60-Hertz power line frequency as a time base. This frequency was divided electronically by six to provide the 10-Hertz pulse stream. Thus, each units digit on a counter represented one-tenth of a second.

Due to the nature of the bandpass filter circuits, the output signals from these filters would be a function of both frequency and loudness. We had to cancel out the effect of loudness from these output signals if our frequency data were to remain uncontaminated by the variations in signal level. In designing a complex speech-processing system, one group of researchers used what they termed a normalizing input system, which effectively kept the gain of the apparatus constant over a certain preset range (Olson, Belar, and DeSobrino 1962). Bandpass filters were used, and the output voltages obtained in each frequency band were proportional to the signal envelope. The output of each channel was quantized by operating a relay above a specific predetermined threshold. By using a similar "automatic gain stage" in our device, the effects of loudness on the output signals of our filters could be negated.

Construction of the Audio Analyzer

The audio analyzer was constructed using a chassis and standard nineteen-inch rack panel, allowing the experimenter some flexibility of installation. In our case, we used the device as a "table model." Three separate power supplies, a 10-Hertz pulse stream generator, five active bandpass filters with a common automatic gain stage, a Schmitt trigger/relay driver section, and five high-speed relays were built into the chassis. A frequency/loudness mode selector, five audio level controls, five filter sensitivity controls, and five output data counters were mounted on the front panel. Following construction, the unit was calibrated using an audio signal generator (General Radio type 1309A), an oscilloscope (Tektronix type 564), and an A.C. voltmeter (Heath model IM-21).

Operating Procedures

The standard procedure for an audio analysis included the following steps.
1. The audio samples to be analyzed were rerecorded onto high-quality audio tape at 7.5 inches per second, using a stereo tape deck (Sony model TD-252D).
2. The new tape was played back on a second stereo tape deck (Sony model 666D) through a stereo amplifier (Realistic model SA-175C), and the audio output was monitored on the detachable speakers of a stereo tape recorder (Wollensak model 5740).
3. The amplifier controls were set so as to provide a maximum input signal of 1.0 volt, peak to peak, at the input jack of the analyzer.

At the start of an analysis run, all output counters were reset to zero and the audio tape was cued to the beginning of the appropriate sample. A pulse stream interrupt switch on the analyzer allowed the experimenter to prevent any spurious noises or other undesired audio signals (such as scene identification numbers) from activating the counters prior to the occurrence of the actual audio signals to be analyzed. After each analysis run, the playback tape deck was stopped, the data on the counters recorded, and the counters reset for the next run. For each analysis, six data collections were made: three in the frequency mode and three in the loudness mode. This repetition reduced the possibility of error and furnished data for a reliability test (see chapter 2). Since the audio samples were of varying length, the figures read from the counters were a function of time as well as frequency or loudness. A correction procedure was therefore used; the data for each counter were expressed as a percentage of the whole by dividing the figure for that counter by the total for all five counters for a given analysis run.

3 | Normative Data

THE NORM GROUP

To evaluate the performance of the many samples that have taken the PONS test, we found it essential to provide a standard or a norm to which a given sample's performance could be compared. This normative sample had to be sufficiently large to provide stability of statistical characteristics and had to be relevant to the other samples for which we would use the norm group as a standard for evaluation.

Ideally, separate norms should be provided for every kind of group with which those who are administered the test are likely to be compared. For instance, the score of a sixty-year-old man who is a physician should be compared with a normative group of men, a normative group of sixty-year-old persons, and a normative group of physicians. Although we report only one main standardization group against which major comparisons are made, it will become clear to the reader that our comparisons of each group's scores are made with the scores of all other relevant groups so that a network of comparisons for each sample is developed. In addition, data for grade school and junior high school norm groups are provided in chapter 8.

As our main standardization group, we used 492 public senior high school students from three parts of the United States. The test was administered to 234 students in a midwest public high school, 136 in a west coast public high school, and 122 in an east coast public high school.[1] No significant differences on any PONS scores were found among the three samples, so they were pooled to form a single large norm group. IQ and aptitude data collected for the midwest and east coast students indicated that they were of average intelligence and ability. The students in our three sample groups tended to come from primarily middle-class families.

At the first stage of our norm development, only two of these three samples

---

1. In some analyses, the data from a few students were eliminated for various reasons, such as the subjects' omission of a large number of the test items.

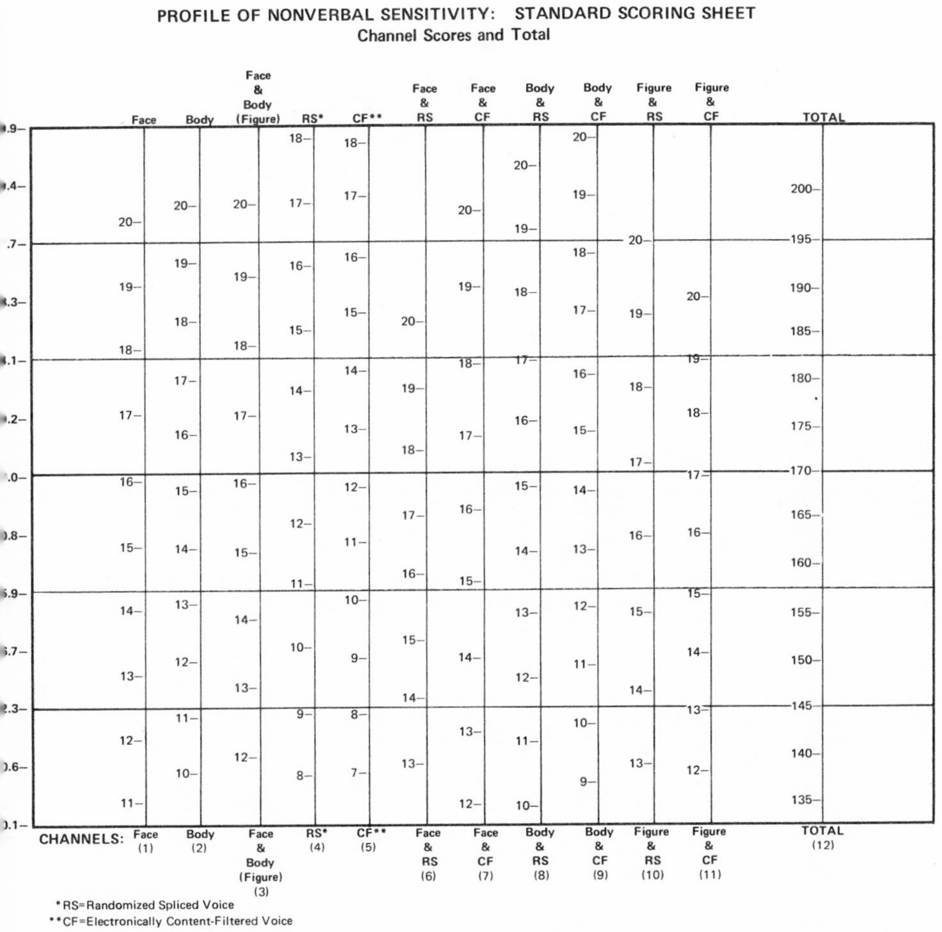

PROFILE OF NONVERBAL SENSITIVITY: STANDARD SCORING SHEET
Channel Scores and Total

	Face	Body	Face & Body (Figure)	RS*	CF**	Face & RS	Face & CF	Body & RS	Body & CF	Figure & RS	Figure & CF	TOTAL
9.9				18—	18—				20—			
9.4	20—	20—	20—	17—	17—		20—	19—				200—
9.7		19—	19—	16—	16—			19—	18—	20—		195—
9.3	19—	18—		15—	15—	20—	19—	18—	17—	20—		190— 185—
9.1	18—	18—	14—	14—	18—	19—	18—	17—	16—	19—	19—	180—
9.2	17—	17—	17—	13—	13—	19—	17—	16—	15—	18—	18—	175—
8.0	16—	15—	16—	12—	12—	18—	16—	15—	14—	17—	17—	170
8.8	15—	14—	15—	12— 11—	17— 16—	16— 15—	15—	14—	13—	16—	16—	165— 160—
6.9	14—	13—	14—	10—	15—		13—	12—	15—	15—		155—
6.7	13—	12—	13—	10—	9—	15— 14—	14—	13—	11—	14—		150—
2.3	12—	11—	12—	9—	8—	14— 13—	13—	11—	10—	13—	13—	145—
0.6	11—	10—		8—	7—	13— 12—	12—	10—	9—	13—	12—	140— 135—
0.1												

CHANNELS: Face (1)   Body (2)   Face & Body (Figure) (3)   RS* (4)   CF** (5)   Face & RS (6)   Face & CF (7)   Body & RS (8)   Body & CF (9)   Figure & RS (10)   Figure & CF (11)   TOTAL (12)

*RS=Randomized Spliced Voice
**CF=Electronically Content-Filtered Voice

FIGURE 3.1. Standard scoring sheet for the Profile of Nonverbal Sensitivity: Channel scores and total

were available to us. These were the midwest and the west coast high school students. This preliminary norm group consisted of 359 males and females. The mean credited[2] scores and standard deviations were computed for this group on each of the channels and marginals, the total, the individual scenes,

2. As described in chapter 2, we distinguish raw from credited scores on the PONS test, and we always report credited scores. A raw score consists simply of the number of items that the subject answered correctly. When subjects omit items, a problem in comparing scores exists, since omitted items are marked wrong. The credited score consists of the number correct plus half of the number omitted (thus giving ½ point, the chance level of accuracy for a two-choice answer, for each omitted item). This procedure has been especially useful in scoring samples of alcoholics or psychiatric patients who tend to leave a number of items blank.

and the four quadrants. Using the means and standard deviations from this preliminary norm group, we constructed standard scoring sheets for channel scores and totals (figure 3.1) and for pooled channels and affective quadrants (figure 3.2). On the standard scoring sheets, the 50-percentile line represents the mean score for the preliminary norm group on the individual channels, total, marginals, and affect quadrants. The 84.1 and 15.9 percentiles represent the +1 and −1 standard deviations, and the 97.7 and 2.3 percentiles represent the +2 and −2 standard deviations. The standard scoring sheets figure very highly in the evaluation of the performance of individuals and groups against a standard and in the comparison among the performances of various related samples.

PROFILE OF NONVERBAL SENSITIVITY: STANDARD SCORING SHEET

Pooled Channels and Type of Scene

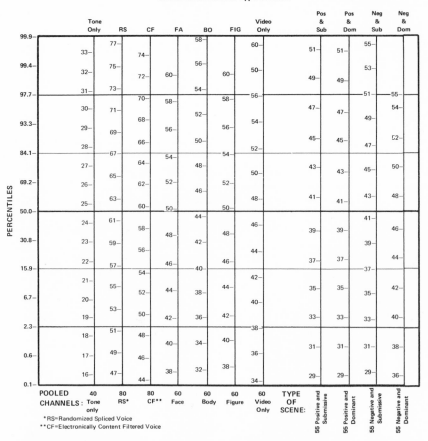

FIGURE 3.2. Standard scoring sheet for the Profile of Nonverbal Sensitivity: Pooled channels and type of scene

TABLE 3.1. Means and Standard Deviations of Norm Group on Channels, Marginals, and Total (N = 480)

Audio Channel		Video Channel				
		None	Face	Body	Figure	Total
None	Mean		16.153	15.474	16.064	47.691
	SD		1.748	2.026	1.787	4.216
Randomized spliced	Mean	12.541	17.674	15.265	16.773	62.252
	SD	1.946	1.882	1.814	1.557	4.828
Content-filtered	Mean	12.182	16.482	14.381	17.064	60.109
	SD	2.012	1.625	1.931	1.968	5.189
Total	Mean	24.723	50.309	45.120	49.900	170.052
	SD	2.965	3.980	4.321	4.235	12.389

Often in this book, we present the mean performance of a sample by showing its profile on the standard scoring sheet. The profile is simply a line connecting the performance levels of a group or individual on each of the PONS scales. Thus, a PONS channel profile would consist of the eleven channel scores plotted on the standard scoring sheet. The similarities and differences on various PONS measures between various groups and the norm group as well as among the individuals in a given group become readily apparent when the profiles are compared visually.

Not long after the development of the standard scoring sheets, we collected data from the sample of senior high school students on the east coast, completing our standardization sample. The mean scores of this sample of 121 male and female students were almost identical to those of the preliminary norm group. By pooling the data from the east coast high school with those of the preliminary norm group, we increased the stability of the means and variances of the PONS normative data. These summary statistics appear in tables 3.1 and 3.2. The means and standard deviations of all the PONS scales were computed separately for males and females. Although the sex difference in PONS accuracy will be discussed in more detail in chapter 7, we present the accuracy scores for 171 males and 309 females in tables 3.3 and 3.4. Note that in ten of the eleven channels, the mean for female subjects exceeded the mean for male subjects.

It was important to determine that the percentage of correct answers was neither too high nor too low. If the subjects' accuracy were close to 50 percent, they would be performing merely at chance level. If subjects' accuracy were close to 100 percent, it would also be clear that the test items could not discriminate between individuals in terms of their nonverbal sensitivity. For the entire norm group the average total accuracy was 77.29 percent (SD =

TABLE 3.2. Means and Standard Deviations of Norm Group on Quadrants and Scenes (N=480

Positive			Negative		
	Mean	SD		Mean	SD
Submissive			*Submissive*		
Helping a customer	8.027	1.182	Talking about death	8.609	1.39
Ordering food	8.730	1.090	Talking about divorce	7.607	1.51
Expressing gratitude	8.790	1.313	Returning faulty item	8.193	1.19
Expressing deep affection	8.252	1.132	Asking forgiveness	8.727	1.34
Seducing someone	7.267	1.326	Prayer	8.176	1.24
Total Positive-Submissive	40.159	3.799	Total Negative-Submissive	42.392	4.48
Dominant			*Dominant*		
Talking about wedding	7.234	1.391	Criticizing someone for being late	8.626	1.29
Leaving on a trip	8.300	1.153	Nagging a child	8.761	1.42
Expressing motherly love	9.232	1.314	Strong dislike	9.148	1.20
Admiring nature	8.980	1.130	Threatening someone	8.709	1.21
Talking to a lost child	8.380	1.061	Jealous anger	9.654	1.32
Total Positive-Dominant	40.339	4.081	Total Negative-Dominant	47.162	3.94

5.63 percent), indicating that our average scores were well above chance but with no danger of a ceiling effect.

In order to examine more carefully these normative data and to specify the differences in mean accuracy among the channels and quadrants, we computed a five-way repeated measures analysis of variance. The factors were face (present/absent), body (present/absent), audio (none/RS/CF), dominance (submissive/dominant), and positivity (negative/positive). The empty cell (no face, no body, no audio) was filled in with the chance level of accuracy. Because each of 480 subjects provided data for the full $2 \times 2 \times 3 \times 2 \times 2$ repeated measures design, the error terms were very small, making the F-tests very powerful and resulting in many significant effects. Thirteen of the fifteen possible main effects and first order interactions were significant at the .001 level, but we were less interested in significance testing than in examining various effect sizes. (Effect size is here defined as the difference between the means of the conditions being compared divided by the common standard deviation of the two conditions [Friedman 1968; Cohen 1969; see also chapter 7].) Because of the number and complexity of the higher order interactions, we report only the main effects and various first order interactions.

Accuracy on items where face was present (i.e., face and figure, in both pure and mixed channels) was higher than on items where face was not present (effect size = 6.81σ). The same was true of body (effect size = 3.57σ). These two effects were the result of higher accuracy on channels containing video information than on those containing only RS or CF voice (or no information at all, where the score would have been at the chance level

TABLE 3.3. Means and Standard Deviations of Norm Group on Channels and Total, Sexes Separately (171 males, 309 females)

		Video Channel									
		None		Face		Body		Figure		Total	
Audio Channel		Male	Female	Male	Female	Male	Female	Male	Female	Male	Female
None	Mean			15.939	16.272	14.848	15.820	15.550	16.348	46.336	48.440
	SD			1.762	1.732	2.046	1.933	2.006	1.586	4.471	3.877
Randomized spliced	Mean	12.588	12.515	17.196	17.938	14.895	15.469	16.576	16.882	61.254	62.804
	SD	2.024	1.904	2.115	1.685	1.944	1.707	1.632	1.506	5.170	4.544
Content-filtered	Mean	11.737	12.429	16.102	16.693	14.053	14.563	16.699	17.265	58.591	60.950
	SD	2.174	1.876	1.707	1.541	2.050	1.841	2.164	1.823	5.702	4.683
Total	Mean	24.325	24.943	49.237	50.903	43.795	45.853	48.825	50.495	166.181	172.194
	SD	3.199	2.808	4.356	3.629	4.494	4.047	4.715	3.824	13.454	11.220

TABLE 3.4. Means and Standard Deviations of Norm Group on Quadrants and Scenes, Sexes Separately (171 males, 309 females)

	Positive				Negative			
	Male		Female		Male		Female	
	Mean	SD	Mean	SD		Mean	SD	Mean	SD
Submissive					*Submissive*				
Helping a customer	8.044	1.226	8.018	1.160	Talking about death	8.398	1.516	8.727	1.306
Ordering food	8.614	1.210	8.794	1.045	Talking about divorce	7.281	1.500	7.788	1.493
Expressing gratitude	8.447	1.454	8.979	1.188	Returning faulty item	8.175	1.345	8.202	1.108
Expressing deep affection	8.170	1.167	8.298	1.111	Asking forgiveness	8.518	1.511	8.843	1.228
Seducing someone	7.012	1.362	7.408	1.286	Prayer	8.064	1.308	8.238	1.212
Total Positive-Submissive	39.772	4.044	40.374	3.646	Total Negative-Submissive	40.921	4.905	43.205	4.012
Dominant					*Dominant*				
					Criticizing someone				
Talking about wedding	7.006	1.327	7.361	1.411	for being late	8.447	1.434	8.725	1.196
Leaving on a trip	8.050	1.223	8.439	1.090	Nagging a child	8.535	1.426	8.887	1.415
Expressing motherly love	8.965	1.448	9.380	1.211	Strong dislike	8.766	1.420	9.359	1.018
Admiring nature	8.743	1.209	9.112	1.064	Threatening someone	8.520	1.334	8.814	1.127
Talking to a lost child	8.216	1.197	8.471	0.968	Jealous anger	9.520	1.333	9.728	1.319
Total Positive-Dominant	39.313	4.216	40.906	3.896	Total Negative-Dominant	46.175	4.304	47.709	3.627

of accuracy). Accuracy on items containing RS voice was greater than accuracy on items containing CF, and accuracy on items containing any tone was greater than accuracy on items containing no tone (effect size $= 1.85\sigma$). Dominant affect was easier to read than submissive (effect size $= 1.73\sigma$), and negative affect easier than positive (effect size $= 2.48\sigma$).

In channels where the face was present, dominant affect was easier to read than submissive, and positive affect easier than negative. When face was not present, submissive affect was easier than dominant and negative easier than positive. Finally, overall, negative-dominant plus positive-submissive affects were easier to read than negative-submissive plus positive-dominant affects.

One hundred fifty-six subjects (none from the standardization sample, and mostly college students) took the PONS test twice, with an interval of six to eight weeks between testings. We were primarily interested in assessing the test-retest reliability of the PONS (which will be discussed later), but we also wished to establish norms for the increase in accuracy from first to second testing. This increase in accuracy may be the result of an increase in exposure to the stimulus person as well as familiarity with taking the test. We were particularly interested in whether there would be differential improvement in the various channels. The percentage accuracy scores on the first testing for this sample did not differ significantly from the accuracy scores of the standardization group. In addition, the rank order correlation between the channel scores of these two groups was .98.

Subjects gained in accuracy on all eleven channels from first to second testing. An analysis of variance revealed that it was a significant gain (effect size $= 1.48\sigma$, $p < .001$). In addition, there was a greater increase in accuracy for channels including content-filtered speech than for channels including randomized spliced speech ($p < .008$) and a greater increase for body-present channels than for those not containing body ($p < .001$). Accuracy increased more when body appeared without face than when body appeared with face ($p < .002$).

RELIABILITY

Reliability refers to the consistency and stability of measurements (Fiske 1971). A certain degree of score dependability is a necessary condition before the PONS can be considered valuable for use in either research or practical situations. This section presents reliability data for the various channels, marginals, and quadrants, and for the total.

Internal consistency reflects the extent to which the items of a scale or test represent a homogeneous set of measurements of some trait. If a test is internally consistent, it yields consistent results throughout much of the test in a single administration. Stability or test-retest reliability reflects the extent to which the test yields consistent results from testing to testing. High test-retest reliability means that individuals maintain their rank positions relatively well over time in whatever psychological functions the test measures. The reliability of a test is expressed as a reliability coefficient that can range from 0.00 (zero reliability) to +1.00 (perfect reliability).

INTERNAL CONSISTENCY. On the data from 492 high school students in the standardization sample, we computed internal consistency correlations for the total, channels, quadrants, and marginals using the KR-20 formula (Guilford 1954). These coefficients appear in table 3.5. For each channel, marginal, or affect quadrant consisting of less than 220 items, the Spearman-Brown prophecy formula (Walker and Lev 1953) was used to determine the "effective" reliability equating for length of 220 items (Rosenthal 1973).

In order to determine the factors along which the test items varied that contributed to the internal consistency of the norm group data, an analysis of variance was performed on KR-20 values computed for each of the forty-four "quadrant by channel" combinations (e.g., positive-dominant affect in face + RS channel). Each of these forty-four subscores was the mean of five items. The design was a five-way analysis of variance of the same design as described above. The empty cell (where voice, face, and body were absent) was assigned a reliability of 0.00.

The analysis revealed two clear and interesting results. Negative affect was more reliable than positive affect ($F(1,11) = 8.75$, $p < .05$, $r = .66$), and dominant affect was more reliable than submissive affect ($F(1,11) = 9.60$, $p < .05$, $r = .68$).

For the high school norm group (N = 492), we computed another measure of internal consistency using a method suggested by Armor (1974). When different items in a set measure an underlying dimension unequally, certain

TABLE 3.5. Effective Reliability Coefficients: Internal Consistency As Measured by KR-20

	Video Channel				
Audio Channel	None	Face	Body	Figure	Total
None		.88	.86	.84	.90
Randomized spliced	.06	.94	.79	.86	.89
Content-filtered	.57	.86	.79	.94	.87
Total	.68	.92	.88	.91	.86

Quadrant	
Positive-submissive	= .78
Positive-dominant	= .84
Negative-submissive	= .87
Negative-dominant	= .87

TABLE 3.6. Values of θ: A Measure of Internal
Consistency

Scale	θ
Total (220 items)	.920
Quadrants × channels (44 items)	.837
(Positive + negative) × channels (22 items)	.789
(Dominant + submissive) × channels (22 items)	.786
20 scenes	.759
Channels	.696

modifications in reliability formulas may be necessary. Armor's method
solves this problem using factor scaling. Since "principal component" factor
loadings indicate the magnitude of the contribution of each variable to the
underlying continuum or factor, this method can be used to determine the
degree of relationship between the items in a scale. The coefficient, θ, is
computed as follows: $[(p - 1)/p] [1 - (1/\lambda)]$, where p is the number of items
in the scale and λ is the latent root of the first principal components factor (in a
factor analysis of the p items). Theta is always greater than or equal to zero,
and the greater the proportion of variance accounted for by factor 1 in the
principal components analysis, the greater is the internal consistency of the
scale. The values of θ are reported in table 3.6. As expected, θ increases as
the number of items upon which it is based increases ($r(4) = .86$, $p < .03$).

STABILITY RELIABILITY. Stability or retest reliability was assessed in six
samples with test-retest intervals of ten days to ten weeks. The subjects were
56 U.S. college students (ten days), 17 U.S. college students enrolled in a
course in group processes (six weeks), 29 U.S. college students (six weeks),
74 Australian college students (six weeks), 36 U.S. high school students
(eight weeks), and 81 U.S. college students (ten weeks). The median retest
reliability coefficients obtained from these samples appear in table 3.7. These
coefficients are relatively substantial. Of course, the scales with more items
(such as the marginals) are more stable than the scales with fewer items (such
as the individual channels). The stability of the quadrants is also rather high.
In general, channels with higher retest reliability tended also to have higher
internal consistency ($r(9) = .43$, $p < .10$, one-tailed).

A further look at reliability involved the shapes of the PONS profiles over
time. We wish to determine whether the shape of the profile—the differential performance on certain channels—remained relatively constant from first
to second testing. To accomplish this, we correlated the pretest profile (z-
scores of the eleven channels) with the posttest profile for each of four samples and compared the median of these four correlations ($r = .41$) with the
median correlation of each sample's pretest profile with the posttest profile of
the other three samples ($r = .13$). In these correlations, the eleven channels
were the "sampling units," so that each correlation was based on nine de-

TABLE 3.7. Median Test-Retest Reliability Coefficients from Six Samples (N=293)

Audio Channel	Video Channel				
	None	Face	Body	Figure	Total
None		.24	.34	.24	.52
Randomized spliced	.18	.43	.26	.20	.50
Content-filtered	.27	.20	.24	.27	.50
Total	.32	.49	.54	.51	.69

Quadrant	
Positive-submissive	= .42
Positive-dominant	= .56
Negative-submissive	= .52
Negative-dominant	= .48
All negative	= .63
All positive	= .62
All submissive	= .55
All dominant	= .68

grees of freedom. These results show clearly that a sample's posttest profile bears a greater resemblance to that sample's pretest profile than it does to the profile of an independent group of subjects.

RELIABILITY OF PONS AFFECT DIMENSIONS: THE ANALYSIS OF INCORRECT RESPONSE ALTERNATIVES

We recall that the 20 scenes of the PONS were divided equally into two dimensions of affect: positive-negative and dominant-submissive. Therefore, there were five scenes assigned to each of the four quadrants formed by the intersection of these two dimensions. Of the total 220 items of the PONS, 55 correct answers (5 scenes × 11 channels) are found in each of the four quadrants. We will gain a further understanding of the reliability of the assignment of scenes to quadrants by examining the effects on accuracy of the quadrant locations of the incorrect alternatives with which the correct answers were randomly paired in the preparation of the PONS answer sheet.

If the scenes were placed into quadrants unreliably (i.e., randomly), there would be no relationship between accuracy and the quadrant location of the incorrect answer relative to the quadrant location of the correct answer. If the scenes were placed into quadrants reliably, there would be a specifiable effect on accuracy of the quadrant location of the incorrect answer relative to the quadrant location of the correct answer. That is, if the incorrect alternative fell in the same quadrant as the correct alternative, they should be most difficult to distinguish and accuracy should be lowest. If the incorrect alternative fell into an adjacent quadrant, i.e., one that differed from the correct alternative on one of the affect dimensions but did not differ on the other affect dimension, it should be easier to distinguish the correct from the incorrect alternative, and accuracy should be higher. If the incorrect alternative fell into the opposite quadrant, i.e., one that differed from the correct alternative on both of the affect dimensions, it should be still easier to distinguish the correct from the incorrect alternative, and accuracy should be higher still.

Table 3.8 shows the mean accuracy scores, in percentages, obtained by the preliminary norm group of 359 high school students, simultaneously considering the quadrant locations of both the correct and incorrect response alternatives on the PONS answer sheet. The notes [a], [b], and [c] indicate the accuracy scores obtained when the response alternatives were from the same quadrants, adjacent quadrants, or opposite quadrants, respectively.

The first row of table 3.9 summarizes the data of table 3.8 and shows that there is a linear increase in accuracy as the incorrect response alternative is moved from the same quadrant to the opposite quadrant. The correlation coefficient shown as the fourth entry represents the correlation associated with the predicted linear trend and may be interpreted as a kind of reliability coefficient (Friedman 1968). The F shown as the fifth entry is the F associated with the test for the predicted linear regression of the three means shown. The next three rows of table 3.9 present the analogous results of three replications based on a sample of additional high school students, psychiatric patients, and alcoholic patients. The four reliability coefficients are remarkably similar, ranging from .902 to .937, with a median of .917. Figure 3.3 shows graphically the effects of the quadrant location of the incorrect alternative on the accuracy scores of all four samples.

TABLE 3.8. Accuracy on Quadrants As a Function of Quadrant Location of Incorrect Alternative (N=359)

		Correct Alternative			
		Dominant		Submissive	
		Incorrect Alternative		Incorrect Alternative	
Correct Alternative	Incorrect Alternative	Dominant	Submissive	Dominant	Submissive
Positive	Positive	69.8%[a]	74.7%[b]	74.7%[b]	63.9%[a]
	Negative	73.0[b]	76.5[c]	89.2[c]	59.6[b]
Negative	Positive	83.3[b]	91.2[c]	85.9[c]	78.2[b]
	Negative	74.6	92.6[b]	86.0[b]	52.5[a]

[a]incorrect alternative located in same quadrant as correct alternative
[b]incorrect alternative located in quadrant adjacent to quadrant of correct alternative
[c]incorrect alternative located in quadrant opposite to quadrant of correct alternative

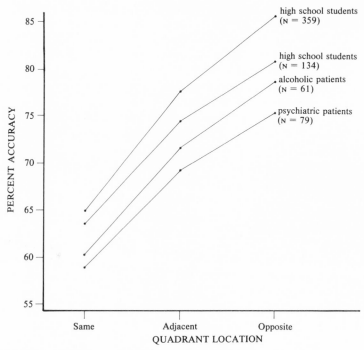

FIGURE 3.3. Mean accuracy obtained at three levels of similarity of incorrect alternative to correct alternative for four samples

It is also possible to ask which of the two affect dimensions contributed more heavily to the high reliabilities shown in table 3.9. Table 3.10 displays the mean accuracy obtained for each of the two affect dimensions depending upon whether the incorrect alternative was from the same end of the dimension or from the other end of the dimension as the correct alternative. For all

TABLE 3.9. Accuracy at Three Levels of Similarity of Incorrect Alternative to Correct Alternative for Four Samples

	Quadrant Similarity			Quadrant Reliability Data	
Sample	Same	Adjacent	Opposite	r	F (linear)
High school students ($N = 359$)	65.2%	77.8%	85.7%	.937	2579
High school replication ($N = 134$)	63.6	74.6	81.0	.913	668
Psychiatric patients ($N = 79$)	59.3	69.4	75.5	.902	342
Alcoholic patients ($N = 61$)	60.6	71.8	78.8	.921	338
Median	62.1	73.2	79.9	.917	505

TABLE 3.10. Accuracy at Two Levels of Similarity of Incorrect Alternative to Correct Alternative for Two Dimensions of Affect

Sample	Positive-Negative				Dominant-Submissive			
	Same	Different	r	F	Same	Different	r	F
High school students (N = 359)	73.6%	79.6%	.748	456	69.4%	83.9%	.939	2680
High school replication (N = 134)	70.8	76.1	.678	113	67.3	79.5	.904	597
Psychiatric patients (N = 79)	65.4	71.4	.723	85	63.3	73.5	.873	249
Alcoholic patients (N = 61)	68.1	73.4	.680	52	64.2	77.3	.916	313
Median	69.4	74.8	.702	99	65.8	78.4	.910	455

four samples, the magnitude of the effect, or the reliability of the dimension, was substantially greater for the dominant-submissive dimension than for the positive-negative dimension. For the PONS test, therefore, the distinction between dominant and submissive scenes is easier than the distinction between positive and negative scenes.

So far in our analysis of the effect of the type of affect of the incorrect alternative, we have examined that effect only in relation to the type of affect of the correct alternative. It was also of interest, however, to examine the effect of the type of affect of the incorrect alternative quite apart from the type of affect of the correct alternative. Table 3.11 shows the results of this analysis for both affect dimensions, for four samples of subjects. There was a tendency for items in which the incorrect alternative was positive in affect to be judged more accurately, though this effect was not large in magnitude. However, there was a very large effect on accuracy of the dominant versus submissive nature of the incorrect alternative. Why a dominant affect incorrect response alternative should increase accuracy so substantially is not at all clear. Perhaps the dominant scene descriptions were more arousing and served to keep subjects more alert in their judgments.

TABLE 3.11. Accuracy As a Function of the Affect Dimension of the Incorrect Alternative

Sample	Positivity				Dominance			
	Positive	Negative	r	F	Dominant	Submissive	r	F
High school students (N = 359)	77.7%	75.5%	.361	54	79.6%	73.7%	.736	424
High school replication (N = 134)	74.0	72.9	.191	5	75.6	71.1	.615	81
Psychiatric patients (N = 79)	69.7	67.1	.425	17	70.3	66.5	.552	34
Alcoholic patients (N = 61)	70.2	71.3	−.176	2	73.4	68.1	.682	52
Median	72.1	72.1	.276	11	74.5	69.6	.648	66

ADDITIVITY OF CUES

How stimuli are combined by a judge in order to make an integrative response has been studied in a large variety of formats in psychology (Hastorf, Schneider, and Polefka 1970). Studies in impression formation have examined the use of a stimulus person's individual traits in the formation of an overall attitude toward him. Some researchers have attempted to develop models of clinical judgment to understand how particular symptoms and test results are weighted and combined to arrive at a final diagnosis. The question has been studied in the areas of communication as the process of combining verbal and nonverbal cues (Kozel 1969). Many researchers have found that a linear additive model accounts well for the relationship between cues and response (Anderson 1968). As the simplest form of the stimulus combination rule, it expresses the response as a linear combination of cues.

The question of the additivity of cues has relevance for the PONS test if we consider it in a modified perspective. Is the information conveyed in one channel plus the information conveyed in another channel equal to the information conveyed when transmission is through those two channels simultaneously? For instance, does the information transmitted by face in each scene added to the information transmitted by RS in each scene equal that transmitted by the face + RS channel? The best way for us to examine the amount of information transmitted in the PONS test is to examine accuracy.

Our first step in the analysis was to construct a 3 × 4 table using the mean accuracy scores on each of the eleven channels obtained by the standardiza-

TABLE 3.12. Procedure for Investigating Additivity of the PONS

	Means			
	Video Channel			
Audio Channel	None	Face	Body	Figure
None		16.2	15.5	16.1
Randomized spliced	12.5	17.7	15.3	16.8
Content-filtered	12.2	16.5	14.4	17.1

	Effects and Residuals				
	Video Channel				
Audio Channel	None	Face	Body	Figure	Row Effects
None		− .20	.90	0.0	0.0
Randomized spliced	− .15	.60	0.0	0.0	− .05
Content-filtered	.07	0.0	− .38	.72	− .65
Column effects	−3.40	1.05	− .75	.75	16.1 = grand median

tion sample of 480. These data appear in table 3.12. Using a procedure known as "median polish" (Tukey 1970), we "removed" the row and column effects as well as the overall level of the scores as reflected in the grand median of the eleven scores in the table. The procedure left us with a table of residuals (residual = score minus row effect minus column effect minus grand median), the magnitude of which tells us how the table departs from additivity. If the table were completely additive, the residuals would all be zero (that is, if 0 = residual = score − row effect − colum effect − grand median, then score = grand median + row effect + column effect). Hence, residuals that are not zero indicate interaction between (nonadditivity of) channels. Furthermore, the nonzero row and column effects indicate main effects of audio or video modes on accuracy.

From table 3.12 the main effects of marginals are rather clear. Content-filtered voice resulted in lower accuracy than expected. The presence of the face in the video channels resulted in higher accuracy than did the absence of face, and video information generally was a very important factor in performance. What is really important for the question of additivity is an examination of the channel residuals, five of which are zero or very close to zero. Three of these five involved mixed channels indicating that face + CF, body + RS, and figure + RS were additive.

Interactions were indicated for face + RS and figure + CF, such that accuracy in reading the nonverbal content of a scene presented in the audio and video channels was enhanced when both channels were judged simultaneously. Performance on body + CF was slightly lowered when both channels were presented together. Accuracy on body was higher when no audio information accompanied it.

FACTOR STRUCTURE OF THE PONS TEST

In order to examine further the structure and psychometric characteristics of the PONS test, we employed principal components analysis, a method that maximizes the amount of variance explained (Armor and Couch 1972). The factor extraction continued either until the maximum number of factors requested was reached (the requested limit determined by the number of factors we thought we could interpret) or until the additional percentage of variance explained by adding another factor was too low. Rotation was then undertaken to make the factors more interpretable. Kaiser's varimax method (1958) was used, which will usually tend toward "simple structure," a factor matrix in which each variable loads highly on only one factor. Simple structure makes it possible to name the factors more easily. An orthogonal rotation was tried using two, three, four, five, etc., factors (up to the number of factors extracted), and each was examined.

FACTORING CHANNELS. For our norm group of 492 male and female high school students, the eleven channel accuracy scores were intercorrelated and factor analyzed. Although six factors were extracted and rotated orthogonally, a four-factor solution was by far the simplest to interpret. Table 3.13 shows the rotated factor loadings for these four factors. The first factor was characterized by high loadings (.60 or higher) on the six channels in which the face was shown. Persons scoring high on this factor, then, were those who were more accurate in decoding nonverbal communication when the face was available as a source of cues. This factor, based on six channels, or 120 scenes, accounted for 28 percent of the total variance.

The second and third factors were both quite specific to the decoding of purely auditory cues. Factor 2 was defined by accuracy in the twenty items of the randomized spliced channel and factor 3 was defined by accuracy in the twenty items of the content-filtered channel. Each of these quite specific factors accounted for about 9 percent of the total variance.

The fourth factor was characterized by high loadings (.55 or higher) on the three channels in which the body was shown without the face. Persons scoring high on this factor, then, were those who were more accurate when only visual cues from the body were available. This factor, based on three channels, or sixty scenes, accounted for 15 percent of the total variance.

On the basis of this factor analysis, we can suggest, at least as a hypothesis for further investigation, that skill at decoding the eleven channels of nonverbal cues of the PONS can be divided into four subskills: (a) decoding facial

TABLE 3.13. Factor Analysis of Eleven Channels: Four-Factor Solution (N = 492)

| Variable | Rotated Factor Loadings | | | | |
	1	2	3	4	Communality
Face	.616[a]	.119	.095	.147	.425
Body	.468	−.045	.020	.589[a]	.569
Figure	.682[a]	.071	.110	.242	.541
Randomized spliced	.142	.950[a]	.032	.116	.937
Content-filtered	.202	.040	.965[a]	.142	.994
Face + Randomized spliced	.704[a]	.022	.063	.219	.548
Face + Content-filtered	.651[a]	−.033	.092	.204	.476
Body + Randomized spliced	.334	.066	.125	.572[a]	.459
Body + Content-filtered	.114	.133	.080	.825[a]	.718
Figure + Randomized spliced	.674[a]	.300	.086	.051	.554
Figure + Content-filtered	.699[a]	.061	.105	.318	.604
Sum squares	3.113	1.042	1.007	1.662	6.824
Percentage of variance	28	9	9	15	
Number of variables defining factor	6	1	1	3	
Number of items defining factor	120	20	20	60	

[a]Variables defining factor

cues, (b) decoding randomized spliced cues, (c) decoding content-filtered cues, and (d) decoding cues from the body without the face.

FACTORING POSITIVE AND NEGATIVE CHANNELS. For the same sample of 492 high school students, the channel scores were computed separately for positive and negative affect scenes. The resulting twenty-two positive and negative channel scores were then intercorrelated and factor analyzed. Although other factor solutions were also sensible, the most parsimonious solution was the rotated factor structure based on three factors. The first factor was characterized by high loadings (.30 or higher) on the eleven negative affect channels. Persons scoring high on this factor, then, were those who were more accurate in decoding nonverbal cues in any channel so long as the affect being communicated was negative. This factor, based on eleven "semi" channels, or 110 scenes, accounted for 15 percent of the total variance.

The second factor was characterized by high loadings (.35 or higher) on the nine positive affect channels that provided visual cues. Persons scoring high on this factor were those who were more accurate in decoding visual cues of either face or body so long as the affect being communicated was positive. This factor, based on nine "semi" channels, or ninety scenes, accounted for 17 percent of the total variance.

The third factor was characterized by high loadings (.55 or higher) on the two positive affect channels that provided exclusively audio cues. Persons scoring high here were those who were more accurrate in decoding auditory cues unassisted by visual cues so long as the affect being communicated was positive. This factor, based on two "semi" channels, or twenty scenes, accounted for 6 percent of the total variance.

On the basis of this factor analysis of the twenty-two positive and negative "semi" channels, we can suggest as a hypothesis that three skills may be involved in the decoding of positive and negative affects in the various channels: (a) decoding negative cues in any channel, (b) decoding positive cues in any visual channel, and (c) decoding positive cues from audio information alone without the help of any visual cues.

FACTORING DOMINANT AND SUBMISSIVE CHANNELS. For the same sample of 492 high school students, channel scores were also computed separately for dominant and submissive affect scenes. The resulting twenty-two dominant and submissive channel scores were intercorrelated and factor analyzed. Once again, although other factor solutions were interpretable, the most parsimonious solution was the rotated factor structure based on three factors. The first factor was characterized by high loadings (.25 or higher) on submissive affect scenes providing facial cues and on randomized spliced audio cues of either affect. Persons scoring high on this factor, then, were those who were more accurate in decoding (a) facial cues when the affect was submissive and

(b) randomized spliced vocal cues of either affect. This factor, based on eight "semi" channels, or eighty scenes, accounted for 14 percent of the total variance.

The second factor was characterized by high loadings (.30 or higher) on all of the dominant channels with the exception of randomized spliced cues. This single exception, it will be recalled, had loaded highly on the first factor. This second factor, almost a pure factor of accuracy in decoding dominant affect cues, was based on ten "semi" channels, or 100 scenes, and accounted for 14 percent of the total variance.

The third factor was characterized by high loadings (.30 or higher) on submissive affect scenes in which visual cues were provided only by the body and auditory cues were provided only by content-filtered speech. Persons scoring high on this factor were those who were more accurate in decoding submissive affect when cues were transmitted only by the body or by content-filtered speech. This factor, based on four "semi" channels, or forty scenes, accounted for 8 percent of the total variance.

On the basis of this factor analysis of the twenty-two dominant and submissive stimuli of all of the channels, we can suggest, again as a hypothesis, that three skills may be involved in the decoding of dominant and submissive affects in the various channels: (a) decoding submissive affects providing facial cues and/or randomized spliced audio cues (either dominant or submissive), (b) decoding dominant cues in all channels except randomized spliced speech, and (c) decoding submissive affects in which visual cues come only from the body channel and audio cues only from the content-filtered channel.

FACTORING QUADRANT BY CHANNEL COMBINATIONS. For the same sample of 492 high school students, channel scores were computed separately for each of the four affect quadrants (i.e., combinations of the positive-negative and dominant-submissive dimensions). The forty-four resulting quadrant × channel scores were intercorrelated and factor analyzed. Only three factors were extracted. The first rotated factor was characterized by high loadings (.25 or higher) on the negative-submissive scenes of all eleven channels and was, therefore, based on fifty-five scenes; it accounted for 8 percent of the total variance.

The second factor was characterized by high loadings (.30 or higher) on all but three (face, CF, face + CF) of the eleven channels of the positive-submissive scenes. We may interpret it, then, as approximately representing skill at decoding positive-submissive scenes. This factor, based on eleven channels and fifty-five scenes, accounted for 8 percent of the total variance.

The third factor was characterized by strongly negative loadings (−.35 or lower) on all but three (face, RS, face + RS) of the eleven channels of the negative-dominant scenes. We may interpret it, then, as approximately representing lack of skill at decoding, or insensitivity to, negative dominant affects. This factor, also based on eleven channels and fifty-five scenes, accounted for 8 percent of the variance.

On the basis of this factor analysis of the forty-four quadrant by channel combinations, we can suggest as a hypothesis that three skills may be involved in the decoding of the various quadrant by channel combinations: (a) decoding negative-submissive affects, (b) decoding positive-submissive affects, and (c) decoding negative-dominant affects, or, more precisely, decoding negative-dominant affects poorly.

It will be useful to have a summary of the results of the four factor analyses presented so far, and table 3.14 provides such a summary. For each of the analyses, the interpreted factors are listed. For each of the factors, eight columns of data are provided: (1) the range of the factor loadings of the interpreted factor; (2) the median factor loading of the variables defining the factor; (3) the median factor loading of the variables not a part of the factor; (4) the difference between these two medians (the larger the difference between these two medians, the clearer is the definition of the factor in terms of relative magnitude of factor loading); (5) the percentage of variance accounted for by the factor; (6) the number of variables entering into the interpretation of the factor; and (7) the number of items entering into the interpretation of the factor.

Examination of the summary table suggests a very clear picture of the factor structure of the eleven channels, disregarding affects. There appeared to be four factors representing four skills at decoding the nonverbal cues represented in our eleven channels: (a) face reading skill, (b) randomized spliced audio skill, (c) content-filtered audio skill, and (d) body (without face) reading skill.

The remaining three factor analyses subdivide the channels by affect dimensions, and the results suggest the following easily interpreted factors: (a) a negative affect decoding skill; (b) a positive affect, video channel skill; (c) a positive affect, audio channel skill; (d) a dominant affect skill; (e) a negative-submissive affect skill; (f) a positive-submissive affect skill; and (g) a negative-dominant affect skill. In a general way, these factor structures lend some further validity to our conception and construction of the PONS as being composed of scenes located on both a positive-negative dimension and a dominant-submissive dimension.[3]

3. An additional factor analysis was carried out on the matrix of intercorrelations of all 220 items of the PONS. Six factors were extracted, but since all six together accounted for less than 14 percent of the total variance, no attempt was made to interpret these factors. Individual items of the PONS probably lack the reliability required for a more satisfactory factor analysis. There is some indication that this relative unreliability was somewhat increased by the 33 items (15 percent) for which the norm group's mean accuracy did not exceed 50 percent. The median loading of all 220 items on the first principal component (unrotated) was +.19, and all 33 of these low-accuracy items showed loadings below that value; 22 (67 percent) of the 33 showed negative loadings, while only 6 (3 percent) of the remaining 187 items showed negative loadings. Before

TABLE 3.14. Summary of Factor Analyses (N = 492)

Factor Analysis	Range of Factor Loadings	Median Loading	Median Residual Loading	Factor Clarity (2–3)	Percent of Variance	Number of Variables	Number of Items
1. Channels							
Face	.62–70	.68	.20	.48	28	6	120
Randomized spliced	.95	.95	.06	.89	9	1	20
Content-filtered	.96	.96	.09	.87	9	1	20
Body only	.57–82	.59	.18	.41	15	3	60
Median	.78–88	.82	.13	.68	Total 61	11	220
2. Channels by positivity							
Negative	.32–65	.44	.19	.25	15	11	110
Positive Visual	.40–62	.53	.25	.28	17	9	90
Positive Audio	.60–65	.62	.07	.55	6	2	20
Median	.40–65	.53	.19	.28	Total 38	22	220
3. Channels by dominance							
Submissive face, any RS	.29–69	.50	.22	.28	14	8	80
Dominant (except RS)	.34–67	.49	.14	.35	14	10	100
Submissive body only plus CF	.33–65	.53	.15	.38	8	4	40
Median	.33–67	.50	.15	.35	Total 36	22	220
4. Channels by quadrants							
Negative-Submissive	.25–56	.38	.17	.21	8	11	55
Positive-Submissive	.05–56	.34	.16	.18	8	11	55
Negative-Dominant	-.10–-69	-.39	-.14	-.25	8	11	55
Median	.10–56	.38	.16	.21	Total 24	33	165

FACTORING TWENTY SCENES. For the same 492 high school students whose responses had been factor analyzed by channels and affects, we computed accuracy scores for each of the twenty scenes adding over the eleven channels. These twenty scene accuracy scores were intercorrelated and factor analyzed. Six factors were extracted and were found to be relatively interpretable on the basis of the nature of the scenes defining each factor. The first rotated factor was characterized by high loadings (.40 or higher) on five scenes that appeared to have in common a tendency for the portrayer to be in a position of dominance, authority, or control. Persons scoring high on this factor, then, were those who were more accurate in decoding nonverbal cues of control. This factor, based on five scenes or fifty-five items, accounted for 11 percent of the total variance.

The second factor was characterized by strong negative loadings ($-.55$ or lower) on the two scenes in which the portrayer apologetically told a customer that the items in question were no longer available or asked for forgiveness. Persons scoring high on this factor, then, appear to be relatively insensitive to nonverbal cues of contrition. This factor, based on two scenes or twenty-two items, accounted for 7 percent of the total variance.

The third factor was characterized by strong negative loadings ($-.30$ or lower) on the five scenes that appeared to have in common that they communicated strong affects in a controlled manner (talking about a divorce, expressing motherly love, nagging a child, expressing deep affection, and threatening someone quietly). Persons scoring high on this factor were those who tended to be relatively insensitive to nonverbal cues of strong but controlled affects. This factor, based on five scenes or fifty-five items, accounted for 9 percent of the total variance.

The fourth factor was characterized by strong negative loadings ($-.55$ or lower) on the two scenes in which the portrayer was discussing the death of a friend or leaving on a trip. Persons scoring high on this factor appeared to be relatively insensitive to nonverbal cues of separation. This factor, based on two scenes or twenty-two items, accounted for 7 percent of the total variance.

The fifth factor was characterized by strong negative loadings ($-.50$ or lower) on the three scenes in which the portrayer was criticizing someone for having kept her waiting, saying a prayer, or trying to seduce someone. Per-

---

deciding whether to drop these 33 items from future analyses, we examined the correlation of each item with the total PONS score based on all 220 items. The majority (18) of the 33 items showed positive correlations, and of the 10 items showing a significant correlation ($\pm$ .09) with total score, 7 showed a significant positive correlation. In addition, the correlation of PONS accuracy based on all 220 items with PONS accuracy based on the 187 items remaining after removal of the 33 low accuracy level items was very high (.97), as were the analogous correlations computed channel by channel (median $r = .91$). For these reasons and to preserve the orthogonality or balance of the PONS design ($2\times2\times3\times2\times2\times5$), we decided to retain all 33 items.

sons scoring high on this factor appeared to be relatively insensitive to non-verbal cues of dependence on others. This factor, based on three scenes or thirty-three items, accounted for 10 percent of the total variance.

The sixth and final factor was characterized by strong negative loadings ($-.55$ or lower) on the two scenes in which the portrayer was describing her impending wedding or describing a faulty item being returned to a store. Per-sons scoring high on this factor appeared to be relatively insensitive to non-verbal cues associated with description, narration, or recitation. This factor, based on two scenes or twenty-two items, accounted for 7 percent of the total variance.

On the basis of this factor analysis we can suggest at least as a hypothesis for further investigations that skill at decoding the nonverbal cues of the twenty scenes of the PONS can be subdivided into six subskills: (a) decoding cues of interpersonal control, (b) decoding cues of contrition, (c) decoding cues of strong but controlled affects, (d) decoding cues of separation, (e) decoding cues of dependence, and (f) decoding cues associated with recitation.

4 | Grouping Samples

A FACTOR ANALYTIC APPROACH TO GROUPING SAMPLES

The PONS has been administered to persons of both sexes, many age groups, many nationalities and ethnic groups, many levels of education, and many occupations. We explored some underlying dimensions of nonverbal sensitivity using principal components analysis to group samples on the basis of similarity of the shapes of their PONS profiles. This step in our research served as a means of data reduction and as an attempt to understand the relationship between structural characteristics such as age, sex, education, or culture and the shape of the PONS profile.

Three criteria were used for selecting samples to be included in the factor analysis: (1) each sample had to contain both male and female subjects; (2) no sample could have fewer than two members of each sex; and (3) no sample would be included that was heterogeneous with respect to national origins, age, occupation, or education.[1] These criteria reduced the number of acceptable samples to 71.[2] In the analysis, the males and females of each sample were considered as separate samples, so that the total number of samples was 142.

In the first analysis, the "cases" or "units" were the eleven channels of the PONS, and the "variables" for each case were the 142 mean scores of the samples for that case (that is, channel). This type of factor analysis is called Q-type (Harman 1967), to distinguish it from the more common type of factor analysis (R-type) in which a "case" would be a person (or sample) and "variables" would be the person's (sample's) scores across a set of items (channels). The factor analysis technique used was the principal components model. The principal components were then rotated by Kaiser's varimax

---

1. A partial exception is the Mexican sample, which represented a broader age range than usual.
2. All subject samples used an English-language answer sheet except for Israelis, Mexicans, and the larger German sample, who used native language answer sheets.

method, which yielded orthogonal factors, since we sought independent dimensions on which to classify our samples.

Because the ordering of difficulty of the eleven channels tended to be similar for nearly all of the samples, their profiles were highly positively correlated. In order to prevent obtaining a factor structure that merely reflected the ordering of difficulty of the eleven channels (a property of the PONS test), we equated the channels for level of difficulty using standardized scores. The means and standard deviations of the 142 samples on the eleven channels were computed, and these were used to construct eleven z scores for each of the 142 samples.

The factor solution consisted of six factors (the factor extraction being stopped after six because the seventh factor accounted for a minimal amount of variance). This solution accounted for a substantial total of 77.7 percent of the variance in the PONS profiles of the 142 samples.

Not all of the six orthogonally rotated factors were equally interpretable, and we will report only those two factors that we felt we could interpret easily. For each factor we examined the samples whose rotated loadings on that factor were equal to or greater than .50 in absolute value. The figure associated with each factor presents a profile of the median channel performance of the five extreme positive and the five extreme negative loading samples on that factor. That is, a point on the profile of the five highest loading samples represents the median of the mean scores on that channel of the five samples that had the highest loadings on that factor.

Factor 1 was the strongest factor, accounting for 20.3 percent of the variance after rotation (figure 4.1). It was relatively easy to interpret this factor. Of the twenty positive loading samples ($r \geq .50$), twelve were high school, junior high, or grade school students, and eight were college age and older (including psychiatric patients and foreign samples). On the other hand, of the twenty-five negative loading samples ($r \leq -.50$), only two were high school students and the others consisted of college students and professionals such as teachers, nurses, psychiatrists, and social workers. This pattern was found to be significantly different from chance occurrence ($\chi^2(1) = 11.70, p < .01, \phi = .51$). We called this factor the "unsophisticated-sophisticated" dimension. The "sophisticated" samples, those loading negatively, included the college and professional samples, while those loading positively, the "unsophisticated" samples, including children, exotic (foreign) groups, and psychiatric patients.

The graph in figure 4.1 reveals that the profiles of the positive and negative loading samples cross only on the audio channels (RS and CF), while their performance on the other channels tends to be quite disparate. The positive loading samples ("unsophisticated") tend to exhibit relatively good performances on the two audio channels, but poorer performances on the other channels. The negative loading samples ("sophisticated") tend to exhibit

PROFILE OF NONVERBAL SENSITIVITY: STANDARD SCORING SHEET

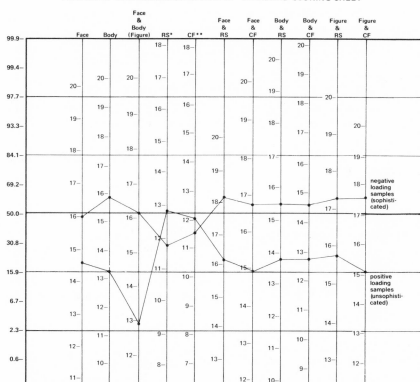

FIGURE 4.1. Factor 1: "Unsophisticated-sophisticated" factor. Median channel scores of five highest ($\geq +.83$) and five lowest ($\leq -.73$) loading samples on factor 1.

relatively poor scores on the tone channels but better scores on channels involving video cues.

We do not know for sure why the profiles of these two groups of samples differ as they do. Perhaps vocally communicated cues of emotion are more universal and less culturally determined than visual cues. Perhaps in less modernized cultures and among children there is more reliance placed on auditory cues. In chapter 8 a somewhat similar pattern of auditory and visual skills emerged from a cross-sectional analysis of samples' relative accuracies on these channels, with younger samples showing a relative (but not absolute) advantage on auditory cues. In that chapter we speculate further on possible determinants of this developmental pattern.

The second interpretable factor accounted for 11.4 percent of the variance after rotation. Eight of the nine samples with high positive loadings were foreign male samples, and eleven of the sixteen samples with high negative loadings were female samples (both American and foreign) ($\chi^2(1) = 5.53$, $p < .02$, $\phi = .47$). This suggests a sex-linked dimension, perhaps one characterized by "equalitarian" versus "traditional" attitudes toward sex roles. This interpretation is based on the notion that the nationalities represented by the high positive loading samples are characterized by more traditional attitudes toward women. We suggest that Irish men, Eskimo men, Alaskan Indian men, Mexican men, Australian men, and New Guinean men may be, to a great extent, uninfluenced by the changing attitudes toward women. Among the most negatively loading samples we find American college women and graduate students, female Israeli college students, Australian artists (both sexes)—all groups probably characterized by relatively equalitarian attitudes toward sex roles.

The profile sheet (figure 4.2) clearly reveals that the high positive loading samples have high accuracy on pure tone and quite low accuracy on pure video and that the high negative loading samples have high scores on pure video and somewhat lower scores on pure audio. This pattern may be related to an earlier finding in which female experimenters communicated more warmly to male subjects in tone of voice than visually and male experimenters communicated more warmly to female subjects in visual channels than in tone of voice (Rosenthal 1967). Perhaps "traditional" males are accustomed to evoking warm and positive responses from females in tone of voice and hence develop greater sensitivity to it, relative to the other channels and relative to females and nontraditional males. We believe that this possibility is sufficiently intriguing to merit further examination.

This analysis was useful both in categorizing our many samples along dimensions and in giving us better insight into the relationship between the structural characteristics of our samples and the shape of their PONS profiles. We examined further the factor structure of these samples using measures from the PONS that were more stable than the eleven channel scores and that, unlike the eleven channels, were relatively orthogonal to one another.

In chapter 3, the factor analysis was described that reduced the eleven channels to four orthogonal measures: RS (20), CF (20), body present without face (60), and face present (120). All 220 items of the PONS are included in these four measures. The second Q-type factor analysis again involved the 142 samples as variables, but treated these four PONS measures as cases instead of the eleven channels. The procedure of z-scoring the four measures was again used to equate for difficulty of dimension and for the number of items in each. Principal components analysis was also used, and the factors obtained were rotated using Kaiser's varimax method. Because the number of cases was four, a maximum of three components could be extracted.

PROFILE OF NONVERBAL SENSITIVITY: STANDARD SCORING SHEET

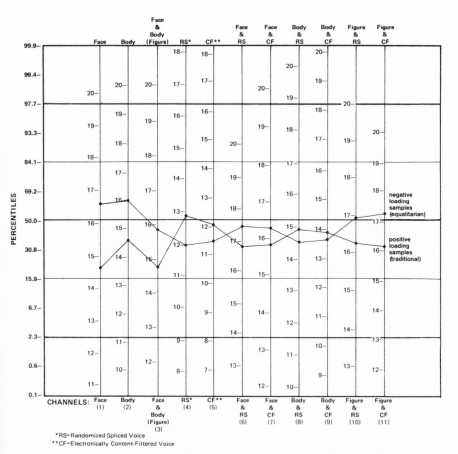

FIGURE 4.2. Factor 2: "Traditional-equalitarian" factor. Median channel scores of five highest ($\geq + .60$) and five lowest ($\leq - .69$) loading samples on factor 2.

Factor 1 accounted for 42.7 percent of the total variance after rotation. There were forty-two samples with factor loadings greater than or equal to $+.50$ and forty-one samples with loadings less than or equal to $-.50$. Of the positively loading samples, twenty-six were U.S. and sixteen were non-U.S. samples. Of the negatively loading samples, thirteen were from the United States and twenty-eight were not. Since this is a significant grouping ($\chi^2(1) = 6.43$, $p < .02$, $\phi = .28$), we named factor 1 the "American versus non-American" factor.

In figure 4.3 we present a graph of the mean z scores on the four measures of the samples with factor loadings $\geq +.85$ or $\leq -.85$ on factor 1. The graph

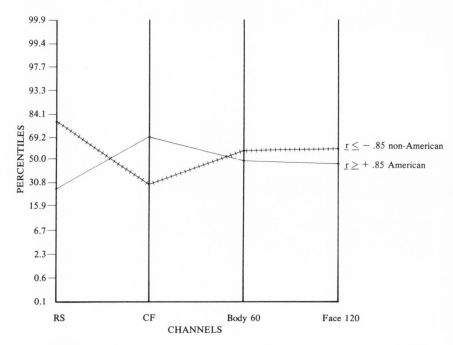

FIGURE 4.3. Mean scores of most extreme positive and negative loading samples on factor 1

shows clearly that Americans obtained higher accuracy scores on CF than on RS, while non-Americans obtained higher accuracy on RS than on CF. We might suggest that our non-American samples who knew English only as a second language (or did not know it at all and took the PONS test with an answer sheet translated into their native language), or who were unaccustomed to American-spoken English, listened more carefully to the audio segments of the PONS than did Americans (who may have been less attentive and interested). Since RS may require more careful listening than CF for successful performance, we might expect non-American samples to receive higher RS scores. It is also possible that sequence cues, which are preserved in CF but not in RS, convey culturally shared information about affect, and hence sequence would be more important to persons from the same culture as the sender than to persons from different cultures. American subjects, if they relied heavily on such cues, may have been simultaneously advantaged on CF and disadvantaged on RS relative to the foreign subjects.

Factor 2, which accounted for 41.6 percent of the total variance after rotation, was essentially a replication of factor 1 in the earlier analysis using the eleven channels. We again named this factor the "unsophisticated-sophisticated" factor. Of the high positively loading samples, thirty-five were college students, clinicians, and professional artists and one was a sample of psychiatric patients. Of the high negatively loading samples, eighteen were junior high school students, psychiatric patients, and foreign (exotic) groups; only eight samples were college students and clinicians. This grouping was highly significant ($\chi^2(1) = 28.32$, $p < .001$, $\phi = .68$).

In figure 4.4, the mean z scores of the most extreme positive ($r \geq +.85$) and most extreme negative ($r \leq -.85$) loading samples are graphed. It is clear from this graph that the results dealing with differential channel performance from the earlier analysis have also been replicated. As before, the "sophisticated" samples obtained high video but relatively low audio scores, while the "unsophisticated" samples obtained relatively high audio but low video scores.

Factor 3, which accounted for 15.7 percent of the variance after rotation, seemed to be a sex-linked dimension. Of the twenty high positive loading samples, twelve were female and eight were male (these male samples were high school and college students [$N=5$], clinicians [$N=2$], and artists [$N=1$]). Of the ten extreme negative loading samples, two were female and eight were male. This grouping was significant at the .10 level ($\chi^2(1) = 2.83$, $p < .10$, $\phi = .31$).

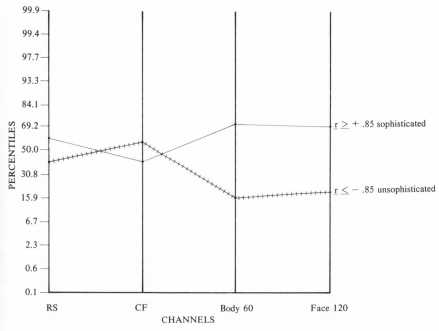

FIGURE 4.4. Mean scores of most extreme positive and negative loading samples on factor 2

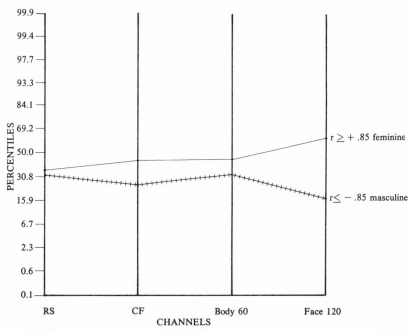

FIGURE 4.5. Mean scores of most extreme positive and negative loading samples on factor 3

TABLE 4.1. Summary of Second Grouping of 142 Samples on Four Measures of the PONS

Factor	Negative Loading	Positive Loading
1 Effect size $\phi = .28$ Profile characteristics:	*non-American* high scores on RS low scores on CF	*American* high scores on CF low scores on RS
2 Effect size $\phi = .68$ Profile characteristics:	*unsophisticated* high scores on audio low scores on video	*sophisticated* high scores on video low scores on audio
3 Effect size $\phi = .31$ Profile characteristics:	*masculine* higher scores on RS than CF lower scores on face 120 than on body 60	*feminine* higher scores on CF than RS higher scores on face 120 than on body 60

TABLE 4.2. Accuracy on PONS Total for Fourteen Types of Samples

Sample Type	Number of Samples	Number of Persons	Mean Accuracy
U.S. college students, general	9	545	80.8%
U.S. college students, psychology	8	157	80.8
Psychologists and clinicians	13	319	80.5
Art, design, and theater groups	11	184	79.1
North American adults	8	130	78.9
Commonwealth college students	15	980	78.8
U.S. teachers	4	133	78.1
U.S. high school students	13	500	77.4
Non–U.S. teachers	9	195	76.9
Non-English speaking college students	5	317	75.7
U.S. junior high school students	3	365	74.4
"Exotic" (non-Western) groups	11	279	71.5
Psychiatric patients and alcoholics	7	143	70.9
U.S. children	10	211	67.5
Median	9	245	77.8
Total	126	4,458	

Figure 4.5 presents the graph of the mean z scores on the four measures of the most extreme positive ($r \geq +.85$) and most extreme negative ($r \leq -.85$) loading samples on factor 3. It is clear from the graph that the female samples had higher scores on the face than the body factor and performed slightly better on CF than on RS. The male samples received higher scores on body than on face and performed slightly better on RS than on CF. The result in the audio channels is consistent with the hypothesis that females perform better on CF because it requires a global, empathic mode of responding, while males perform better on RS because this channel requires a more analytic, molecular mode of responding. Accuracy in reading the face may also be a more analytic skill, and we might expect males to excel at this channel too. Our face measure, however, contains all figure (face + body) items as well as all face-only items, so that these results do not necessarily invalidate our hypothesis; for example, perhaps the females raised their scores on the face

TABLE 4.3. Accuracy in Two Types of Samples for Two Types of Channels

Channels	Type of Sample		Difference
	Sophisticated	Unsophisticated	
Some video	81.9%	72.8%	9.1%
Tone only	62.2	57.8	4.4
Difference	19.7	15.0	4.7

PROFILE OF NONVERBAL SENSITIVITY: STANDARD SCORING SHEET

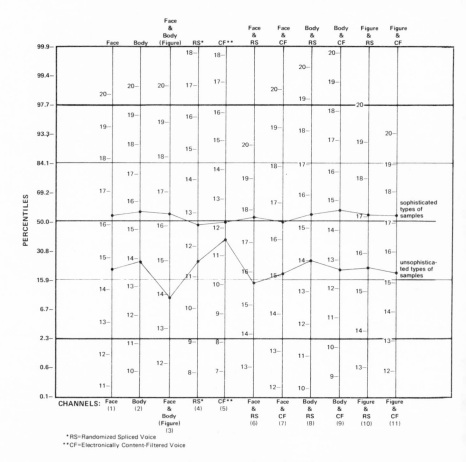

FIGURE 4.6. Mean accuracy of two types of samples: Channel scores and total

TABLE 4.4. Accuracy in Two Types of Samples for Two Types of Quadrants

Quadrants	Type of Sample		
	Sophisticated	Unsophisticated	Difference
Some negative or dominant	80.0%	70.5%	9.5%
No negative or dominant (positive-submissive)	73.3	67.1	6.2
Difference	6.7	3.4	3.3

120 measure by performing exceptionally well at reading the body portion of the figure channel. As chapter 7 points out, for the high school norm group females performed relatively worse on audio and relatively better on video than males, and relatively better on items showing the body.

Table 4.1 presents a summary of the three factors obtained in this analysis. We note the replication of one of the earlier factors (the unsophisticated-sophisticated factor) and the fact that another sex-linked dimension was obtained (masculine-feminine factor). We emphasize that the labels chosen for our factors and our interpretations of the PONS performances of the samples defining the various dimensions are intended only to be hypothesis generating.

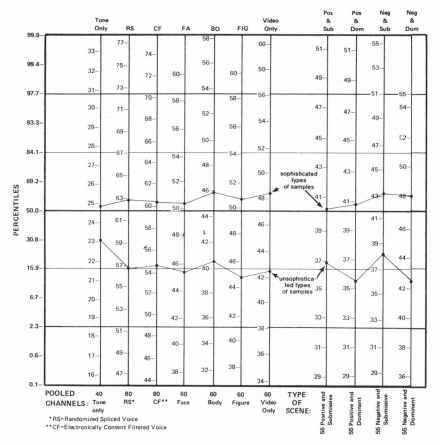

PROFILE OF NONVERBAL SENSITIVITY: STANDARD SCORING SHEET

Pooled Channels and Type of Scene

FIGURE 4.7. Mean accuracy of two types of samples: Pooled channels and type of scene

MORE ON THE SOPHISTICATED AND UNSOPHISTICATED. As part of an earlier analysis, we had categorized our earliest-obtained 126 samples into the fourteen types of groups listed in table 4.2. We noted that three of our categories, the last three listed in table 4.2, corresponded to the types of groups defining the "unsophisticated" end of the unsophisticated-sophisticated factor. Therefore, as an additional check on the results of the factor analyses, we compared the last three types of samples of table 4.2 with all other types of samples for the tone-only channels and for all other channels combined. Table 4.3 and figure 4.6 show that although the "sophisticated" types of samples scored much higher overall than the "unsophisticated" types of samples, their superiority was much greater on channels offering some video cues than on channels offering no video cues. The interaction was significant statistically and substantial in magnitude ($F(1,1232) = 116.62$, $p < .001$, effect size $= .65\sigma$). Relatively speaking, then, the more unsophisticated types of samples were best at tone-only channels, while the more sophisticated types of samples were best at video cue-bearing channels. This result supports the results of the factor analyses yielding the unsophisticated-sophisticated dimension.

As a complement to the factor analyses, it was of interest to compare the "sophisticated" and "unsophisticated" types of samples on their performance on the four quadrants. Of the interaction between the two types of samples and the four quadrants, 97.3 percent of the variance was due to the relative superiority of the unsophisticated types of samples on the positive-submissive quadrant. Table 4.4 and figure 4.7 show this result, which was both significant statistically and substantial in magnitude ($F(1,300) = 58.46$, $p < .001$, effect size $= .88\sigma$). Why these less sophisticated types of samples should be relatively more accurate at decoding positive and submissive nonverbal cues is not at all obvious.

Appendix 4A gives our most up-to-date listing of data from samples that took the full PONS, with the samples grouped according to a revised fifteen-category system.

Appendix 4A

GROUPING SAMPLES INTO FIFTEEN CATEGORIES

In chapter 4, table 4.2 lists fourteen a priori categories to which samples were assigned. In tables 4.5 and 4.6, we present scores on the full PONS test for all samples that we analyzed and that fit into this category system. Each sample is listed in only one category.

The category system used here is exactly like that used in table 4.2, with one exception: the category "Psychologists and Clinicians" has now been subdivided into "Psychologists (graduate students and faculty)" and "Clinicians." Hence, there are fifteen rather than fourteen categories in tables 4.5 and 4.6. In these tables and in table

4.2, the males and females of each sample are not separated into two separate samples, as was done in the factor analytic studies reported earlier in chapter 4. Only a handful of samples did not fit any of the categories and are therefore not listed.

What follows is a brief description of the types of samples included in each category and the number of *samples* in each.

1. U.S. children: Grades 3-6 (N=16).
2. U.S. junior high school students: Grades 7-9 (N=3).
3. High school students: Grades 10-12, from the United States, Israel (Hebrew answer sheets), and Australia (N=15).
4. U.S. college students (general): U.S. college students in introductory psychology courses or with unknown academic concentrations (N=32).
5. U.S. college students (advanced psychology): U.S. college students in middle- or upper-level psychology courses (N=8).
6. Commonwealth college students: College students from Canada, Australia, Northern Ireland, New Zealand, and Hong Kong (N=19).
7. Non-English speaking college students: College students in Mexico, Israel, and Germany, all of whom used PONS answer sheets translated into their own language (N=5).
8. Art, design, and theater: College students, graduate students, and professionals in visual studies, acting, architecture, sculpture, painting, art teaching, interior design, and industrial design (N=11).
9. Adults (general): Adults who were not full-time students and who were neither teachers, psychologists, mental patients, clinicians, nor employed in the arts. Includes samples of married couples, attendees at an international conference on nonverbal communication, magazine staff, forest rangers, and business executives; predominantly from the United States (N=15).
10. U.S. teachers: U.S. undergraduate and graduate students in teacher education, classroom teachers, and school administrators (N=11).
11. Psychologists (faculty and graduate students): Graduate students in nonclinical areas of psychology, psychology faculty, attendees at American Psychological Association convention; predominantly U.S. samples (N=5).
12. Clinicians: Medical students, physicians, and nursing faculty; psychiatrists, clinical and counseling psychologists and graduate students, psychiatric nurses, community psychologists, occupational therapy trainees, dance therapy graduate students, alcoholism counselors, mixed staff in psychiatric hospitals. Samples are from the United States, Northern Ireland, Australia, and Canada (N=31).
13. New Guinean, Australian Aborigine, Alaskan Eskimo, Alaskan Indian: Samples of those four ethnic groups (includes junior high school, high school, college, and adults) (N=11).
14. Psychiatric patients and alcoholics: Patients in mental hospitals in the United States, Northern Ireland, and Australia; U.S. alcoholics (N=8).
15. Non-U.S. teachers: Secondary and college level teachers and teachers in training from Europe, Australia, and Singapore (N=8).

Table 4.5 gives for each sample its category, N, mean age, mean total accuracy for the full PONS, variance for the total, and mean accuracy scores for the four quadrants. Table 4.6 gives for each sample its category and mean accuracy scores on the eleven channels.

TABLE 4.5. Mean Total and Quadrant Scores for 198 Samples, Grouped into Fifteen Categories

Sample	N	Age	Total	S^2 of Total	Positive-Submissive	Positive-Dominant	Negative-Submissive	Negative-Dominant
1. U.S. children								
(N=16)								
1	17	9.00	149.647	285.463	36.206	34.971	36.324	42.147
2	18	10.36	151.028	195.402	37.083	35.278	36.250	42.417
3	13	11.53	152.154	365.399	36.808	36.538	37.077	41.731
4	31	11.45	158.370	220.863	39.222	35.611	38.018	45.519
5	23	10.73	142.217	265.322	34.543	32.391	35.630	39.652
6	7	9.60	149.214	79.347	36.071	33.500	35.571	44.071
7	30	10.63	151.350	276.585	36.383	34.417	37.650	42.900
8	23	11.60	151.042	271.894	36.479	35.583	36.979	42.000
9	9	10.00	147.944	197.580	36.611	31.889	36.500	42.944
10	43	8.00	132.872	176.838	31.209	29.546	33.291	38.826
11	15	9.200	144.933	88.462	35.767	30.300	34.433	44.433
12	6	9.000	139.417	120.535	34.750	30.333	32.917	41.417
13	27	9.192	137.796	150.949	32.963	29.574	34.426	40.833
14	24	10.125	150.250	135.500	36.938	32.354	36.688	44.271
15	13	10.077	149.462	208.556	35.462	32.731	36.462	44.808
16	69	11.250	147.696	227.117	36.072	32.558	35.370	43.696
2. U.S. junior high school students								
(N=3)								
1	109	13.05	164.468	150.046	39.532	38.528	40.761	45.647
2	128	13.844	159.711	274.368	37.516	37.961	39.461	44.773
3	129	14.22	166.512	176.563	39.581	38.577	42.182	46.171
3. High school students								
(N=15)								
1	55	15.0	171.554	125.821	40.945	41.118	41.718	47.773
2	58	16.0	176.034	61.472	41.414	42.241	43.474	48.905
3	73	15.47	167.199	249.744	39.952	39.781	41.185	46.281
4	30	17.12	165.433	197.357	38.983	38.983	41.533	45.933
5	17	16.35	168.676	94.123	39.353	39.324	42.265	47.735
6	22	16.72	173.636	89.314	41.023	40.136	43.682	48.795
7	15	16.6	165.567	201.817	40.267	38.867	40.733	45.700
8	7	18.85	172.429	86.952	39.429	41.000	42.429	49.571
9	82	17.24	169.658	183.560	39.396	39.774	43.555	46.933
10	123	16.63	169.622	110.481	40.114	40.467	42.321	46.719
11	22	16.84	169.500	68.727	40.977	40.795	42.091	45.636
12	40	15.200	173.087	122.199	40.375	41.275	43.912	47.525
13	55	16.34	172.064	92.046	40.791	40.118	43.073	48.082
14	52	16.56	174.346	70.909	40.779	42.202	43.519	47.846
15	70	14.086	166.728	110.276	38.107	37.879	43.950	46.793
4. U.S. college students (general)								
(N=32)								
1	83	27.78	171.584	109.870	39.741	41.325	42.777	47.741
2	50	20.56	178.580	49.954	41.630	42.690	44.960	49.300
3	82	21.59	147.707	93.213	41.287	41.854	42.579	48.988
4	105	17.94	177.119	79.706	41.238	42.390	44.471	49.019
5	133	18.45	175.707	82.737	41.507	41.925	43.793	48.481
6	10	18.00	183.150	57.803	42.750	45.000	46.700	48.700
7	50	19.41	178.420	78.974	41.880	42.130	44.770	49.640
8	23	19.087	175.174	59.600	39.696	41.783	43.956	49.739

Table 4.5. *Continued.*

Sample	N	Age	Total	S² of Total	Positive-Submissive	Positive-Dominant	Negative-Submissive	Negative-Dominant
4. U.S. college students (general) (N=32)								
9	34	23.353	170.765	115.062	41.088	40.618	41.662	47.397
10	9	24.000	171.667	162.944	40.389	41.222	42.389	47.667
11	106	18.124	176.566	123.377	40.830	42.264	44.462	49.009
12	60	18.450	178.250	67.928	42.000	42.650	44.692	48.908
13	51	18.653	176.147	164.208	41.627	42.441	43.510	48.569
14	12	21.250	168.958	154.311	41.250	41.208	41.167	45.333
15	8	24.750	178.750	78.938	43.250	42.375	44.875	48.250
16	148	18.151	170.615	117.408	40.216	41.061	42.233	47.105
17	22	19.182	175.773	96.085	41.318	42.318	43.636	48.500
18	22	18.273	180.614	57.589	42.409	43.932	44.864	49.409
19	29	19.897	169.758	294.234	40.965	39.828	42.638	46.328
20	12	19.500	175.917	22.118	40.458	40.542	43.833	51.083
21	11	21.545	175.000	52.045	42.500	41.545	42.818	48.136
22	32	18.344	178.531	70.608	41.344	42.953	45.234	49.000
23	19	19.684	174.763	31.983	40.868	42.000	43.737	48.158
24	21	19.238	176.738	32.515	40.452	41.952	45.238	49.095
25	12	17.667	179.958	44.936	42.458	42.917	44.750	49.833
26	96	21.812	171.068	141.976	39.875	40.615	42.984	47.594
27	139	17.935	176.669	91.437	41.108	42.482	44.295	48.784
28	28	20.857	174.071	64.745	39.714	41.696	43.982	48.679
29	28	21.500	174.000	105.000	40.036	41.768	43.268	48.929
30	295	20.500	178.819	73.521	41.558	42.829	45.030	49.402
31	33	19.0	177.379	85.454	41.758	42.985	44.545	48.091
32	41	17.95	182.122	57.160	42.951	43.610	46.098	49.463
5. U.S. college students (advanced psychology) (N=8)								
1	32	26.40	174.734	145.564	39.812	41.422	44.578	48.922
2	21	24.70	184.175	103.432	42.050	45.100	45.900	51.125
3	34	23.0	176.559	79.247	41.265	41.603	44.662	49.029
4	12	23.8	178.083	60.368	41.792	42.333	44.250	49.708
5	8	21.5	180.313	47.353	41.750	43.688	45.250	49.625
6	9	21.13	179.667	83.055	41.611	42.167	45.667	50.222
7	33	24.23	179.939	96.163	40.909	43.697	45.621	49.712
8	14	19.44	178.071	67.495	40.714	42.429	45.321	49.607
6. Commonwealth college students (N=19)								
1	76	19.25	172.928	77.590	41.046	40.197	43.460	48.224
2	12	21.83	177.917	55.035	41.917	40.792	44.583	50.625
3	24	22.38	171.813	100.350	41.333	39.396	43.271	47.812
4	30	22.30	175.550	61.056	40.650	42.517	43.233	49.150
5	128	20.21	169.172	66.048	39.965	40.801	40.781	47.625
6	156	20.12	170.359	103.213	39.849	40.349	42.641	47.519
7	75	22.08	174.400	64.887	41.167	41.000	43.533	48.700
8	67	21.85	171.754	118.779	41.468	40.403	43.710	49.355
9	15 ⎫		180.333	92.256	41.667	43.000	45.800	49.867
10	15 ⎪ 25.87		176.800	156.127	42.267	42.300	42.867	49.367
11	15 ⎬		176.200	56.960	42.367	42.267	43.533	48.033
12	15 ⎭		177.533	106.749	41.100	42.000	45.100	49.333
13	44	25.66	171.670	83.840	40.295	39.955	42.841	48.580

Table 4.5. *Continued.*

Sample	N	Age	Total	S² of Total	Positive-Submissive	Positive-Dominant	Negative-Submissive	Negative-Dominant
6. Commonwealth college students (N=19)								
14	34	24.77	172.706	57.825	41.676	40.132	43.147	47.750
15	45	25.29	172.133	62.414	40.333	41.022	42.911	47.867
16	64	20.64	169.719	98.319	40.305	39.453	42.727	47.234
17	47	20.96	175.734	81.201	41.968	41.362	44.053	48.351
18	64	20.47	179.547	46.615	41.578	42.469	45.023	50.477
19	96	19.17	174.271	69.373	41.406	41.109	43.161	48.594
7. Non-English speaking college students (N=5)								
1	25	24.92	169.000	45.580	39.360	39.800	42.020	47.820
2	55	. . .	167.045	93.539	. . .	. . .	. . .	. . .
3	68	. . .	164.809	170.499	37.404	38.882	42.522	46.000
4	106	19.75	166.509	70.349	38.538	38.802	42.396	46.774
5	63	20.05	164.778	72.188	38.175	38.032	42.103	46.468
8. Art, design, and theater (N=11)								
1	24	23.45	176.104	33.458	41.625	41.625	43.292	49.562
2	6	21.33	166.167	130.723	41.333	39.750	39.000	46.083
3	8	20.11	177.188	19.184	43.563	41.813	43.750	48.063
4	19	22.33	165.737	206.983	39.526	38.947	41.210	46.053
5	10	24.11	159.950	90.523	37.150	38.850	39.050	44.900
6	31	19.86	175.339	67.635	41.339	40.661	44.468	48.871
7	35	19.31	170.129	93.819	40.186	39.429	42.857	47.657
8	29	20.63	171.483	75.163	41.207	39.845	42.465	47.965
9	7	23.85	186.500	54.786	43.214	45.286	47.571	50.429
10	11	24.0	180.773	14.153	41.636	44.455	45.591	49.091
11	4	19.75	183.625	47.422	43.250	42.250	47.250	50.875
9. Adults (general) (N=15)								
1	15	44.13	172.067	73.262	40.667	41.467	43.067	46.867
2	16	26.0	177.467	70.124	41.233	42.300	44.633	49.300
3	12	25.3	171.875	119.597	40.167	41.750	41.208	48.750
4	13	31.92	176.769	75.485	40.692	42.192	44.577	49.308
5	13	28.46	179.577	23.302	42.077	42.769	45.731	49.000
6	18	32.17	171.028	79.791	39.056	39.806	43.694	48.472
7	20	26.43	174.275	86.187	40.375	42.625	43.125	48.150
8	30	30.96	167.883	65.945	38.083	39.800	42.650	47.350
9	6	. . .	180.500	94.917	40.667	43.500	46.833	49.500
10	36	. . .	169.875	135.699	39.056	41.236	42.736	46.847
11	40	34.950	174.012	81.531	40.775	41.587	42.675	48.975
12	136	. . .	173.243	81.360	40.397	41.191	43.485	48.169
13	4	33.000	183.000	12.000	41.500	45.000	44.500	52.000
14	24	41.667	170.646	55.697	39.062	40.750	42.458	48.375
15	23	38.14	168.261	65.215	39.152	39.696	42.804	46.609
10. U.S. teachers (N=11)								
1	16	27.2	174.125	88.417	40.656	41.437	43.781	48.250
2	45	43.10	166.689	200.957	38.589	39.522	41.600	46.978

Table 4.5. *Continued.*

Sample	N	Age	Total	S² of Total	Positive-Submissive	Positive-Dominant	Negative-Submissive	Negative-Dominant
10. U.S. teachers (N=11)								
3	59	32.04	171.754	87.520	40.492	40.746	42.466	48.051
4	13	27.07	175.038	54.748	40.538	42.115	43.346	49.038
5	52	22.308	179.077	53.686	42.048	42.442	44.779	49.808
6	39	54.500	160.141	295.409	37.667	36.872	40.615	44.987
7	83	29.224	176.114	80.664	40.976	42.193	43.765	49.181
8	56	23.179	172.884	56.964	41.062	40.991	43.018	47.812
9	53	23.057	177.641	112.428	41.708	42.802	44.094	49.038
10	65	32.822	166.177	127.687	39.338	39.069	41.223	46.546
11	86	25.106	172.924	163.240	41.163	40.512	42.692	48.558
11. Psychologists (faculty and graduate students) (N=5)								
1	89	34.64	174.045	73.751	39.966	41.062	43.888	49.129
2	14	23.3	186.767	51.531	43.400	45.100	47.433	50.833
3	9	26.11	182.278	30.062	41.389	44.889	45.833	50.167
4	7	28.500	176.643	99.909	40.071	42.571	46.143	47.857
5	5	25.2	185.200	4.160	43.200	46.200	45.000	50.800
12. Clinicians (N=31)								
1	7	26.16	169.172	66.048	38.429	36.857	42.071	47.786
2	12	49.91	176.542	17.561	40.833	41.833	44.875	49.000
3	8	32.75	178.937	31.152	42.375	43.625	43.375	49.562
4	6	28.00	176.500	82.000	41.917	43.083	43.333	48.167
5	7	23.28	179.357	59.765	42.214	42.786	44.000	50.357
6	29	29.76	174.000	88.759	39.672	40.017	44.638	49.672
7	33	28.18	175.823	28.525	41.387	40.758	43.919	49.758
8	61	30.76	171.106	91.493	40.066	40.418	42.484	48.139
9	8	26.30	175.000	30.000	41.250	41.188	43.375	49.188
10	16	27.167	180.781	39.874	41.844	43.188	46.000	49.750
11	38	28.816	176.408	92.011	41.158	41.408	44.447	49.395
12	39	32.36	167.95	100.60	39.86	39.88	42.06	46.14
13	53	23.423	169.802	116.324	39.915	39.613	42.755	47.519
14	16	28.4	174.97	85.75	41.75	41.47	43.66	48.09
15	18	19.611	177.528	31.958	41.583	42.111	44.583	49.250
16	12	28.333	180.417	56.910	42.417	41.083	46.417	50.500
17	14	25.143	177.679	49.593	41.000	41.929	44.143	50.357
18	33	. . .	172.560	62.588	39.909	41.242	43.151	48.258
19	14		179.286	66.374	42.071	43.286	45.214	48.714
20	3	35.10	176.333	126.333	39.333	42.667	43.667	50.667
21	9		174.000	97.313	41.944	40.778	43.444	47.833
22	14		176.036	47.633	40.036	42.143	45.000	48.857
23	16	24.500	179.625	59.234	42.812	41.937	44.437	50.438
24	32	26.187	173.000	208.468	40.266	40.781	43.078	48.875
25	18	40.389	176.750	31.007	40.306	42.333	44.944	49.167
26	40	39.200	174.125	127.934	40.312	41.425	43.937	48.450
27	47	. . .	171.670	62.253	39.340	39.330	43.936	49.064
28	11	30.636	177.909	70.492	42.000	42.500	44.636	48.773
29	18	34.778	171.500	155.583	38.583	40.611	43.500	48.806
30	18	24.056	166.972	89.569	37.944	40.417	43.000	45.611
31	13	28.769	169.654	166.669	37.962	39.500	43.231	48.962

Table 4.5. *Continued.*

Sample	N	Age	Total	S^2 of Total	Positive-Submissive	Positive-Dominant	Negative-Submissive	Negative-Dominant
13. New Guinean, Australian, Aborigine, Alaskan Eskimo, Alaskan Indian								
(N=11)								
1	18	14.5	161.472	166.455	38.167	38.250	40.806	44.250
2	23	14.6	151.978	204.874	36.804	35.130	38.522	41.522
3	30	25.58	154.117	156.461	38.600	35.500	38.817	41.200
4	23	30.78	148.891	92.782	36.456	35.022	37.174	40.239
5	27	24.67	155.037	111.239	38.018	35.259	38.648	43.111
6	22	16.18	153.386	233.862	37.114	35.409	38.432	42.432
7	28	17.70	163.232	85.883	39.768	37.143	41.714	44.607
8	54	19.89	146.009	148.846	34.018	34.148	37.056	40.787
9	34	18.62	163.794	129.017	39.044	39.221	40.515	45.015
10	12	25.0	165.667	86.515	39.458	38.583	41.250	46.375
11	8	28.0	167.438	141.603	40.938	38.813	42.563	45.125
14. Psychiatric patients and alcoholics								
(N=8)								
1	17	35.58	151.147	312.649	36.471	36.176	36.765	41.735
2	15	35.7	151.533	274.731	37.367	34.700	38.333	41.133
3	82	37.850	154.244	383.250	37.116	35.939	38.518	42.671
4	24	27.91	149.583	416.160	35.000	34.562	38.500	41.521
5	50	45.21	158.110	288.932	37.470	37.480	39.550	43.610
6	9	19.88	161.444	163.025	38.167	38.167	39.556	45.556
7	11	36.90	158.591	315.264	38.409	36.864	38.636	44.682
8	17	46.93	169.029	101.640	37.412	37.853	42.176	44.588
15. Non-U.S. teachers								
(N=8)								
1	21	24.45	169.738	56.610	39.357	40.119	42.905	47.357
2	8	21.13	174.750	63.875	42.125	40.500	44.000	48.125
3	15	23.06	172.100	50.173	40.333	40.100	43.400	48.267
4	4	34.50	167.750	75.313	38.000	41.000	41.375	47.375
5	6	42.16	174.000	50.417	39.167	41.417	44.750	48.667
6	5	34.20	165.100	6.240	39.900	38.300	41.100	45.800
7	69	34.22	164.101	194.445	37.993	39.536	40.964	45.609
8	50	33.08	167.870	136.396	38.900	39.230	42.460	47.280

TABLE 4.6. Mean Channel Scores for 198 Samples, Grouped into Fifteen Categories

Sample	Face	Body	Figure	RS	CF	Face & RS	Face & CF	Body & RS	Body & CF	Figure & RS	Figure & CF
1. U.S. children (N=16)											
1	14.735	13.324	13.676	11.382	11.059	14.647	14.824	14.147	11.588	15.176	15.088
2	14.444	13.250	12.944	11.833	10.556	15.333	15.611	13.306	12.083	16.083	15.583
3	14.231	13.423	14.192	10.923	11.385	15.423	15.346	13.846	12.154	15.731	15.500
4	14.741	14.611	14.296	11.870	12.241	15.685	15.574	14.167	12.333	16.573	16.315
5	13.957	13.913	13.065	10.261	10.804	14.261	14.283	12.087	10.674	14.043	14.870
6	14.929	14.000	13.214	10.429	11.500	14.643	15.429	13.786	10.571	14.786	15.929
7	15.117	14.233	13.617	10.300	11.400	15.533	14.767	13.483	12.583	15.283	15.033
8	14.583	13.625	13.875	10.750	11.938	15.646	15.354	13.146	11.396	15.500	15.229
9	14.889	13.111	12.889	11.667	10.667	14.444	14.556	13.222	11.611	15.667	15.222
10	12.360	11.698	11.558	10.535	10.628	12.977	12.919	12.372	11.256	13.884	12.686
11	14.500	12.633	12.800	10.667	11.233	15.200	14.400	13.333	11.700	15.300	13.167
12	12.750	12.750	13.000	11.167	11.167	13.333	14.000	11.833	11.667	14.083	13.667
13	12.259	12.500	12.056	11.111	11.296	13.056	13.926	12.352	11.500	14.093	13.648
14	14.354	13.333	13.771	11.771	10.938	14.083	14.708	13.917	11.729	15.708	15.938
15	14.385	13.115	12.423	11.615	10.962	14.846	14.769	14.000	12.308	15.769	15.269
16	13.978	13.308	13.884	10.522	11.746	14.319	14.457	13.080	12.275	15.094	15.036
2. U.S. junior high school students (N=3)											
1	16.261	15.055	15.087	12.583	10.986	16.940	15.995	14.528	13.344	16.752	16.936
2	15.262	14.453	14.488	12.062	12.012	16.699	15.590	14.398	13.379	15.562	15.805
3	16.244	14.957	15.527	12.504	11.554	17.473	16.488	14.814	13.977	16.484	16.488
3. High school students (N=15)											
1	15.864	15.127	16.227	13.964	12.291	17.855	16.582	15.245	14.082	17.118	17.200
2	16.681	16.121	16.922	13.060	12.414	18.414	17.103	15.793	14.638	17.259	17.629
3	15.781	15.411	15.925	12.110	11.979	17.247	16.075	14.870	14.130	16.630	17.041

Table 4.6. *Continued.*

Sample	Face	Body	Figure	RS	CF	Face & RS	Face & CF	Body & RS	Body & CF	Figure & RS	Figure & CF
3. High school students (N=15)											
4	15.800	14.383	15.717	12.517	12.400	16.233	16.400	14.850	14.217	16.067	16.850
5	15.588	15.029	15.794	11.794	12.029	17.824	16.706	15.824	14.147	16.765	17.176
6	16.432	15.386	16.705	11.727	13.273	17.932	16.864	15.614	15.000	17.318	17.386
7	16.533	15.067	15.467	10.933	11.667	17.333	17.200	15.200	13.367	16.400	16.400
8	16.286	16.143	16.000	11.286	11.857	18.286	16.571	16.286	15.286	17.286	17.143
9	16.256	15.543	15.884	12.262	12.591	17.835	16.165	15.329	14.646	16.524	16.622
10	16.252	15.654	15.878	12.622	11.699	17.687	16.443	15.146	14.419	16.703	17.118
11	16.182	15.364	16.205	12.273	11.341	18.136	16.932	14.795	13.977	16.773	17.523
12	16.712	15.212	16.475	12.825	12.475	18.150	16.700	15.675	14.062	17.500	17.300
13	16.382	15.809	16.536	13.018	11.527	17.909	16.618	15.327	14.627	16.809	17.500
14	16.692	15.962	16.385	13.135	12.192	18.385	16.625	15.471	14.394	17.519	17.587
15	16.414	15.314	15.114	11.864	11.621	17.486	15.679	15.171	14.471	16.600	16.993
4. U.S. college students (general) (N=32)											
1	16.030	15.681	16.259	12.476	12.494	17.723	16.512	15.313	14.880	17.072	17.145
2	16.770	16.450	17.350	13.080	12.570	18.280	16.990	15.770	15.790	17.460	18.070
3	16.445	15.780	16.689	12.805	12.585	17.683	16.659	15.457	15.713	17.262	17.628
4	17.062	16.209	17.219	13.214	12.314	18.409	16.886	15.424	15.190	17.409	17.781
5	16.695	16.184	16.865	12.741	12.526	18.203	16.865	15.244	15.383	17.274	17.726
6	16.800	17.000	17.700	13.950	14.400	19.000	16.700	17.000	15.500	17.400	17.700
7	16.630	16.490	16.950	12.960	13.250	18.360	16.900	16.060	15.680	17.340	17.800
8	17.000	15.652	17.109	12.348	12.543	17.696	17.087	15.522	15.000	17.261	17.956
9	15.779	15.456	16.603	12.191	12.794	17.794	16.588	15.324	14.618	16.765	16.853

10	16.611	16.111	15.778	12.889	12.167	18.222	17.000	15.000	14.444	16.444	17.000
11	16.849	16.302	17.104	12.660	12.519	18.123	16.670	15.849	15.481	17.283	17.726
12	17.100	16.400	17.208	13.133	12.975	18.083	17.083	15.892	15.300	17.433	17.642
13	16.510	16.216	17.108	13.529	12.382	18.471	16.971	15.716	15.000	16.637	17.608
14	16.083	15.667	15.292	11.833	11.542	18.083	15.708	15.583	14.917	17.000	17.250
15	17.125	17.000	17.000	13.125	12.500	18.500	18.000	15.000	15.000	17.875	17.625
16	15.986	15.615	15.997	12.807	12.220	17.642	16.470	15.463	14.882	16.574	16.959
17	16.727	15.682	16.955	12.682	12.727	18.318	16.818	15.636	15.182	17.136	17.909
18	17.136	16.591	17.682	12.818	13.477	18.045	16.818	16.409	15.955	17.500	18.182
19	15.759	15.759	16.414	12.207	12.431	17.397	16.241	15.241	14.966	16.483	16.862
20	17.417	16.750	16.833	12.542	13.000	18.125	16.917	16.042	15.125	16.667	16.500
21	16.227	16.545	16.636	13.000	12.545	17.636	17.136	15.818	14.091	17.455	17.909
22	16.953	16.594	17.312	13.109	12.969	18.219	16.875	15.750	15.781	17.094	17.875
23	16.895	15.526	16.842	12.789	12.395	18.210	16.789	15.763	15.158	16.868	17.526
24	16.952	16.905	16.976	12.952	12.857	17.905	16.714	15.762	15.048	17.238	17.429
25	17.000	16.292	16.833	13.750	12.917	18.417	17.583	15.667	15.833	17.917	17.750
26	16.411	14.880	16.646	12.792	12.734	17.542	16.318	15.177	14.370	16.880	17.318
27	16.903	16.388	17.043	12.835	12.687	18.223	17.054	15.288	15.198	17.083	17.968
28	16.929	15.696	16.768	12.482	12.696	17.661	16.857	15.286	15.393	16.911	17.393
29	16.893	15.339	16.714	12.821	12.982	17.696	16.679	15.518	14.661	17.268	17.429
30	16.880	16.119	16.958	13.525	13.234	18.490	17.010	15.920	15.512	17.512	17.659
31	17.030	16.015	17.151	13.652	12.379	18.318	16.788	15.788	14.864	17.788	17.606
32	16.854	16.659	17.683	13.561	13.537	18.390	17.171	16.341	16.073	17.683	18.171

5. U.S. college students (advanced psychology) (N=8)

1	16.375	15.859	16.406	13.109	13.094	18.125	16.437	15.406	15.312	17.141	17.469
2	17.225	16.975	17.525	14.150	13.950	18.675	17.700	16.200	15.775	17.950	18.050
3	16.941	16.015	17.397	11.853	12.294	18.750	16.941	16.044	14.500	17.941	17.882
4	17.042	16.583	17.292	12.542	12.708	18.375	17.542	15.750	14.917	17.833	17.500
5	17.500	17.000	17.125	13.000	13.375	18.500	16.750	16.063	15.375	17.500	18.125
6	16.611	16.333	17.111	12.889	12.278	18.333	16.889	16.556	16.000	18.222	18.444
7	17.394	16.727	17.030	13.697	12.303	18.394	17.091	16.030	15.348	17.803	18.121
8	17.857	16.643	17.107	13.286	12.571	17.929	16.536	15.286	15.464	17.286	18.107

Table 4.6. *Continued.*

Sample	Face	Body	Figure	RS	CF	Face & RS	Face & CF	Body & RS	Body & CF	Figure & RS	Figure & CF
6. Commonwealth college students (N=19)											
1	16.329	15.895	16.553	13.020	12.033	18.085	16.211	15.704	14.855	17.204	17.039
2	16.292	17.083	16.667	13.917	12.458	18.667	16.417	16.083	15.333	17.625	17.375
3	16.271	15.333	16.771	13.042	12.479	17.521	16.229	15.396	14.729	17.167	16.875
4	16.550	16.033	16.300	13.833	12.333	18.133	16.817	16.300	14.283	17.533	17.433
5	15.844	16.125	15.969	12.051	11.316	17.930	16.070	15.430	14.562	16.902	16.973
6	16.442	15.452	16.048	12.615	12.122	17.641	16.465	15.196	14.603	16.888	16.888
7	16.200	15.813	16.587	13.573	11.673	18.207	16.667	15.800	14.693	17.627	17.560
8	16.952	15.516	16.984	13.129	11.935	18.161	16.758	15.887	14.516	17.726	17.371
9	17.067	16.733	17.467	13.133	13.133	18.600	17.133	15.867	15.267	17.800	18.133
10	17.000	16.133	16.667	13.333	13.167	17.867	17.333	15.567	15.133	17.200	17.400
11	16.600	17.000	16.533	12.867	12.933	18.700	16.333	15.533	15.167	17.000	17.533
12	16.600	17.067	16.833	12.933	12.333	18.133	17.400	15.633	15.267	17.667	17.667
13	16.182	15.375	16.580	12.864	11.477	18.091	16.636	15.500	14.773	17.080	17.114
14	16.426	15.294	16.397	12.382	11.500	18.132	16.882	15.765	15.132	17.456	17.338
15	16.289	15.433	16.489	13.389	11.478	18.311	16.378	15.333	14.444	17.067	17.522
16	15.766	15.289	15.992	11.883	11.812	17.750	16.672	15.375	14.484	17.172	17.523
17	16.553	15.681	16.947	13.426	11.915	18.383	16.511	16.394	15.394	17.191	17.340
18	17.078	16.664	17.234	13.469	12.594	18.672	17.359	16.109	15.344	17.281	17.742
19	16.573	15.755	16.292	13.021	11.964	18.208	16.745	15.891	14.969	17.474	17.380
7. Non-English speaking college students (N=5)											
1	15.520	14.880	15.720	12.680	12.240	17.860	16.980	14.640	14.660	16.760	17.060
2	16.191	15.273	15.527	12.555	11.291	16.591	15.664	14.927	14.400	17.200	17.427
3	16.243	15.176	15.088	12.154	11.515	16.390	15.515	14.875	14.390	16.397	17.066
4	15.670	15.193	15.958	12.047	11.863	17.174	16.014	15.321	14.132	16.042	17.094
5	15.024	15.206	15.992	11.500	12.040	16.802	16.627	15.786	13.937	15.516	17.349

8. Art, design, and theater
(N=11)

	1	2	3	4	5	6	7	8	9	10	11
1	16.583	15.937	16.896	13.417	13.333	17.750	16.958	15.937	14.729	17.292	17.271
2	15.750	15.083	14.667	13.333	12.417	17.667	15.667	14.000	13.500	16.750	17.333
3	16.625	16.875	18.000	11.750	12.688	17.813	17.000	15.375	14.875	17.813	18.375
4	16.316	15.974	15.921	11.806	11.500	16.816	16.079	14.632	13.000	16.737	17.132
5	15.950	15.150	15.350	11.700	10.050	16.150	15.000	14.150	13.850	16.450	16.150
6	16.694	15.742	16.710	13.032	12.258	18.161	16.629	16.161	15.048	17.339	17.564
7	16.114	15.471	16.071	12.557	12.157	17.700	16.329	15.314	14.743	16.914	16.757
8	16.207	15.224	16.086	12.707	11.241	17.862	16.448	15.793	14.948	17.966	17.000
9	17.857	16.857	18.500	14.143	13.000	18.571	18.286	16.714	17.143	17.571	17.857
10	16.227	16.682	17.182	14.000	12.273	18.091	17.364	16.227	15.909	18.091	18.727
11	18.250	17.250	17.125	14.750	13.250	18.250	17.000	17.000	16.250	17.250	17.250

9. Adults (general)
(N=15)

	1	2	3	4	5	6	7	8	9	10	11
1	16.200	15.867	17.067	13.000	12.733	17.600	16.000	15.933	13.733	17.000	16.933
2	16.300	16.267	17.067	13.233	13.000	18.300	17.200	15.800	15.533	17.433	17.333
3	16.208	15.750	16.333	12.250	12.792	17.917	16.250	15.042	15.083	16.833	17.417
4	16.654	15.269	17.192	13.269	13.769	18.346	16.423	15.808	15.077	17.500	17.462
5	16.692	17.269	17.885	13.077	12.462	18.231	16.692	16.000	15.423	18.154	17.692
6	16.111	15.889	16.278	12.833	11.667	18.333	15.500	15.639	14.528	17.417	16.833
7	16.225	16.075	17.225	12.950	12.025	18.100	16.250	15.425	14.925	17.175	17.900
8	16.100	14.717	16.900	11.933	11.833	17.767	16.283	14.667	13.817	16.833	17.033
9	17.500	16.167	16.667	12.500	14.500	18.500	17.833	15.167	16.000	17.500	18.167
10	16.181	15.569	16.361	13.139	11.625	17.611	16.583	15.347	14.236	16.528	16.694
11	16.562	15.812	16.675	13.575	12.150	17.775	16.425	15.612	15.300	17.050	17.075
12	16.500	16.007	16.956	12.426	12.169	17.875	16.787	15.346	14.882	16.831	17.463
13	17.750	17.500	17.250	13.500	14.500	18.750	17.750	15.750	15.000	16.750	18.500
14	16.229	15.792	15.833	12.750	11.979	17.750	16.792	15.875	14.271	16.750	16.625
15	15.870	15.478	16.196	11.935	11.739	17.783	16.239	15.478	14.413	16.652	16.478

10. U.S. teachers
(N=11)

	1	2	3	4	5	6	7	8	9	10	11
1	16.750	16.125	16.781	12.437	11.187	18.250	17.187	15.531	14.500	17.562	17.813
2	16.011	15.311	15.878	12.067	12.222	17.100	16.033	14.822	14.433	16.356	16.456

Table 4.6. *Continued.*

Sample	Face	Body	Figure	RS	CF	Face & RS	Face & CF	Body & RS	Body & CF	Figure & RS	Figure & CF
10. U.S. teachers (N=11)											
3	16.373	15.907	16.729	12.542	11.678	18.017	16.542	15.127	14.602	17.203	17.034
4	16.731	16.808	16.962	12.615	12.346	17.962	16.846	16.269	14.577	17.231	16.692
5	17.115	16.462	17.404	12.942	12.942	18.135	16.981	15.750	15.750	17.385	18.135
6	15.462	13.936	14.667	11.397	12.000	16.654	15.372	14.949	13.628	16.385	15.692
7	16.476	15.904	16.657	13.349	12.729	18.373	17.018	15.898	14.819	17.470	17.422
8	16.679	15.929	16.393	13.107	12.187	17.750	16.473	15.741	14.589	17.027	17.009
9	16.491	16.547	16.887	13.226	13.038	18.236	16.632	15.953	15.538	17.396	17.698
10	15.838	15.085	15.877	12.254	11.777	17.346	16.108	14.846	13.931	16.600	16.515
11	16.366	15.599	16.628	12.564	12.006	17.919	16.459	15.948	14.936	17.122	17.378
11. Psychologists (faculty and graduate students) (N=5)											
1	16.594	15.844	16.781	13.406	11.562	18.396	16.729	16.031	15.063	17.469	17.302
2	18.133	17.467	17.767	13.833	12.900	18.333	18.000	16.733	16.567	17.867	19.167
3	17.222	16.444	18.111	13.000	13.722	18.556	17.333	15.667	15.000	18.222	19.000
4	16.286	17.143	16.857	12.714	13.143	18.286	17.071	15.143	15.143	17.429	17.429
5	17.200	17.600	17.600	14.200	12.600	19.400	17.000	15.800	17.200	17.600	19.000
12. Clinicians (N=31)											
1	15.857	15.071	16.071	11.000	11.857	17.786	15.286	15.714	13.429	16.571	16.500
2	16.500	16.167	17.750	12.958	12.375	18.750	17.000	15.333	14.667	17.250	17.792
3	17.375	16.750	17.500	13.250	11.750	18.750	17.875	14.937	14.750	18.250	17.750
4	17.667	16.000	16.000	12.917	12.500	18.417	16.667	15.833	15.417	17.167	17.917
5	17.286	17.000	16.857	12.857	14.357	17.643	16.714	16.643	16.000	16.571	17.429
6	16.379	15.707	16.621	13.190	12.121	18.155	16.690	15.138	15.017	17.448	17.534
7	16.823	16.081	16.952	13.242	12.839	18.242	16.468	15.484	15.177	16.919	17.597
8	16.287	15.172	13.393	12.762	11.828	17.992	16.377	15.279	14.811	17.049	17.156

9	15.937	16.125	16.875	14.625	12.375	18.250	16.250	15.375	14.812	17.625	16.750
10	17.500	17.094	17.594	13.219	12.875	18.438	16.625	16.125	16.000	17.500	17.813
11	16.539	16.763	17.158	13.158	12.421	18.355	16.895	15.526	14.750	17.197	17.645
12	15.40	15.18	15.90	12.20	11.73	17.37	15.59	15.54	14.63	17.15	17.26
13	16.321	15.311	16.113	12.066	11.943	17.726	16.538	15.396	14.245	17.019	17.123
14	16.47	15.81	17.06	12.81	12.44	17.78	17.03	15.03	15.34	17.25	17.94
15	16.944	15.611	16.444	13.250	12.694	18.583	17.194	16.194	14.972	17.639	18.000
16	16.833	17.333	17.607	11.750	13.667	18.333	17.250	15.917	16.167	17.667	17.833
17	16.821	15.143	17.607	13.464	13.321	17.929	17.000	16.000	15.571	17.214	17.607
18	16.000	15.848	16.318	12.530	12.318	18.015	16.409	15.318	15.061	17.121	17.621
19	17.286	16.643	17.071	12.929	12.857	18.429	17.429	16.071	14.643	17.714	18.214
20	17.000	17.000	17.333	11.667	12.333	18.000	17.000	15.333	14.000	17.000	19.000
21	16.333	15.722	16.500	12.778	13.444	18.278	16.643	15.111	14.000	17.389	17.444
22	16.750	16.571	16.679	12.429	12.643	18.214	17.250	15.643	15.179	17.786	17.500
23	16.625	17.125	17.250	12.937	13.500	18.250	16.500	16.312	14.937	17.625	17.812
24	16.500	16.141	16.141	12.922	12.047	18.078	16.722	15.016	15.687	16.812	17.156
25	16.889	16.194	16.889	13.000	12.556	18.778	16.722	16.000	14.917	17.306	17.500
26	16.300	16.400	16.950	12.337	12.475	18.000	17.112	15.212	15.250	17.025	17.062
27	16.064	15.277	16.043	12.660	12.894	18.191	16.851	15.681	15.191	16.617	16.149
28	17.227	15.409	16.818	13.682	12.545	17.909	17.364	16.045	16.182	17.091	17.636
29	16.417	15.000	16.472	12.694	12.778	17.833	16.944	15.278	14.194	17.056	16.833
30	15.528	15.750	15.083	11.917	12.333	18.083	15.111	15.944	14.444	15.056	17.722
31	16.538	15.231	15.962	12.577	12.538	17.692	16.000	15.038	14.692	16.077	17.308

13. New Guinean, Australian Aborigine, Alaskan Eskimo, Alaskan Indian (N=11)

1	15.167	14.250	13.528	13.944	12.889	16.694	15.556	14.250	13.694	15.889	15.611
2	14.935	13.196	12.870	12.304	12.174	15.674	14.870	13.435	12.348	15.326	14.848
3	14.367	13.750	13.633	12.250	11.650	15.717	14.817	14.883	12.367	15.583	15.100
4	14.391	12.630	13.239	11.522	11.196	14.804	14.891	13.783	12.522	15.196	14.717
5	14.926	13.926	13.815	12.000	11.111	15.574	14.852	14.796	13.630	15.093	15.315
6	14.614	13.659	13.705	11.818	11.364	15.705	14.750	13.795	12.977	15.636	15.364
7	14.696	14.679	14.893	12.929	12.018	16.893	15.929	14.893	13.786	16.429	16.089
8	13.556	13.833	13.241	10.833	10.565	14.972	14.269	14.213	11.519	14.911	14.019
9	15.309	15.721	14.324	12.265	11.265	17.015	15.471	15.544	13.868	16.426	16.588

Table 4.6. *Continued.*

Sample	Face	Body	Figure	RS	CF	Face & RS	Face & CF	Body & RS	Body & CF	Figure & RS	Figure & CF
13. New Guinean, Australian Aborigine, Alaskan Eskimo, Alaskan Indian (N=11)											
10	15.292	15.208	15.917	11.875	12.792	16.792	16.042	15.125	14.292	16.167	16.167
11	14.875	14.438	15.125	13.063	11.875	16.625	17.125	15.313	15.313	17.188	16.500
14. Psychiatric patients and alcoholics (N=8)											
1	14.206	13.265	14.059	10.469	11.176	15.941	14.765	14.529	12.294	15.441	15.029
2	14.533	13.667	13.633	11.400	11.500	16.200	14.933	13.700	11.900	15.200	14.867
3	14.677	13.738	14.372	11.646	11.207	16.152	15.079	14.018	12.750	15.628	14.976
4	14.104	13.250	13.729	11.896	11.563	14.813	14.854	13.479	12.688	15.438	13.771
5	15.040	14.580	14.830	11.530	11.330	16.690	15.080	14.150	13.080	16.050	15.750
6	15.111	14.778	14.722	11.611	12.444	16.722	15.222	14.111	14.333	16.556	15.883
7	15.409	15.545	14.818	11.318	11.500	15.227	15.364	14.227	13.500	15.773	15.909
8	15.676	14.353	14.941	11.353	12.618	16.971	14.794	14.441	13.735	16.118	17.029
15. Non-U.S. teachers (N=8)											
1	15.857	14.857	16.095	13.000	11.452	17.690	16.333	15.542	14.238	17.167	17.524
2	15.562	16.125	16.437	13.187	13.375	18.375	16.937	15.875	13.875	17.125	17.875
3	15.967	15.633	16.000	13.767	12.000	17.800	16.067	15.467	15.267	16.933	17.200
4	16.375	17.250	16.250	11.750	12.125	15.750	16.250	15.000	13.500	16.500	17.000
5	17.250	16.500	16.667	11.667	12.167	18.500	17.167	16.500	15.167	16.750	15.667
6	16.400	15.100	16.200	12.200	10.100	17.000	15.000	14.900	15.000	16.600	16.600
7	15.406	14.841	15.304	11.674	11.478	17.036	15.985	15.261	13.754	16.384	16.978
8	15.470	15.440	15.620	11.580	12.370	17.540	16.340	15.170	14.990	16.440	16.910

5 | Length of Communication Exposure

During the early video tape stages of the development of the PONS, we discovered that when the twenty scenes were shown for about five seconds, our pilot study subjects from Harvard University were able to achieve nearly perfect accuracy. By shortening the exposure time to two seconds we were able to bring the average accuracy level of a roughly comparable group of Harvard University students down to about 84 percent. Such a level of accuracy often tends to increase the potential for higher levels of reliability than either higher or lower levels of mean accuracy, given that each item has two response alternatives (Guilford 1954, p. 391).

Still, we were surprised that subjects obtained so much useful information from scene exposures of only two seconds. It led us to wonder how much further we would have to decrease length of visual exposure to obtain a chance level of accuracy. Accordingly, we constructed a new version of the PONS test, the brief exposure PONS, employing the twenty face-only scenes and the twenty body-only scenes, and employing the pairs of response alternatives that accompanied these scenes in the full PONS. These forty scenes were systematically divided into four groups of ten scenes each, each group having a different length of exposure. The four lengths were $1/24$th, $3/24$ths, $9/24$ths, and $27/24$ths of a second (that is, 1, 3, 9, and 27 frames, where 24 frames are shown in one second). These particular values were chosen such that their logarithms would be equally spaced, because we felt that differences in length of exposure would be more important at the lower levels of exposure length (e.g., 1 versus 3 frames) than at the higher levels of exposure length (e.g., 9 versus 27 frames). Within each of these four levels of exposure length, five of the scenes were in the face channel and five in the body channel. Within each of the 4×2 cells formed by the crossing of exposure length with channel, the five scenes were arranged in order of increasing difficulty to form a third factor made up of five levels of difficulty. Difficulty was defined by the mean performance on each item of 148 university students (several samples) who had been tested on these 40 items as part of their taking the full 220-item

PONS test. The eight scenes shown within each level of difficulty were presented in random order, and levels of difficulty were presented in the following order: (a) second hardest, (b) easiest, (c) hardest, (d) second easiest, and (e) medium difficulty. Level of difficulty thus was only trivially related to order of presentation ($\rho = .10$). To summarize the design of the new film: each subject's forty responses were arrayed as a $4 \times 5 \times 2$ analysis of variance with four levels of exposure length, five levels of item difficulty, and two channels. Appendix 5A shows which items from the full PONS were used in this test.

CONTROLLING FOR RESPONSE BIAS

David Kenny suggested to us that it might be advisable to check our shortened forty-item answer sheet for any possible response bias. Despite our having blocked on level of item difficulty, it might still be possible that small biases in test takers' choices or in the answer sheet itself (e.g., of base rate preferences for certain response alternatives, or of item sequence, item order, item sequence $\times$ order interactions) might distort, however slightly, the results of studies employing the new film. A small response bias would be of little consequence for most purposes of the PONS and its short forms, but since the brief exposure PONS had been designed especially to find the chance level of performance as a function of exposure length, it was especially important to detect and correct any possible response bias. What we needed was a group of persons to take our test but with no stimuli. Five small samples of high school students, college students, and adults were invited to take this "test": they were to try to get the right answer on the basis of no ostensible information. We felt that perhaps the nature of the item's placement on the answer sheet and the particular pairing of correct and incorrect response alternative might unintentionally affect their responses.

The median accuracy of the five samples was 51.0 percent, but some evidence of possible response bias was found in the weighted mean accuracy of all fifty-seven subjects, which was 52.3 percent rather than the expected 50.0 percent, a bias that was significant statistically but not huge in magnitude ($t = 2.07$, $p < .05$, effect size $= .55\,\sigma$). In addition, we found that fifteen of the forty items were answered correctly or incorrectly more often than could be easily ascribed to chance (at $p = .05$). In the absence of any response bias we would expect to find only about two such items instead of fifteen. Direction of bias, however, was balanced, with eight items answered correctly and seven items answered incorrectly by significantly more than 50 percent of the subjects. Such a result suggested that there might well be a bias in some of the main effects and interactions in which we were interested.

The "test" responses were analyzed by means of a $5 \times 4 \times 5 \times 2$ analysis of variance with the five samples as levels of the between-subjects factor and the three within-subject factors arrayed as the $4 \times 5 \times 2$ described above. The results showed no significant main effect for samples ($F = 0.76$) nor any interaction involving sample at $p < .05$ and no F as large as 1.7. Samples were, therefore, collapsed and the $4 \times 5 \times 2$ analysis was computed with all fifty-seven subjects as replicates. Almost all effects were found to be significant, five at $p < .001$, one at $p < .05$, and one at $p < .10$. These results provided convincing evidence that there was indeed a bias built into our forty-item answer sheet, a bias for which we would want to correct in the analysis of any data based on these answer sheets. To give an indication of the magnitude of this bias a very representative value is the F, for all forty items, of 4.86, with $df = (39,2180)$, p very small. An F of such magnitude is associated with an intraclass correlation of .063, meaning that the average subject is likely to show a correlation of only that size with any other subject in his or her pattern or profile of correct and incorrect responses. If there were no response bias whatever, there would be no agreement or similarity between subjects in their pattern or profile of correct and incorrect responses and the correlation obtained would have been still closer to zero and F would have been closer to 1. The response bias we found, then, was modest in magnitude but quite real in the sense of statistical significance.

ACCURACY AT HIGH SPEED

The brief exposure PONS was administered to 137 undergraduate and graduate students enrolled in four different colleges and universities in New York City and Boston. The New York sample was comprised of 90 graduate students of education and the three Boston samples were comprised of both graduate and undergraduate students of education or social science ($N = 24$, 12, 11).

A preliminary $4 \times 4 \times 5 \times 2$ analysis of variance was computed with the four samples as levels of the between-subjects factor and the $4 \times 5 \times 2$ representing the within-subjects factors of length of exposure, level of difficulty, and channel (face vs body). Although there was a significant difference ($t(126) = 2.79$, $p = .006$, effect size $= .50\sigma$) between the sample of eleven students enrolled in a seminar on nonverbal communication and the rest of the samples (which did not differ among themselves), none of the interactions involving sample was significant, so that all subsequent analyses were conducted on all subjects disregarding their sample membership. Table 5.1 shows the effects on accuracy of length of stimulus exposure for each of the four samples and for all subjects combined, disregarding sample membership (weighted mean). These values have been corrected for response bias and for chance by subtracting the "pseudoaccuracy" rates obtained in our study of response bias from

TABLE 5.1. Accuracy at Brief Exposures (Corrected for Response Bias)

	Exposure Length (in Frames; 1 Frame = $^1/_{24}$ second)				
Sample	1	3	9	27	Mean
N=82[a]	1.5%	16.4%	17.5%	18.1%	13.4%
N=24	9.4	15.0	15.2	16.8	14.1
N=11[b]	14.8	15.4	18.7	19.1	17.0
N=11[c]	4.4	25.4	28.9	23.6	20.6
Median	6.9	15.9	18.1	18.6	15.6[d]
Unweighted mean	7.5	18.0	20.1	19.4	16.3
Weighted mean[e]	4.3[f]	16.9	18.2	18.4	14.4[g]
Predicted	3.0	7.0	16.0	25.0	12.8
Error in prediction	−1.3	−9.9	−2.2	+6.6	−1.6

[a]Eight subjects did not answer all items and were omitted from the Anova.
[b]One subject did not answer all items and was omitted from the Anova.
[c]Students enrolled in a course on nonverbal communication.
[d]The means of the four samples differed moderately among themselves ($\eta = .27, F(3,124) = 3.13, p < .03$).
[e]The analogous values of this row for a more recent set of five samples (N=378) were: 6.7, 27.1, 24.6, 26.2, and 21.1.
[f]Differs from zero at $p < .001, t(135) = 31.88$.
[g]Corrections for response bias employed for each exposure length (1, 3, 9, 27) were −5.5, −4.6, −1.1, and +1.8, respectively. The correlation between accuracy in face and body channels was .45, $p < .001$.

the raw accuracy rates obtained for each of the forty items in the present study. The "pseudoaccuracy" scores are composed of two components: one based on chance level of responding (.50) and one based on response bias.

The next to last row of table 5.1 shows the median accuracy that five of us predicted for each level of exposure time, and the last row shows how wrong we were. Although we had accurately predicted a monotonic increase in accuracy as length of exposure time increased, we had substantially underestimated performance at the shorter exposure times (375 milliseconds or less) and we had substantially overestimated performance at the longer exposure time of twenty-seven frames (1125 milliseconds).

Perhaps we should not have been surprised at how well subjects could decode nonverbal cues at such brief exposure times. Sperling (1969) reported that four symbols could be reported after having been exposed for only 15 milliseconds, and that increasing exposure time to 500 milliseconds did not improve performance when a report could be made right away. These results, based on more discrete stimulus materials than a facial expression or a body position, may nevertheless help to account for the good performance at the brief exposure levels. Perhaps because of the difference in stimulus materials or because our task does not allow as quick a response as Sperling's, our results did show improved performance in going from 41.7 to at least 375 milliseconds. The largest improvement came in going from one to three frames of exposure, with relatively little subsequent increase in accuracy. The primary difference, of course, between the one-frame exposure and the other exposures is the presence of movement. At one frame we have no movement whatever, while even at three frames we often do have movement, however briefly shown. A natural followup experiment, then, would be to repeat the present study adding a factor of motion versus no motion. That would require the addition of three groups of single-frame stimuli projected for $^3/_{24}$ths, $^9/_{24}$ths, and $^{27}/_{24}$ths of a second. The results of such a study might help us decide whether it is motion or increased exposure time that improves performance when exposure time is increased from the $^1/_{24}$th of a second baseline. Either or both may help.

Table 5.2 shows the results of the $4 \times 5 \times 2$ analysis of variance computed for all subjects disregarding the sample to which they belonged (because sample membership showed no significant [$p \leq .05$] interaction with any other variable). For each of the forty items comprising the $4 \times 5 \times 2$ array, the correction for response bias was applied by subtracting the mean "pseudoaccuracy" rate from the raw obtained accuracy rate. The average performance in decoding body (14.0) was very similar to the performance in decoding face (14.9), but all other main effects and interactions were substantial and significant at $p < .001$. The enormous effect of difficulty level simply confirms the value of having blocked on that variable and the very large linear trend shows

TABLE 5.2. Analysis of Variance of Brief Exposure PONS Accuracy ($N = 128$)

	Effect		Error			
Source	df	MS	df	MS	F	η
Channel	1	0.112	127	0.127	0.88[a]	.08
Difficulty level	4	26.935	508	0.186	145.10	.73
Linear trend	1	73.289	508	0.186	394.03	.66
Residual	3	11.483	508	0.186	61.74	.52
Length	3	5.938	381	0.187	31.76	.45
Linear trend	1	12.334	381	0.187	65.96	.38
Quadratic	1	4.841	381	0.187	25.89	.25
Residual	1	0.639	381	0.187	3.42[a]	.09
Channel × difficulty	4	8.384	508	0.190	44.06	.51
Channel × difficulty linear	1	27.054	508	0.190	142.37	.47
Residual	3	2.160	508	0.190	11.37	.25
Channel × length	3	9.066	381	0.169	53.51	.54
Channel × (27 vs. 1+3+9)	1	21.410	381	0.169	126.69	.50
Residual	2	2.894	381	0.169	17.16	.29
Difficulty × length	12	4.475	1524	0.195	22.99	.39
Channel × difficulty × length	12	4.942	1473	0.172	28.68	.44
Subjects	127	0.245				

[a] $p > .05$; all other $p < .001$

that, on the whole, the items that had been the most difficult on the full PONS for our earlier group of 148 college students were also the most difficult on the brief exposure PONS for the 128 students of the present analysis. This result is essentially further evidence for the reliability of the level of difficulty of the forty items in going from the full PONS to the brief exposure PONS.

The large effect of length of exposure shows that the differences in (unweighted) mean accuracy shown in table 5.1 are substantial, and the large component of this effect that is due to a linear increase as we go from the first to the fourth level of exposure time is reflected in the large effect for linear trend in length of exposure. The significant but smaller quadratic trend in length of exposure is due to the finding that the three- and nine-frame exposure lengths resulted in relatively better performance than did the one- and twenty-seven-frame exposure lengths. This quadratic trend reflects the relatively maximal difficulty of the one-frame exposure as well as the relative lack of benefit derived in going from the nine- to the twenty-seven-frame exposure length.

The channel × difficulty level interaction is due for the most part to the interaction between channel and the linear trend component of level of difficulty. The direction of this effect is such that more difficult scenes are relatively more difficult in body than face, while the easier scenes are relatively easier in body than face. The reason for this is not at all clear.

The channel × length of exposure interaction is due for the most part to the contrast in which the three shorter exposure levels (1, 3, and 9) are compared to the longest exposure level (27) for the two channels. The direction of this contrast was such that decreasing exposure length to nine or fewer frames from twenty-seven frames actually increased accuracy for body but greatly decreased accuracy for face. Perhaps body cues are relatively well apprehended at high-speed exposures in an intuitive, global, nonanalytic manner, with additional small increases in exposure length serving more to confuse than to assist decoding. Between nine and twenty-seven frames there may be a shift from a more global, nonanalytic orientation to a more analytic orientation, but twenty-seven frames of exposure may not supply enough information to permit the successful operation of the more analytic orientation. Further increases in exposure time ought to lead to increased accuracy, however, since more information would be provided upon which the analytic mode might operate. An indirect examination of this possibility could be undertaken by considering the results obtained from two additional samples.

Table 5.3 shows, in the first two columns, the mean accuracy obtained for face and body at two levels of exposure length of the present study. The third column shows that for the 148 college students whose data provided the definition of item difficulty for the present study, an exposure length of 48 frames (two seconds) was associated with a net accuracy in face of 36.3 percent (i.e., 86.3 percent accuracy − 50.0 percent, correcting for chance

TABLE 5.3. Accuracy in Two Channels for Four
Levels of Exposure Length

Channel	Exposure Length (in Frames)			
	1,3,9[a]	27[a]	48[b]	120[c]
Face	9.8%	30.1%	36.3%	45%
Body	16.4	6.8	33.1	45
Mean	13.1	18.4	34.7	45

[a]based on the present sample of 128 students
[b]based on the earlier sample of 148 students
[c]based on pilot video tape version data; values given are
only approximations

performance). Based on our video tape pilot version of the PONS, we would
expect still further increases in accuracy to about 45 percent as exposure
length increased to about five seconds. For face, then, there appears to be a
steady increase in accuracy as the length of exposure is increased. For body,
there was a steady increase in accuracy only from the twenty-seven-frame
exposure length onward, with the very fast exposure lengths showing the
unusually high level of accuracy discussed above.

The level of difficulty × length of exposure interaction and the three-way
interaction, each with 12 *df* in the numerator, were deemed uninterpretable
and are, therefore, not described here.

HIGH-SPEED ACCURACY AND INTERPERSONAL
RELATIONSHIPS

All subjects of the four samples taking the brief exposure PONS were also
asked to rate their relationships with persons of the same and opposite sex.
The eight variables rated for relationships with each sex were: Warm, Honest,
Enduring, Satisfying, I understand friends' feelings, Friends understand my
feelings, Quick to make friends, and Number of intimate friends. These
sixteen variables were correlated with accuracy at each of the four levels of
exposure length and with accuracy for each channel. Because there were no
stable differences among correlations based on the various exposure lengths
and channels, the sixteen relationship variables were correlated with the brief
exposure PONS total score for all subjects (disregarding sample membership).
Because of a few omitted ratings, the sample size ranged from 134 to 137.
The nine subjects who had omitted a few PONS items were included in this
analysis; they were given 0.5 credit for each item omitted from the brief
exposure PONS.

Table 5.4 shows the resulting correlations. In general, they tended to be

TABLE 5.4. Correlations between Brief Exposure
PONS Accuracy and Interpersonal Relationships

	Relationships with	
Variable	Same Sex	Opposite Sex
Warm	−.21[a]	−.12
Honest	.05	.07
Enduring	−.13	−.07
Satisfying	−.11	−.06
I understand friends	−.25[b]	−.06
Friends understand me	−.19[a]	.02
Make friends quickly	−.21[a]	−.13
Number of friends	.02	−.01
Median	−.16[c]	−.06[d]

[a] $p < .05$
[b] $p < .01$
[c] For an additional sample of 58 college students, the
analogous median $r = -.02$, but the median r based only on
single-frame exposure accuracy was $-.19$.
[d] For an additional sample of 58 college students, the
analogous median $r = -.16$, but the median r based only on
single-frame exposure accuracy was $-.26, p < .05$.

negative, suggesting that those who were more accurate at decoding brief
exposures reported less satisfactory relationships with other people. Specifically, those who were more accurate reported their relationships with others of
the same sex to be significantly less warm; they also reported that they were
significantly less understanding of their friends, were significantly less understood by their friends, and were significantly less likely to make new friends.
Essentially the same results are obtained if accuracy on just the fastest two (1
and 3 frames) or fastest three (1, 3, and 9 frames) exposure lengths is employed rather than the total of all four exposure lengths.

For an interpretation of these surprising results, we suggest that perhaps
those persons who are most accurate at the fastest speeds become aware of too
much "leakage" (Ekman and Friesen 1969a) from other people. To employ a
different idiom, that of Goffman (1956), high-speed accuracy permits access
to the backstage regions that are best kept from members of the audience. In
short, people who are especially accurate at very high speeds may simply
"know too much" about others to make them "socially acceptable" interactants. The idea that being "overly" accurate at decoding nonverbal cues
might be associated with problems of interpersonal relationships has also been
proposed by Davitz (1964), who measured accuracy in the audio rather than
the video channels, and by Brown (1965), who was discussing interpersonal
sensitivity in general.

In chapter 11, correlations of these same relationship ratings with the full PONS test are discussed. These correlations tended to be very weak but generally positive. In chapter 6 are found the correlations of the brief PONS with the full PONS and the still PONS.

Appendix 5A

ITEMS IN FORTY-ITEM BRIEF EXPOSURE PONS

TABLE 5.5. Items in Forty-Item Brief Exposure PONS

Item Number	Item Number in Full PONS	Item Number	Item Number in Full PONS
1	116	21	107
2	18	22	8
3	37	23	103
4	42	24	135
5	57	25	51
6	194	26	14
7	60	27	172
8	16	28	138
9	74	29	119
10	52	30	203
11	212	31	30
12	155	32	197
13	201	33	181
14	43	34	122
15	5	35	15
16	45	36	213
17	149	37	140
18	70	38	123
19	146	39	176
20	192	40	185

NOTE: Using this table in conjunction with appendix 2E, an answer sheet and scoring key can be constructed. Instructions to test takers should be appropriately modified from those in appendix 2F.

6 | Short PONS Tests

For practical and theoretical reasons, we developed a still photo version of the PONS. If this short form of the PONS showed promising correlations with the full PONS, it would enable many more investigators to have access to the test, with greater convenience and lower cost.

The research dealing with short exposure times (chapter 5) had shown that motion was not required for better-than-chance accuracy at PONS-type tasks in the video channels. Research was therefore planned in which video stimuli were to be presented with and without motion, for varying lengths of time, to study the effects on accuracy of adding motion to stimuli varying in exposure lengths. This type of research also required a still photo version of the PONS.

TEST DEVELOPMENT. The still photo version of the PONS test comes in two forms. One is a set of sixty 4″ × 5″ photographs, the other a set of 35-mm slides made from these photographs, each taken from one of the sixty scenarios comprising the face, body, and figure (face + body) channels in the full PONS. The order of presentation of the sixty photographs (slides) is identical to the order of the sixty face-only, body-only, and figure-only scenes in the full PONS, and the sixty response alternatives are identical to the response alternatives for these sixty items in the full PONS. The photo test is administered with an overhead (opaque) projector, and the slide test is administered with a slide projector. Appendix 6A lists the sixty items with the corresponding item numbers from the full PONS.[1]

The order of presentation of the sixty photos was checked to see whether

---

1. For the first sample tested, one of the items was misprinted so that the correct alternative was accidentally omitted. This error was not discovered until all the analyses were completed. In view of the high correlation between the sixty-item and corrected fifty-nine-item versions ($r = .994$ for pretest and .995 for posttest), we have presented the results of all analyses based on all sixty items.

scenes from the three channels were equitably distributed over the first fifteen, the second fifteen, the third fifteen, and the last fifteen scenes. The resulting χ^2 of 5.2, $df = 6$, $p > .50$, suggested that scenes from the three channels were fairly equally distributed over the four blocks of fifteen scenes each. An additional check was made to determine whether level of item difficulty was comparable across these four blocks. Item difficulty was defined in terms of the quadrant location of the incorrect alternative (see chapter 3). Items were most difficult when the incorrect alternative was from the same quadrant as the correct alternative and least difficult when the incorrect alternative was from the quadrant opposite to the quadrant of the correct alternative. Items were intermediate in difficulty when the incorrect alternative was from a quadrant adjacent to that of the correct alternative, i.e., differing either in the dimension of dominance or of positivity, but not in both. This check yielded a χ^2 of 5.8, $df = 6$, $p > .45$, suggesting that difficulty level was fairly equally distributed over the four blocks.

PHOTOGRAPHING THE SCENES. The PONS master video tape containing the unedited scenarios (averaging 5.5 seconds in length) was played on an Ampex model 7500 one-inch video recorder in a darkened room. A Setchell-Carlson model 2100-SD twenty-three-inch monitor was set up at a height that allowed the center of the camera lens to be aimed at the exact center of the image on the screen. Contrast and brightness controls were adjusted to produce a medium-high contrast, average brightness picture.

By using the index for scene locations originally made with the PONS master video tape, the fast-forward mode of tape advance was employed to move to those scenes desired. Once the proper scene was located, it was previewed and timed in order to locate the central portion. The video tape was then rewound to a cue position, usually several seconds in timing length before the start of the selected scene. The photographer gave a ready signal and the machine was started. The scene was photographed when the central portion of the previewed playback again occurred. Whenever there was any doubt as to the probable quality of a given shot, due to the possible coincidence of "sync" lines in the video picture at the time of shutter release or some other reason, the tape was rewound and the same scene shot again. In these cases, the shutter was released at a very slightly different location in the central portion of the scene. This procedure was continued until all sixty scenes had been photographed.

The photographs were taken with a Kodak Medalist II camera tripod-mounted 3½' from the monitor. Video scanning lines did not appear in the photographs thanks to the camera's leaf shutter and the exposure used. Kodak Tri-X roll film was exposed at f5.6 for $^1/_{25}$ second for each photograph and developed in Kodak HC110 Dilution B developer. The enlargements were made with a 100-mm lens on a Beseler 23C II enlarger. The $4'' \times 5''$ prints were made on Kodak Polycontrast Rapid RC F surface paper using Polycontrast filters 2½, 3, 3½, and 4, and developed in Kodak Dektol 1:1 water dilution.

The slides (black and white transparencies) were made by photographing the sixty photos with a 35-mm camera and were commercially developed and mounted.

PERFORMANCE ON QUADRANTS AND CHANNELS. The still photo PONS was administered with an overhead projector to fifty-three high school students in a New England town. Of these students, thirty-five were females, seventeen were males, and one could not be identified as to sex.

Accuracy in the four quadrants was as follows: positive-submissive 78.2 percent, positive-dominant 76.1 percent, negative-submissive 80.8 percent, negative-dominant 69.1 percent. Accuracy was significantly greater in the submissive than in the dominant scenes ($F(1,50) = 24.03$, $p < .001$; effect size $= 1.39\,\sigma$). There was a tendency for accuracy to be greater in the positive than in the negative scenes and there was a significant interaction such that positive-dominant and negative-submissive scenes were more accurately judged than the scenes of the other two quadrants ($F(1,50) = 7.80$, $p = .008$; effect size $= .79\,\sigma$).

These subjects had been administered the full PONS as well as the still photo PONS, so it was possible to compare their performance on the three still channels with their performance on the three moving channels of the full PONS. Overall accuracy on the still photo PONS was 76.0 percent, and overall accuracy on the full PONS (three corresponding channels) was 81.5 percent, suggesting that the addition of movement and/or the addition of adjacent frames may add appreciably to subjects' accuracy ($F(1,50) = 29.44$; effect size $= 1.53\,\sigma$ or $r = .61$). Frijda (1953) also found significantly greater accuracy for film-presented than for photo-presented facial expressions. However, for the somewhat different conditions of his research compared to ours, the size of the effect he obtained was smaller (effect size $= .70\,\sigma$ or $r = .33$). A still earlier study by Dusenbury and Knower (1938), however, suggested that the advantage of film-based over still photo–based accuracy might be even greater ($2.15\,\sigma$ or $r = .73$) than the advantage we obtained.

Some light might be shed on the question of the extent to which it is the addition of movement per se or simply the increase in number of different frames shown that improves accuracy by comparing accuracy on the motion picture PONS with accuracy based on an increasing number of different still photos drawn from the forty-eight frames (two seconds' worth) of the PONS scenes. From this we might learn how many still photos or frames drawn from a two-second film clip (and shown at what exposure lengths) are equivalent in information to a moving two-second clip.

There was only one very large two-way interaction of full versus still PONS

TABLE 6.1. Accuracy in Three Channels on Still
Photo PONS for Each Level of Positivity and
Dominance (N=53)

Video Channel	Negative	Positive	Mean
Face	70.6%	82.0%	76.3%
Body	81.1	70.0	75.6
Figure	73.0	79.5	76.3
Mean	74.9	77.2	76.0[a]

Video Channel	Dominant	Submissive	Mean
Face	70.7%	81.9%	76.3%
Body	74.5	76.7	75.6
Figure	72.6	80.0	76.3
Mean	72.6	79.5	76.0[b]

[a]interaction $F(2,100) = 27.07, p < .001$
[b]interaction $F(2,100) = 3.37, p < .04$

with the variables of channel, dominance, positivity, or order. That was the interaction with the dominance dimension. For the still PONS, accuracy was higher for submissive (79.5 percent) than for dominant (72.6 percent) scenes. For the full PONS, the difference was reversed (78.5 percent vs 84.5 percent) and the effect was very large ($F(1,50) = 47.68$, effect size $= 1.95\sigma$, or $r = .70$). Why still photos should aid in the decoding of submissive cues while motion pictures should aid in the decoding of dominant cues is not at all obvious, however. Perhaps the accurate assessment of dominance cues requires the opportunity to note not only appearance but change in appearance as well.

As the last column of table 6.1 shows, there was essentially no difference in the level of accuracy obtained in each of the three channels of the still photo PONS ($F = 0.11$). However, channel did interact significantly with both the positivity and the dominance of the scene. The channel × positivity interaction showed that when the face was shown (face and figure channels), accuracy was greater on positive scenes, but when the face was not shown, accuracy was greater on negative scenes. The channel × dominance interaction showed that for the face channel, submissive scenes were relatively easier than dominant scenes, while for the body channel, dominant scenes were relatively easier than submissive scenes. For the figure channel there was essentially no difference between the submissive and dominant scenes except the difference associated with the main effect of dominance.

SEX. Just as is the case for the full PONS, females' performance (77.8 percent) on the still photo PONS was superior to males' performance (74.3

percent) ($t = 1.70$, $p < .05$, one-tailed; effect size $= .48\sigma$). The magnitude of the effect of sex on still PONS accuracy was quite comparable to the effect we have generally obtained of sex on full PONS accuracy (see chapter 7).

LEARNING. The five replications found within each of the three channels for each of the four quadrants of the still photo PONS were blocked into five levels of order corresponding to the first, second, third, fourth, and fifth replications of all combinations of quadrant $\times$ channel. Since item difficulty was equitably distributed throughout the early and late sections of the test, changes in accuracy over time may be viewed as an index of learning.

Table 6.2 shows the mean accuracy obtained in each of the five blocks of order of presentation of the scenes. These order of presentation effects are shown for the total, for each of the three channels, and for each level of the two dimensions of affect. For each row of table 6.2, a contrast for linear regression was computed and the resulting r, F, and associated p levels are shown in the last three columns. For all channels and affects combined there was a significant linear trend such that accuracy increased over time.

There was, however, a significant interaction of order $\times$ channel ($F(8,400)$ $= 17.02$, $p < .001$), which showed that learning differed dramatically in the three channels. For figure, there was a very large positive linear effect (r $= .60$ as shown in column 6 of table 6.2), for body there was a moderate positive linear effect, and for face there was a large negative linear effect.

TABLE 6.2. Accuracy in Five Time Blocks for Three Channels and Two Dimensions of Affect of Still Photo PONS

| | Time Block | | | | | | | |
	1	2	3	4	5	r^a	F (linear)	p
Channel								
Face	83.5%	75.0%	79.0%	73.5%	70.6%	−.40	9.32[b]	.003
Body	85.5	49.2	85.1	77.9	80.0	.27	3.92	.05
Figure	64.5	78.9	69.2	81.8	87.0	.60	28.68	.001
Total	77.8	67.7	77.8	77.8	79.2	.34	6.60	.02
Affect								
Dominant	66.9%	63.5%	79.0%	75.3%	78.2%	.57	23.67	.001
Submissive	88.7	71.9	76.5	80.2	80.2	−.17	1.51[b]	.25
Positive	78.5	62.0	85.0	80.0	80.3	.40	9.33	.003
Negative	77.2	73.4	70.5	75.6	78.1	.08	0.32	

$$^a r = \sqrt{\frac{F}{F + 50}}$$

[b]Indicates that accuracy decreased over time. In all other rows accuracy increased over time.

Thus, in the two channels in which the body was shown, subjects showed improvement over time, while in the channel showing only the face their performance actually worsened over time. This latter result was quite unexpected and is not easy to understand. We may speculate that the still photos of the face appeared fairly easy to the subjects so that their level of effort and concentration may have dropped off, leading to worsened performance. For still photo scenes showing the body, early performance was substantially more difficult and may have led to the maintenance of higher levels of effort and concentration, permitting more learning to occur.

There was also a significant interaction of order × dominance ($F(4,200)$ = 8.87, $p < .001$), which showed that there was a very large positive linear learning effect for the dominant scenes while for the submissive scenes there was a small tendency for performance to worsen over time. Finally, there was also a significant interaction of order × positiveness ($F(4,200)$ = 7.84, $p < .001$), which showed that there was a large positive linear learning effect

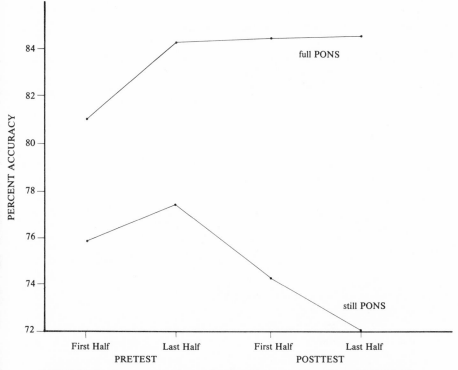

FIGURE 6.1. Accuracy for first and second halves of the still and full PONS on two testing occasions (N = 36)

for the positive scenes while for the negative scenes there was only a small tendency for performance to improve over time.

To summarize the evidence on learning during the course of the administration of the still photo PONS, we can say that subjects generally did improve their performance during the course of the test. This improvement, or learning, was most dramatic for dominant scenes, for positive scenes, and for scenes in which the body was shown with or without the face. When only the face was shown, performance actually deteriorated over time, perhaps for motivational reasons.

So far, our discussion has been of learning during the course of a single administration of the still PONS. However, for thirty-six of our subjects it was possible to obtain retests about two months later on both the still PONS and the full PONS. We could, therefore, examine the likelihood of the occurrence of learning over successive testings. Figure 6.1 shows the pretest and posttest results for the still and full PONS (three corresponding channels) with a separate data point given for the first half and last half of the items administered at each testing. Although both tests showed improvement from the first half to the last half of the pretest, only the full PONS showed a further improvement in going from the pretest to the posttest. The still PONS performance actually worsened in going from the pretest to the posttest relative to the full PONS (interaction $F(1,35) = 15.79$, $p < .001$, effect size $= 1.34\sigma$, $r = .56$). Perhaps a single testing is optimal for the still PONS, since further study of a still photo may not add much information compared to further study of even a very brief motion picture. The greater complexity of the full PONS may make it more possible to improve with additional study or practice.

RELIABILITY. For the fifty-three subjects of the present study, a measure of internal consistency based upon the latent root of the first unrotated principal component was computed. This index of reliability, developed by Armor (1974), is called θ (see chapter 3). The reliability of the 60-item still photo PONS was found to be .76. As a basis for evaluating this theta coefficient relative to the reliability of the full PONS, we computed theta for the entire high school norm group. That θ, based upon 220 items, was .92. When the Spearman-Brown correction was applied to the still photo PONS to predict the reliability to be obtained if the 60 items were increased to 220, the resulting coefficient was identical (.92). This result suggests that the internal consistency of the still PONS is about the same as that of the full PONS, taking into account the shorter length of the photo test.

About two months after the fifty-three subjects of the present study were administered the full PONS and the still photo PONS, thirty-seven of them were available to take both tests again. Table 6.3 shows the retest reliabilities of various subsections of both tests. The first four rows list reliabilities that are directly comparable from still to full PONS in that these correlations are based on identical numbers of items. For all three channels, and for the sum of these three channels, the still PONS retest reliabilities were somewhat higher than the comparable full PONS reliabilities.

The fifth through eighth rows of table 6.3 show the retest reliabilities for the four quadrants. Here the reliabilities of the still PONS and full PONS are not directly comparable, however, since the quadrant reliabilities are based on only fifteen items in the case of the still PONS but on fifty-five items in the case of the full PONS. Thus, while the latter retest reliabilities are higher, the Spearman-Brown correction shows that the still PONS correlations tend to be higher when a correction is made for number of items. The same result is obtained when we consider the two levels of each of our two orthogonal affect dimensions shown in rows nine to twelve. Correcting for number of items, the still PONS tends to be somewhat more reliable in the retest sense.

It is also of interest to note the retest reliabilities of each of the twenty scenes of the still PONS. Because each scene is based on only three items, one from each of the three pure video channels, we do not expect individual scenes to show large retest reliabilities. It is instructive, therefore, to note that there are a number of individual scenes with substantial reliabilities. Table 6.4 shows the retest reliabilities for the scenes of both the still and full PONS. We expect higher reliability for the latter, of course, since each scene is based on eleven items rather than on the three items of the still PONS scenes. For the

TABLE 6.3. Retest Reliabilities of Still Photo PONS and Full PONS ($N=37$)

Channel or Affect	Still PONS		Full PONS	
	r	Number of Items	r	Number of Items
Face	.31	20	.05	20
Body	.53[a]	20	.50[b]	20
Figure	.42[b]	20	.12	20
Total of three channels	.58[a]	60	.50[b]	60
Positive-submissive	.57[a]	15	.58[a]	55
Positive-dominant	.43[b]	15	.58[a]	55
Negative-submissive	.41[c]	15	.51[b]	55
Negative-dominant	.15	15	.51[b]	55
Submissive	.63[a]	30	.63[a]	110
Dominant	.43[b]	30	.62[a]	110
Positive	.51[b]	30	.64[a]	110
Negative	.49[b]	30	.63[a]	110
Full PONS total			.71[a]	220

[a]$p \leqslant .001$
[b]$p \leqslant .01$
[c]$p \leqslant .05$

TABLE 6.4. Retest Reliabilities of Still Photo PONS and Full PONS
Scenes (N=36)

Scene	Still Photo PONS	Full PONS
Expressing deep affection	.68[a]	.58[a]
Seducing someone	.67[a]	.62[a]
Admiring nature	.58[a]	.54[a]
Talking to a lost child	.55[a]	.27
Jealous anger	.41[b]	.33[c]
Threatening someone	.39[b]	.51[b]
Order food	.37[c]	.26
Asking forgiveness	.30[c]	.19
Leaving on a trip	.28[c]	.41[b]
Expressing gratitude	.27	−.07
Prayer	.19	.62[a]
Returning faulty item	.15	.03
Talking about divorce	.13	.31[c]
Nagging a child	.04	.51[b]
Talking about wedding	.02	.38[c]
Talking about death	.01	−.01
Strong dislike	−.00	−.03
Expressing motherly love	−.05	.38[c]
Criticizing someone for being late	−.05	.45[b]
Helping a customer	−.06	.19

[a]$p \leq .001$, one-tailed
[b]$p \leq .01$, one-tailed
[c]$p \leq .05$, one-tailed

full PONS, 60 percent of the scenes are ''significantly'' reliable, while for the still PONS 45 percent are equally reliable.

In general, scenes that were found more reliable for the full PONS were also found more reliable for the still PONS ($r = .41$). For the still PONS, all four of the scenes with reliabilities exceeding .50 were of positive affect, and three of these four scenes were among the most reliable of the full PONS scenes as well.

ANALYSIS OF INCORRECT RESPONSE ALTERNATIVES. We recall that the twenty scenes of the still PONS (like the full PONS) were divided equally into two orthogonal affect dimensions: positive-negative and dominant-submissive. Therefore, of the total sixty items of the still PONS, fifteen correct answers (5 scenes × 3 channels) are found in each of the four quadrants. It will help us to gain a further understanding of the reliability of the placement of scenes within quadrants of the still PONS if we examine the effects on accuracy of the quadrant locations of the incorrect alternatives with which the correct answers were randomly paired in the preparation of the original PONS answer sheet. (For the same analysis based on full PONS data, see chapter 3.) If the scenes were placed into quadrants unreliably (i.e., randomly) there would be no relationship between accuracy and the quadrant location of the incorrect answer relative to the quadrant location of the correct answer. If the scenes were placed into quadrants reliably, there would be a specifiable effect on accuracy of the quadrant location of the incorrect answer relative to the quadrant location of the correct answer. That is, if the incorrect alternative fell in the same quadrant as the correct alternative, they should be most difficult to distinguish and accuracy should be lowest. If the incorrect alternative fell into an adjacent quadrant (one that differed from the correct alternative on one of the affect dimensions but did not differ on the other affect dimension), it should be easier to distinguish the correct from the incorrect alternative, and accuracy should be higher. If the incorrect alternative fell into the opposite quadrant (one that differed from the correct alternative on both of the affect dimensions), it should be still easier to distinguish the correct from the incorrect alternative and accuracy should be yet higher.

Figure 6.2 shows the effects of the quadrant location of the incorrect alternative on the accuracy of both the still PONS and the three moving channels of the full PONS. For both forms of the PONS there is a very substantial and very significant ($p < .001$) linear trend showing that accuracy increases as the incorrect alternative becomes more dissimilar from the correct answer. For the

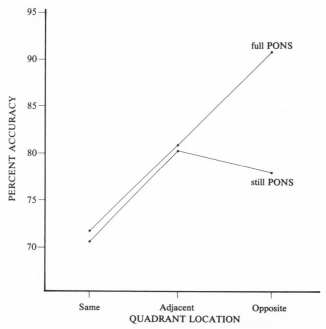

FIGURE 6.2. Accuracy obtained at three levels of similarity of incorrect alternative to correct alternative for still PONS and analogous channels of full PONS

still PONS the magnitude of the linear trend corresponded to an r of .43, while for the full PONS version of the same three channels r was .78.

FACTOR STRUCTURE. In computing the θ index of reliability, a principal components analysis of all 60 items was computed, but this analysis (like the earlier analysis of all 220 items of the full PONS in chapter 3) yielded no readily interpretable factors after orthogonal rotation. The 60 variables were then reduced to 12, each composed of the sum of the scores on the five scenes of each affect quadrant for each channel. These 12 variables, listed in the first column of table 6.5, were then factor analyzed and five easily interpretable factors emerged after rotation. Table 6.5 shows the rotated factor loadings, the sums of the squares of the factor loadings, the median factor loadings for those variables defining each factor, and the median factor loadings for those variables not defining each factor.

A well-defined factor is one in which the median loadings of variables defining a factor are substantially higher than the median loadings of variables not defining a factor. The first factor will serve as illustration. Three of the four largest factor loadings involved body-related variables, and so the factor was defined as a ''body'' factor. The median factor loading of the four body-related variables was found to be .50, which was substantially larger than the median of the remaining eight factor loadings ($-.04$).

The next four factors corresponded to the four affect quadrants, or doing well (positive loadings) at the two negative quadrants and poorly (negative loadings) at the two positive quadrants. The four quadrant factors are orthogonal to each other but, as table 6.5 shows, each is related to the ''body'' factor because each of the four quadrants is represented once in the four body variables. The median correlation of the accuracy score on the twenty items of the body channel correlated with each of the four quadrants, each based on fifteen items, was .43, while the median intercorrelation of the four quadrant scores was only .20.

Our factors, then, though not independent of each other, tell us at least two important things. First, there was a substantial body factor to be found in the factor analysis of the three channels; and second, the four affect quadrants developed originally for the film version of the PONS were relatively well reproduced in the still photo version of the PONS.

CHANNEL VALIDITY. If a single correlation coefficient could be employed to express the concurrent validity of the still photo PONS, it would have to be the correlation between the still PONS and the 220-item PONS. For our fifty-three subjects that correlation was .53, and for the thirty-seven of these subjects who were retested two months later the correlation was then .59 (both $p < .001$). For both the pretest and the posttest, the still photo PONS showed the highest correlation with the body channel of the full PONS ($r = .51$

TABLE 6.5. Factor Analysis of Still Photo PONS

		Rotated Factor Loadings			
Variable	Body	Negative-Submissive	Negative-Dominant	Positive-Dominant	Positive-Submissive
Face–positive-submissive	-.04	-.07	+.04	-.08	-.87[a]
Face–positive-dominant	+.06	-.09	+.12	-.75[a]	+.13
Face–negative-submissive	-.08	+.75[a]	+.03	+.00	-.07
Face–negative-dominant	-.04	+.03	+.84[a]	+.07	-.04
Body–positive-submissive	+.54[a]	-.47	+.10	-.18	-.31[a]
Body–positive-dominant	+.47[a]	+.36	+.13	+.14[a]	-.47
Body–negative-submissive	+.21[a]	+.64[a]	-.28	-.39	+.05
Body–negative-dominant	+.82[a]	+.13	+.18[a]	-.18	+.05
Face + body-positive-submissive	+.12	-.21	+.58	-.25	-.15[a]
Face + body-positive-dominant	-.66	+.08	+.19	-.42[a]	-.06
Face + body-negative-submissive	-.06	+.16[a]	-.04	-.64	-.21
Face + body-negative-dominant	+.23	+.51	+.53[a]	-.00	+.14
Sum squares	1.75	1.69	1.53	1.46	1.18
Percentage of variance	15	14	13	12	10
Median factor loadings					
Variables defining factors	+.50	+.64	+.53	-.42	-.31
Variables not defining factors	-.04	+.03	+.10	-.18	-.04

[a] Loadings defining factor labels

TABLE 6.6. Intercorrelations among Channels of Still Photo PONS and Full PONS
(N=53)

	Full PONS			Still Photo PONS	
	Face	Body	Figure	Face	Body
Full PONS					
Body	.14				
Figure	.36ᵃ	.06			
Still Photo PONS					
Face	.05	.26	.11		
Body	.17	.52ᵇ	.17	.19	
Figure	−.10	.29ᶜ	.04	.45ᵇ	.16

ᵃp ≤ .01
ᵇp ≤ .001
ᶜp ≤ .05

and .58). That result is consistent with the finding of the factor analysis that
the first factor of the still PONS was a body accuracy factor.

If the still photo PONS were measuring very much the same sort of thing as
the full PONS, we would expect the various subsections of the still PONS to
correlate about as highly with the analogous subsections of the full PONS as
with each other. Table 6.6 shows the intercorrelations among the face, body,
and figure channels of the still PONS and full PONS. The median channel
intercorrelations for the full and still PONS were .14 and .19, respectively,
while the median intercorrelation between still and full PONS channels
was .17. Thus, channel scores of the two tests were about as highly correlated
with each other as were channel scores of the same test.

Essentially the same results were obtained when the four quadrants were
intercorrelated. The median quadrant intercorrelations for the full and still

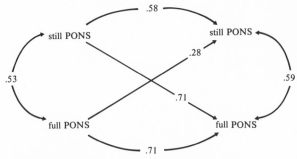

FIGURE 6.3. Cross-lagged correlations of still photo PONS and full PONS (220
items)

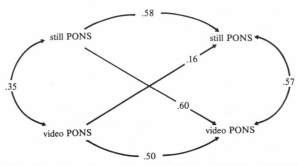

FIGURE 6.4. Cross-lagged correlations of still photo PONS and full PONS on video channels only (60 items)

PONS were .22 and .20, respectively, while the median intercorrelation be-tween still and full PONS quadrants was .25. Just as was the case with chan-nels, then, quadrants of the two tests were about as highly correlated with each other as were the quadrant scores of the same test.

Further evidence that the subtests of the still and full PONS were measuring essentially the same kind of performance came from a consideration of the cross-lagged correlations. Figure 6.3 shows that the full PONS score on a two-month follow-up testing was as well predicted by the still PONS taken two months earlier as by the full PONS taken two months earlier. Similarly, figure 6.4 shows that the sum of the three video channels of the full PONS was as well predicted by the still PONS taken two months earlier as by the sum of the three video channels of the full PONS taken two months earlier. In short, the still photo PONS appears to be measuring just about the same type of skill as that measured by the full PONS and its component parts.

SCENE VALIDITY. We wanted to know for the twenty scenes whether those subjects who were especially accurate at any particular scene of the still PONS would also be especially accurate at the corresponding scene of the full PONS. Scene accuracy could take on values from 0 to 3 for the still PONS and 0 to 11 for the full PONS. All twenty still PONS scene scores were correlated with all twenty full PONS scene scores (median $r = .18$). For the remaining 380 correlations between the twenty scenes of the still PONS and the twenty scenes of the full PONS ($20 \times 20 - 20$) the median correlation was .04. Of the 20 correlations between the same scenes in each of the tests, 16 were larger than that value and three were smaller, suggesting that, on the whole, subjects more accurate at still PONS scenes were also more accurate at those same scenes on the full PONS. Nine of the scenes, or 45 percent, showed a signifi-cant ($p \leq .05$) degree of relationship, with a correlation of .25 or higher. At least some of the individual scenes appear to show a modest degree of indi-vidual validity despite their being based on only three items each.

CORRELATIONS WITH BRIEF EXPOSURE PONS. In the chapter dealing with length of communication exposure (chapter 5) there is a description of a modification of the face and body channels of the full PONS so that the length of exposure was only one, three, nine, or twenty-seven frames. This brief exposure form of the PONS was administered to the thirty-six high school students who had also been administered the 220-item PONS and the still photo PONS for a second time. The top half of table 6.7 shows the intercorrelations among the three forms of the PONS (still, brief, and full) for the face and body channels. For the face channel the three forms of the PONS showed a median intercorrelation of .22 (top two rows of table 6.7) and for the body channel the analogous median correlation was .59 (last two columns of table 6.7). Both sets of intercorrelations, those for face and those for body, were quite homogeneous, suggesting that all three measures were equally similar to one another within each channel but more similar to one another in the body channel than in the face channel.

The bottom half of table 6.7 shows the median correlations of each of the six variables (i.e., face and body channels for full, brief, and still PONS) with the remaining five variables. Comparing the medians of the two columns shows that the body channel correlations were substantially higher than the face channel correlations. Comparing the medians of the three rows shows

TABLE 6.7. Intercorrelations among Face and Body Channels of Still Photo PONS, Brief Exposure PONS, and Full PONS ($N=36$)

	Face			Body	
	Full PONS	Brief PONS	Still PONS	Full PONS	Brief PONS
Face					
Brief PONS	.22				
Still PONS	.36[a]	.21			
Body					
Full PONS	.13	.15	.45[b]		
Brief PONS	.26	.36[a]	.17	.62[c]	
Still PONS	.20	.14	.52[c]	.59[c]	.45[b]

	Median Correlations		
	Face	Body	Median
Full PONS	.22	.45[b]	.34[a]
Brief PONS	.21	.36[a]	.28
Still PONS	.36[a]	.45[b]	.40[a]
Median	.22	.45[b]	.34[a]

[a] $p \leq .05$
[b] $p \leq .01$
[c] $p \leq .001$

that the median correlations of the three forms of the PONS were fairly similar to each other with the median for the still PONS slightly higher than the medians for the full and fast PONS.

In sum, when we consider the relationships of the face and body channels measured by three alternative forms of the PONS we find that the pattern of relationships was quite similar for the three measures and that, especially for the body channel, all three appeared to be measuring the same underlying construct to a great extent.

PHOTO BOOKLET PONS

With the help of Samuel Livingston we developed a self-administered forty-item booklet version of the still PONS, employing the twenty face-only and twenty body-only items of the still photo PONS (see appendix 6B for list of items). The booklet photo PONS was administered to a sample of twenty-four business executives (twenty-three males, one female) and, by Frankie Phillips, to a sample of sixty-two classroom teachers (forty-five females, seventeen males). Table 6.8 shows the mean accuracy scores obtained by both samples for the two channels, the four quadrants, and the total of the booklet PONS. The total accuracy scores obtained were slightly higher than the total mean accuracy score obtained on the nonbooklet form of the photo test form of the PONS (76.0). For the sample of teachers we compared the total booklet form score of the males and females. Just as with the nonbooklet form and the full PONS, the performance of the women was superior, though the difference was neither significant nor large (effect size $= .16\sigma$, $t = 0.63$).

Both samples taking the booklet form of the PONS test had also taken the full PONS, and table 6.9 shows the correlation of the total score on the full PONS with the channel scores of the booklet form and of the full PONS. Among the teachers, each channel of the booklet PONS showed a strong

TABLE 6.8. Accuracy in Two Channels and Four Quadrants on Booklet Form PONS for Two Samples

	Teachers (N = 62)	Business Executives (N = 24)
Face	79.7%	78.2%
Body	74.7	77.9
Positive-submissive	76.8	79.4
Positive-dominant	76.5	78.3
Negative-submissive	78.8	80.0
Negative-dominant	76.6	74.6
Total	77.2%	78.1%

TABLE 6.9. Correlations of Full PONS Total with
Channels of Booklet Form PONS and Full PONS for
Two Samples

	Teachers (N = 62)	Business Executives (N = 24)
Booklet PONS		
Face 20	.49[a]	−.40[b]
Body 20	.60[a]	.46[b]
Total 40	.64[a]	.05
Full PONS		
Face 20	.79[a]	.22
Body 20	.80[a]	.57[c]
Video 60	.91[a]	.60[c]

[a] $p \leq .001$
[b] $p \leq .05$
[c] $p \leq .01$

relationship to the full PONS, but among the executives the face channel inexplicably showed a significantly negative correlation with the full PONS, although the body channel showed the predicted positive relationship. Rows 4, 5, and 6 of table 6.9 show that parts of the full PONS correlated more highly with the full PONS total among the teachers than among the executives.

We can conclude for the booklet form of the PONS that the body channel correlates well with the full PONS total regardless of sample, while the total booklet PONS score correlated well with the full PONS total only for the larger sample of teachers.

FACE AND BODY PONS

In order to explore the practicality of using a short form video PONS test, we made a film consisting of the twenty face-only and twenty body-only items from the full PONS. In this film, the forty items were arranged in a new random order and the response alternatives for these items were the same as those of the PONS answer sheet. Appendix 6C lists the items and their corresponding items from the full PONS.

In order to examine the reliability of the face and body PONS, we administered it to a sample of twenty-two male and seventy female teachers-in-training at an eastern U.S. university. The θ reliability of the face and body PONS was .63 overall. The KR-20 reliability for the 40 items was .28 and .60 when scaled up to 220 items using the Spearman-Brown formula. The KR-20 coefficients for face and body were .15 and .26, respectively, and the corrected coefficients (scaled to 220 items) were .65 and .80. These reliabilities

TABLE 6.10. Means and Standard Deviations on Face and Body PONS

Scale	Males (N=22)		Females (N=70)		Total (N=92)	
	Mean	SD	Mean	SD	Mean	SD
Face	15.205	2.074	15.786	1.552	15.647	1.698
Body	15.023	1.665	15.250	2.014	15.196	1.930
Total	30.227	2.702	31.036	2.728	30.842	2.729
Positive-submissive	7.727	1.288	7.929	1.272	7.880	1.272
Positive-dominant	7.250	1.251	7.236	1.203	7.239	1.208
Negative-submissive	6.705	1.241	7.171	1.139	7.060	1.174
Negative-dominant	8.545	1.262	8.700	1.111	8.663	1.144

NOTE: For 68 married people from the greater Boston area, accuracies were: face, 15.51 (SD = 1.66); body, 14.46 (SD = 1.53); total, 29.97 (SD = 2.35). For 51 grade school children of these 68 married people, accuracies were: face, 13.40 (SD = 1.61); body, 13.85 (SD = 1.96); total, 27.26 (SD = 2.64).

were slightly lower than those obtained for face and body channels of the full PONS.

In table 6.10 are the means and standard deviations of the scores on the face and body PONS obtained by this sample. They are reported for the whole sample and for the male and female subsamples. As in the full PONS, the mean score of the females exceeded that of the males.

The face and body PONS has also been administered to a large sample of fourth and fifth graders and to children with learning disabilities. The results for these children and for adults are discussed in chapter 8.

BRIEF EXPOSURE PONS

Chapter 5 is devoted entirely to describing the development and use of a video test in which the exposure lengths of the stimuli are shortened to one, three, nine, and twenty-seven frames (at a film speed of twenty-four frames per second). In the full PONS and the face and body PONS, all stimuli are forty-eight frames long.

ORIGINAL SENDER AUDIO PONS

This test is simply the twenty RS-only and the twenty CF-only items from the full PONS, randomly reordered. The answer sheet contains the same pairs of alternatives that appeared with these items in the full PONS. Appendix 6D contains the forty items with their corresponding item numbers from the full PONS.

This test has been used in several studies as a short form of the PONS. Data on the test are presented below, where the male audio PONS is described. In addition, chapter 13 describes the use of this test in a validity study and chapter 14 describes its use in a study of practice effects.

MALE AUDIO PONS

This test was made on exactly the same format as the audio test employing the original PONS sender (see above). A man was recruited who was similar to the original sender in demographic ways (white, married with no children, twenty-five years old, college graduate, middle class, from the northeastern United States). This man was fully informed of the purpose of the study and of which situations he was to portray, but he was not informed of how to portray them. He did not hear or see any portions of the PONS test. An informal panel of judges selected his most authentic sounding portrayals for content filtering and randomized splicing. The scenes were not rerated as to their locations in the four affective quadrants.

The male audio PONS has the same scoring key as the original sender audio test (appendix 6D). The answer sheet is identical except that "fatherly" is substituted in "expressing motherly love."

Since this instrument has been used as a measure of paralinguistic sensitivity independently of the full PONS test, we have developed norms for performance on the male audio PONS and have investigated the relationship of accuracy on this test to accuracy on the audio channels of the full PONS.

The first sample to which the audio male PONS was administered consisted of forty-six male and thirty-four female college students from the United States. This sample served as a preliminary norm group. The means and standard deviations for it appear in table 6.11. On all of the measures except the positive-submissive affect quadrant, the performance of females exceeded that of males.

TABLE 6.11. Means and Standard Deviations on Male Audio PONS for College Students (46 males, 34 females)

Scale	Males		Females		Total	
	Mean	SD	Mean	SD	Mean	SD
Randomized spliced	13.52	1.43	14.12	1.72	13.78	1.58
Content-filtered	11.49	2.12	12.71	1.75	12.01	2.05
Total	25.01	2.85	26.82	2.52	25.78	2.85
Positive-submissive	5.96	1.66	5.87	0.90	5.92	1.38
Positive-dominant	5.40	1.45	6.06	1.36	5.68	1.44
Negative-submissive	7.22	1.50	7.87	1.33	7.50	1.46
Negative-dominant	6.44	1.27	7.03	1.49	6.69	1.39

The scores of this group of college students provided useful information about expected levels of performance on the male audio PONS, but to use these data as the final normative data would have posed two problems. First, scores on the male audio PONS could not be meaningfully compared with scores on the audio channels of the full PONS (with a female sender) since in the full PONS, subjects receive more than the forty exposures to the CF and RS voice available in the male audio version. In the full PONS, subjects are exposed to the RS or CF voice in all the mixed channel items in addition to the twenty pure RS and twenty pure CF items. Second, subjects in the college sample were somewhat older than the subjects in the norm group for the full PONS.

We administered both the male and original sender audio PONS tests to sixty male and fifty-nine female high school students from the same east coast public high school that our PONS norm group came from. None of these subjects had ever taken the full PONS. Approximately half of the subjects took first the female and then the male audio test. The remaining subjects took the male and then the female audio test.

In table 6.12 we present the means and standard deviations of scores on both tests. Since various systematic patterns in those means became evident, we computed an analysis of variance to determine the size of such effects and their significance. One striking pattern was that mean accuracy scores on the female audio test were significantly higher than those on the male audio test $(F(1,129) = 27.44, p < .001, r = .42$, effect size $= .92\sigma)$. Thus, subjects found it easier to decode the voice of the female sender than the male sender. We cannot tell whether the affect in a female's voice tone is easier to judge than the affect in a male's (perhaps females are more expressive) or whether the particular female sender was more nonverbally expressive than the particular male sender. In a recent review, Hall (1978b) concluded that although female senders are markedly more accurate in their nonverbal encoding than male senders for *visual* channels, for auditory channels the results were quite equivocal. However, only a few published studies on auditory decoding were available for review.

A significant interaction $(F(1,129) = 8.42, p < .005, \eta = .25$, effect size $= .51\sigma)$ indicated that on the male audio test, randomized spliced voice was easier to decode than content-filtered voice. For the female audio PONS, the opposite was true. Scores on the two negative quadrants tended to be higher than those on the two positive quadrants on both tests $(F(1,129) = 143.95, p < .001, \eta = .73$, effect size $= 2.11\sigma)$. Finally, the mean score of female subjects was significantly higher than the mean score of male subjects on channels $(F(1,129) = 4.44, p < .04, \eta = .18$, effect size $= .37\sigma)$ and on quadrants $(F(1,129) = 6.20, p < .02, \eta = .21$, effect size $= .44\sigma)$ of male and female audio tests combined.

At the same time that we collected the data from the audio norm sample, we

TABLE 6.12. Means and Standard Deviations on Male and Original Sender Audio PONS for High School Students (60 males, 59 females)

Scale	Subjects	Male Voice		Female Voice[a]	
		Mean	SD	Mean	SD
RS	All	12.59	1.78	13.04	1.89
	Males	12.52	1.75	12.99	1.91
	Females	12.66	1.82	13.09	1.90
CF	All	12.20	1.98	13.79	1.82
	Males	11.88	1.98	13.80	1.72
	Females	12.52	1.94	13.78	1.94
Total	All	24.79	2.72	26.83	2.62
	Males	24.40	2.59	26.79	2.74
	Females	25.18	2.81	26.87	2.51
Positive-submissive	All	5.85	1.30	5.87	1.36
	Males	5.92	1.11	6.07	1.40
	Females	5.78	1.48	5.68	1.30
Positive-dominant	All	5.39	1.24	6.03	1.43
	Males	5.48	1.28	5.98	1.43
	Females	5.29	1.19	6.08	1.45
Negative-submissive	All	7.03	1.50	7.37	1.20
	Males	6.62	1.45	7.27	1.10
	Females	7.46	1.44	7.48	1.30
Negative-dominant	All	6.52	1.47	7.56	1.00
	Males	6.38	1.38	7.48	0.89
	Females	6.65	1.55	7.63	1.10

[a]For 68 married people in the greater Boston area, accuracies were: RS, 13.90 (SD = 1.71); CF, 13.15 (SD = 1.68); total, 27.04 (SD = 2.50). For 51 children of these 68 married people, accuracies were: RS, 12.67 (SD = 1.88); CF, 12.82 (SD = 2.06); total, 25.49 (SD = 2.93).

administered both audio tests to twenty-six students (eleven males and fifteen females) who had taken the full PONS a few months earlier. A significant interaction ($F(1,129) = 4.16, p < .05, \eta = .18$, effect size $= .36\sigma$) indicated that having taken the full PONS test previously aided performance on the female audio test but relatively handicapped performance on the male audio test. Previous exposure to the paralinguistic cues of a particular stimulus person may enhance future understanding of *that* person but interfere with the decoding of such cues from a different person. A second interaction ($F(1,129) = 4.68, p < .04, \eta = .19$, effect size $= .38\sigma$) indicated that accuracy on the randomized spliced channel of *both tests* was increased by prior experience with the full PONS, while accuracy in content-filtered speech was relatively diminished by having previously taken the full PONS.

In order to examine the extent to which the various scales were related within each audio test, we computed the intercorrelations for each test using the data from the audio norm sample of 119 students. On each test, accuracy

TABLE 6.13. Median Correlations of Channels of Male Audio PONS with Audio Channels of Full PONS for Three Samples ($N = 155$)

Female Voice (Full PONS)	Male Audio PONS		
	RS	CF	Total (RS + CF)
Randomized spliced	.21	.05	.29
Content-filtered	.06	.14	.15
Tone 40 (RS + CF)	.23	.19	.30

on RS voice and accuracy on CF voice were relatively orthogonal abilities as they are for the full PONS, as shown by the factor analysis of the eleven channels (chapter 3). For the female audio PONS the correlation between CF and RS was $-.01$ and for the male audio PONS this correlation was .06. On each test the four quadrants were also uncorrelated.

The intercorrelations of the male and female audio tests for the audio norm group were very low. These correlations were: male total with female total, $r = .03$; male RS with female RS, $r = -.04$; male CF with female CF, $r = .18$. The median of the four quadrant-to-quadrant correlations was .05. The intercorrelations of the male and female audio tests are not zero in all studies, however. In table 6.13 we present the median intercorrelations of scores on the channels of the male audio PONS and the audio channels of the full PONS for three additional samples (eighty male and female U.S. college students, twenty-nine male and female Australian college students, and forty-six female Australian teachers-in-training).

As with the full PONS, we examined the internal consistency of the male audio PONS test. Using the data from the norm group of 119 male and female high school students who took only the audio tests, we computed internal consistency measures of θ and KR-20. The θ reliability of the male test was .56, obviously considerably lower than that of the 220-item full PONS. We must remember, however, that the θ reliability coefficient of a scale decreases as the number of items in the scale decreases. Since the audio PONS test contains only 40 items, we would expect the value of θ to be lowered.

The KR-20 values for total male audio PONS, the RS and CF channels, and the four quadrants appear in table 6.14. These values were all rather low. This fact can, of course, be partially accounted for by the fact that so few items are contained in each scale. In order to determine the effective reliability equating each channel and quadrant for length with the total male audio PONS (40 items), we employed the Spearman-Brown prophecy formula. Then, in order to equate the audio PONS with the full PONS for length (220 items) to compare it meaningfully to the full PONS reliabilities, we again employed the Spearman-Brown formula (Walker and Lev 1953).

TABLE 6.14. KR-20 Reliabilities of Male Audio PONS for Audio Norm Group
(N=119)

Scale	KR-20	Equated for 40 Items Using Spearman-Brown Formula	Equated for 220 Items Using Spearman-Brown Formula
Total (40 items)	.086	.086	.341
Randomized spliced (20 items)	.029	.056	.246
Content-filtered (20 items)	.058	.110	.405
Positive-submissive (10 items)	.000[a]	.000	.000
Positive-dominant (10 items)	.000[a]	.000	.000
Negative-submissive (10 items)	.262	.587	.887
Negative-dominant (10 items)	.216	.524	.858

[a]Due to sampling fluctuation resulting from the small number of items in these scales, the obtained KR-20 reliabilities were slightly less than zero. Such negative values indicate reliability coefficients that are effectively zero.

Table 6.14 shows that the internal consistency of the male audio PONS was rather low (although the reliability of the negative quadrants was substantial). A possible consequence of this low internal consistency is that the validity coefficients of the male audio PONS (i.e., correlations with other measures) may be low. However, since θ reliability was higher ($+.56$) and the stability of the test (the test-retest reliability, which we have not yet assessed) may be more substantial, the size of the validity coefficients for the male audio PONS, while probably lowered by relative unreliability, may not be zero.

More on the male audio PONS can be found in chapter 7, where the generality of sex effects for other senders besides the original sender is discussed, and in chapter 14, where its use in a study of practice effects is discussed.

CHILD SENDER AUDIO PONS

An audio test on exactly the same format as the male and original sender audio tests was made using an eight-year-old girl. The order and response alternatives are identical to the other two audio tests (appendix 6D).

Since this test has been used mainly with children (both with and without learning disabilities), readers are referred to chapter 8 for more information on this test. In addition, the test is discussed in chapter 7, where we deal with generality of sex effects on the full PONS.

Appendix 6A

ITEMS IN SIXTY-ITEM STILL PHOTO PONS

TABLE 6.15. Items in Sixty-Item Still Photo PONS

Item Number	Item Number in Full PONS	Item Number	Item Number in Full PONS	Item Number	Item Number in Full PONS
1	5	21	60	41	149
2	8	22	70	42	155
3	13	23	74	43	157
4	14	24	77	44	168
5	15	25	80	45	172
6	16	26	82	46	176
7	18	27	86	47	178
8	20	28	103	48	181
9	26	29	107	49	185
10	29	30	113	50	191
11	30	31	114	51	192
12	37	32	116	52	194
13	42	33	119	53	197
14	43	34	122	54	201
15	44	35	123	55	202
16	45	36	131	56	203
17	51	37	135	57	205
18	52	38	138	58	211
19	56	39	140	59	212
20	57	40	146	60	213

NOTE: Using this table in conjunction with appendix 2E, an answer sheet and scoring key can be constructed. Instructions read to test takers should be appropriately modified from those in appendix 2F.

Appendix 6B

ITEMS IN FORTY-ITEM PHOTO BOOKLET PONS

TABLE 6.16. Items in Forty-Item Photo Booklet PONS

Item Number	Item Number in Full PONS	Item Number	Item Number in Full PONS
1	5	9	42
2	8	10	43
3	14	11	45
4	15	12	51
5	16	13	52
6	18	14	57
7	30	15	60
8	37	16	70

Table 6.16. *Continued*.

Item Number	Item Number in Full PONS	Item Number	Item Number in Full PONS
17	74	29	155
18	103	30	172
19	107	31	176
20	116	32	181
21	119	33	185
22	122	34	192
23	123	35	194
24	135	36	197
25	138	37	201
26	140	38	203
27	146	39	212
28	149	40	213

NOTE: Using this table in conjunction with appendix 2E, an answer sheet and scoring key can be constructed. Instructions read to test takers should be appropriately modified from those in appendix 2F.

Appendix 6C

ITEMS IN FORTY-ITEM FACE AND BODY PONS

TABLE 6.17. Items in Forty-Item Face and Body PONS

Item Number	Item Number in Full PONS	Item Number	Item Number in Full PONS
1	16	21	107
2	15	22	30
3	122	23	212
4	185	24	51
5	138	25	149
6	119	26	70
7	18	27	140
8	60	28	146
9	116	29	74
10	213	30	194
11	155	31	37
12	57	32	176
13	197	33	172
14	135	34	123
15	103	35	42
16	181	36	45
17	14	37	201
18	43	38	5
19	52	39	192
20	8	40	203

NOTE: Using this table in conjunction with appendix 2E, an answer sheet and scoring key can be constructed. Instructions read to test takers should be appropriately modified from those in appendix 2F.

Appendix 6D

ITEMS IN FORTY-ITEM MALE, CHILD, AND ORIGINAL SENDER AUDIO
PONS

TABLE 6.18. Items in Forty-Item Male, Child, and Original Sender
Audio PONS

Item Number	Item Number in Full PONS	Item Number	Item Number in Full PONS
1	160	21	94
2	105	22	190
3	62	23	11
4	66	24	3
5	33	25	91
6	139	26	152
7	1	27	4
8	81	28	55
9	145	29	171
10	151	30	96
11	93	31	167
12	153	32	220
13	193	33	219
14	112	34	158
15	47	35	145
16	7	36	23
17	216	37	31
18	144	38	132
19	88	39	73
20	61	40	95

NOTE: Using this table in conjunction with appendix 2E, an answer sheet and
scoring key can be constructed. Instructions read to test takers should be
appropriately modified from those in appendix 2F.

7 | Gender and PONS Skill

In our culture, it is widely believed that women tend to be socially and emotionally oriented—that they are interested in and sensitive to other people's needs and feelings. Men, on the other hand, are believed to be less socially oriented and more concerned with activities, particularly instrumental ones. The nature of these beliefs and the degree to which they are justified have been the subject of much theoretical and empirical work (e.g., Maccoby and Jacklin 1974; Parsons and Bales 1955; Spence, Helmreich, and Stapp 1974). Though people may not agree on whether these kinds of differences are learned or innate, nevertheless there are pervasive assumptions made about differences in males' and females' social orientations.

In order to measure such differences and to understand them if they exist, we must differentiate, conceptually at least, among the kinds of behaviors that may be involved. In particular, interest level (sociality or attentiveness) should be distinguished from social skill, and social skill should be differentiated into at least two components, judging ability and ability to behave appropriately or facilitatively toward others.

A tendency to pay attention to other people and to value their experiences may be differentially reinforced early in the lives of women and men, in keeping with cultural norms. Following from this differential level of social interest, differential skill at judging others or in behaving sensitively toward others may develop through practice. At any one point in time it would be hard to say how much the accuracy of a person's social judgments and the appropriateness of his or her interpersonal behavior depend on these two conceptually distinct factors of interest and skill. It would be important to try to assess how behavioral differences (for example, in amount of interpersonal attention or in amount of time spent with others) contribute to performance differences over time (for example, in ability to understand other people's feelings).

150

Within the performance or social skill category, we should distinguish between accuracy of social-interpersonal judgment and the ability to "act wisely" toward others. Further, "acting wisely" can be thought of as the ability to encode one's feelings and thoughts in a way that can be understood *and* the ability to decide when and what feelings and thoughts to convey. Finally, the distinction between strictly nonverbal and mixed verbal-nonverbal skills must be made, for both the judging and communication of messages in social situations.

Because of our own interest in decoding, which is an intentionally narrow operational definition of social sensitivity, our review of previous studies is confined to studies in which decoding of strictly nonverbal cues was measured. We are aware that using a different definition of social sensitivity could result in drawing a different conclusion from the literature (e.g., Maccoby and Jacklin 1974). Our review is limited to studies using instruments that required judges to identify the affective meanings of nonverbal stimuli (face, body, or voice tone) and in which an "objective" assessment of judging skill could be made.

It might be instructive to give examples of the kinds of studies we have *excluded*. Shanley, Walker, and Foley (1971) found females to perform significantly better than males on two of the six Guilford Tests of social intelligence; these, however, are paper-and-pencil tasks whose relationship to decoding of nonverbal cues is unknown. Rothenberg (1970) found no significant difference in the ability of grade-school boys and girls to judge affect from tape-recorded dialogues; in that study, the nonverbal cues were combined with verbal cues in the stimulus materials, making an inference about purely nonverbal skill impossible. Cline (1955), using sound-film interviews as stimuli, found females to be better than males at postdicting personality characteristics of senders; this study not only involved mixed verbal-nonverbal cues, but also its concern was with the ability to judge personality, not with the ability to tell one kind of communication or one affect from another.

Some studies involving strictly nonverbal cues have also been excluded from our review. In Buck et al. (1972), nonverbal communication was more accurate in female dyads than in male dyads, but we cannot know whether this was due to better sending or judging ability among females or both. Scherer (1974) found females to be more accurate judges of the affective meanings of electronically synthesized tones than males; intriguing though this finding is, we cannot safely generalize from it to human nonverbal communication. Kleck and Nuessle (1968) found females to be better than males at noticing instances of eye contact in dyads; however, this does not mean that females also make more accurate inferences about people's feelings or about the meanings of nonverbal cues. Finally, although the abilities of males and females to encode (send) nonverbal cues have been compared (e.g.,

Thompson and Meltzer 1964; Zuckerman, Lipets, Koivumaki, and Rosenthal 1975), this literature is not reviewed here.

In a paper by Hall (1978a), all of the known studies relevant to gender differences in decoding accuracy, including studies using the PONS test, are summarized. Here we present a summary based on data provided by Hall (1978a) of only those studies that did not use the PONS test or one of its derived forms, to provide a standard for comparing results based on the PONS. All of the summarized studies required judges to decode nonverbal affective stimuli in the face, body, or voice channels.

First we will consider the direction of outcome—whether males or females scored more accurately on the decoding task. Excluding studies for which the direction could not be ascertained, 80 percent (40/50) showed females to be more accurate decoders than males. This proportion did not vary appreciably with the sex of the sender; females were more accurate in 78 percent (7/9) of studies with female senders, 80 percent (8/10) of studies with male senders, and 81 percent (25/31) of studies with both male and female senders. Looked at by modality of sending, females were more accurate in 82 percent (33/40) of studies using visual nonverbal cues, 57 percent (4/7) of studies using audio cues, and 100 percent (3/3) of studies using both visual and audio cues.

In terms of magnitude of effect (d or standard deviation units; Cohen 1969), the median gender effect of the thirty-five studies for which d was known or could be computed was $.30\sigma$. The median effect was $.14\sigma$ for female senders, $.22\sigma$ for male senders, and $.36\sigma$ for studies with both male and female senders. The median effect was $.30\sigma$ for visual studies, $-.14\sigma$ for auditory studies, and 1.12σ for studies with visual and auditory cues.

Thus, it appears that for both indices (direction and magnitude of effect), females scored higher than males in general, and there was no evidence that the difference varied with the sex of the senders of the cues. Females seemed to be relatively more accurate than males on visual cues than on auditory cues.

GENDER EFFECTS IN PONS RESEARCH

SEX DIFFERENCES ON CHANNELS AND TOTAL. As table 3.3 showed, the high school norm group (N = 480) showed female advantage on all but one channel (RS). In an analysis of variance performed on these data, sex was a between-subjects factor, and audio (absent/RS/CF), face (absent/present), body (absent/present), dominance (submissive/dominant), and positivity (negative/positive) were repeated measures factors. The effect on performance attributable to sex was significant ($F(1,478) = 26.46$, $p < .001$; r between sex and total = .23; effect size (d) = $.47\sigma$).

For the high school norm group (chapter 3), the junior high school norm group (chapter 8), and the children's norm group (chapter 8), males tended to exhibit slightly more variability in their PONS scores than did females. This phenomenon is not peculiar to the PONS test; on tests of cognitive abilities, at least, males' scores are often more variable than females' scores (Maccoby and Jacklin 1974).

The interactions of sex with the three channel factors (audio, face, and body) were nonsignificant for the high school norm group for audio and face ($F < 2; p > .14$), but highly significant for sex $\times$ body ($F(1,478) = 8.06$, $p = .005$; $r = .13$; effect size $= .26\sigma$). Females profited significantly more than males from the addition of body cues in the stimuli to be judged. (A recent replication by Karen Fischer showed a similar effect for a sample of 160 college students, effect size $= .14\sigma$.)

Collapsing the channels in order to examine tone-only (RS + CF) versus video-only (pure face, pure body, and pure figure), it was apparent that high school norm group males performed relatively well on audio and relatively poorly on video, compared to females ($F(1,5258) = 8.86$, $p < .005$; $r = .13$; effect size $= .27\sigma$). We should bear in mind that the reliability of the PONS audio channels is lower than that of the video channels (see chapter 3), thus reducing our power to detect differences between groups in the audio channels. This tendency for males to score relatively well compared to females in audio skill is, however, quite consistent with our review of earlier literature.

In addition, sex interacted with channels in two three-way interactions. The sex $\times$ face $\times$ body interaction ($F(1,478) = 7.95$, $p = .13$; effect size $= .26\sigma$) showed that females did relatively too well when either face or body was present but too poorly when both or neither was present. The sex $\times$ audio $\times$ body interaction was also significant ($F(2,956) = 8.31$, $p < .001$; $\eta = .13$), and this interaction showed that females did relatively too well when either audio or body cues were present but too poorly when both or neither was present.

In order to examine gender differences across several age groups, an analysis of variance was performed on the mean scores of males and females in samples of four different age levels (grade school, junior high school, high school, and adults older than college age). In this analysis, each sample of subjects was treated as one unit of analysis whose scores were means across subjects within the samples. Means were computed for each channel separately for males and females, creating a within-units repeated-measures design as follows: audio (none/RS/CF) $\times$ body (absent/present) $\times$ face (absent/present) $\times$ sex (males/females). Sample sizes and descriptions of samples are in appendix 7A. No sample was used in which there was only one member of either sex.

A main effect for sex ($F(1,17) = 23.72$, $p < .001$; $r = .76$; effect size $= 2.36\sigma$) showed females to excel over males, collapsing over all age levels. Table 7.1 presents the percentage of PONS accuracy, channel by channel, for males and females. Females did better by at least two percentage points on every channel.

There was no sex $\times$ audio or sex $\times$ face interaction. The sex $\times$ body

TABLE 7.1. Accuracy on Eleven PONS Channels, for Males and for
Females (Age Levels Analysis of Variance)

Audio Channel	Sex	Video Channel			
		None	Face	Body	Figure
None	Males	50.0%[a]	76.7%	72.0%	74.7%
	Females	50.0	79.4	76.2	78.3
	Female advantage	0	2.7	4.2	3.6
RS	Males	59.6	82.2	71.2	80.3
	Females	62.3	84.8	75.1	83.1
	Female advantage	2.7	2.6	3.9	2.8
CF	Males	58.2	77.9	65.6	80.4
	Females	60.6	80.8	69.3	84.3
	Female advantage	2.4	2.9	3.7	3.9

NOTE: N=23 samples (units). Since each sample was divided into male and
female components, effective N was 46.
[a]theoretical accuracy

interaction, however, was very significant ($F(1,17) = 10.54$, $p = .005$; $r = .62$; effect size $= 1.57\sigma$); it showed that females profited significantly more than males from the addition of body cues in the stimuli to be judged. This replicates the sex $\times$ body effect found when the high school norm group (included in this sample as nine separate samples) was examined by itself. In addition, the age $\times$ sex $\times$ body interaction, though not significant, showed that males were at their greatest disadvantage in utilizing body cues compared with females when they were of grade school age ($F(3,17) = 1.64$, $p = .22$; $\eta = .47$).

In another analysis of variance, the grade school category of the preceding analysis was broken down into third, fourth, fifth, and sixth grades (grade school norm group, chapter 8). The design of the analysis of variance was identical to the preceding analysis, except that the units of analysis were individual children and not whole samples, and therefore sex was now a between-units factor rather than a repeated-measures factor. The main effect for sex was again strong ($F(1,192) = 18.19$, $p < .001$; $r = .29$; effect size $= .62\sigma$). As in the preceding analysis, the sex $\times$ audio and sex $\times$ face interactions were small ($F(2,384) = .21$, $p > .50$; $F(1,192) = 2.24$, $p < .14$), but the sex $\times$ body interaction was very significant again ($F(1,192) = 10.27$, $p = .002$; $r = .23$; effect size $= .46\sigma$). As in the preceding analysis, for all items in which body was present, girls did relatively too well taking into account the sex and body main effects.

It is not immediately clear why this differential accuracy at judging body cues shows up. Perhaps the sexual connotations of the woman's body distract males from the judging task. Perhaps males are embarrassed or inhibited about watching the female sender's body. If either of these suggestions is true, then males' performance on the PONS test may be an underestimate of their actual skill in judging body cues in settings where observation can be more covert and in which body cues are embedded in a larger context (and therefore not so salient). Furthermore, when the sender is a male, another pattern of gender differences may result. Clearly, there is need for developing PONS-like instruments using male senders, as well as more female senders.

The detailed analyses reported in the last few pages have demonstrated the existence of an overall difference in PONS accuracy in favor of female subjects as well as some differential effects on certain channels, in several large samples of grade school children, junior high school and high school students, and adults. It was also important to determine the stability of the obtained sex difference for the test as a whole across our entire pool of subject samples in which both males and females participated.

Figure 7.1 displays the magnitude of the gender difference on PONS total score for 133 samples tested with the full PONS test, excluding samples for which there were not at least two males or two females. The value indicated for each sample is the effect size, or standardized difference, calculated as ($\overline{X}$ females $-$ $\overline{X}$ males)/pooled within-sex standard deviation (Cohen 1969). As discussed earlier, the standardized difference is an estimate of effect size in standard units, which enables the researcher to compare results across studies that use different scales of measurement or that differ in subject variability. In figure 7.1, positive values show that females performed better than males, and negative values show that males performed better than females.

A χ^2 test was performed to see whether the number of samples showing female advantage was significantly different from the expected number, which would be half under the null hypothesis. Eighty percent (106/133) showed female advantage, compared to 20 percent (27/133) showing male advantage or no difference ($\chi^2(1) = 45.74$, $p < .001$). This 80 percent can be compared to the 80 percent showing female advantage on earlier instruments. If the PONS test measures nonverbal skill more precisely than earlier instruments, then we would predict that the magnitude of the sex difference (or any between-subjects effect) would be higher because of the increased power of the instrument to detect effects that, in fact, exist. The range of effects in figure 7.1 was from -0.97σ to 2.36σ, and the median effect size for the 133 samples was .42 σ (unweighted mean $=$ .41 σ). The sex effect obtained for our high school norm group was .47 σ; .49 σ for the junior high school norm group; and .62 σ for the grade school norm group. Since the median effect size computed for the non-PONS decoding literature (Hall 1978a) was .30σ, we can tentatively conclude that the PONS is a more precise measuring instrument.

In addition, the magnitude of the sex effect was calculated for the three occupation/interest groups for which several samples were available. These

FIGURE 7.1. Frequency distribution of sex effects on PONS total score (N = 133 samples)

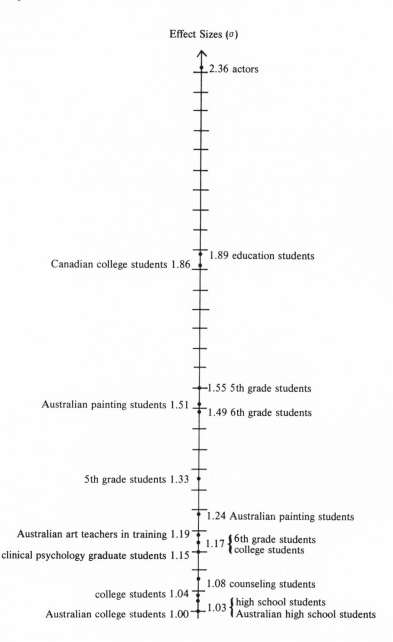

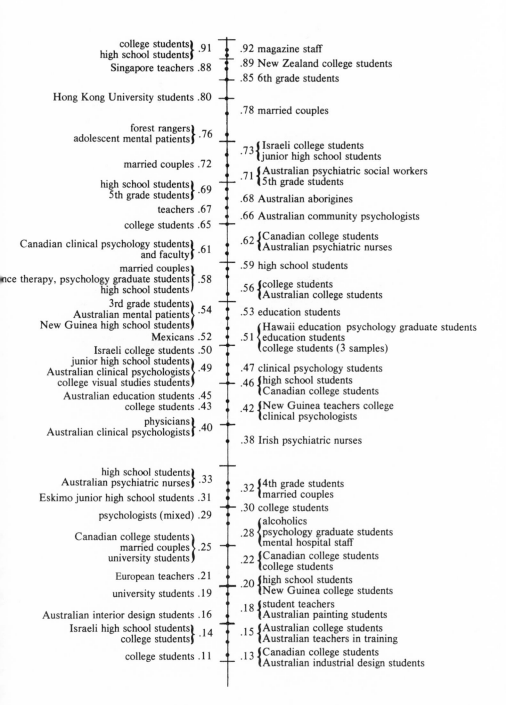

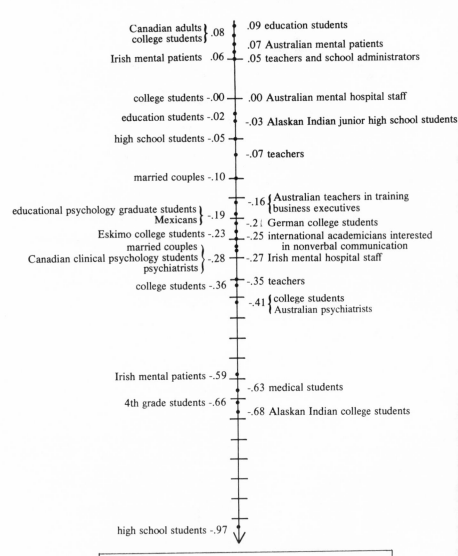

Canadian adults ⎱ .08   .09 education students
college students ⎰

                            .07 Australian mental patients

Irish mental patients .06   .05 teachers and school administrators

college students -.00   .00 Australian mental hospital staff

education students -.02   -.03 Alaskan Indian junior high school students

high school students -.05

                             -.07 teachers

married couples -.10

                       -.16 ⎰ Australian teachers in training
                              ⎱ business executives

educational psychology graduate students ⎱ -.19
Mexicans ⎰   -.21 German college students

Eskimo college students -.23   -.25 international academicians interested
married couples ⎱   in nonverbal communication
Canadian clinical psychology students ⎰ -.28 -.27 Irish mental hospital staff
psychiatrists ⎰

college students -.36   -.35 teachers

                        -.41 ⎰ college students
                             ⎱ Australian psychiatrists

Irish mental patients -.59

                       -.63 medical students

4th grade students -.66

                       -.68 Alaskan Indian college students

high school students -.97

Effect size (σ) = ($\bar{x}$ of females-$\bar{x}$ of males)/pooled within-sex standard deviation. No sample included has fewer than two members of each sex. All are from continental United States unless otherwise indicated. The scale is condensed for values greater than .80σ or less than -.10σ.

groups were: (1) "artistic," comprising actors and students of visual studies, art, art teaching, music, interior design, dance, and writing;[1] (2) "teaching," comprising education students, student teachers, teachers, and school administrators (all teaching below college level); and (3) "clinical," comprising medical, clinical psychology, and educational psychology students, clinical psychologists, community psychologists, psychiatrists, physicians, psychiatric nurses, and psychiatric social workers. For comparison purposes, we computed the magnitude of the sex effect for two unspecialized groups: (1) college students in the United States, Canada, Israel, Germany, Australia, New Guinea, New Zealand, and Hong Kong; and (2) high school students in the United States, Australia, and New Guinea. As table 7.2 shows, the magnitude of the sex difference for artistic groups is appreciably greater than in the other four groups, who differ little from each other.

For the thirty-four college samples, sex effects were examined separately for seventeen U.S. culture and seventeen non-U.S. culture samples (from the countries listed above and including Alaskan Indians and Alaskan Eskimos). For the U.S. samples (833 persons), the median effect was .30 σ (weighted mean effect = .40 σ). For the non-U.S. group (892 persons), the median effect was .46 σ (weighted mean effect = .48 σ). In the seven samples from non-English-speaking cultures (Israel, New Guinea, Hong Kong, Alaskan Indians, and Alaskan Eskimos), the effect was similar to that found for the whole foreign group of samples. Thus, we did not pick up an overall difference between U.S. and non-U.S. cultures, nor between English-speaking and non-English-speaking cultures. Perhaps college students are too homogeneous a population for cultural effects to show up. It is still possible that differences between the sexes in judging ability may vary with the relative status of each sex or with the gender-role customs in different cultures.

SEX DIFFERENCES ON AFFECTIVE QUADRANTS. Table 3.4 showed how males and females in the high school norm group performed on the four quadrants (type of affect). There was a tendency for females to perform better, relatively, on negative scenes than on positive scenes. There was no sex $\times$ dominance interaction ($F < 1$), but the sex $\times$ positivity interaction was significant at $p = .005$ ($F(1,478) = 8.33$; $r = .13$; effect size = .26 σ). In addition, the sex $\times$ dominance $\times$ positivity interaction was significant at $p = .004$; females did relatively too well on negative-submissive and positive-dominant and too poorly on negative-dominant and positive-submissive affect ($F(1,478) = 8.76$; $r = .13$; effect size = .27 σ).

1. One of these eight samples consisted of sixty undergraduates from the University of California, Santa Cruz, fifty-three of whom were artistic and seven of whom were control subjects. Because of the small number of nonartistic subjects in this sample, we felt justified in labeling this sample as artistic. The sample is not included in figure 7.1 because the subjects were able to take only the first eighty items of the PONS test.

TABLE 7.2. Median and Weighted Mean Effects of Sex (σ) for Five Kinds of Samples

Sample Group	N (Samples)	N (Persons)	Median Effect (σ)	Weighted Mean Effect (σ)
Artistic	8	171	.88	.71
Teaching	16	785	.20	.36
Clinical	22	536	.39	.34
College	34	1725	.36	.44
High school	12	581	.56	.57

An independent sample of 119 high school students took the tone-only portions of the full PONS (forty items) and the forty-item male audio PONS test (see later in this chapter, and chapter 6). The sex × positivity interaction was again found (positivity means being computed across both tests), with $F(1,115) = 6.28$, $p < .01$, effect size $= .47\sigma$. Examination of the means revealed that females again performed better on negative affect, compared to the males.

In a sample of college students tested by Karen Fischer, the interaction of sex with positivity was again significant ($F(1,158) = 8.48$, $p = .005$, effect size $= .46\sigma$), with females scoring relatively better on negative scenes than males.

Among 200 children in grades three through six who took the full PONS test, the sex × positivity interaction was again significant ($F(1,198) = 9.97$, $p = .002$, effect size $= .45\sigma$), with females performing relatively better on negative scenes than males.

In a sample of 275 fourth and fifth graders who took the face-only and body-only portions of the full PONS (forty items) and the forty-item child sender PONS audio test (see later in this chapter, and chapter 8), the sex × positivity interaction did not emerge ($F(1,270) = .19$, $p > .50$). Lowered reliability of the short tests (see chapter 8) may have contributed to this failure to replicate.

JUDGES' PREDICTIONS OF SEX EFFECTS. It seemed interesting to see if judges could predict the direction of sex effects and the PONS scenes on which such sex effects would be most pronounced, without actually seeing the PONS film but rather by judging the scene labels. Predictions of male and female accuracy on the twenty PONS scene descriptions were obtained by Lauri Fidell from fifty-two high school students (thirty-one males and twenty-one females). Each judge was given the twenty labels, taken directly from the PONS answer sheet, and was asked to predict males' and females' actual performance on nine-point scales (extremely poor to extremely good). These ratings revealed that both sexes predicted that females would be more accurate than males across the twenty scenes. The entire group of judges predicted an overall accuracy of 69 percent for males and 80 percent for females $(F(1,50) = 55.09, p < .001; r = .72;$ effect size $= 2.10\sigma)$. It is interesting to note that this predicted sex effect is much greater in magnitude (2.10σ) than the actual sex effect for the high school norm group $(.47\sigma)$. There was no main effect of judge's sex and no interaction of judge's sex with the sex for whom the predictions were made, nor with the affective quadrant of the scene. Judges predicted that both sexes would judge positive affect more accurately than negative affect $(F(1,50) = 36.77, p < .001; r = .65;$ effect size $= 1.72\sigma)$; this is opposite to the actual performance of the high school norm group (chapter 3). Judges also predicted that females would be differentially better at positive affect compared to males $(F(1,50) = 4.52; p < .04; r = .29;$ effect size $= .60\sigma)$; this, too, is not the pattern obtained for the norm group.

Judges' predictions of male and female performances were correlated with the actual performances of males and females in the high school norm group. The correlations across the twenty scenes between actual accuracy and predicted accuracy for males and females respectively (judges pooled over sex) were $-.13$ and $-.08$ (n.s.). The correlation between actual and predicted *difference* scores between males and females was $-.04$. Not only were judges unable to predict the rank order of the twenty scenes for the two sexes separately, but they were also unable reliably to identify those scenes on which relatively large and relatively small sex effects occurred.

GENERALIZATION OF FEMALE ADVANTAGE TO OTHER SENDERS. One important question was whether the reliable female advantage obtained with the PONS test would replicate with other tests of the same design but having different senders. We cannot offer a comprehensive answer to this question, because of the expense and time required to develop full-scale PONS-like tests. The data we have, however, do suggest that the female advantage is generalizable, as do the findings reported in Hall (1978a).

A forty-item audio-only test (RS and CF) was developed using an eight-year-old girl (see chapter 8). This test was identical in format to the audio portions of the full PONS test, except that the affects portrayed by the child sender were the age-appropriate ones used on the answer sheets in other testings of children. In a sample of 275 fourth and fifth grade children, girls performed significantly better than boys on the test's total score $(t(273) = 2.59, p < .01; r = .15;$ effect size $= .31\sigma)$.

In three samples of adults who took the child sender audio PONS (suburban couples, education students, and a group of psychologists), the sex effects (standardized differences) were $.27\sigma$, $-.22\sigma$, and $.07\sigma$. In three samples who took only the tone-only portions of the full PONS test (high school students, education students, and U.S. Information Agency officers), the sex effects were $.03\sigma$, $.01\sigma$, and $.39\sigma$. For the high school norm group, the magnitude of the female advantage was smaller for audio portions of the full PONS test than for the video portions and the tone 40 sex effect was smaller than the total sex effect ($.21\sigma$ vs $.47\sigma$).

From the start, we recognized that our observation of sex differences in nonverbal skill might be confounded by the fact that the PONS sender was a woman, and similarly by the fact that the PONS child sender was a girl. Women and young girls may have special skill only at reading another female; men and boys might be better than females at judging nonverbal cues sent by a male. Although the earlier literature on decoding does not support this hypothesis, we began an investigation of the question with our own instruments.

To address this hypothesis, the male sender audio PONS test was made. It is a forty-item audio-only (RS and CF) test whose twenty scenes are the same twenty scenes used in the full PONS test (see chapter 6 for more information on this test). Ideally, we would have made a male audiovisual test just like the full PONS. The male sender test that we did make could allow us only to test the hypothesis that males read audio cues from a male sender better than females do. But it could *not* (nor could an audiovisual test with one male sender) permit us to draw conclusions about sex differences in sending ability nor about interactions of sender sex and receiver sex. Such conclusions can be drawn only by using many male and female senders, for only then could the personality and other nongender characteristics of the senders be relatively unconfounded with gender.

It is important to emphasize that with the testing materials we now have, we are still unable to comment on sex differences in sending ability or sending style of our senders, because any differences in the mean accuracy of judges on these tests could be caused by individual (not gender-related) differences among the senders. We are also incapable of detecting a sender sex × receiver sex interaction, if one exists. If such an interaction exists, it means that accurate judgment of nonverbal cues depends *both* on the sender's sex *and* on the receiver's sex.

There may in fact exist a sender sex × receiver sex × sender skill interaction, in which accuracy depends on the judge's sex, the sender's sex, and the sender's sending skill. Because we have only one adult male sender and one adult female sender, we cannot detect these effects. For example, if our female sender is a poor sender relative to other female senders, and if our male sender is a good sender relative to other male senders, then this fact could affect the male and female judges' performances differentially. A good male sender might be judged more accurately by females than by males, whereas a poor or average male sender might be judged more accurately by males than by females. We cannot test for such effects because, in the absence of norms for male and female sending ability, we cannot say how skilled or unskilled our two senders are compared to other senders of their sexes.

TABLE 7.3. Female Decoding Advantage (σ) for Female, Child, and Male Sender

Sender	Number of Samples	Median Effect[a]	Mean Effect[b]
Female	3	.03	.14
Child	4	.17	.11
Male	8	.14	.13

[a]differences tested by $\chi^2(2) = 0.08, p = .96$
[b]differences tested by $F(2,12) = 0.01, p = .99$

Nevertheless, comparing the scores of male and female subjects on the male and female tests will allow us to address at least the hypothesis that females perform better than males only when the sender is also female. In seven samples, the median and mean scores for the male sender total were barely higher for females than for males, and the median effect size was zero (mean weighted according to sample size $= .19\sigma$; unweighted mean $= .10\sigma$).

A twenty-item test (CF only) patterned after the PONS audio tests was developed by David McClelland and Charles Dailey. This test employed a Spanish-speaking male speaker enacting the twenty PONS scenes. It was used with a sample of 131 U.S. Information Agency officers. In this sample, the correlation between sex and performance was .15, with females doing better than males ($t = 1.77$, $p < .10$; effect size $= .32\sigma$).

The results obtained with two male audio senders do not give support to the idea that the magnitude of the sex effect varies with the sender's sex when we keep in mind that the median sex effect for female audio PONS is only .03. This conclusion is consistent with the conclusion based on our review of the earlier decoding literature. Finally, it should be noted that sex effects on audio channels may be attenuated by the lower reliability of the audio channels of both the male and female audio tests (see chapters 3 and 6). Table 7.3 shows that, considering all fifteen relevant samples, the female advantage is not appreciably different among our three audio tests ($F(2,12) = 0.01$, $p = .99$, $\eta = .03$).

SEX DIFFERENCES IN NONVERBAL SENSITIVITY AT DIFFERENT AGE LEVELS. Since we collected PONS data from males and females at several age levels, it was possible to look, cross-sectionally, at sex $\times$ age (or sex $\times$ grade) interactions. Such interactions would tell us whether females in our samples were, relative to their usual advantage, more or less accurate at different age levels.

One hypothesis was that females would be more advantaged at younger ages and become less advantaged with age, relative to males. This hypothesis rested on the idea that girls' cognitive abilities may develop faster than boys' in early life, especially verbal ability (Kagan 1971; Maccoby and Jacklin 1974). The hypothesis that boys would catch up was put forth to explain an obtained effect of sex on nonverbal decoding ability among children as early as 1931 (Kellogg and Eagleson). A recent review (Maccoby and Jacklin 1974) suggests, however, that females' advantage on verbal tasks increases from about age eleven on, and that males' advantage on visual-spatial and mathematical tasks starts to show up around puberty and increases through adolescence. To the extent that such skills are related to nonverbal decoding skill, we should probably not place much confidence in a hypothesis suggesting that boys and girls become more similar in sensitivity as they grow older.

Another hypothesis predicted the opposite trend, that males and females start out equivalent in nonverbal skill and that female children gradually gain their advantage. This hypothesis rests on the assumption that, as they grow older, children learn gender-appropriate behavior via reinforcement, modeling, or differential practice. Gender-appropriate behavior may involve the acquisition of superior nonverbal skills among females; or phrased differently, it may involve punishment and/or negative reinforcement for boys' attending to nonverbal cues. Maccoby and Jacklin (1974), in reviewing the literature on differential socialization, point out that boys tend to be punished for cross-sex behavior more often than girls (p. 328). If too much of an interpersonal orientation is considered girlish or sissy, then considerable pressure may be brought on boys not to develop or to manifest their full potential in this area.

The effect sizes reported earlier in this chapter for grade school, junior high school, high school, and college samples suggest that strong interactions of sex and age are not apparent. The effect sizes for these age groups were: $.62\sigma$ for grade school norm group, $.49\sigma$ for junior high school norm group, $.47\sigma$ for high school norm group ($.57\sigma$ for twelve high school samples [weighted mean effect size]), and $.44\sigma$ for thirty-four college samples (weighted mean effect size).

A more precise analysis was available in the analysis of variance described earlier in which grade school, junior high school, high school, and older-than-college adults were treated. The interaction of age group with gender was very small ($F(3,17) = .36, p > .50; \eta = .24$).

In the analysis of variance described earlier, which treated only the four grades of the grade school norm group, the grade $\times$ sex interaction was again nonsignificant ($F(3,192) = 2.12, p < .10; \eta = .18$). The residuals showed that in the third and fourth grades, males performed relatively better than they should have, given the sizes of the sex and grade main effects. However, it should be kept in mind that the absolute difference between boys and girls in the two younger grades still favored the girls.

In another, independent, sample, 275 fourth and fifth graders took two short PONS tests: a forty-item video-only test comprised of all face-only and body-only items from the full PONS, and the forty-item child sender audio test. Though the sex effect was significant across both tests ($F(1,270) = 4.60$, $p < .04; r = .13$; effect size $= .26\sigma$), the sex $\times$ grade interaction was again very small ($F(1,270) = 1.53, p < .22; r = .08$; effect size $= .15\sigma$). As in the preceding analysis, the younger boys performed relatively better compared with girls than did the older boys.

To summarize, our data have shown no appreciable interactions of age and sex, which suggests that girls must acquire their nonverbal skill at ages younger than those tested with the PONS tests or boys must suffer a decline in theirs. Our results are similar to those of Dimitrovsky (1964), who tested boys and girls in fifth through twelfth grades with a standard content measure of auditory nonverbal sensitivity and also found girls to have a significant advantage across the eight grades, with no significant interaction between age and sex.

Although the tendency that we found for very young boys to perform relatively well compared to how boys usually performed was a weak and nonsignificant effect, it supports the results of Dimitrovsky (1964), who found that girls judged auditory cues more accurately than boys at ages six to twelve but not at age five, and of Kellogg and Eagleson (1931), who found that girls aged seven to fourteen excelled over boys at recognizing facial expressions, but not at younger ages. Kellogg and Eagleson advanced the interpretation that girls mature faster than boys, but if this interpretation were correct, boys would "catch up," which they do not do. These data that suggest that girls' and boys' skills are somewhat more similar at younger ages may be affected by lowered reliability of the testing instruments in younger age groups: the less reliable the test, the less ability it has to discriminate. Kellogg and Eagleson did not report reliabilities; Dimitrovsky's reported reliabilities were considerably lower for her younger age groups. KR-20 reliabilities for the full PONS test for the four grades in our grade school norm group were .54 for third grade, .96 for fourth grade, .80 for fifth grade, and .89 for sixth grade; so here, too, reliability jumps abruptly between the youngest age group and the others.

One thing is clear: our data do not strongly support the hypothesis that females' superiority in reading nonverbal cues decreases with advancing age, at least not according to our cross-sectional analyses. We are left with several unresolved questions. Are females biologically programmed to have or to develop superior nonverbal skill (perhaps because such skill enhances the survival chances of offspring) or do female children develop superior skill as a result of social learning? It is not hard to infer possible social roots of the feminine advantage, and some have been mentioned earlier in this section.

English (1972) and Weitz (1974) have advanced an intriguing variation of a social learning hypothesis, suggesting that because women are oppressed in most societies of the world, they acquire nonverbal skills to an acute degree as an adaptation to an environment in which it is to their advantage to read accurately what more powerful people require of them.

Continued experience in subordinate roles may bring about, over time, differential learning of the meanings of nonverbal cues in the sexes. It has been documented that females engage in more visual monitoring of others' behavior than do males (Exline 1972). Such monitoring may be a requirement, or at least a by-product, of the subordinate role.

In a very beginning way, we examined this hypothesis using the results of a study by Kimes (1975). The number of seconds of eye contact engaged in with another person during a three-minute conversation by each of fifty undergraduate subjects was measured, and those same subjects then took the first eighty items of the full PONS test (the test was abbreviated because the film broke). In this study, females engaged in more eye contact than did males, but the difference was not significant ($r = .17$, $p < .30$). In this sample, females performed better than males ($F(1,38) = 4.05$, $p < .06$; $r = .31$; effect size $= .65\sigma$), and persons who engaged in more eye contact in the experimental situation also scored higher than did persons who engaged in less eye contact ($F(1,38) = 4.04$, $p < .06$; $r = .31$; effect size $= .65\sigma$). When amount of eye contact was partialed out, the relationship of sex to PONS skill was somewhat diminished (partial $r = .24$). Hence, the difference between males' and females' looking behavior was not entirely sufficient to explain the difference between males' and females' PONS scores.

There are other ways in which being in a subordinate role could affect females' nonverbal skill. English has suggested that if males typically dominate social situations by talking more and generally commanding more attention, then the greater amount of time females must spend in watching and listening during their lifetimes might account for their nonverbal decoding advantage.* This would be a pure practice effect brought about by females' having to play a different social role than males, with no necessary component of differential valuation of interpersonal sensitivity per se. In other words, females may be more nonverbally sensitive than males, not because society encourages females to be interpersonally sensitive, but rather because society encourages females to be observers more than participants.

Because the sex effect shows up so early, we would have to assume that differential learning of nonverbal skills occurs very early. PONS-like tests must be developed to assess decoding skill in the very young, and more research relating nonverbal sensitivity to sex-role socialization is necessary before we can begin to understand the origins of the sex differences we have observed.

Some recent evidence suggests the possibility of an inborn differential sensitivity or at least reactivity on the part of males and females to affective cues. Simner (1971) found that in three studies of 3-day-old infants, girls tended to cry more in response to another infant's cry than boys. Sagi and Hoffman (1976) found the same to be true for 1½-day-old infants. In both sets

*P. W. English 1976: personal communication.

of studies, the response was specific to the sound of crying, since control sounds were used for which no sex differences were observed.

SEX DIFFERENCES IN THE RELATIONSHIP OF PONS TO ACHIEVEMENT AND IQ. Chapter 10 explores at some length the correlations between PONS skill and various measures of achievement and intelligence for both sexes combined. It was concluded, by doing a discriminant validity analysis, that the magnitude of the relationship of achievement and intelligence to nonverbal sensitivity as measured by the PONS test was small.

It was possible, in several samples of sufficient size, to compute correlations between PONS and such objective ability measurements separately for the sexes. This was interesting because it seemed possible that a high-scoring male, for example, might earn that high score using a somewhat different style or skill than would a high-scoring female.

Subjects in four samples, one high school and three college, reported their Verbal and Math Scholastic Aptitude Test scores in a questionnaire. Descriptions and N's for these samples appear in table 7.4. This table also contains the median of the four correlation coefficients computed between selected PONS scores and the SAT scores, separately for males and females. The PONS scores used in this table (as well as in subsequent such tables) are RS-only, CF-only, body 60, and face 120 (the four factors derived from factor analysis of the full PONS test; see chapter 3), and total.

TABLE 7.4. Median Correlations between PONS and SAT, for Males and for Females, for Four Samples

	Verbal SAT		Math SAT	
Scale	Males	Females	Males	Females
RS 20	.32	.17	−.05	.06
CF 20	.08	−.01	.15	−.19
Body 60	.18	.15	.25	−.07
Face 120	.18	.12	.21	−.04
Total	.36	.20	.30	.02

NOTE: Each entry is the median of four correlation coefficients. The four samples were: (1) Billerica, Mass., public high school students (N = 17 males, 29 females); (2) Bridgewater State College students, Bridgewater, Mass. (N = 10 males, 18 females); (3) University of Rochester undergraduates, Rochester, N.Y. (N = 69 males, 35 females); and (4) Harvard University summer school students, Cambridge, Mass. (regularly attending many colleges and universities) (N = 43 males, 34 females).

The row labeled total shows that for males and females alike, Verbal SAT predicted PONS score to a moderate degree (but slightly more so for males). The median correlations for Math SAT and PONS total told a different story. The correlation of .30 for males suggested that in order for males to perform well, they tend to have to be high scorers on mathematical aptitude as well. However, for females there was virtually no relationship (median $r = .02$) between mathematical aptitude and PONS total. In other words, for females it tended to make almost no difference, as far as PONS total was concerned, whether one had high or low mathematical aptitude. The difference between males' and females' correlations for the total was significant at $p < .05$, two-tailed.

The top four rows of table 7.4 show correlations between SAT scores and the four relatively orthogonal factors of the PONS test. Each of these factors contains 20, 60, or 120 items, and hence reliability is lower than that of the total, which contains 220 items (see discussion of reliability in chapter 3). In general, the correlations for males and females are similar in magnitude for Verbal SAT, but with males showing consistently higher correlations; for Math SAT we see that the tendency for males to have higher correlations is even stronger.

One interpretation of this difference between males and females is that for females, nonverbal accuracy may be profited more by an intuitive or global strategy than by an analytic strategy, and that the reverse may be true for males. Males who have more analytic skill may profit particularly from the latter strategy. This interpretation is very speculative, of course, but it is not entirely original. In Allport (1924), female judges made their judgments about the meanings of facial expressions in half the time it took his male judges, and he invoked the females' "intuitive" approach as an explanation. Coie and Dorval (1973), in a study of "role-taking ability" in children in grades two through four, used a task in which the child, communicating via conversation only, had to arrange a set of objects on a board to match their arrangement on the confederate's board. For both boys and girls, correlations of accuracy of this task with two tests of verbal intelligence ranged from .21 to .50 ($p < .01$). For boys, correlations with two tests of analytic intelligence were .42 ($p < .01$) and .39 ($p < .01$), whereas for girls the correlations were .15 and .08. Coie and Dorval suggested that some factor other than analytic ability is critical to girls' performance on communication tasks. Though the cues in this task were probably not affective cues, nevertheless it is intriguing to find the same patterns of correlations as we obtained between receiving accuracy and tests of verbal and analytic ability.

High school rank and scores on two vocabulary tests were also correlated with the PONS, and no statistically significant differences occurred between the correlations for males and females.

For samples of 112 and 139 high school students, IQ test scores were correlated with PONS separately for males and females. With the exception of the PONS score body 60, the other factors and the total showed correlations of very similar magnitudes for males and females. The average correlations for males and females between IQ and body 60 were .04 and .24 ($p < .01$) (difference between r's significant at $p < .10$, two-tailed).

SEX DIFFERENCES IN THE RELATIONSHIP OF PONS TO FIELD DEPENDENCE-INDEPENDENCE. In three samples, subjects took the PONS along with Witkin's Group Embedded Figures Test (Witkin et al. 1971). As outlined more fully in chapter 10, scores on field dependence-independence describe the extent of a person's competence at perceptual disembedding and seem to predict aspects of psychological activity other than perceptual functioning (Witkin et al. 1971). One set of psychological variables that appear related to field dependence has to do with responses to socially relevant stimuli. Konstadt and Forman (1965) found that field dependent children under conditions of disapproval looked at other persons during testing significantly more frequently than did field independent children under similar conditions of disapproval. Messick and Damarin (1964), following Witkin's suggestion that field dependent persons are particularly attentive to facial expressions as a source of clues about the other's opinions of the self, found a correlation of $-.29$ ($p < .05$) between field independence and a test of accuracy at recalling human faces (the direction of the correlation indicating that high field depen-

TABLE 7.5. Median Correlations between PONS and Witkin's Group Embedded Figures Test (GEFT), for Males and for Females, for Three Samples

Scale	GEFT	
	Males	Females
RS 20	.16	.13
CF 20	−.09	.06
Body 60	.18	.15
Face 120	.03	.29
Total	.08	.28

NOTE: The three samples were: (1) Billerica, Mass., public high school students (N = 55 males, 59 females); (2) Harvard University summer school students, Cambridge, Mass. (regularly attending many colleges and universities) (N = 46 males, 34 females); and (3) University of Ottawa, Canada, students (N = 118 males, 170 females).

dence went with high recall accuracy). Wolitzky (1973), however, using the Embedded Figures Test and two tests of sensitivity to affective voice tone cues, found that more field independent subjects were more accurate at judging the nonverbal cues.

Table 7.5 shows the correlations between PONS and GEFT in our three samples, separately for each sex. In general, the median correlations were positive for both sexes, indicating that higher scores on the PONS were associated with more field independence. Hence, it would not seem that skill at decoding nonverbal cues is associated with the GEFT in the way that would be predicted from the data on attentiveness to nonverbal cues. Our finding is consistent with Wolitzky's result, suggesting that attentiveness to nonverbal cues and accuracy at decoding them should not be considered conceptually equivalent.

SEX DIFFERENCES IN THE RELATIONSHIP OF PONS TO SELF-REPORTED INTERPERSONAL SUCCESS. Chapter 11 has a full discussion of sixteen interpersonal success questionnaire items, five interpersonal success factors derived from them, and correlations between these factors and PONS scores for both sexes together. When similar relationships for the sexes separately were examined in four samples of high school and college students (total N = 479), the median correlations were all small and of very similar magnitudes for both sexes.

SEX DIFFERENCES IN THE RELATIONSHIP OF PONS TO SELF-REPORTED NONVERBAL SENSITIVITY. Chapter 11 describes in some detail our six-item questionnaire on self-reported nonverbal sensitivity and the correlations between it and PONS scores for the sexes pooled. In general, these questions produced very low correlations with PONS, which were interpreted to mean that people's own opinions about their nonverbal skill were not very accurate.

In this section we explore the accuracy of people's predictions separately for males and females. Three of the questions were general in nature: own warmth, own ability to understand other people, and own ability to understand social situations. These three items were correlated for males and females with PONS total in four samples (twenty-eight Australian clinical psychologists, twenty-eight U.S. college students, and forty-four and thirty-four U.S. married couples). The median of these three correlations for each sample was taken, and then the median of these medians across the four samples was taken, rendering correlations of −.16 for males and .02 for females.

The remaining three questions dealt with own ability to understand tone of voice, body movements, and facial expressions. These three items were correlated with tone 40, body 60, and face 60, respectively, for each sample. The median correlations across the four samples between these ratings and PONS skill were small and of nearly equal magnitudes for males and females.

Appendix 7A

SAMPLE SIZES AND DESCRIPTIONS OF SAMPLES USED IN SEX × AGE
LEVEL ANALYSIS OF VARIANCE

Elementary school students

unit 1 = 3rd graders in Evanston, Ill., public school (N = 43) (one classroom) (8.0
   years)
unit 2 = unweighted means of 2 4th grade classrooms in Niles, Ill., public school (N =
   17,7) (9.0 years, 9.6 years)
unit 3 = unweighted means of 3 5th grade classrooms in Niles, Ill., public school (N =
   19,23,30) (10.4 years, 10.7 years, 10.6 years)
unit 4 = unweighted means of 3 6th grade classrooms in Niles, Ill., public school (N =
   11,31,23) (11.5 years, 11.4 years, 11.6 years)

Junior high school students

unit 1 = junior high school students in Niles, Ill., public school (grades unknown) (N
   = 109) (13.0 years)
unit 2 = junior high school students in Fairbanks, Alaska, public school (grades
   unknown) (N = 127) (13.8 years)

High school students

unit 1 = 11th and 12th graders in Billerica, Mass., public school (N = 123) (16.6
   years)
unit 2 = 12th graders in Billerica, Mass., public school (N = 22) (16.8 years)
unit 3 = high school students in Burnsville, Minn., public school (mixed grades) (N =
   73) (15.5 years)
unit 4 = high school students in Burnsville, Minn., public school (mixed grades) (N =
   30) (17.1 years)
unit 5 = 10th graders in South San Francisco, Calif., public school (N = 55) (15.0
   years)
unit 6 = 11th graders in South San Francisco, Calif., public school (N = 58) (16.0
   years)
unit 7 = high school students in North Ryde, Australia (grades unknown) (N = 55)
   (16.3 years)
unit 8 = 10th graders in Harvard, Mass., public school (N = 40) (15.2 years)
unit 9 = high school students in Billerica, Mass., public school (grades unknown) (N
   = 52) (16.6 years)

Adults (unspecialized)

unit 1 = adults in Natick, Mass., couples club (mostly couples) (N = 30) (31.0 years)
unit 2 = adults in metropolitan Boston, Mass. (couples who had teenage children) (N
   = 16) (43.9 years)

unit 3 = adults in metropolitan Boston, Mass. (couples who had toddlers) (N = 16) (26.0 years)

unit 4 = adults in metropolitan Boston, Mass. (young couples without children) (N = 12) (25.3 years)

unit 5 = adults in Cambridge, Mass. (N = 13) (31.9 years)

unit 6 = adults in Cambridge, Mass. (N = 13) (28.5 years)

8 | Developmental Aspects

Recent discussions of "social competence" in children (Anderson and Messick 1974) and of "psychosocial maturity" (Greenberger and Sørenson 1974) point to the importance of a child's abilities to understand the meanings of nonverbal cues of emotion and to identify what kinds of emotion are typically elicited by various social or personal experiences. These writers do, of course, include many other criteria besides these in their discussions. In particular, it is obvious that the ability or willingness to act appropriately toward others as a result of accurate social judgment must be a critical ingredient in any conception of social competence or psychosocial maturity.

"Social sensitivity" and "empathy" in children, constructs that include the expression and recognition of emotions, have been the topic of considerable but by no means exhaustive research. Charlesworth and Kreutzer (1973) have provided a review of the facial expression and recognition literature on infants and children, and they offer the thesis that expression of emotion may be a more innate ability than is the recognition of emotion, which may require greater cognitive and perceptual development and more social experience than does expression. However, the methodological problems in using infants and young children as subjects make measurement of recognition harder than measurement of expression.

Recognition is difficult to measure unless the subject can label, identify, point out, or otherwise indicate his response to some stimulus; even if the task is designed so that the child's response can be nonverbal, the child must be able to understand verbal task instructions in most cases. And, even in the absence of all indications of differential responses to social or emotional stimuli, the child may still differentiate among affective stimuli in ways that are not apparent to an observer. Despite this unresolved problem, evidence does suggest that recognition requires more social experience and cognitive development than does expression, but we need more research on both.

Relatively few studies have examined a child's ability to recognize purely nonverbal stimuli, compared to the number that have examined "social sensitivity" or "empathy" as a more global ability to understand and describe whole social/interpersonal contexts—a skill that must include the ability not only to understand the meanings of nonverbal cues, but also to infer how people ought to feel on the basis of situational details, description of events, and a general understanding of interpersonal relations. Studies on social sensitivity and empathy in children have employed a wide range of stimuli, including isolated nonverbal cues (such as photos of faces or electronically filtered speech), dramatized recorded episodes involving mixed verbal-nonverbal cues, drawings or photos involving a person's expressions plus contextual cues (such as other persons' expressions or situational details), and purely contextual cues (such as a narrated story whose central character's affect must be inferred only from events in the story).

The most common form of task involves presenting the child with such a stimulus, asking him or her to describe the feelings of the stimulus person(s), and scoring the child's open-ended, spontaneous response for accuracy of inferring the emotions or the psychological states of the stimulus person(s). Among studies using this paradigm with strictly nonverbal cues are Gates (1923, 1925, 1927), Kellogg and Eagleson (1931), Walton (1936), Staffieri and Bassett (1970), and Izard (1971).

Because eliciting a verbal response makes the adequacy of the response so contingent on verbal ability, some studies have involved explicit attempts to enable the child to respond nonverbally. Dashiell (1927) and Izard (1971) both report comparisons of this approach with the verbal labeling approach, and both report that younger children performed more accurately using nonverbal responses than using verbal responses.

In this type of study, the standard procedure is to show the child several facial expressions (photos or drawings of stick figures) that the child may or may not have been trained to recognize; to present the stimulus, which may be facial expressions, voice tone samples, or a narrated story; and then to ask the child to point to the face or stick figure that matches the affect seen or heard in the test stimulus, or the affect that should be aroused in the primary character in the narrated story. Hence, it is a multiple choice task in addition to being nonverbal. This method is not without verbal ability requirements; however, the requirements are for comprehension, not production. Among studies using purely nonverbal stimuli in this way are Dimitrovsky (1964), Gitter, Mostofsky, and Quincy (1971), and McCluskey et al. (1975). Among studies using narrated stories or affect words as stimuli are Honkavaara (1961), Ekman and Friesen (1971), and Borke (1971, 1973).

Other methods of measuring "social sensitivity" or "empathy" have been employed that are less obviously related to the construct of nonverbal sensitivity that is of primary interest in this book. These include vicarious experiencing (Feshbach and Roe 1968), matching expressions to a standard (Odom and

Lemond 1972), and affective role-taking ability (Feffer and Gourevitch 1960).

With respect to the relationship of age to social sensitivity, several authors (Dymond, Hughes, and Raabe 1952; Honkavaara 1961; Gilbert 1969; Savitsky and Izard 1970) observed that younger children appeared to attend more to external details in the stimulus materials (such as colors, clothing, and accessories) than to details of expression, and that older children appeared to use expression cues more in discriminating, matching, or identifying the affective content of the stimulus materials.

Of the more than thirty studies that included cross-sectional age comparison of children's ability to empathize, role-take, or make socially sensitive judgments, the vast majority reported age effects on at least one dependent measure, and such effects were predominantly linear. Among studies using nonverbal stimuli, age effects were found in Gates (1923, 1925), Kellogg and Eagleson (1931), Walton (1936), Dimitrovsky (1964), and Izard (1971).

Though the effect of age is beyond dispute, the question of the age at which children are able to begin making accurate judgments of others' feelings remains open, since in any study the child's ability to perform is so dependent on the difficulty of the perceptual task and the response mode. Some authors (e.g., Borke 1971, 1972) are convinced that a child as young as three years old can make affective judgments that are not the result of mere projection of his or her own feelings onto another. However, we have little understanding of the cognitive or affective mechanisms employed in making judgments about others' feelings; the importance of projection and stereotypy, especially in younger children, has been speculated on (Chandler and Greenspan 1972), but in fact little is known about the relative importance of projection, stereotypy, or vicarious experiencing, or about "figure-ground" relations in making such judgments.

Several factors undoubtedly contribute to the increase of these skills over time, among them increasing perceptual skill (e.g., audiovisual integration; Birch and Belmont 1965), increasing test-taking ability (practice with tests, verbal ability), and increasing experience interacting in a social environment (practice at reading nonverbal cues in everyday life, acquisition of the correct labels for emotional states). The present research using the PONS test and PONS-like instruments has not been an attempt to produce a definitive answer to the relative importance of different kinds of developmental skills; rather, it assumes that the factors named above, at least, all contribute to the observed increase in nonverbal judging ability with advancing age.

What the present research attempts is the establishment of PONS norms for different age levels—childhood through adulthood—on channels and types of affect, using cross-sectional analyses; the examination of the relationship of age to accuracy at judging channels and types of affect; and effects of learning disability in children. Correlations of intellectual achievement with PONS ability in children are discussed in chapter 10; the relationship of sociometric ratings to PONS ability in children is discussed in chapter 11; sex effects among children are discussed in chapter 7; and effects of deafness and blindness in children are examined in chapter 12.

PONS INSTRUMENTS FOR CHILDREN

FULL PONS FOR CHILDREN. Children in the third through sixth grades in two midwestern elementary schools were administered the entire 220-item PONS test, with the following alterations in administrative procedure. In some classrooms, school teachers administering the test allowed an interitem interval of longer than the usual five seconds, and in some instances they administered the test in two separate testing sessions of about one half hour each.

Children used an answer sheet that had ¼" type and twenty scene descriptions designed to describe the same affects as on the adult form, but using vocabulary and social contexts that would be sensible to young children.[1] For example, "criticizing someone for being late" was changed to "Judy is mad at her friend for being late" in the interests of simple vocabulary. "Trying to seduce someone" was changed to "Judy wants a kiss from her boyfriend" in the interests of creating a relevant context for children; for similar reasons, "talking about the death of a friend" was changed to "Judy's best friend just moved away." Table 8.1 presents all of the children's scene labels and the corresponding adult labels. The appropriateness of the choice of children's labels was informally validated by asking six raters to match each children's label with its corresponding adult label. Four raters were able to do this without error; two raters made one matching error each, and the confusing labels were then reworded to prevent subsequent confusion.

Table 8.2 presents the means and standard deviations (in terms of item accuracy), as well as percentage accuracies, for these four grades (sexes pooled) and table 8.3 presents similar data for emotional quadrants. As the means show, even the youngest children performed at a better than chance level. These means may be compared with the norm group means presented in chapter 3.

---

1. Honkavaara (1961) reported that in her studies of children's recognition of emotions, children could identify affective scenes matter-of-factly (that is, they could interpret affects in descriptive, situational terms) earlier than they could identify the emotional labels that accompanied the affective actions or situations. It follows that children's accuracy should be maximized when the response alternatives consist of concrete situational or descriptive labels rather than the more abstract emotional labels.

TABLE 8.1. Scene Names Used in Children's PONS Answer Sheets and Corresponding Scene Names Used in Adults' PONS Answer Sheets

Child	Adult
1. Judy is mad because another girl took her boyfriend.	1. expressing jealous anger
2. Judy is helping a lost child.	2. talking to a lost child
3. Judy likes the pretty flowers.	3. admiring nature
4. Judy's best friend just moved away.	4. talking about the death of a friend
5. Judy is leaving on a trip. She is saying "Good-bye."	5. leaving on a trip
6. Judy is saying her prayers.	6. saying a prayer
7. Judy is mad at her friend for being late.	7. criticizing someone for being late
8. Judy is saying "Thank you."	8. expressing gratitude
9. Judy works in a store.	9. helping a customer
10. Judy is going to her birthday party tonight.	10. talking about one's wedding
11. Judy has just broken up with her boyfriend.	11. talking about one's divorce
12. Judy wants a kiss from her boyfriend.	12. trying to seduce someone
13. Judy loves her baby sister.	13. expressing motherly love
14. Judy loves her boyfriend.	14. expressing deep affection
15. Judy is telling her little brother to pick up his toys.	15. nagging a child
16. Judy is sorry for what she did.	16. asking forgiveness
17. A man broke Judy's clock. She wants him to fix it.	17. returning faulty item to a store
18. Judy says, "Watch out or I will make you sorry."	18. threatening someone
19. Judy hates someone.	19. expressing strong dislike
20. Judy is asking the waiter for food.	20. ordering food in a restaurant

Analysis of variance on the means for channels and quadrants rendered F-tests for main effects and interactions that were almost all highly significant because of the very small error terms that resulted from the five-way repeated-measures design (these five factors being audio, body, face, dominance, and positivity). The direction of effects was very similar to the pattern obtained for the high school norm group.

The KR-20 coefficient of internal consistency (reliability) (Guilford 1954) for the 220-item test, pooling across grades, was .86. For the four grades separately, these reliabilities were .54 for third grade, .96 for fourth grade, .80 for fifth grade, and .89 for sixth grade.

An additional sample of children was tested by Robert Clark in New York City, who computed internal consistency coefficients separately for three age groups. The *alpha* coefficients were .91 for twenty eight-to-nine year olds, .95 for twenty ten-to-eleven year olds, and .91 for twenty twelve-to-thirteen year olds.

FACE AND BODY PONS FOR CHILDREN. Two hundred and seventy-five fourth and fifth graders from six midwestern schools (none of the same chil-

TABLE 8.2. Accuracy on Channels of Full PONS, for Four Grades (N=200)

Audio Channel	Grade	None Mean	None SD[a]	Face Mean	Face SD	Body Mean	Body SD	Figure Mean	Figure SD	Marginals Mean	Marginals SD
						Video Channel					
None	3[b]	10 (50%)[c]	0	12.36 (61.8%)	2.30	11.70 (58.5%)	2.28	11.56 (57.8%)	2.18	35.62 (59.4%)	4.46
	4[d]	10 (50)	0	14.79 (74.0)	2.35	13.52 (67.6)	2.66	13.54 (67.6)	2.64	41.85 (69.8)	6.03
	5[e]	10 (50)	0	14.57 (72.9)	2.05	13.88 (69.4)	2.16	13.27 (66.4)	2.45	41.72 (69.5)	5.21
	6[f]	10 (50)	0	14.52 (72.6)	2.20	13.99 (70.0)	2.32	14.11 (70.6)	2.40	42.62 (71.0)	5.51
	Mean	10 (50)	0	14.10 (70.5)	2.36	13.40 (67.0)	2.45	13.20 (66.0)	2.56	40.70 (67.8)	5.88
Randomized spliced	3	10.54 (52.7)	2.13	12.98 (64.9)	2.38	12.37 (61.8)	2.29	13.88 (69.4)	2.01	49.77 (62.2)	5.96
	4	11.11 (55.5)	2.06	14.65 (73.3)	2.67	14.04 (70.2)	2.23	15.06 (75.3)	2.48	54.85 (68.6)	6.41
	5	10.68 (53.4)	2.18	15.07 (75.4)	2.48	12.99 (65.0)	2.61	15.08 (75.4)	2.49	53.82 (67.3)	7.06
	6	11.20 (56.0)	2.33	15.56 (77.8)	2.43	13.69 (68.4)	2.56	15.98 (79.9)	1.98	56.44 (70.6)	6.90
	Mean	10.86 (54.3)	2.20	14.72 (73.6)	2.63	13.20 (66.0)	2.53	15.10 (75.5)	2.35	53.88 (67.3)	7.08
Content-filtered	3	10.63 (53.2)	2.42	12.92 (64.6)	2.48	11.26 (56.3)	1.99	12.69 (63.4)	2.31	47.49 (59.4)	5.43
	4	11.19 (56.0)	1.80	15.00 (75.0)	1.53	11.29 (56.4)	1.92	15.33 (76.6)	2.23	52.81 (66.0)	5.03
	5	10.99 (55.0)	1.68	14.82 (74.1)	2.14	11.84 (59.2)	2.50	15.12 (75.6)	2.57	52.78 (66.0)	6.05
	6	11.95 (59.8)	1.98	15.38 (76.9)	2.05	11.96 (59.8)	2.28	15.73 (78.6)	2.68	55.02 (68.8)	6.25
	Mean	11.24 (56.2)	2.01	14.61 (73.0)	2.30	11.68 (58.4)	2.26	14.81 (74.0)	2.74	52.34 (65.4)	6.44
Marginals	3	21.16 (52.9)	3.47	38.26 (63.8)	5.49	35.33 (58.9)	4.83	38.13 (63.6)	4.71	132.87 (60.4)	13.46
	4	22.29 (55.7)	2.83	44.44 (74.1)	5.28	38.85 (64.8)	5.54	43.94 (73.2)	5.60	149.52 (68.0)	15.34
	5	21.67 (54.2)	2.95	44.46 (74.1)	5.40	38.70 (64.5)	5.46	43.47 (72.4)	6.36	148.31 (67.4)	16.55
	6	23.15 (57.9)	3.14	45.45 (75.8)	5.77	39.64 (66.1)	5.41	45.82 (77.4)	5.84	154.07 (70.0)	17.10
	Mean	22.10 (55.2)	3.19	43.43 (72.4)	6.13	38.29 (63.8)	5.52	43.11 (71.8)	6.39	146.92 (66.8)	17.65

NOTE: In a sample of 48 fourth graders, 57 fifth graders, and 69 sixth graders in New York City, the overall accuracies were 63.7%, 68.0%, and 67.1%, respectively. For males and females in these three grades, the accuracies were: 4th grade, 61.9% and 65.9%; 5th grade, 66.2% and 69.9%; 6th grade, 64.8% and 68.8%.

[a] standard deviation based on item accuracy
[b] N=43
[c] theoretical accuracy
[d] N=24
[e] N=71
[f] N=62

TABLE 8.3. Accuracy on Affect Quadrants of Full PONS, for Four Grades ($N=200$)

	Grade	Negative		Positive	
		Mean	SD[a]	Mean	SD
Submissive	3[b]	33.29 (60.5%)	4.46	31.21 (56.7%)	4.17
	4[c]	36.10 (65.6)	5.77	36.17 (65.8)	3.20
	5[d]	36.64 (66.6)	5.12	35.96 (65.4)	4.77
	6[e]	37.40 (68.0)	5.18	37.53 (68.2)	5.09
	Mean	35.86 (65.2)	5.28	35.21 (64.0)	5.12
Dominant	3	38.83 (70.6)	6.53	29.55 (53.7)	3.69
	4	42.71 (77.6)	5.84	34.54 (62.8)	4.20
	5	41.72 (75.8)	5.43	33.98 (61.8)	4.52
	6	43.43 (79.0)	5.92	35.72 (64.9)	4.28
	Mean	41.67 (75.8)	6.07	33.45 (60.8)	4.77

[a] standard deviation based on item accuracy
[b] $N=43$
[c] $N=24$
[d] $N=71$
[e] $N=62$

dren who took the full PONS test) took a test consisting of the 20 face-only and the 20 body-only items from the full PONS test (the face and body PONS; see chapter 6). Answer sheets were constructed by selecting the 40 corresponding items from the 220-item children's answer sheet.

Table 8.4 shows the means and standard deviations for children's performance on this short test, and the data in this table can be compared to the face-only and body-only data in table 8.2. This comparison reveals that body-only scores were comparable, but face-only scores were considerably lower for the children taking the short video test. A possible reason is that children taking the full PONS test profited on face-only items from the experience of viewing face + audio items; hearing tone of voice while seeing face probably increases learning (especially with the possibility of lip-reading) more than hearing tone of voice while seeing body.

The KR-20 reliability for the 40-item video-only test was only .11 (much lower than the reliability of these two channels for the high school norm group). When this reliability coefficient was transformed using the Spearman-Brown prophecy formula (Rosenthal 1973) to give an estimate of equivalent reliability for the test if it were the full 220-item length, the reliability was .40.

CHILD SENDER AUDIO PONS FOR CHILDREN. A forty-item test identical in format to the male audio test and to the forty-item audio test extracted from the full PONS was made, whose sender was an eight-year-old Caucasian female (the niece of the original PONS sender). She was well acquainted with

TABLE 8.4. Accuracy for Forty-Item Face and Body PONS, for Grades Four and Five
Pooled, Sexes Pooled and Separately (N=275)

	Video Channel					
	Face		Body		Total	
Subjects	Mean	SD[a]	Mean	SD	Mean	SD
All	13.03 (65.2%)	1.78	13.89 (69.4%)	1.80	26.92 (67.3%)	2.64
Males[b]	13.03 (65.2)	1.89	13.86 (69.3)	1.89	26.88 (67.2)	2.71
Females[c]	13.04 (65.2)	1.65	13.92 (69.6)	1.70	26.96 (67.4)	2.58

NOTE: Among 51 children in grades 2–8 (mostly grades 4–5), the accuracy scores on the two
channels of this test were 67.0% for face and 69.25% for body.
[a]standard deviation based on item accuracy
[b]N=147
[c]N=128

the original sender, but had never seen nor heard any portions of the PONS
test. The recordings of her portrayals were made at her own home. She was
asked to enact situations similar to the children's scene labels. As in the case
of the original PONS sending, no prepared script was used. Her mother, the
original PONS sender, and an additional judge previously unacquainted with
the child were present to judge the authenticity of the portrayals, and these
judges chose the renditions that were acceptably plausible renditions of the
requested affect situations.

The 275 children who took the video-only test also took this test, using
large-print answer sheets. Table 8.5 presents means and standard deviations
for this test; these data can be compared to the audio data in table 8.2, though
it should be remembered that the scores represent accuracies for different
senders. Such comparison shows that scores on the two tests for CF are
comparable, but scores on RS are considerably higher in the case of the child
sender. This is also the case with adult samples taking the child-sender test
(See chapter 6). The KR-20 reliability for the child sender audio test was
only .18, but transformed using the Spearman-Brown prophecy formula to
estimate equivalent reliability at the 220-item length, it was .55 (not a great
deal lower than the reliability of these two channels for the high school norm
group when they heard the original PONS sender).

ANALYSES OF FACE AND BODY PONS AND CHILD SENDER AUDIO PONS.
The KR-20 reliability for the two short tests together was .16 for the 80 items,
and the Spearman-Brown correction to 220-item length brought this coefficient up to .36. In addition, Armor's θ (1974) (coefficient of internal consistency using a factor analysis approach) for the 80-item test was .66.

Intercorrelations of the scores of the 275 children who took both of these
short tests revealed that the face and body channels were only minimally

correlated ($r = .09$), as were RS and CF ($r = .08$). Of special interest is the fact that RS and CF showed different relationships to visual scores. The correlations of RS with face, body, and video total were .16 ($p < .01$), .13 ($p < .05$), and .19 ($p < .01$), whereas the correlations of CF with the same three scores were $-.10$, $-.10$, and $-.14$ ($p < .05$). High scores on RS, therefore, were positively related to video scores, but high scores on CF were negatively related to video scores. It is interesting that being relatively good at CF, the harder of the two audio channels, should predict video scores negatively. We will speculate later in this chapter that knowing a lot about auditory nonverbal cues may make one distrustful of the apparent meanings of visual nonverbal cues, because people who can interpret the difficult nonverbal audio cues may realize, as a result, that it is easier to "fake" visual cues than audio cues. The correlations reported here suggest that RS and CF perhaps do not tap identical knowledge of audio nonverbal cues; and the factor analysis of the eleven PONS channels reported in chapter 3 showed that RS and CF emerged as orthogonal factors (at least for the full PONS).

Analysis of variance was performed on the scores of the 275 children who were administered both of these tests. Between-subjects factors were sex (see chapter 7) and grade (to be discussed later in this chapter); within-subjects (repeated-measures) factors were modality (audio/video), relative difficulty of channels (easier = face, RS/harder = body, CF), dominance (submissive/dominant), and positivity (negative/positive). Effects involving modality could not be interpreted, since differences in the apparent difficulty of audio versus video were confounded with the fact that audio and video were portrayed by different senders (child sender versus original PONS sender). A strong main effect of easiness ($F(1,270) = 48.87$, $p < .001$; $r = .39$; effect size = $.85\,\sigma$) showed that the two channels labeled as easy (face and RS) were in fact easier than the two channels labeled as hard (body and CF). A strong main effect for positivity ($F(1,270) = 116.50$, $p < .001$; $r = .55$; effect size

TABLE 8.5. Accuracy for Forty-Item Child Sender Audio PONS, for Grades Four and Five Pooled, Sexes Pooled and Separately (N=275)

| Subjects | Audio Channel | | | | | |
| | Randomized Spliced | | Content-Filtered | | Total | |
	Mean	SD[a]	Mean	SD	Mean	SD
All	13.66 (68.3%)	2.12	11.30 (56.5%)	2.04	24.96 (62.4%)	3.05
Males[b]	13.34 (66.7)	2.20	11.18 (55.9)	1.83	24.52 (61.3)	3.08
Females[c]	14.02 (70.1)	1.97	11.44 (57.2)	2.25	25.47 (63.7)	2.94

[a] standard deviation based on item accuracy
[b] N=147
[c] N=128

= 1.32 σ) showed that negative scenes were judged more accurately than positive scenes (parallels Dimitrovsky 1964 and PONS norm group performance).

In addition, a strong main effect of dominance ($F(1,270)$ = 195.60, p < .001; r = .65; effect size = 1.70 σ) showed that submissive affect was judged more accurately than dominant affect in both audio and video. The direction of this effect was the reverse of the predicted direction: for the full PONS, dominant affect was judged more accurately than submissive affect by all four grades tested (three through six); this was true for the test as a whole and also for the two analogous modes (face-only + body-only and RS-only + CF-only). Inspection of the means of the short tests for submissive and dominant, for the two modalities, revealed that for video, submissive affect was judged 1.6 percentage points more accurately than dominant affect (68.2 percent versus 66.6 percent), whereas for audio, submissive affect was judged 14.3 percentage points more accurately than dominant affect (69.7 percent versus 55.4 percent) (F for interaction of modality and dominance = 127.66, df = 1,270, p < .001; r = .57; effect size = 1.39 σ). It appears that our child sender was a better sender of submissive affect than our original PONS sender (or, conversely, a worse sender of dominant cues). This also raises the possibility that children in general send dominant affect relatively poorly and submissive affect relatively well compared with adults. Such a hypothesis is congruent with common sense, since we would predict that young children are required to behave submissively far more often than they are required to behave dominantly. However, with data generated by only one child sender and one adult sender, we offer this hypothesis with understandable caution.

Two additional, independent, samples of subjects took both of these forty-item tests (forty-two grade school children and thirty adults). For these two groups pooled, submissive affect was again judged significantly more accurately than dominant affect ($F(1,68)$ = 9.51, p = .003; r = .35; effect size = .75 σ); and inspection of the means revealed that submissive affect was judged more accurately than dominant affect for each sample taken separately as well, and the age × dominance interaction was not significant. Submissive affect was judged more accurately than dominant affect for both children and adults on the audio test; but on the video test, submissive affect was judged more accurately than dominant affect by the children but dominant affect was judged more accurately than submissive affect by adults (the pattern we would expect for judgments of the original PONS sender) (age × modality × dominance interaction, $F(1,68)$ = 4.30, p = .042; r = .24; effect size = .49 σ). This finding not only supports the earlier hypothesis that our child sender may be better at sending submissive cues than our adult sender, but it also suggests that children are more attuned to reading submissive affect in adult senders than are adults, and, conversely, adults are more attuned to reading dominant affect in other adults than are children. This could be because children are used to behaving submissively and therefore recognize submissive affect, or

TABLE 8.6. Accuracy on Channels of Full PONS, for Junior High School Norm Group, Sexes Pooled and Separately (N=109)

| Audio Channel | Subjects | Video Channel | | | | | | | | | |
| | | None | | Face | | Body | | Figure | | Marginals | |
		Mean	SD[a]	Mean	SD	Mean	SD	Mean	SD	Mean	SD
None	All	10 (50%)[b]	0	16.26 (81.3%)	1.81	15.06 (75.3%)	1.88	15.09 (75.4%)	2.24	46.26 (77.1%)	4.24
	Males[c]	10 (50)	0	16.06 (80.3)	1.99	14.66 (73.3)	1.91	14.90 (74.5)	2.35	45.51 (75.8)	4.44
	Females[d]	10 (50)	0	16.48 (82.4)	1.59	15.49 (77.4)	1.76	15.29 (76.4)	2.13	47.08 (78.5)	3.88
Randomized spliced	All	12.58 (62.9)	1.93	16.94 (84.7)	2.24	14.53 (72.6)	2.15	16.75 (83.8)	1.60	60.73 (75.9)	5.42
	Males	12.31 (61.6)	1.84	16.46 (82.3)	2.43	14.62 (73.1)	2.27	16.63 (83.2)	1.67	59.96 (75.0)	5.44
	Females	12.88 (64.4)	2.01	17.47 (87.4)	1.88	14.42 (72.1)	2.03	16.88 (84.4)	1.52	61.58 (77.0)	5.33
Content-filtered	All	10.99 (55.0)	2.09	16.00 (80.0)	1.67	13.34 (66.7)	1.95	16.94 (84.7)	2.11	57.15 (71.4)	4.75
	Males	10.61 (53.0)	2.10	15.80 (79.0)	1.88	12.99 (65.0)	2.04	16.65 (83.2)	2.06	55.91 (69.9)	4.84
	Females	11.39 (57.0)	2.02	16.21 (81.0)	1.39	13.73 (68.6)	1.78	17.25 (86.2)	2.13	58.50 (73.1)	4.30
Marginals	All	23.52 (58.8)	2.92	49.10 (81.8)	4.39	42.82 (71.4)	4.24	48.70 (81.2)	4.85	164.47 (74.8)	12.25
	Males	22.88 (57.2)	2.89	48.21 (80.4)	4.97	42.19 (70.3)	4.36	48.10 (80.2)	4.76	161.69 (73.5)	12.11
	Females	24.23 (60.6)	2.80	50.08 (83.5)	3.44	43.50 (72.5)	4.04	49.35 (82.2)	4.91	167.51 (76.1)	11.78

[a] standard deviation based on item accuracy
[b] theoretical accuracy
[c] N=57
[d] N=52

because the affects sent from adult to child in daily life may actually be more submissive in tone than affects sent from adult to adult, and therefore children might be more on the lookout for those kinds of cues on the part of an adult.

JUNIOR HIGH SCHOOL FULL PONS TESTING. Three large samples and two small samples of junior high school students have been tested with the adult form of the full PONS test. These samples were 129 females from Marblehead, Mass. (mean age 14.2 years); 127 Alaskan Caucasian males and females (mean age 13.8 years); 18 Alaskan Indian males and females (mean age 14.5 years); 23 Alaskan Eskimo males and females (mean age 14.6 years); and 109 males and females from Niles, Illinois (mean age 13.0 years). The normative data presented for junior high level will be those from the Niles, Illinois, testing (N = 109). The decision to use only this sample was based on the atypical cultural and ethnic composition of the Alaskan samples and the all-female composition of the Massachusetts sample. In all apparent ways, the Illinois sample was the most "ordinary" junior high school sample tested.

Table 8.6 shows the means and standard deviations for the eleven channels, seven marginals, and the total, for the sexes both pooled and separately. Table 8.7 shows the means and standard deviations for affect quadrants.

HIGH SCHOOL FULL PONS TESTING. Sixteen samples of tenth, eleventh, and twelfth graders have been tested in the United States, Australia, and New Guinea. The high school norm group, consisting of three samples of American students (one eastern, one midwestern, and one western public high school; N = 492), is described fully in chapter 3.

TABLE 8.7. Accuracy on Affect Quadrants of Full PONS, for Junior High School Norm Group, Sexes Pooled and Separately (N=109)

	Subjects	Negative		Positive	
		Mean	SD[a]	Mean	SD
Submissive	All	40.76 (74.1%)	4.58	39.53 (71.9%)	3.49
	Males[b]	40.02 (72.8)	5.02	39.37 (71.6)	3.23
	Females[c]	41.58 (75.6)	3.93	39.71 (72.2)	3.77
Dominant	All	45.65 (83.0)	4.13	38.53 (70.0)	4.32
	Males	45.17 (82.1)	4.49	37.14 (67.5)	3.99
	Females	46.17 (83.9)	3.66	40.05 (72.8)	4.19

[a]standard deviation based on item accuracy
[b]N=57
[c]N=52

MAIN EFFECTS OF AGE

Several analyses were performed to assess the effect of age on PONS performance, not only for the younger age groups but also for the entire span of ages tested in the course of PONS research (third grade through early middle age).

In an analysis involving just the third through sixth graders who took the full PONS test ($N = 200$), the main effect for grade was highly significant ($F(3,196) = 13.87$, $p < .001$; $\eta = .42$). A linear trend tested on the total scores of these four grades was highly significant ($F(1,196) = 38.0$, $p < .001$; $r = .40$; effect size $= .87\sigma$), showing that PONS scores improved significantly linearly from third to sixth grade.

Another analysis of variance (described in chapter 7) involved these four grades, plus junior high school students, high school students. and adults (unspecialized), with samples rather than subjects as the units of analysis. Age was a highly significant main effect ($F(3,17) = 20.03$, $p < .001$; $\eta = .88$), and a linear trend tested on the total scores showed that the improvement on PONS performance with advancing age was highly significant ($F(1,17) = 54.88$, $p < .001$; $r = .87$; effect size $= 3.59\sigma$). Figure 8.1 shows the eleven-channel profiles and totals for these four groups.

A final and exhaustive analysis was performed using all full PONS samples tested as of this writing for which the sample's mean age could be computed (but excluding psychiatric and alcoholic samples). For 124 such samples, the correlation between mean PONS total score and mean age (rounded to the nearest whole year) was .34 ($df = 122$, $p < .001$). When non-native-English-speaking samples were removed, this correlation was .40 ($df = 103$, $p < .001$); and when all non-continental-U.S. samples were removed, this correlation was .47 ($df = 64$, $p < .001$). These correlations show that performance improved linearly with age. Similarly, Walton (1936), using a facial affect decoding task with 461 children ranging in age from six to sixteen, found a correlation of .42 between age and decoding accuracy.

Figure 8.2 shows the mean percentage accuracy at five age levels. As this figure shows, the clearest linear relationship was in the 8–25 age group. In older samples, PONS performance leveled off. Analysis of variance of the accuracy rates of figure 8.2 showed very significant and very large linear ($F(1,119) = 37.08$, $\eta = .49$) and quadratic ($F(1,119) = 33.40$, $\eta = .47$) trends that together accounted for 91 percent of the between age levels variance.

Finally, the correlations between age and PONS performance were examined on a within-samples basis, in all forty-three samples in which such correlations were computed. The median correlation was $-.02$. That this median coefficient was close to zero attests to the limited age range in most of the samples. In a more recent sample of adults with a larger age range, Myron

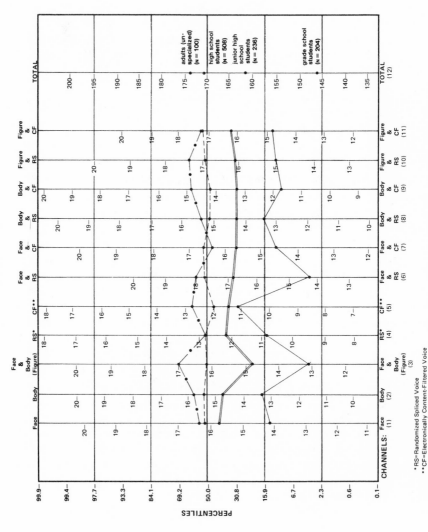

PROFILE OF NONVERBAL SENSITIVITY: STANDARD SCORING SHEET
Channel Scores and Total

FIGURE 8.1. Eleven-channel profiles and totals for four age levels, sexes pooled

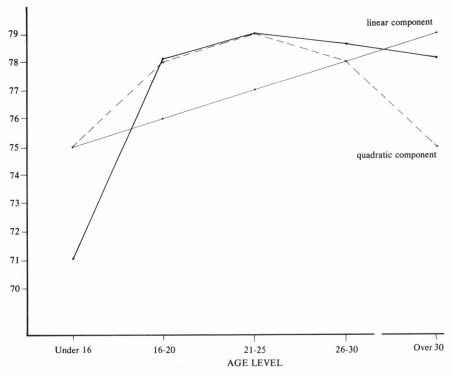

FIGURE 8.2. Mean accuracy at five age levels

Wish found older adults to perform less well than younger adults ($r(152) = -.36$, $p < .0001$), a result consistent with our finding of an overall quadratic trend.

INTERACTIONS OF AGE AND OTHER FACTORS

AGE-CHANNEL INTERACTIONS. In an analysis of variance, grade (third through sixth) and sex were between-subjects factors, and audio (none/RS/CF), face (absent/present), body (absent/present), dominance (submissive/dominant), and positivity (negative/positive) were within-subjects (repeated-measures) factors. Grade interacted significantly with face ($F(3,196) = 11.36$, $p < .001$; $\eta = .38$), but not with audio or body ($F = 1.09$ and $1.24, p > .30$), which showed that different ages of children did not manifest significantly different degrees of audio or body skill. Inspection of the residuals of the significant grade × face interaction revealed that the youngest children (third graders), compared to the fourth through sixth graders, profited significantly too little from facial cues and showed a relatively greater degree of accuracy on items involving no face.

In the "age levels" analysis of variance referred to earlier in this chapter, involving these same grade school children plus junior high school, high school, and adults (unspecialized), the age $\times$ audio interaction was again small ($F(6,34) = 1.25$, $p < .31$). The age $\times$ face interaction was considerably larger ($F(3,17) = 4.17$, $p < .03$; $\eta = .65$). This time, the age $\times$ body interaction was substantial as well ($F(3,17) = 8.39$, $p = .002$; $\eta = .77$). The residuals revealed that the younger two groups (grade school and junior high school) performed at a relative disadvantage when face or body cues were present and that the two older age groups (high school and adults) performed at a relative advantage when face or body cues were present. In each interaction, the largest such effects occurred at the grade school level.

Summarizing, we found that the effect of age on the ability to make use of audio cues seems to be considerably smaller than the effect of age on the ability to make use of visual cues.

In both the grade school and age levels analyses, the age $\times$ face $\times$ body interactions were notable (for grade school analysis, $F(3,192) = 2.36$, $p = .074$; $\eta = .19$; for age levels analysis, $F(3,17) = 5.91$, $p = .006$; $\eta = .71$). In both cases, the residuals indicated that the youngest age level—third grade in the first case, grade school in the second case—differed from the older three age levels. The youngest age level was "too good," relatively speaking, when either no face and no body were present or when both face and body were present, and "too poor" when either face or body was present without the other. In both analyses, the age $\times$ audio $\times$ face and age $\times$ audio $\times$ body interactions were either significant or marginally significant. However, no meaningful interpretation of these effects has been made.

We might propose that younger children's apparent relative disadvantage at reading facial cues from an adult might be related to their small stature; very young children (infants, toddlers) would ordinarily be crouched down to or picked up by an adult, and older children (high school) would presumably be tall enough to communicate with adults on a face-to-face basis, as would adults. Children between these ages (5–13, let us say) might find themselves always towered over by adults who are, quite literally, talking down to them. This could possibly account for the age $\times$ face effects found in both the grade school analysis and the age levels analysis, but which was considerably stronger in the grade school analysis.

Taking together the age $\times$ face interaction, the age $\times$ body interaction, and the age $\times$ face $\times$ body interaction apparent in the age levels analysis, we should attempt to provide a more comprehensive hypothesis to account for these effects, since small stature probably does not result in a lack of access to adult bodies, as it might to adult faces.

An interesting hypothesis draws on some work by Bugental and her colleagues that suggests that children derive qualitatively different kinds of information from adult-sent nonverbal cues than do adults. Bugental et al. (1970) found that, in general, for young children visual channels of communication had less evaluative impact than either verbal (script) or tone of voice (content-filtered speech). Their more specific finding was that youngest children (ages 5–8) discounted women's (but not men's) smiles—that is, they perceived them as less positive than did older children (13 and up). Bugental, Kaswan, and Love (1970) also found that children responded more negatively than adults did to cue combinations sent by female senders (but not male senders) that involved positive visual cues and negative tone-of-voice cues. In other words, children discounted the cue content of the female face and placed relatively more weight on the auditory channel. Finally, Bugental, Love, and Gianetto (1971) found that for mothers communicating with their children, the mothers' smiles did not reflect the affective content of their speech message, whereas for fathers communicating with their children, the fathers' smiles indicated that they were making friendly or approving comments. The first two studies suggested that children tend to tune out visual, particularly facial, information sent by adult women, and the third study suggested one reason why this might be the case: female faces may not be accurate reflectors of female emotions.

We might, therefore, expect that the performance of younger children might show relative decrement for visual information compared with auditory information, if in fact children "trust" the veridicality of audio nonverbal information more than visual nonverbal information. This interpretation takes on added credibility when we remember that subjects taking the PONS test must respond to adult female cues only. (We might, on the basis of Bugental's studies, speculate that children's PONS performance would show a different pattern of effects for a male sender.)

Figure 8.3 displays the unweighted mean percentage accuracy scores for pure audio and pure video (means of two and three channels, respectively) for the four grade school groups, the junior high school norm group, the high school norm group, and eighteen college groups tested in the United States, as well as single mode performance for samples of blind and deaf subjects. This figure demonstrates that as age advances, the groups' accuracy on pure video channels increases at a faster rate than does their accuracy on pure audio channels (ρ computed between age level and video − audio = .86, p = .02), which indicates that younger children are *relatively* more sensitive to audio cues than older subjects.

In Bugental et al. (1970), children thirteen and up saw women's smiles as more positive than did children aged five to eight; in other words, the older children seemed to be accepting the meanings that the senders *wanted* them to receive. This apparent reluctance of younger children to perceive smiles as positive—or, put more broadly, to accept the intended messages—may be

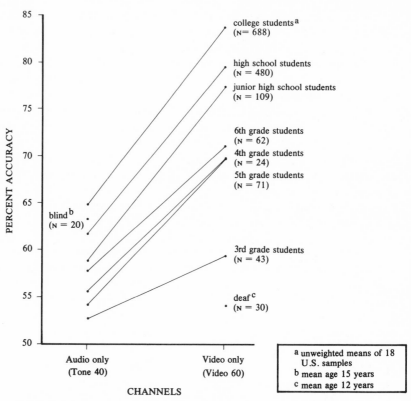

FIGURE 8.3. Accuracy on pure tone and pure video channels for seven age levels

seen by adult senders as a kind of subversion of the communication process. We may hypothesize that socialization includes the child's learning to attend to "proper" cues, those whose meanings the sender wants read, and no others.[2]

We suggest that the channels for which such socialization would be most effective are those channels that are under the least conscious control of the sender (in other words, those channels in which nonverbal "leakage" is most likely). Hence, we propose that audio nonverbal cues may be under less conscious control than are visual cues, and that within the visual mode, body cues may be under less conscious control than face cues (this has been suggested by Ekman and Friesen 1969*a*, 1974). Following from this, the too-accurate reading of such cues by children would be likely to be suppressed

---

2. Schachtel (1949) suggested that people forget their early childhood experiences because such memory would disrupt the restrictive social order of modern civilization, and that such forgetting is taught as part of the socialization process. Our hypothesis is a variant of Schachtel's.

or at least not expected to develop beyond a certain level during socialization. An alternative, but not incompatible, hypothesis to explain the tone-video-age interaction displayed in figure 8.3 is that as children become more and more verbally oriented, either the social pressure to pay attention to verbal messages or the effort required to decipher them may contribute to a relative inattention to nonverbal audio cues.[3]

Before leaving to future researchers our hypothesis that children learn not to attend too well to audio nonverbal communication (for whatever reasons), we shall briefly describe four additional findings that might bear on the hypothesis.

In chapter 10, we examine the relationship between attention to cues in different channels and accuracy on the different channels of the PONS test. Our question was this: if a person pays particular attention to, say, face cues in a task designed to measure the degree of such attention, will that person be likely to perform particularly well on the face channel of the PONS test? The study we did (employing college students) showed that for face and body, attention and accuracy were positively related, but for audio there was no such relationship. Paying more or less attention to audio cues did not predict audio accuracy. This finding may support our childhood socialization hypothesis. Let us say that children gradually stop improving their ability to read information conveyed by tone of voice (or improve slower than on video). We might expect that by the time they reach college, the habit of "tuning out" some audio cues may be so ingrained that close listening, by itself, is not sufficient to allow the extraction of added amounts of information from the voice. The findings of our children's analyses and our attention study are consistent with this hypothesis, though they do not "prove" it by any means.

A second relevant finding has to do with effects of practice, retesting, and training on PONS accuracy. In chapter 14, we note that audio accuracy was generally less amenable to improvement with practice than video accuracy.

In the attention study, attention did not predict audio accuracy; in the studies on practice and training, audio accuracy improved less than video accuracy. Both of these findings are consistent with the hypothesis that people learn not to extract all of the information available in audio. Of course, this line of reasoning assumes that audio channels contain as much information to be extracted as the video channels do—an untested assumption. The fact that audio items on the PONS test are harder to judge accurately than video items can be adduced as evidence to support two (not mutually exclusive) hypoth-

3. Some parallel data pertain to the expressive behavior of infants and children. Charlesworth and Kreutzer (1973), reviewing the literature on expression of emotion, report that "in general, infants and very young children are believed to be more expressive than older children and adults" (p. 127). The probable reasons they give are the development of fine muscular control, social pressure, and the development of cognitive abilities that enable the child to replace emotional outbreak by instrumental and cognitive acts (for instance, rationalization).

eses: (1) Audio items do not contain as many nonverbal cues that can be judged at all (perhaps because our filtering methods remove cues, or because people learn not to send or just do not send as many meaningful nonverbal audio cues, or both). (2) Audio items do not contain as many nonverbal cues that people *know how to judge* (a psychological matter on the judge's part, not a characteristic of the sent message). A provocative, but very inconclusive, support for the latter position came when the audio scores of blind teenagers were compared to the audio scores of sighted teenagers (figure 8.3 and chapter 12). The blind teenagers scored very well on the audio test, better than their seeing cohorts, which suggests that under some conditions (in this case, blindness), children continue to learn auditory nonverbal cues. Deaf children (figure 8.3) did not show such an added learning on video, compared to hearing cohorts.

The third relevant finding is the study on effects of knowing the sender, described in chapter 13. In that study, friends and family of the PONS sender performed relatively better than a matched group of strangers on audio, whereas the strangers performed relatively better on video. If it can be presumed for the moment that socialization brings with it a form of "taboo" on reading audio cues, then we might hypothesize that friendly acquaintanceship or family relationship allows the taboo to be relaxed. One might propose that the degree of mutual trust incurred by such a relationship implies, tacitly, that the interpretation of additional audio cues will be utilized in the interests of the sender.

The fourth relevant finding was described in chapter 4. That chapter described two factor analyses carried out as a way of clustering samples according to similarities in the shapes of the eleven-channel and four-factor profiles (see chapter 3 for description of the four orthogonal PONS factors). It will be recalled that these two analyses both produced a strong factor that was labeled the "sophisticated-unsophisticated" dimension. Sophisticated samples included college students, mental health clinicians, and artists, while unsophisticated samples included young children and teenagers, psychiatric patients, and foreign (particularly exotic foreign) groups. The profile characteristics of these two types of group were such that sophisticated samples scored high on video channels and unsophisticated samples scored high on audio channels. This finding suggests that the less westernized and less well socialized samples had the same advantage on audio channels that we observed among young children.

To summarize these arguments, we have described five findings that, taken together, suggest that social propriety and/or the processes of verbalization and socialization incur a relative disadvantage at interpreting nonverbal audio cues. Certainly, the cross-sectional nature of our studies, and the fact that we use studies on adults as supporting evidence, makes our conclusions very tentative indeed. Briefly restated, the five findings are: (1) younger children performed at a relative advantage on audio channels, compared to older children and adults; (2) paying extra attention to audio cues did not predict audio accuracy for adults, but such attention paid to video cues did predict video accuracy; (3) practice helped video accuracy more than it helped audio accuracy; (4) acquaintanceship with the sender was related to a relatively greater degree of audio skill than that found among strangers; and (5) samples other than children that can be characterized as "unsophisticated" performed relatively better on audio cues than samples characterized as "sophisticated." This network of findings supports the hypothesis that greater socialization brings a reduced rate of learning for audio cues, but none of these studies was designed specifically to test such a hypothesis. Clearly, more research is necessary.

Returning now to the relationship of age to channels, we also examined the data for the 275 children who took the video-only test and the child-sender audio test, using both analysis of variance and correlational techniques. The analysis of variance revealed a significant grade $\times$ easiness interaction ($F(1,270) = 7.49$, $p = .007$; $r = .16$; effect size $= .32\sigma$). This showed that younger children (fourth grade) performed relatively better on the "harder" channels (body and CF) than did the older children (fifth grade), and that the older children performed relatively better on the "easy" channels (face and RS) than did the younger children.

The correlational analysis showed correlations of virtually zero between grade and RS, CF, video total, and audio total, but significant and opposite-sign correlations between grade and face ($r = .18$, $p < .01$) and between grade and body ($r = -.12$, $p < .05$). This grade-related difference between face performance and body performance was therefore probably mainly responsible for the significant interaction of grade and easiness described above. Hence, this result is consistent with the grade school and age level analyses of variance of the full PONS test, which showed no age $\times$ audio channels interaction but which did show age $\times$ visual channels interactions. However, the negative correlation between grade and body ($-.12$) shows a reverse trend not observed previously. These results suggest that younger children are relatively more accurately attuned to the more difficult, perhaps more unconscious (implied by Bugental, Love, and Gianetto 1971), perhaps more veridical, channels, which older children seem to find more difficult, either absolutely (in the case of body in this analysis) or relatively (older children improve much more on face than on tone). That CF scores for this sample predicted video scores negatively (earlier in this chapter) may indicate that special skill at the possibly more unconscious audio mode (CF) causes children to discount or to disbelieve video cues, perhaps because such children know that the face and voice can send discrepant cues, and, knowing that the face may be easier to manipulate than the voice, they may distrust the video messages.

AGE-QUADRANT INTERACTIONS. In the four-grade analysis, the grade $\times$ dominance interaction was not significant ($F < 1$, $p > .50$), but the grade $\times$

positivity interaction was significant ($F(3,196) = 3.02$, $p = .032$; $\eta = .21$). The residual effects showed that the third grade differed from the older three grades in being "too good" on negative affect and "too poor" on positive affect. The grade × dominance × positivity interaction was small ($F < 1$, $p > .50$).

Interactions of grade and channel with quadrants were nonsignificant for grade × face × dominance and grade × body × dominance ($F < 1$, $p > .46$), but significant for grade × audio × dominance ($F(6,392) = 3.30$, $p = .004$; $\eta = .22$). The residuals indicated that for submissive affect, third and fourth graders performed relatively "too well" on CF and relatively "too poorly" on no audio and RS, compared to the fifth and sixth graders; and for dominant affect, the third and fourth graders performed relatively "too poorly" on CF and relatively "too well" on no audio and RS.

All three interactions involving grade, channel, and positivity of affect were significant (grade × audio × positivity, grade × face × positivity, and grade × body × positivity). For grade × audio × positivity ($F(6,392) = 3.60$, $p = .002$; $\eta = .23$), no meaningful interpretation of the effect has been made. For grade × face × positivity, the residuals associated with the means showed that third graders differed from the older three grades in being "too good" when face showed negative affect and "too poor" when face showed positive affect, compared to the three older grades, who showed the reverse pattern ($F(3,196) = 5.42$, $p = .002$; $\eta = .28$). This finding offers some corroboration of Bugental et al. (1970), who showed that children aged five to eight perceived women's smiles as less positive than did children aged thirteen and up. If our third grade children were inclined to be confused by or to discount the positive affect scenes in face, then it follows that they might have obtained lower accuracy scores on such scenes.

The grade × body × positivity interaction was weaker than the two just described ($F(3,196) = 2.28$, $p = .081$; $\eta = .18$), and it showed that the third and fourth graders differed from the older two grades in performing relatively "too well" when the body showed negative affect and relatively "too poorly" when the body showed positive affect, compared to the fifth and sixth graders, who showed the reverse pattern. This effect can be interpreted similarly to that of the grade × face × positivity interaction: we might hypothesize that positive cues were discounted or misinterpreted by younger children when they were sent by the body.

CHILDREN WITH LEARNING DISABILITIES

As part of her continuing research with children who have learning disabilities, Tanis Bryan became interested in the question of differences in sensitivity to nonverbal cues between these special children and normal controls (Bryan 1974, 1975, 1977; Bryan and Wheeler 1972). As her measure of sensitivity to nonverbal cues she employed the forty-item face and body PONS test, which is comprised of the same forty items that make up the face and body channels of the full-length PONS. In addition, she used the forty-item audio PONS test that employed a female child as the sender.

The selection of a four-channel test battery was based in part on the need for a shorter form than the full-length PONS, and these particular four channels were selected because of the factor analytic evidence based on the full-length PONS that face, body, RS, and CF were all relatively independent of one another and might, therefore, be tapping substantially different skills. This mutual independence was also found for the four channels of the present battery. For the norm group of 275 children, the mean intercorrelation among the four channels was .04, the median was .09, and the range was from $-.10$ to .16. The internal consistency reliability, θ, based on a factor analysis of the eighty items, was .66 (Armor 1974). The development of this battery of tests for use with children was greatly facilitated by Tanis Bryan's experience and consultation.

The basic children's norm group for this particular subtest battery was a sample of 275 fourth and fifth graders from the Chicago area who were tested by Bryan and who were discussed earlier in this chapter. A standardized profile sheet was developed for the four-channel battery on the basis of this norm group. Figure 8.4 shows the profile sheet, which was designed in a manner analogous to the profile sheet for the 220-item PONS. Just as in the case of the 220-item PONS profile sheet, the mean performance of the norm group in raw score units can be read for any channel, quadrant, or marginal by noting the raw score value falling at the fiftieth percentile line that runs across the sheet. Each percentile reading in the left hand margin corresponds to half a standard deviation. Tables 8.4 and 8.5 gave the means and standard deviations for channels and marginals for all 275 children. Females performed better than males overall (about $.23\,\sigma$), as is usual in most such comparisons. There were no very dramatic interactions between sex and channel, quadrant, or marginal, however, with the two most extreme differences (in direction of difference), occurring for the RS channel ($.32\,\sigma$ favoring girls) and the positive-dominant quadrant ($.04\,\sigma$ favoring boys).

Three other samples were administered the test battery under discussion: one sample of children and two samples of adults. The children ($N = 48$) were third, fourth, and fifth graders from the Chicago area who were also tested by Tanis Bryan. The smaller sample of adults ($N = 30$) was comprised of members of a Jewish temple's club for married couples in the greater Boston area. The larger sample of adults ($N = 100$) was comprised of professional educators attending a workshop on education at Fordham University.

To form clearer groups of normal children and learning disabled children, the two samples of children ($N = 275$ and $N = 48$) were merged and then

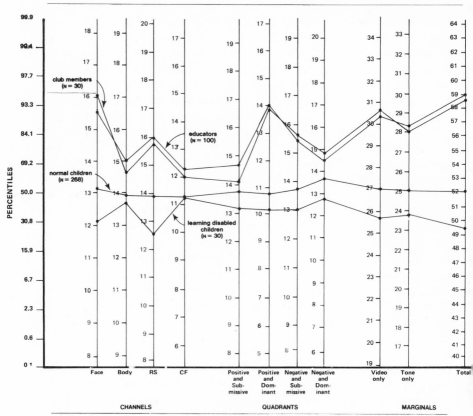

FIGURE 8.4. Mean accuracy in channels, quadrants, and marginals for four samples

divided into those who were clearly learning disabled (N = 30) and those who were relatively normal (N = 268), setting aside children who had been identified as brain-damaged or as potentially learning disabled. Because there were so few of them, third graders were also not included in this analysis. Fig. 8.4 summarizes the performance of the two groups of adults and the two groups of children. Because of the small sizes of some of the samples and because there were no appreciable interactions of sex with channels or quadrants for this battery, data for males and females are not reported separately.

The most striking result in figure 8.4 is the very marked difference in performance between the children and the adults. Overall, adults were markedly superior to even the normal children (t = 9.75, effect size = 1.69 σ), a result expected on the basis of the data yielded by the full-length, 220-item PONS. Compared to the normal children, the adults were particularly superior at the face and randomized spliced channels. Both of these channels can be hypothesized to be more amenable to an attentive and analytic approach, the kind of approach adults might be expected to have learned.

Compared to the normal children, the adults were also particularly superior at the positive-dominant and negative-submissive affect quadrants. Interestingly, these are the two quadrants at which foreign service officers were particularly superior to the norm group of high school students on the female audio PONS test. The positive-dominant items tend to be supportive in expressive tone and the negative-submissive items tend to evoke support in expressive tone. Perhaps sensitivity to support offered and support requested is of particular benefit to those with special interpersonal concerns, such as foreign service officers, educators, and adult members of couples' social clubs. We should emphasize that the results for the foreign service officers were based on forty items (female adult sender) of audio PONS that were different from the forty items (female child sender) that constituted the audio half of the test battery under discussion here.

Although the effect is not very large, compared to the normal children, the adults were superior in the video channels more than in the audio channels. That same result has also been found using the full-length PONS with various samples of adults and children. Earlier, in the chapter dealing with the factor analysis of samples, we noted that more sophisticated samples generally showed such a relative advantage of video over audio nonverbal sensitivity.

Before leaving our discussion of the adult samples, we may note that their performance on the two video channels was very similar to that of the norm group for the analogous two channels of the 220-item PONS. That is not surprising, however, since the same 40 video stimuli were employed in both tests. Somewhat more surprising was the result that for the CF channel the adult samples also performed very similarly to the CF channel of the full-length PONS despite the difference in senders between those subtests. Adult performance on the randomized spliced subtest of the present battery was very much superior (nearly two σ's) to the performance of the norm group on the RS channel of the full-length PONS. Direct comparisons between performance on the present battery and performance on the full-length PONS, then, should be attempted only with the greatest caution.

Figure 8.4 also shows that the overall performance of the normal children was appreciably superior to that of the learning disabled children ($t = 3.01$, effect size $= .60\sigma$). That is the result we would expect, but we cannot tell just what about learning disabled children would lead to lowered performance. One simple interpretation might be that since most of these children have attention and performance problems they simply cannot manage the taking of the PONS test as effectively as the normal children. That interpretation, however, could not explain the finding that these children show their PONS disadvantage primarily in the face and RS channels. This relative disadvantage had been predicted by Mary Lu Rosenthal on the basis of an attention, or

TABLE 8.8. Correlations of Sociometric Attractiveness with PONS and Learning Disability Status

Channel	Sample 1 (N = 40)	Sample 2 (N = 275)	Combined (Weighted)
Face 20	.18	.06	.07
Body 20	.16	.06	.07
RS 20	.33[a]	.18[b]	.20[c]
CF 20	−.42[b]	−.01	−.06
Positive-submissive	.09	.21[c]	.20[c]
Positive-dominant	.17	.04	.06
Negative-submissive	.07	.02	.03
Negative-dominant	.05	.11	.10
Video total	.23	.08	.10
Audio total	.04	.12[a]	.11[a]
Total	.16	.14[a]	.14[a]
Learning disability status	−.26	−.25[c]	−.25[c]

[a] $p \leq .05$
[b] $p \leq .01$
[c] $p \leq .001$

information-processing, hypothesis. She suggested that, compared to normal children, the learning disabled children would find the grosser movements of the body, arms, and hands easier to attend to and process than the smaller, more subtle, finer-grained movements of the face and that the content-filtered scenes would be simpler phenomenologically, i.e. would ''feel'' less confusing, than the randomized spliced scenes. Looking again at figure 8.4, we note that it is precisely on these channels, those with which learning disabled children had the most trouble, that adults performed best, perhaps because they were able to be both more attentive and analytic than the normal children, who in turn may have been able to be more attentive and analytic than the learning disabled children.

For both samples of children tested by Tanis Bryan, sociometric ratings of social attractiveness were available. Table 8.8 shows the correlations between these ratings and accuracy in the various channels, quadrants, and marginals of the eighty-item form of the PONS, and between these ratings and learning disability status. Children with learning disabilities were found to be significantly less socially attractive to other children, a finding that is consistent with classroom experience. Socially more attractive children were found to be better at decoding nonverbal cues in general but especially at RS and at positive-submissive scenes. Perhaps the analytic skill that may be required to decode randomized spliced speech is associated with those analytic skills required for successful interpersonal relations. In addition, it may be that children who are well attuned to positive-submissive cues from others are

TABLE 8.9. Correlations of PONS with Ethnic Status among Children

Channel	Sample 1 ($N = 48$)	Sample 2 ($N = 275$)	Combined (Weighted)
Face 20	−.13	−.11	−.11[a]
Body 20	.06	−.13[a]	−.10
RS 20	−.04	−.19[b]	−.17[b]
CF 20	.26	.15[a]	.17[b]
Positive-submissive	.00	−.17[b]	−.14[a]
Positive-dominant	.06	−.01	.00
Negative-submissive	.08	−.08	−.06
Negative-dominant	−.03	.01	.00
Video total	−.04	−.16[b]	−.14[a]
Audio total	.10	−.04	−.02
Total	.05	−.13[a]	−.10

[a] $p < .05$
[b] $p < .01$

more likely to recognize and reinforce the emission of those cues, thereby leading them to be treated more often as a well-liked leader.

About one third of the children of Tanis Bryan's samples were black. Race (black or white) was coded as a binary (1 or 0) variable and correlated with PONS accuracy. Table 8.9 shows that there was no consistent overall relationship between PONS accuracy and ethnic status. However, black children tended to be consistently better than white children on CF channels but not as good on RS or face. Black children also tended to be less sensitive to positive-submissive affects. Perhaps this is due to their receiving a relative dearth of such cues in their interactions with adult white women. Ethnic differences in PONS performance are further discussed in chapter 9.

9 | Cultural Variation

Social scientists have long been interested in the degree to which nonverbal expressions can be interpreted correctly by members of different cultures. One of the first researchers in the area was Charles Darwin; in 1872, he published *The Expression of the Emotions in Man and Animals.* Much of Darwin's book is devoted to careful description of the physical movements that accompany emotional expressions—for example, the constricting of the muscles that surround the eye during crying, shouting, or periods of extreme stress. However, one of the central questions of Darwin's undertaking was whether or not expressions and gestures were cross-culturally identical.

From Darwin's perspective, the question seemed to represent a choice between explanations of gestures and expressions that were genetic or biological in nature and explanations that were social and cultural in nature. To answer this question, Darwin undertook what was probably the first questionnaire approach to the study of nonverbal communication. He submitted a list of sixteen questions to individuals who had lived for a time in various non-Western and, in some cases, preliterate cultures, and he received thirty-six replies.

Darwin's questionnaire items described in some detail his observations of various nonverbal expressions and gestures in his own culture. He asked his respondents to determine whether or not individuals in the cultures with which they had worked exhibited similar patterns of expression and behavior. Darwin urged them not to rely upon memory but, instead, to conduct fresh observations on each of the sixteen points he raised. For example, the second question on Darwin's list was ''Does shame excite a blush when the colour of the skin allows it to be visible? and especially how low down the body does the blush extend?'' Similarly, question 4 was ''When considering deeply on any subject, or trying to understand any puzzle, does he frown or wrinkle the skin beneath the lower eyelids?'' (p. 15).

Many of the questions in Darwin's questionnaire reflected his quite specific interest in the muscular and somatic changes that accompanied various emotional states or expressive gestures. However, some of Darwin's interest was

200

focused upon the degree to which expressions could be interpreted in various cultures. Question 15 was "Can guilty, or sly, or jealous expressions be recognized? though I know not how these can be defined" (p. 16), and question 8 was "Can a dogged or obstinate expression be recognized, which is chiefly shown by the mouth being firmly closed, a lowering brow and a slight frown?" (p. 16).

Darwin's hypothesis, in advance of his data collection, seems to have been that there was a great consistency across cultures in forms of expression and gesture. He wrote, "I have endeavored to show in considerable detail that all the chief expressions exhibited by man are the same throughout the world" (p. 359). Based upon the replies of his respondents, Darwin did, in fact, conclude that most forms of expression and gesture were characteristic of the species rather than of the cultures. While concluding that the major expressive actions of humans are biological, however, Darwin still suggested that some aspects of expression were the inventions of individual cultures, such as kissing, nodding, and shaking the head. These expressions, he concluded, were not biological or universal and thus would not be interpreted in the same way by members of different cultures.

Twentieth-century researchers have continued to find Darwin's questions interesting. Much of the research since Darwin concerning the similarities or differences in the expression of emotions in various cultures is summarized by Ekman (1972), Ekman, Friesen, and Ellsworth (1972), Ekman (1973), and Harrison et al. (1972). In a discussion of possible flaws in Darwin's century-old classic, Ekman (1973) has suggested that one source of bias was the fact that Darwin's thirty-six respondents knew from the questions he sent them what particular muscular pattern Darwin thought was associated with each emotion. That is, rather than ask, "What movements of the face are there when a person is considering deeply on any subject, or trying to understand any puzzle?," Darwin instead provided a suggestion of an answer within the question ("does he frown or wrinkle the skin beneath the lower eyelid?"). But Darwin himself was aware of some of the problems in his method, as Ekman has pointed out. Darwin appears to have known of the effects that a researcher's expectations can have on his findings.

The principal division among researchers on the relationships between culture and expression, beginning with Darwin, seems to have been between relativists and universalists. Ekman (1972) has summarized the general form of these two approaches:

> Most universalists maintain that the same facial muscular movement is associated with the same emotion in all peoples through inheritance. Relativists view facial expression as in no way innate, but akin to language and learned within each culture; therefore, only through a highly unlikely coincidence would a facial expression be found to have the same emotional meaning in two independent cultures. (pp. 207–8)

Before discussing relevant research from the relativist and universalist perspectives, it is perhaps important to note that this disagreement has been somewhat muddied by a failure to draw several distinctions. A general discussion of some of these problems is given by Ekman, Friesen, and Ellsworth (1972) and Ekman (1973).

First, there is a problem with the word "expression." A wide variety of behaviors have been referred to as expressions—from a blush of embarrassment to the highly stylized motions of a theatrical performance. Ekman (1972) has urged that a distinction be made between "facial expressions of emotion" and "facial gestures" (p. 209). Ekman and Friesen (1972) and Ekman (1973) have also used the term "emblem" to refer to gestures. In making this distinction, Ekman (1973) suggests that "expressions of emotion" be used to refer to behaviors that are relatively less intentional, which "may occur when an individual is completely alone, as for example, while watching television." By contrast, gestures or emblems are more intentional behaviors and are "used only to send messages to another person." An example of an expression in Ekman's terms might be the raising of the eyebrows in surprise, while an example of an emblem is the "gun-to-temple" gesture for suicide. Ekman and Friesen (1972) suggest that emblems are nonverbal acts that have a direct verbal translation, and that people are usually aware of their use of emblems.

Something like this distinction is also suggested by Leach (1972), who suggests that there may be nonverbal behaviors that are similar to a gestural language, and he gives the example of gestures used in religious ceremonies. This distinction between expressions and emblems is of considerable relevance to the disagreement between relativists and universalists, as Ekman (1972, 1973) and Hinde (1972) have pointed out, since it is possible that emblems may be more subject to cultural variation than expressions. In particular, Ekman (1973) has suggested that Darwin was referring to expressions, while many cultural relativists refer to emblems.

A second distinction that may be important in the argument between relativists and universalists concerns whether they have studied nonverbal behavior using a "components" or a "judgment" approach (Ekman 1973). In the components approach, the focus is generally upon the precise meaning of various muscle movements or relatively microscopic behaviors; an example would be an interest in how an individual's eyebrows move while asking a question. The judgment approach involves asking an audience or panel of judges to try to interpret the meaning or implications of a specimen of nonverbal behavior. An example of this approach would be asking a panel of judges to interpret a photograph of a face as showing either happiness or anger.

A third distinction is whether the nonverbal behaviors considered are posed or spontaneous. In a small judgment study reported by Darwin, the pictures he used were of spontaneous emotion, in the sense that the facial expression was obtained by a real stress (electricity) rather than a portrayed stress. At least two writers, Landis (1924) and Hunt (1941) have criticized posed expressions, saying that they are a learned language that is unrelated to real or spontaneously experienced emotional expression. Ekman (1973) adds that there are also differences within posed expressions between a simulation of an actual expression as it would occur in nature and a display of an emblematic expression. Ekman, Friesen, and Ellsworth (1972) suggest that when the individual is trying to simulate an actual expression as it would occur in nature, such posed behavior is largely similar to spontaneous behavior.

A fourth complicating factor in the debate between cultural relativists and universalists is that they have discussed different channels of nonverbal behavior. Darwin and Ekman have focused primarily on facial expression. Most anthropologists (e.g., Hall, LaBarre, and Birdwhistell) have focused upon body movement, body position, or gesture. It is possible that this focus on radically different nonverbal channels has been partially responsible for the fact that researchers on facial expressions have tended to emphasize universalist findings, while researchers on body movement or gestures have tended to favor relativist findings.

Finally, a fifth factor that may have complicated the disagreement between relativists and universalists seems to be the lack of consensus about the validity of evidence. This problem may be inherent when an area is of interest to (at least) sociologists, psychologists, anthropologists, and ethologists. As an example of this type of problem, the case study or ethnographic methods employed by anthropologists in this area have been criticized as "anecdotal" by some researchers (e.g., Eibl-Eibesfeldt 1972). Conversely, the use of quantitative analyses of judgments of posed expressions in a laboratory setting (which is the preferred technique of many researchers in this area) has been criticized as artificial or unrealistic by some more anthropologically oriented researchers (Leach 1972). Given the variations in methodology, therefore, one wonders if the "evidence" of an experimental psychologist can ever convince an anthropologist, and vice versa.

All of these conceptual and methodological issues tend to undercut the comparability of research on the cultural variability or universality of nonverbal behavior. It may be that the question of universality can meaningfully occur only on a quite specific level (e.g., are the hand gestures for victory the same in all cultures?). Some examples of research on the question of the relativity or universality of nonverbal behaviors are discussed briefly below, first for the relativity perspective and second for the universality perspective.

CULTURAL RELATIVITY

The position of the cultural relativists has generally been either (a) that the same nonverbal behaviors are used in such radically different (and even opposite) fashions in different cultures that they are virtually unrecognizable across cultures, or (b) that the same nonverbal behaviors are used with differences that are distinct but small, and the behaviors are therefore recognizable across cultures.

An example of the first, more adamantly relativist perspective has been given by Birdwhistell (1970, p. 42):

> Insofar as I have been able to determine, just as there are no universal words, no sound complexes, which carry the same meaning the world over, there are no body motions, facial expressions, or gestures which provoke *identical* responses the world over. A body can be bowed in grief, in humility, in laughter, or in readiness for aggression. A ''smile'' in one society portrays friendliness, in another embarrassment, and, in still another may contain a warning that, unless tension is reduced, hostility and attack will follow.

Other writers (e.g., Klineberg [1938, 1940], LaBarre [1947], and Argyle [1969]) have also focused on variations across cultures in the nonverbal behavior displayed during various situations. Klineberg specifically discussed occasions when grief was, in some cultures, masked by feigned joy.

Some of the best-known relativist research has focused on the specific differences across cultures in the use of a single channel of nonverbal behavior. Briefly, we will review a few findings of research on four channels of nonverbal behavior: spatial behavior, gesture and body movement, the voice, and the face.

One of the first to write about spatial behavior, or proxemics, was Edward Hall (1959, 1969). Some of Hall's observations on the importance and variety of spatial relations in various cultures have been pursued systematically by Watson (1970, 1972). Watson studied conversations between two members of six cultural groups: Arabs, Latin Americans, Southern Europeans, Asians, Indians/Pakistanis, and Northern Europeans. He measured several aspects of nonverbal behavior in the conversations: axis, closeness, touch, eye contact, and voice loudness. Watson found that Arabs, Latins, and Southern Europeans faced each other more directly, had more intense eye contact, and touched each other more. Another researcher on cultural variations in proxemic behavior, Little (1968), asked members of various national groups to place dolls in spatial relationship to one another to portray a variety of social situations. He found consistent differences among the cultures in his samples in the distances they chose for the hypothetical conversations.

There have been a number of important investigations of cross-cultural variations in gesture and movement. One of the earliest was done by Efron (1941), who studied Eastern European Jews and Southern Italians who had immigrated to New York City. Efron found that the more assimilated the individuals were in their adoptive American culture, the less their gestural traits were characteristic of their culture of origin. Another early work on cultural differences in gestural traits was the wide-ranging book by Ruesch and Kees

(1972), first published in 1956. An empirical study of cross-cultural variation in "emblematic" hand movements has been reported by Ekman and Friesen (1972). The authors concluded that the "origin of emblems is culture specific learning" (p. 358) and gave examples of this variation.

There has been little cross-cultural research on the voice. Beier and Zautra (1972) reported a study on the identification of emotions in three cultures from a tape recording of American speakers. The speakers were asked to say one-, two-, and three-word phrases as well as a short paragraph. The content of the phrases was kept the same ("hello," "good morning," "how are you," and "There is no answer. You have asked me that question a thousand times and my reply has always been the same. It will always be the same."), and speakers were asked to portray various emotions while reading the same phrases. Beier and Zautra reported that Japanese and Polish students were much less accurate than Americans at judging the emotion in the voices for short phrases, but no less accurate on the short paragraph. McCluskey et al. (1975) compared Mexican and Canadian children on ability to judge the affect in the electronically filtered speech of Canadian and Mexican women, and found Mexican children to excel.

The nonverbal channel that has been studied cross-culturally most frequently is facial expression. Darwin was one of the first to study facial expression, and most of his 1872 book focused on facial expression rather than other channels of nonverbal behavior. Although Darwin is generally thought of as having drawn universalist conclusions concerning facial expression, there were a number of facial behaviors that he regarded as variable across cultures, as mentioned earlier.

A review of empirical research on facial expression across cultures has been given by Ekman, Friesen, and Ellsworth (1972) and Ekman (1973). Five of the studies reviewed were concerned with cultural specificity, and will be mentioned briefly here.

Dickey and Knower (1941) showed pictures of American actors to Mexican and American children and found that Mexican children were better able to identify the Americans' emotional expressions than American children—a difference the authors attributed to the more frequent experience of "expressiveness" in Mexican culture. Vinacke (1949) and Vinacke and Fong (1955) showed pictures intended to be spontaneous facial expressions of Caucasians and Asian-Americans to groups of Caucasian, Chinese-American, and Japanese-American students at the University of Hawaii. Vinacke did not find differences among the three groups of subjects, and attributed this to the high degree of contact among the cultural groups in Hawaii. Triandis and Lambert (1958) obtained ratings from American and Greek university students and from rural Greek villagers of photographs of expressions posed by a professional actress. The researchers found no differences between the Greek and American university students, but both these groups differed from the rural Greek villagers—a difference the researchers attributed to the greater exposure of the students to film and other media. Cüceloglu (1970, 1972) showed drawings of faces to college students in the United States, Japan, and Turkey, and reported some differences across the three cultures but also some similarities. Winkelmayer et al. (1971) employed as stimuli silent motion pictures of ten normal and ten "schizophrenic" U.S. women, as each told about one happy, one sad, and one anger-related personal experience. They showed the films to American and British psychology students and to Mexican medical students. No cultural differences in accuracy were found when judging the films of "schizophrenic" women, but in judging the films of normal women, the U.S. and British judges were more accurate than the Mexican judges.

A final example of research on cultural variation is Ekman (1973), who showed neutral or stressful films to Japanese and American subjects, while recording their facial expressions with a concealed camera. The film was shown under two conditions: with the viewer alone in a room, and with the viewer accompanied by an interviewer. The facial expressions in the first condition were strikingly similar for Japanese and American subjects. With an interviewer in the room, however, Japanese subjects showed more positive emotions and fewer negative emotions than did American subjects. Ekman interpreted this cultural variation as due to the operation of display rules—that is, culturally determined norms governing the appropriateness of various emotional reactions.

CULTURAL UNIVERSALITY

Despite Darwin's evident belief that some nonverbal behaviors (weeping, prayers, kissing, signs of affirmation or negation, etc.) were strongly influenced by culture, he has generally been regarded as a strong believer in the universality and innateness of nonverbal expressions. Ekman and Friesen (1969b) and Ekman (1973) have pointed out that Darwin failed to make a distinction between finding that emotional expressions are universal and concluding that they are innate.

Darwin mentioned, as evidence for his belief that emotional expression was the result of innate forces, observation of the expression of various emotions in a blind and deaf woman. Darwin reported that she blushed, and he interpreted this as evidence that she could not have learned blushing and that blushing was, therefore, an innate expression. Since Darwin, other researchers have studied blind and deaf persons. Goodenough (1932) published an article containing descriptions and photographs of expressions in a blind and deaf ten-year-old girl. Similarly, Eibl-Eibesfeldt (1972) mentioned filming blind and deaf children, and drew the conclusion that their expressions were innate.

Eibl-Eibesfeldt (1972) has also used film to make observations of the expression of various emotions in several cultures. But despite the generally universalist interpretation that he has drawn from his observations, he has also reported exceptions to his generally universalist conclusions. He states that "in some cultures the eyebrow flash is suppressed. In Japan, for example, it is considered as indecent" (p. 299).

A number of studies have been done to see whether members of various cultures can recognize the expressions of persons from other cultures. Of all the research done in the universalist tradition, these are the most relevant to the PONS paradigm, which involves a test of whether an individual can decode information through various nonverbal channels. Most of these studies have involved showing still photographs of various facial expressions to members of several cultures. A review of much of this research can be found in Ekman (1972, 1973) and Ekman, Friesen, and Ellsworth (1972).

Izard (1969) chose thirty-two photographs on the basis of agreement among several judges in a pretest. These photographs were then shown to eight different cultural groups, and each member was asked to choose from several labels describing the emotion shown in the pictures. In most cases, a majority of the judges in each culture identified the pictures in agreement with the pretest judges' opinions.

A similar study was conducted by Ekman, Sorenson, and Friesen (1969), who studied judgments of photographs of facial expression in five countries including the United States. The authors chose the photographs for their study according to a theory about the precise muscular movements involved in various facial expressions (Ekman, Friesen, and Tomkins 1971). The results of the Ekman, Sorenson, and Friesen study were similar to Izard's; a majority of the judges in each culture chose the "expected" emotions. In summarizing the results of this study, Ekman (1973) interpreted the findings as strong evidence of the universality of facial expressions.

The studies by Izard and by Ekman, Sorenson, and Friesen could not, however, discount the possibility that members of the cultures studied had been influenced by extensive direct or media contact with members of other cultures. Because of this possibility, Ekman and his colleagues (Ekman and Friesen 1971; Ekman, Heider, Friesen, and Heider, undated) selected two linguistic and cultural groups in New Guinea as "visually isolated" samples. Because the two groups were preliterate, Ekman and his colleagues used a technique invented by Dashiell (1927) that involved reading a story to an individual and asking the individual to choose from among three photographs to indicate the person described in the story. The judges from the Fore group (a New Guinea culture) did quite well on the selection task, and a majority chose the picture of the "expected" emotion for five of the six emotions used in the study. The one selection task for which a majority did not agree involved distinguishing fear from surprise.

Ekman (1973) also reported that the degree of contact with Caucasians did

not seem to relate to performance on the picture task; Fore judges who had
been to mission school and read and spoke English did no better on the task
than less westernized Fore judges. This comparison is of considerable importance, because a visually isolated group may be impossible in pure terms—
any group that can be researched is, by definition, in contact with the outside
world.

The findings with the Fore judges, Ekman (1973) has reported, were supported by similar results obtained among another New Guinea group, the
Dani (Ekman, Heider, Friesen, and Heider, undated).

In addition to the study of decoding abilities among the Fore, Ekman and
his colleagues (Ekman and Friesen 1971; Ekman 1972) also asked some
members of the Fore group to encode various emotions. The persons chosen
for this study had not participated as judges in the other study. They were
asked to show how their own faces would look if they were the person in one
of the stories. Video tapes of these posed expressions were then shown to
thirty-four U.S. college students, who were asked to identify which emotion
was being portrayed. Performance on this task was not extremely high: the
median recognition score for the six intended expressions was only 48.5
percent (calculated from Ekman 1972, p. 275). However, four of the six
emotions were recognized at better than the chance level, which was 16.7
percent (happiness, anger, disgust, and sadness). Interestingly, the two emotions that were not recognized at significantly better than chance level were
surprise and fear—the emotions that were confused by the Fore themselves
when judging Caucasian faces.

AN INTERACTIONIST PERSPECTIVE

All evidence seems to point to the inevitability of an interactionist approach, since no relativist researcher has produced evidence that all the nonverbal expressions in one culture are completely unfathomable to members of
all other cultures. At the same time, a close reading of the evidence of
researchers in the universalist tradition provides at least some evidence of the
importance of cultural factors.

For example, a close reading of Ekman, who is often identified as a universalist, demonstrates that he is really an interactionist theorist with a belief (and
evidence) that the origins of expression almost certainly include both cultural
and pan-cultural factors. While much of his research has been directed toward
demonstrating that there is a pan-cultural element in nonverbal expression,
Ekman has certainly not demonstrated or suggested either that cultural variation in nonverbal expression is unimportant or trivial, or that the pan-cultural
element is a sufficiently pervasive ingredient in expression that it enables all
expressions to be recognized unerringly in all cultures.

Ekman (1972) has called his theory of facial expressions a "neuro-cultural" theory, and has suggested that there are two quite different sets of determinants of facial expressions—one that is responsible for universals and a second that is responsible for cultural differences.

Ekman seems to suggest that the effect of cultural factors on the recognizability of facial expressions will be of considerable magnitude. This distinction between the relative contributions of cultural and pan-cultural factors to the recognizability of expressions across cultures is important, particularly since much of the research on this question has employed procedures that intentionally reduced the role of cultural factors in the expressions chosen as stimulus materials.

In Ekman's research on recognizing facial expressions in five literate cultures, for example, efforts were made to avoid sampling procedures that "would be vulnerable to the inclusion of facial expressions which were culture-specific" (Ekman 1972, p. 261). Instead, the sampling of pictures for this study was done purely in terms of the muscular movements present in each photograph. This procedure, while an excellent strategy for the isolation of potentially pan-cultural expressions, also (by design) reduces the presence of culture-specific information in the facial expressions and may also sacrifice a great number of expressions too subtle to be associated with major facial movements. For these reasons, this sampling procedure may place limitations on the inferences to be drawn from levels of accuracy obtained with these pictures in various cultures. For example, if a sample of Brazilians gets a median score of 80 percent accurate in recognizing American facial expressions that have been sampled in this way, we cannot infer that Brazilians would be 80 percent accurate in judging American facial expressions in general; they are only this accurate on judging facial expressions that have been selected precisely because they contain little or no culturally specific information.

Despite the restricted sampling procedures used in many cross-cultural studies of facial expression, at least some researchers have still obtained some indication of variation among cultures. In the study by Izard (1969), for example, although most of the nine cultural groups studied chose the expected emotion, some variation still occurred. The median percentage accuracy scores for the nine college student samples were (our figures): American, 83.5%; German, 82.5%; Swedish, 82.5%; French, 80.5%; English, 80%; Swiss, 77.5%; Greek, 75.5%; Japanese, 54%; African, 50%. The five literate samples described by Ekman showed less variation among samples—ranging from (our figures) a median accuracy of 78 percent for the Japanese sample to 86.5 percent for the Chilean sample. This may have been due to several factors, including the more restricted sampling procedures used to select stimulus photographs and the more limited number of cultures involved.

In summary, most theorists—even those who have worked to establish the existence of at least some cross-culturally recognizable expressions—acknowledge the importance of cultural variables for the accurate recognition of nonverbal behaviors. In addition, although research on this issue has employed a number of different approaches, almost all empirical research in this area has been characterized by the following limitations: (1) the nonverbal behavior studied has almost always been limited to a single channel, with most studies employing still photographs of facial expressions; (2) the number of cultural samples has generally been small, with most studies comparing two or three samples and the largest study comparing nine; and (3) no consistent patterns have been discerned concerning the variation among several cultures in the interpretation of the same nonverbal materials.

CULTURAL VARIATION AND THE PROFILE OF NONVERBAL SENSITIVITY

From the perspective of the PONS test, the question of the relativity or universality of nonverbal expression is of great interest. The PONS paradigm overcomes at least some of the shortcomings of earlier research in this area because it presents nonverbal behavior in several channels (including facial expression, body movement, and qualities of the voice). The PONS film also includes movement—an aspect of nonverbal behavior not included in cross-cultural studies employing still photographs.

In addition, there are a number of other possible sources of variation inherent in cross-cultural testing with the PONS film. One of these, for which the PONS paradigm is an advantage, involves the possibility that different cultures favor information in different channels. In a culture in which hand movement and gestures are extremely important, for example, it is possible that members of this culture would do better than other cultures (better even, perhaps, than Americans) in the interpretation of channels including the sender's hands but not her face. At the same time, of course, members of this culture might do quite badly on PONS channels that omit hand movement.

Another possible source of variation in cross-cultural use of the PONS involves the nature of the decoding task. The viewer is asked to identify an affective situation (e.g., expressing deep affection) from information contained in one or two nonverbal channels. Successful decoding on the PONS, then, requires some recognition of the affective connotations and meaning of the eliciting situations. It is possible that different cultures are relatively less familiar with the affective meaning of some situations. This may be inherent in all cross-cultural inquiry in this area, unless the investigator limits the situations to those that are entirely universal, like birth and death. Even then, the affective connotations of these situations are almost certain to be culturally variable.

Stated succinctly, cross-cultural testing with the PONS film could lend support to one of the following interpretations of the nonverbal communication contained in the film: (1) cultural specificity: that the film contains only an American idiom that is equally incomprehensible to all other cultures; (2) cultural universality: that the film contains universal nonverbal communication, equally interpretable by members of all cultures; or (3) cultural proximity—an interactionist perspective: that the PONS film may contain some pan-cultural elements, but that variance among cultures will be a function of the similarity of that culture to American culture.

RESULTS: (1) VARIATION AMONG CULTURES. In order to help us choose among these three interpretations, the PONS film was shown to a total of 2,300 individuals outside the continental United States. Nationals from twenty[1] countries were included in the testing, and fifty-eight samples were tested to obtain the total cross-cultural sample of 2,300. In addition to the English answer sheet, the cross-cultural testing used PONS answer sheets translated into Spanish, Hebrew, and German.[2]

Briefly, the results of the PONS cross-cultural studies tend to support the cultural proximity interpretation. That is, there was a wide variation in the degree to which other cultures were able to interpret the nonverbal behavior of the American woman in the PONS. In addition, the variation seemed to be nonrandom. The cultures best able to decode the PONS film were those most similar to or most closely associated with American culture.

The first or cultural specificity hypothesis, which suggested that only Americans would be able to interpret the behavior in the PONS, can be considered as disproved. Some cultural samples did virtually as well as Americans. However, at least some elements of the PONS film probably contain an American nonverbal idiom, since American samples did somewhat better than cross-cultural samples.

The second or cultural universality hypothesis, which suggested that all cultures would do equally well due to the universality of nonverbal behavior, can also be considered disproved by the data. There was a wide variation among cross-cultural groups in their levels of accuracy in decoding the PONS film. However, at least some elements of the PONS film may contain behaviors that are panculturally recognizable, since even the lowest scoring cross-cultural samples performed at better than the chance level.

A complete list of the cross-cultural samples, with their sample sizes and

1. This counts two Scandinavian countries as a single country, and four East European countries as one (because of small sample sizes).
2. To maximize equivalence of the foreign language answer sheets, the English answer sheet was translated into the foreign language and then back-translated into English by an independent translator before the foreign language version was accepted.

total PONS scores, is given in table 9.1. The samples are ranked in order of performance, from the highest scoring to the lowest. In general, the cross-cultural samples did less well than the American samples. Of the 117 samples tested as of this analysis, only 9 of the top-scoring third were cross-cultural samples; 24 of the middle third were cross-cultural; and 25 of the bottom third were cross-cultural. This relative disadvantage of the cross-cultural samples is significant ($\chi^2(2) = 16.48$, $p < .001$).

The difference is greater if samples of children are removed from the analysis, since the five worst American samples were grade school children. This restriction is probably justified, since none of the cross-cultural samples involved grade school children. When only 112 samples are considered, the relative disadvantage of the cross-cultural samples becomes larger. Only 8 of the top third of the 112 samples were cross-cultural, 23 of the middle third were cross-cultural, and 27 of the bottom third were cross-cultural ($\chi^2(2) = 21.30$, $p < .001$). The advantage of the American samples also appears in extreme-scoring samples. Of the 112 samples, the best 10 were American, and 9 of the worst 10 were cross-cultural.

A comparison of the median scores of American samples and cross-cultural samples also favors American samples. The median total PONS score of the fifty-eight cross-cultural samples was 169.086 (76.85 percent), while the median total PONS score of the fifty-nine American samples was 174.700 (79.40 percent). If only the fifty-four nonchildren American samples are used for comparison, the median of the American samples is 175.871 (79.94 percent).

Even natively English-speaking samples were at a disadvantage compared to American samples, although, as discussed below, English-speaking samples did better than other cross-cultural samples. There were thirty-two non-American samples for whom English was the first language, and they came from Canada, New Zealand, Australia, and Britain.[3] The median of these English-speaking samples is 171.939, which is still below the median of the fifty-four American samples (175.871). This suggests that the nonverbal behaviors of English speakers from different countries are measurably different and that American nonverbal behavior (in the PONS film) is more difficult for non-American English speakers to interpret than it is for Americans.

Perhaps the most striking aspect of the cross-cultural samples was the wide range in their performances. To illustrate this range, the PONS profiles of the means of four cross-cultural samples—including the best and worst scoring— are shown in figure 9.1. The best scoring of the fifty-eight cross-cultural samples was a group of education students at the University of Sydney in Australia,

---

3. Because of the need to restrict this comparison to individuals for whom English was a first language, the thirty-two samples did not include samples whose members spoke English as a second language: persons in Hong Kong, teachers of English in Singapore, etc.

TABLE 9.1. Cross-Cultural Samples, with Sample Sizes and PONS Total Score

Sample	Sample Size	PONS Total Score	Percent Accuracy
Australia: education I students, U. of Sydney	64	179.500	81.6%
Canada: 4th-year social psychology under-graduates, Nova Scotia	12	177.917	80.9
Australia: painting II students, E. Sydney Tech.	8	177.002	80.5
Australia: architecture III students, E. Sydney Tech.	24	176.104	80.0
Hawaii: education and counseling psychology graduate students	33	175.823	79.9
Australia: 3rd-year students, Sydney Kinder-garten Teachers College	47	175.734	79.9
Australia: undergraduates	30	175.550	79.8
Australia: 2nd-year art teachers, Randwick Technical College	31	175.339	79.7
Australia: secondary teachers in training (ASOPA)	8	174.707	79.4
Australia: undergraduates, U. of New England at Armidale	75	174.400	79.3
Australia: students, Sydney Kindergarten Teachers College	96	174.175	79.2
Australia: faculty, Sydney Kindergarten Teachers College	9	174.000	79.1
Australia: clinical psychologists, Sydney	29	174.000	79.1
Canada: undergraduates, Nova Scotia	76	172.928	78.6
Canada: students, St. Boniface Col., Manitoba	34	172.706	78.5
Australia: primary teachers in training (ASOPA)	15	172.200	78.2
Canada: undergraduates, U. of Manitoba	45	172.133	78.2
Australia: students, North Ryde high school	55	172.064	78.2
New Zealand: undergraduates, U. of Waikato	24	171.813	78.1
Canada: undergraduates, U. of Manitoba	44	171.670	78.0
Alaska: Caucasian university students	83	171.584	78.0
Australia: industrial design students, Rand-wick Technical College	29	171.483	77.9
Australia: staff, North Ryde Psychiatric Center	61	171.106	77.8
Canada: students, Port Hawkesbury, Nova Scotia	18	171.028	77.7
Canada: undergraduates, Nova Scotia	156	170.359	77.4
Australia: interior design students, Randwick Technical College	34	170.129	77.3
Australia: secondary teachers in training, liberal arts (ASOPA)	21	169.738	77.2
Ireland: nurses in training	64	169.719	77.1
Hong Kong: university students	128	169.172	76.9
Germany: university students	25	169.000	76.8
Europe: European teachers of English	52	167.870	76.3
Australia: faculty, E. Sydney Teachers College	4	167.750	76.2
Alaska: Indian university students	8	167.438	76.1

Table 9.1. *Continued.*

Sample	Sample Size	PONS Total Score	Percent Accuracy
Israel: university students	56	167.045	75.9
Australia: welfare officers in training (ASOPA)	14	166.643	75.8
Mexico: students	106	166.509	75.7
Australia: sculpture students, E. Sydney Tech.	6	166.167	75.5
Australia: painting III students, E. Sydney Tech.	19	165.737	75.3
Alaska: Eskimo university students	12	165.667	75.3
Ireland: psychiatric hospital staff	7	165.143	75.1
Australia: staff, Randwick Technical College	7	165.100	75.0
Israel: university students	68	164.809	74.9
Mexico: students	63	164.778	74.9
Singapore: teachers of English	69	164.101	74.6
New Guinea: undergraduates, U. of Papua New Guinea	34	163.794	74.4
New Guinea: students, Sogeri high school	28	163.232	74.2
Alaska: Indian junior high students	18	161.472	73.4
Australia: painting IV students, E. Sydney Tech.	10	159.950	72.7
Alaska: Caucasian junior high students	127	159.831	72.7
New Guinea: administrators in training (ASOPA)	30	155.037	70.5
New Guinea: administrators in training (ASOPA)	27	154.117	70.0
Australia: Aboriginal sample	22	153.386	69.7
Alaska: Eskimo junior high students	23	151.978	69.1
Ireland: psychiatric patients	15	151.533	68.7
Ireland: psychiatric patients	17	151.147	68.7
Australia: psychiatric patients	24	149.583	68.0
New Guinea: New Guinean teachers in training (ASOPA)	23	148.891	67.7
New Guinea: students, Port Moresby Teachers College	54	146.009	66.4

with a PONS total of 179.500 (81.59 percent). The lowest scoring cross-cultural group, with a PONS total of 146.009 (66.36 percent), was a group of students at a teachers college in Port Moresby, New Guinea. The total range of the cross-cultural samples, then, was 33.491 points.

By comparison, the range of the fifty-nine American samples available at the time of these analyses was from the 186.767 (84.89 percent) scored by a group of social psychology graduate students[4] to the 132.872 (60.39 percent) scored by a group of third grade students. The range of these American

4. This does not include a sample of undergraduates who saw a preliminary video tape version of the PONS and who scored 187.000 (85.00%).

PROFILE OF NONVERBAL SENSITIVITY: STANDARD SCORING SHEET
Channel Scores and Total

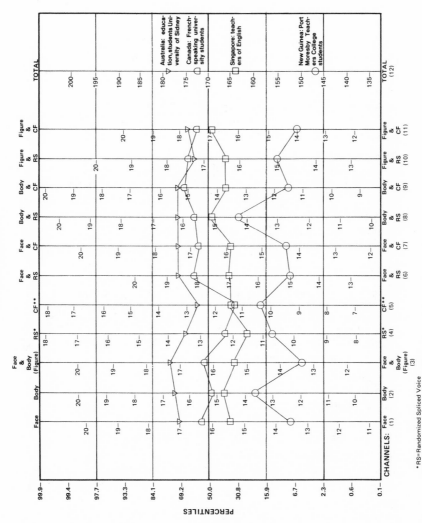

*RS=Randomized Spliced Voice
**CF=Electronically Content-Filtered Voice

FIGURE 9.1. PONS channel scores and total scores for four cross-cultural samples

samples, then, was 53.895. However, when the five samples of grade school students are removed from the American samples, the range is appreciably narrowed. Without the grade school samples, the lowest American sample score is 158.110 (71.86 percent), the score obtained by a group of fifty persons being treated for alcoholism.

In terms of the distribution of sample scores, both the cross-cultural and American samples are skewed. For the fifty-eight cross-cultural samples, 68.90 percent of the range in their scores occurs below their median score. For the fifty-nine American samples, 77.61 percent of the range in their scores occurs below their median score. For the fifty-four nonchildren American samples, 61.97 percent of the range in their scores occurs below their median score. For both cross-cultural samples and American samples, therefore, the worst samples are roughly twice as far below the median as the best samples are above it.

The American norm group of high school students (chapter 3) had a total PONS score of 170.052. The fifty-eight cross-cultural samples ranged around this norm group score, with twenty-six achieving a higher PONS score and thirty-two achieving a lower PONS score. Even the lowest scoring cross-cultural sample, the students at the Port Moresby Teachers College in New Guinea, with a PONS total score of 146.009 (66.36 percent), did better than 110.00 (50.000 percent), which is what might be expected by chance alone on a test of 220 items with two alternatives for each item.

We are unable to conclude whether this finding provides evidence for the idea that at least some aspects of nonverbal behavior are universally intelligible. It is a certainty, for example, that our sample of Port Moresby Teachers College students had some contact with Australians, Americans, and other foreigners. The thirty-six items that this sample decoded accurately above the chance level could have been due to direct contact with foreigners or to indirect cross-cultural contact in the form of magazines, radios, movies, and newspapers. Only if a researcher were able to locate a culture that had experienced no contact whatsoever with Americans (and perhaps any other foreign culture as well), and the members of this hypothetical culture still did better than the chance level on the PONS test or some other multiple-channel decoding instrument, could this be interpreted as evidence for a pan-cultural element in nonverbal communication. This had been the approach pursued by Ekman (1972), although, as indicated earlier in this chapter, he reports that his very remote samples did have contact with foreigners.

RESULTS: (2) CULTURAL PROXIMITY. Our interpretation of the PONS studies as evidence for the interactionist hypothesis is based primarily on two points of evidence: (1) great variation was observed in the decoding abilities of our cross-cultural samples, and (2) even the lowest scoring sample performed at better than the chance level.

A corollary of the interactionist perspective, which we have called the cultural proximity hypothesis, involves an effort to discover whether a discernible pattern occurs in the variation of decoding accuracy among the cross-cultural samples—with the cultures most similar to or most closely associated with the United States doing better on the PONS test. We decided to see whether ratings of cross-cultural samples on a dimension of "cultural similarity to Americans" would correlate with the performance of those samples on the PONS test. Our first test of this rating approach to cultural proximity was conducted when we had the PONS results for only seven samples: Irish nurses, Canadian college students, Irish psychiatric patients, Alaskan Eskimo college students, Alaskan Caucasian college students, Alaskan Indian college students, and European teachers of English.

We asked twenty judges to rate these seven samples on a scale measuring "cultural similarity to the typical American college student." The scale ranged from -10 (very dissimilar) to $+10$ (very similar). To obtain a composite score of the degree of cultural similarity to Americans for the seven samples, we calculated the means of the ratings of the judges. We then correlated the rank order of the cultural similarity to Americans ratings with the total PONS scores obtained for each of the samples. The ratings and PONS total scores are shown in table 9.2.

The results indicate a significant positive relationship between the two rank orders ($\rho = .79$, $p = .02$).[5] This means that the samples with the relatively higher ratings on the dimension of cultural similarity to Americans tended to have higher PONS scores. For example, Canadian college students, who were rated as the most similar to Americans of the seven samples in table 9.2, had the highest PONS score. Irish psychiatric patients, however, were rated as the least similar to Americans, and they had the lowest PONS score.

The cultural similarity to Americans analysis was also applied to the various nations represented within our sample of European teachers of English. Twelve nations were included in this sample, counting three Scandinavian teachers as coming from one country and five East European teachers as coming from one country because of very small sample sizes. Ratings were collected to measure how similar to Americans the twelve national groups were thought to be. In this study, three judges were asked to rank the nations from one (very dissimilar) to twelve (very similar). The composite measure of similarity was obtained by calculating the mean of the rankings made by the three judges. The similarity scores and the PONS total scores of the twelve samples of teachers of English are shown in table 9.3.

The results of this second analysis were like those of the first: a significant positive relationship was found between the ratings of cultural similarity to Americans for the twelve countries and the PONS total scores obtained by

5. All the significance values reported for the ranking studies in this chapter are one-tailed.

TABLE 9.2. Cultural Similarity to Americans Scores and PONS Total Scores for Seven Samples

Sample	Cultural Similarity to Americans Score[a]	PONS Total Score
Canadian university students	5.60	171.859[b]
Alaskan Caucasian university students	3.95	171.584
European teachers of English	0.50	167.870
Alaskan Indian university students	0.00	167.438
Alaskan Eskimo university students	−0.10	165.667
Irish nurses	−1.05	169.719
Irish psychiatric patients	−2.75	151.340[c]

NOTE: $\rho = .79, p < .05$
[a]mean of ratings by twenty judges
[b]unweighted mean of the two samples of English-speaking Canadian university students
[c]unweighted mean of the two samples of Irish psychiatric patients

nationals of those countries ($\rho = .68$, $p < .02$). Again in this analysis, the higher the rated similarity to Americans, the higher the obtained PONS score for the country.

In addition, if the twelve nations are divided into Northern European, Southern European, and Eastern European, a descending pattern of PONS performance can be discerned. The categories for this division were as fol-

TABLE 9.3. Cultural Similarity to Americans Scores and PONS Total Scores for the Twelve National Samples of Teachers of English

Sample	Cultural Similarity to Americans Score[a]	PONS Total Score
England	11.67	170.90
Scandinavia	10.00	176.50
Holland	10.00	165.25
France	8.67	172.44
Germany	8.33	174.33
Scotland	8.33	171.25
Italy	6.00	164.21
Spain	4.33	164.25
Greece	4.00	172.00
Portugal	3.67	159.00
East Europe	2.00	163.50
Turkey	1.00	144.75
Northern Europe	9.50	171.778
Southern Europe	4.50	164.865
Eastern Europe	1.50	154.125

NOTE: $\rho = .68$, $p < .02$ for the 12 national samples
[a]The similarity score is the mean of ratings made by three judges. The interjudge rank correlations were .88, .88, and .91, and the intraclass r was .897.

lows: Northern European included England, Scandinavia, Holland, France, Germany, and Scotland; Southern European included Italy, Spain, Greece, and Portugal; and Eastern European included East Europe countries and Turkey. The mean cultural similarity ratings given these three groups, and the mean PONS scores obtained by nationals from the three groups, are also shown in table 9.3. These regional differences suggest that groups of nations sharing some common cultural elements may be equally able (or unable) to decode the PONS film. One such common cultural element, language family, is considered later in this chapter.

The cultural similarity to Americans analysis was repeated at other points in the data collection process, as additional cross-cultural samples became available. One of these analyses involved collecting ratings on cultural similarity to Americans for twelve samples. The mean ratings and the total PONS scores are shown in table 9.4.

Again in this analysis a significant and positive relationship was found between the ratings of similarity and the total PONS scores for the twelve groups ($\rho = .83$, $p < .001$). Samples rated as more similar culturally to the United States again tended to have higher PONS scores. For example, college and university students from New Zealand and Australia received the highest ratings in this analysis on the dimension of cultural similarity to Americans, and these samples also had the highest PONS scores in this group of samples. By contrast, Australian aborigines, Australian psychiatric patients, and Papua New Guinea Civil Service trainees received the lowest ratings on the similar-

TABLE 9.4. Cultural Similarity to Americans Scores and PONS Total Scores for Twelve Cross-Cultural Samples

Sample	Cultural Similarity to Americans Score[a]	PONS Total Score
Australian teachers college students	7.67	175.703
Australian university students	7.33	179.500
New Zealand university students	6.00	171.813
German university students	4.33	169.000
Australian psychiatric staff	3.33	171.106
New Guinea university students	3.33	163.794
Hong Kong university students	2.33	169.172
New Guinea teachers college students	2.00	146.009
Mexican students	1.67	165.644[b]
Papua N.G. civil service trainees	0.00	152.680[c]
Australian psychiatric patients	−4.66	149.583
Australian Aborigines	−6.00	153.386

NOTE: $\rho = .83$, $p < .001$
[a]The similarity score is the mean of ratings made by three judges. The interjudge rank correlations were .60, .52, and .30.
[b]unweighted mean of the two samples of Mexican students
[c]unweighted mean of the three samples of Papua New Guinea civil service trainees

TABLE 9.5. Cultural Similarity to Americans Scores and PONS Total Scores for Thirty Cross-Cultural Samples

Sample	Cultural Similarity to Americans Score[a]	PONS Total Score
Canadian university students	29.50	171.86[b]
Alaskan Caucasian university students	27.87	171.58
Australian university students	25.87	177.60[b]
German university students	25.00	169.00
New Zealand university students	24.75	171.81
Israeli university students	24.00	165.93[b]
England teachers of English	22.00	170.90
Mexican students	19.62	165.64[b]
Scotland teachers of English	19.50	171.25
Alaskan Eskimo university students	19.50	165.67
Alaskan Indian university students	19.12	167.44
Hong Kong university students	18.12	169.17
Australian psychiatric staff	18.00	171.11
France teachers of English	17.75	172.44
Holland teachers of English	16.12	165.25
Germany teachers of English	15.87	174.33
Scandinavia teachers of English	14.87	176.50
Irish nurses	12.00	169.72
Spain teachers of English	11.62	164.25
New Guinea teachers college students	11.37	146.01
New Guinea university students	10.87	163.79
East Europe teachers of English	10.37	163.50
Italy teachers of English	10.12	164.21
Greece teachers of English	9.75	172.00
Portugal teachers of English	9.12	159.00
Australian psychiatric patients	7.75	149.58
Turkey teachers of English	6.87	144.75
Irish psychiatric patients	5.62	151.34[b]
Papua N.G. civil service trainees	3.00	152.68[c]
Australian Aborigines	1.25	153.39

NOTE: $\rho = .66, p < .001$

[a]The similarity score is the mean of rankings made by eight judges. The intraclass correlation was .71 among the three anthropology graduate student judges, .81 among the other five judges, and .74 for all eight.

[b]unweighted mean of two groups

[c]unweighted mean of the three samples of New Guinea civil service trainees

ity scale, and these samples had three of the four lowest PONS scores in this analysis.

Thirty of the previously analyzed cross-cultural samples were ranked by eight judges (three anthropology graduate students and five nonanthropology college students). The judges were asked to rank the samples according to their degree of cultural similarity to American college students. The mean of the judges' rankings was calculated to obtain a cultural similarity to Americans score for each of the samples.[6] The mean rankings and the total PONS scores are shown in table 9.5.

The results of this fourth analysis are not different from the first three: there was a significant positive relationship between the ratings of cultural similarity to Americans and the PONS scores ($\rho = .66$, $p < .001$). Cross-cultural samples that were rated most similar to Americans tended to have the highest PONS scores.

Both anthropology graduate students and nonanthropology college students seemed to agree fairly well in their ratings on the dimension of cultural similarity. The mean rankings of the anthropologists were significantly correlated with the mean rankings of the nonanthropology college students ($\rho = .72$, $p < .001$). Partly for this reason, rank correlations between the similarity ratings and the PONS scores were similar for the two groups of judges: .66 ($p < .001$) for the anthropology graduate students and .63 ($p < .001$) for the nonanthropology college students.

Finally, ratings of cultural similarity to Americans were collected for each of the twenty nations represented in our fifty-eight cross-cultural samples. Twenty-one undergraduates rated twenty nations using the -10 to $+10$ scale of perceived cultural similarity. The mean of the twenty-one judges' ratings was calculated to obtain a similarity score for each of the twenty nations. For each nation, a total PONS score was obtained by computing the unweighted mean of all the samples tested for that country.[7] The mean similarity ratings for these twenty nations and their total PONS scores are shown in table 9.6.

The results of this final analysis support the cultural proximity interpretation: there was a significant positive relationship between the ratings of cultural similarity to Americans for the twenty nations and the PONS scores of nationals from those countries ($\rho = .74$, $p < .001$). Nations that judges rated as most similar to Americans (Canada, Britain, Australia, etc.) tended to have the highest PONS scores. Nations rated as most dissimilar to the United States (Turkey, New Guinea, Singapore) tended to have the lowest PONS scores.

RESULTS: (3) LINGUISTIC PROXIMITY. The variation among nations in the fifty-eight cross-cultural samples also seems to be associated with formal properties of the language groupings represented in the twenty nations. Four

6. Due to judge errors (repeated use of a rank), the mean of the thirty ranks made by eight judges is 15.572, instead of 15.500.

7. In this analysis, and throughout this chapter, the total PONS scores for a nation are unweighted means for all samples tested for that country. There are two exceptions to this general procedure: in Australia, samples of psychiatric patients and of aborigines were not included in the mean for Australia; in Ireland, psychiatric patients were not included in the mean for that country. These three samples were not included in the country means because samples from other countries did not include comparable groups.

TABLE 9.6. Cultural Similarity to Americans Scores and PONS Total Scores for Twenty Nations

Nation	Number of Samples	Cultural Similarity to Americans Score[a]	PONS Total Score[b]
Canada	7	8.05	172.677
Britain	2	6.90	171.075
Australia	23	5.45	171.677
Scandinavia	1	5.38	176.500
Germany	2	5.19	171.666
France	1	5.05	172.436
New Zealand	1	4.58	171.813
Holland	1	4.48	165.250
Ireland	2	3.10	167.431
Israel	2	3.05	165.927
Italy	1	1.86	164.208
Spain	1	1.10	164.250
East Europe	1	0.62	163.500
Mexico	2	0.38	165.644
Hong Kong	1	0.38	169.172
Greece	1	0.33	172.000
Portugal	1	−0.10	159.000
Turkey	1	−1.48	144.750
New Guinea	6	−2.04	155.180
Singapore	1	−2.57	164.101

NOTE: $\rho = .74, p < .001$
[a]mean of ratings by twenty-one judges
[b]unweighted mean of all samples

different language groups are represented in the cross-cultural samples, and they can be ranked linguistically in order of their genetic proximity (i.e., in terms of a more immediate descent relation from a common parent language) to the language of the speaker in the PONS film, English.

The highest level of classification for the English language is at the level of language family.[8] English is a member of the Indo-European language family, as are most (but not all) of the languages represented in our fifty-eight cross-cultural samples. The next highest level of classification for English is at the level of the two major branches within the Indo-European language: the Centum and Satem branches. English is a Centum language. The next level of classification for English is the level of subbranches within the Centum branch: three of these are the Germanic, Italic, and Hellenic subbranches. English is a member of the Germanic subbranch.

The four language groups contained in the PONS cross-cultural samples are shown ranked in order of genetic proximity to English in table 9.7, along with: (1) the languages in each group that are present in our samples, (2) the

8. We are grateful to Will Vroman for the information about languages upon which this section is based.

TABLE 9.7. Four Language Groups and PONS Scores for Twenty Nations

Language Group and Type	Languages Present in Samples	Nations Present in Each Language	PONS Total Score	Language Group PONS Mean
1. Germanic (Centum, Indo-European)	English	Canada	172.677	170.935
		New Zealand	171.813	
		Australia	171.677	
		Britain	171.075	
		Ireland	167.431	
	German	Germany	171.666[a]	
	Dutch	Holland	165.250	
	Swedish	Scandinavia	176.500	
2. Italic and Hellenic (Centum, Indo-European)	French	France	172.436	166.256
	Spanish	Spain	164.250	
		Mexico	165.644[a]	
	Italian	Italy	164.208	
	Portuguese	Portugal	159.000	
	Greek	Greece	172.000	
3. Slavic (Satem, Indo-European)	Polish	East Europe	163.500	163.500
	Czecho-Slovak			
	Serbo-Croatian			
4. Non-Indo-European	Chinese	Hong Kong	169.172	159.826
		Singapore	164.101	
	Hebrew	Israel	165.927[a]	
	Turkish	Turkey	144.750	
	New Guinea	New Guinea	155.180	

[a] tested in native language

nations from each group that are present in our samples for each language, and (3) the PONS scores of the nations in each language grouping and their unweighted mean.

As table 9.7 indicates, the best-scoring national samples were those with languages most closely related to English; the worst-scoring national samples were those with languages most remote from English (F for linear trend $=$ 10.40, df 2,17, $p < .005$, $r = .60$). This finding raises the interesting possibility that the similarities among verbal languages in a given language group may be paralleled by similarities among the nonverbal behaviors of speakers of those languages. Nonverbal similarities within a language group could include paralanguage, as well as other nonverbal behaviors like facial expressions, body movements, gestures, etc.

In terms of the history of languages, it might be that nonverbal behaviors are transmittable or "heritable" among languages in a manner similar to the transformation of specific words among related languages. For example, the Italic and Hellenic language subbranches have words in their member languages that are, although altered or changed, somewhat recognizable to speakers of any language in this group. An example is the word for "name":

name (English), Name (German), nom (French), nombre (Spanish), nome (Italian), nome (Portuguese), and onoma (Greek).[9]

It is interesting to speculate whether various elements of nonverbal behavior repertoires or "vocabularies," although altered among the various member languages of a language group, are still somewhat recognizable to speakers of any language in the group. Although it is difficult to give concrete examples of actual nonverbal variation among related languages, it might be that words have close nonverbal analogues. For example, it might be that the word for "love" varies recognizably in form or pronunciation among related languages and also in the facial expression (or softened voice, etc.) that often accompanies the speaking of the word.

There might be several nonverbal behaviors that are descended from a common parent nonverbal "language." Members of closely related linguistic groups, therefore, might be as able to interpret the nonverbal behavior of speakers of related languages as they are able to interpret some of their words. This idea is, of course, speculative; but it is consistent with our finding that speakers of languages closely related to English did better on the PONS test than speakers of languages remote from English.

RESULTS: (4) MODERNIZATION, COMMUNICATIONS, AND CONTACT. It is also interesting to ask whether there are other characteristics of the nations in our sample that are related to the ability of members of those nations to decode the PONS test. For the twenty separate nations represented in our PONS samples, an effort was made to collect data on variables of three general types that were thought (on a priori grounds) to be of possible importance to the ability to interpret the nonverbal behavior in the PONS film: (1) general measures of modernization, (2) measures of communications development and sophistication, and (3) measures of direct contact with the United States or with Americans.

Several specific indices were obtained for each of the three general types of measures. A total of eleven indices were selected from various statistical sources:

A. General modernization
   1. Steel: steel consumption in kilograms per capita[10]
   2. Cars: motor vehicles in use per capita[11]
   3. Doctors: physicians per capita[12]
B. Communications development
   4. Energy: energy consumption, in kilogram equivalents of coal per capita[13]

9. The Greek example is shown with a romanized alphabet, as in Algeo and Pyles (1966).
10. *U.N. Statistical Yearbook*, 1972, pp. 539–40.
11. Motor vehicle information from *Statistical Abstract of the United States*, 1972, pp. 827–28; population estimates from same source, pp. 803–5.
12. *U.N. Statistical Yearbook*, 1971, pp. 747–50.
13. Ibid., 1972, pp. 353–56.

5. Newsprint: kilograms of newsprint consumption per capita[14]
6. Telephones: telephones in use per capita[15]
7. Televisions: television sets per capita[16]
8. Radios: radios per capita[17]
C. Contact with Americans or the United States
   9. Trade: ratio of imports from the United States to total imports[18]
  10. Tourists: ratio of touring Americans to total tourists[19]
  11. Mail: ratio of foreign letters received to total domestic mail[20]

The choice of the specific eleven indicators was partly a function of availability. In general, the specific indicators seemed to have face validity for the dimensions they were intended to measure. The one exception was an insufficiently precise indicator. The measure Mail was the ratio of foreign letters received to total domestic mail. The ideal measure of contact with Americans, the ratio of American mail to total domestic mail, was unavailable.

The listing of the variables under the three broad categories shown above was on the basis of the face value of the measures—for example, the five measures under the category of communications development are all measures or correlates of various communications media and devices.[21] The eleven measures were also factor analyzed to see whether the face value clusters corresponded to those obtained through factor analysis.[22]

A number of different factor analytic strategies were followed, including both orthogonal and oblique rotation methods. Although the different methods produced different factor loadings for the eleven variables, the essential factor structure remained the same under all methods. In general, the various factor analyses agreed with the a priori division of the measures, but there were some differences. The first factor consisted of four of the five communications measures (Energy, Telephones, Newsprint, and Televisions) as well as the general modernization variables of Cars and Steel. The second factor consisted of two contact measures (Trade and Tourists), as well as the remaining communications measure, Radios. The third factor consisted of the variables Doctors and Mail. Since the eleven variables are of intrinsic interest in terms of their relationships to the PONS scores of various national samples, they were preserved as eleven distinct measures rather than combined into three factors.

14. Ibid., pp. 550–51.
15. Ibid., pp. 505–8.
16. Ibid., pp. 836–40.
17. Ibid., pp. 836–40.
18. J. Paxton, Ed., *The Statesman's Yearbook: 1972–1973* (London: MacMillan, 1972).
19. *U.N. Statistical Yearbook, 1971*, pp. 458–73.
20. Ibid., pp. 477–82.
21. One variable in the communications category, energy, could also be regarded as an index of general modernization. McClelland (1961, 1963) concluded that electric power production was the best index of comparative rates of modern economic growth.
22. It should be noted that the ratio of variables to units (11/20) is higher than generally thought desirable in factor analysis.

TABLE 9.8. Rank Correlations between PONS Total and Eleven Measures for Twenty Nations

General Modernization		Communications Development		Contact with the United States	
steel	.55[a]	energy	.67[b]	trade	.12
cars	.70[b]	newsprint	.65[b]	tourists	.45[c]
doctors	.37	telephones	.76[b]	mail	−.30
		televisions	.60[a]		
		radios	.61[a]		

[a] $p < .01$
[b] $p < .001$
[c] $p < .05$

For some of the measures, the United States led the other twenty nations in the study. This was true for all five measures of communications development and sophistication. For two of the three measures of general modernization, Steel and Cars, the United States led the other twenty nations in the study.[23] For the general modernization measure Doctors, however, the United States trailed five national samples: Israel, Italy, Germany, Greece, and the East Europe nations. The United States could not be compared with other nations, of course, on the third group of measures, contact with Americans or the United States.

The five measures of communications sophistication and the three measures of general modernization, then, could be relevant to PONS performance in two ways: (1) because they reflect intrinsically important aspects of a culture or nation (e.g., a "high degree of communications awareness"), or (2) simply because they reflect the similarity of the nation to the United States. For example, the nation that is ranked first on Telephones is both (1) the nation in which people are most likely to have used the telephone, and (2) the nation that is most similar to the United States on this variable. If members of this culture did well on the PONS test, it could be because they are relatively sophisticated about one type of communication or because their culture is relatively more similar to American culture.

If all types of variables predict PONS performance equally well, it could be interpreted as support for the similarity hypothesis—that is, nations similar to the United States on these measures do better on the PONS test. However, if some types of variables are better predictors than others (e.g., communications variables are better predictors than general modernization variables), it could mean in addition that the more successful measures are tapping national

23. On the measure of steel consumption, the United States actually trailed Sweden and Czechoslovakia. These two nations, however, were included in the Scandinavian and East Europe samples and the unweighted means of steel consumption for these samples were lower than the U.S. figures.

attributes that are intrinsically advantageous in the decoding of nonverbal information like that in the PONS film.

The relationship between the PONS scores of the twenty nations and their rankings on the eleven measures of general modernization, communications development, and contact with the United States is shown in table 9.8. As the table shows, all five measures of communications development were significantly related to performance on the PONS test, with the best predictor being the number of telephones per capita ($\rho = .76$, $p < .001$). Two of the three measures of general modernization, Steel and Cars, were also significantly related to PONS performance. Only one of the measures of direct contact, Tourists, was significantly related to PONS performance. The contact variable Mail was the only variable negatively related with PONS scores.[24]

The median ρ of the communications measures was .65, the median ρ of the general modernization measures was .55, and the median ρ of the contact measures was .12. In general, then, the measures seemed to be differentially useful as predictors of PONS scores, with the communications measures being more consistently and more strongly related to PONS performance than either measures of general modernization or measures of direct contact with the United States.[25]

Because our national samples vary a good deal on occupation, social class, age, and education, it was desirable to try to hold some of these factors constant while comparing the samples on communications and modernization measures. Fortunately, one of our samples was a group of European teachers of English, which we would presume to be somewhat homogeneous on some of these extraneous variables. This sample was divided up into smaller samples according to national origin (see table 9.3). The samples of teachers from Scotland and England were combined for this analysis, however, since the measures of communications, modernization, and contact were obtained only for all of Britain. There are two additional samples that can be included in this analysis, both of which were collected later. One of these is a sample of teachers of the English language from Singapore. The final sample of the thirteen consists of teachers in New Guinea who were still undergoing training.

24. This variable was constructed from the ratio of foreign letters received to total domestic mail. The denominator of this index was extremely variable and produced extremely high scores for nations with very small domestic mail services.

25. In using aggregate data at the level of a nation to predict performance by individual members of that nation, there is always some danger of an ecological fallacy. That is, one must be careful about attributing performance to a characteristic that may be generally true of a nation but untrue of the persons actually studied. This danger is obviously greater for some variables in this analysis than others. For example, the fact that a nation is high on the contact measure of trade—i.e., the United States supplies much of the nation's imports—may not have had an effect on the nationals we studied from the country. For other variables, however, the aggregate measures are more likely to be meaningful in the lives of individuals. For example, the number of radios in a country almost certainly affected the probability that the nationals from that country in our study had heard a radio.

Table 9.9 shows the correlations of PONS total scores with the eleven nation measures for these thirteen samples of teachers. The relationships in this analysis—with thirteen national samples varying almost not at all on educational or occupational characteristics—are of a larger magnitude than in the first study. Again, the communications measures are most highly correlated with the PONS scores (median ρ = .76), followed by the general modernization measures (median ρ = .75), with the contact measures last (median ρ = .16). This analysis suggests that eliminating variation due to education and occupation may increase the relationship between PONS scores and the communications and modernization variables.

Since some of the samples analyzed in table 9.8 were quite small, we repeated the analysis only using the eleven nations for which the sample size was greater than 10. The sample sizes in this analysis were quite substantial; the median sample size of the eleven national samples was 124. The magnitude of the relationship between PONS and communications measures was larger here than in table 9.8 (median ρ = .79), and about the same for measures of modernization (median ρ = .52) and contact (median ρ = .15).

The results of these analyses do not appear to yield different conclusions. Of the three types of measures, those measuring communications development are clearly the most highly related to the PONS scores of the nations in our cross-cultural testing. The measures of general modernization are also related to PONS performance, but at a considerably lower magnitude. Finally, the measures of direct contact with the United States also appear to be related to PONS performance (negatively in the case of the Mail variable), but least strongly of the three types of measures.

The results of this analysis seem to place primary importance (of the variables we measured) on the level of communications development in a given nation. We generally interpret this as indicating that there seems to be a dimension of communications sophistication that is related to performance on the PONS test. The highest PONS scoring groups were those who came from cultures with the most highly developed systems of communications.

TABLE 9.9. Rank Correlations between PONS Total and Eleven Measures for Thirteen Samples of Teachers of English

General Modernization		Communications Development		Contact with the United States	
steel	.75[a]	energy	.76[b]	trade	.16
cars	.82[b]	newsprint	.80[b]	tourists	.44
doctors	.54[c]	telephones	.82[b]	mail	−.64[c]
		televisions	.70[a]		
		radios	.76[a]		

[a] $p < .01$
[b] $p < .001$
[c] $p < .05$

It could be that the relationship between communications development and PONS performance is a direct function of relatively greater experience at decoding a wide variety of communications in everyday life. In countries with highly developed communications systems, individuals are more likely to be exposed frequently to the single or multichannel communications of a large number of acquaintances (e.g., on the telephone) and strangers (e.g., on radio or television). It is possible that this exposure involves a kind of practice that cultivates an ability to decode.

The relationship between communications development and PONS performance could also involve less direct factors. For example, a number of researchers in the area of comparative aspects of political and economic modernization have concluded that the level of communications development plays a critical role in the process of modernization (Pye 1963; Lerner 1958). In addition to the "practice effect" that communications experience may contribute to decoding skills, highly developed systems of communication in a country may contribute to a set of values in which communication is regarded as important. In a culture high in communications development, then, the individual may be both more oriented toward the interpretation of a wide range of communications and more likely to accumulate decoding experience.

ETHNIC DIFFERENCES

Prior to the development of the PONS, a number of studies had investigated ethnic differences in the decoding of nonverbal cues. George Gitter and his colleagues found in two studies, employing still photographs as stimuli and college students as subjects, that blacks were significantly more accurate decoders than whites ($r = .21$ and $.33$, respectively; Gitter, Black, and Mostofsky 1972a, 1972b). When Gitter and Quincy (1968) employed children ages four to six as subjects, however, they found no difference in decoding accuracy between blacks and whites; nor did Izard (1971) in his study of five- to seven-year-olds. In their research with children ages five to fourteen, Kellogg and Eagleson (1931) found white children to perform better than black children at decoding still photos for seven of the ten age levels ($t(9) = 1.76$, $p = .113$, effect size $= 1.17\sigma$).

In his research employing motion picture stimuli produced by Gitter, Newmeyer (1970) found no overall relationship between race and decoding among adolescent boys, but he did find blacks to be superior at decoding audio cues while whites were superior at decoding video cues. Overall, we must conclude that the relationship between race and decoding of nonverbal cues has not yet been well established although the nature of the stimuli (still photos versus movies), the channel investigated (video versus audio), and the ages of the subjects are all good candidates for the roles of moderator variables.

A good deal of research has addressed the question of cultural differences in PONS performance, but very few data are available in the examination of ethnic differences within the United States. One relevant study was done by Robert McCoid, who administered the PONS to thirty-nine West Virginia teachers, half of whom were black and half of whom were white (see chapter 15 for more detail on this study). Black and white status was coded as 1 and 0, respectively, and was then correlated with channel, quadrant, and marginal performance scores. There were no overall differences in PONS performance between black and white teachers ($r = .00$). Of the twenty-nine different correlations computed, none reached statistical significance; about half (55 percent) favored the black teachers and about half (45 percent) favored the white teachers.

In research on children with and without learning disabilities (N = 316), Tanis Bryan employed an eighty-item short form of the PONS comprised of the face and body channels of the full-length PONS and the CF and RS channels of a specially developed audio PONS in which the sender was a female child (see chapter 8). About one-third of the children were black and two-thirds were white. The first column of table 9.10 shows the correlations between group membership and performance in the four channels of this short form of the PONS. Once again there was no significant or consistent overall relationship between race and sensitivity to nonverbal cues. However, black children were significantly superior to white children in the content-filtered channel and were not as good as the white children in the other channels. The second column of table 9.10 shows the analogous correlations from McCoid's study. We must remind ourselves here that the audio channels of his study employed an adult female sender rather than a child sender. Perhaps because of that difference, or because of the special nature of teacher samples, or because of the instability of small samples, McCoid's results did not parallel Bryan's results.

As a segment of an extensive program of research motivated in part by a desire to find occupational selection instruments that would not discriminate against nonwhites, David McClelland and Charles Dailey administered the adult female sender audio PONS to 83 human service workers and 131 foreign service officers (see chapter 13). The third and fourth columns of table 9.10 show the correlations between nonwhite status and accuracy in CF and RS. Only for the foreign service officers was there a significant relationship, showing nonwhites (primarily but not exclusively blacks) to be superior to whites in decoding content-filtered cues ($r = .21$).

This correlation probably underestimates the actual relationship, since the nonwhite officers were ranked somewhat lower on the criterion variables of effectiveness than the white officers. When the effects of the criterion variable were partialed out, the correlation between CF 20 and nonwhite status increased from .21 to .26 for one criterion variable and to .27 for the other

TABLE 9.10. Correlations of PONS Performance with Nonwhite Status for Four Samples

Channel	Children Grades 3-5[a] (N = 316)	Teachers[b] (N = 39)	Human Service Workers[c] (N = 83)	Foreign Service Officers[c] (N = 131)	Weighted Mean		N
					r	p	
Content-filtered	.17[d]	-.14	-.03	.21[e]	.13[f]	.002	569
Randomized spliced	-.17[d]	-.24	-.12	.00	-.13[g]	.002	569
Face	-.11[e]	-.03			-.10	.06	355
Body	-.10	.03			-.09	.09	355

[a] after Bryan (audio testing was with female child audio PONS)
[b] after McCoid
[c] after McClelland and Dailey
[d] $p \leqslant .01$
[e] $p \leqslant .05$
[f] For a sample of seventy-five U.S. Navy Human Resource Consultants tested by McBer & Co., this correlation was .13.
[g] For a sample of seventy-two U.S. Navy Human Resource Consultants tested by McBer & Co., this correlation was -.17.

criterion variable. Table 9.10 also shows, however, that among human service workers the white workers tended to score slightly higher than the nonwhite workers. Considering both studies together, it appears that neither whites nor nonwhites have a clear advantage in decoding the nonverbal cues of the audio PONS, but occupational category may serve as a moderator variable.

The fifth column of table 9.10 shows the weighted mean correlation between nonwhite status and PONS performance. None of the correlations is large but two are quite significant statistically. In general, the nonwhites (primarily blacks) are superior to whites in decoding content-filtered cues, and whites are superior to nonwhites in decoding randomized spliced cues. Successful decoding of the CF channel may require a more global, intuitive approach, while decoding of the RS channel may require a more molecular, analytical approach; but even if this is correct it does not suggest why such differences in decoding style might be found between white and nonwhite children or adults.

SOCIAL CLASS DIFFERENCES

Not much is known of the relationship between sensitivity to nonverbal cues as measured by the PONS and level of social class. In two studies of high school students, sampled from the eastern and midwestern United States, father's occupational level was available to serve as the operational definition of social class level for most of the students. Table 9.11 shows the correlations between father's occupational level and PONS total score, separately for male and female subjects. The results were quite consistent for the two studies, with females showing a positive correlation between social class and sensitivity to nonverbal cues and males showing a negative correlation.

TABLE 9.11. Correlations of PONS Performance with Level of Father's Occupation for Two Samples of High School Students

	Sex of Subjects					
	Females		Males		Difference	
Sample	r	N	r	N	z	p (two-tailed)
Midwest (N=196)	.27	153	−.14	43	2.35	.02
East (N=107)	.22	56	−.16	51	1.93	.06
Weighted mean (N=303)	.26[a]	209	−.15[b]	94	3.31	.001

[a]p < .0002, two-tailed
[b]p < .16, two-tailed

We might have expected an overall positive correlation between social class and PONS score on the basis of Izard's (1971) research showing that higher social class was associated with more accurate nonverbal decoding in children and Pfaff's (1954) finding that junior high school students of higher socioeconomic status were more sensitive to nonverbal cues than those lower in socioeconomic status. Pfaff's results, however, were based on sensitivity to tone of voice, and he reported no moderating effects of sex of subject. When we examined our results for just the pure tone channels (RS + CF), we again found a positive average correlation between social class and sensitivity for the female subjects of the two samples ($r = .19$). For male subjects, though, the average correlation for the two samples changed to $r = .10$. Thus, for tone of voice alone, our results do appear to be fairly consistent with Pfaff's, suggesting that higher social class predicts higher sensitivity to auditory nonverbal cues. The mystery remains for the full PONS, however, as to why there should be a negative correlation between social class and sensitivity to nonverbal cues for males while the relationship is quite firmly positive for females.

10 | Cognitive Correlates

In this chapter, we will examine the relationship between the PONS test and a variety of measures of cognitive functioning. These measures include IQ tests, Scholastic Aptitude Test (SAT), school grades and class ranks, tests of verbal ability and English language proficiency, Witkin's Group Embedded Figures Test (GEFT), the Dailey Programmed Cases, the Bieri test of cognitive complexity, and differential attention to channels. We will try to address the convergent and discriminant validity of the PONS test (Campbell and Fiske 1959). Demonstration of the convergent validity results in confirmation of scores on the PONS by independent measurement procedures, while the demonstration of discriminant validity provides justification for viewing the PONS as a novel trait measure.

In a number of places in this and other sections we report the correlation of more than one objective measure of ability with PONS. For instance, for a sample of high school students from Minnesota, we collected both verbal and nonverbal IQ scores. In a matrix of intercorrelations, we report the correlation between these two IQ measures, the median intercorrelation of the various PONS measures used in the analysis, and the median correlation between these measures of IQ and the PONS variables. Such a matrix presents the median intercorrelations resulting when a single trait measured by several methods is correlated with the PONS test. (For a detailed discussion of the multitrait, multimethod approach to establishing convergent and discriminant validity, from which our method is derived, see Campbell and Fiske 1959.)

PERFORMANCE MEASURES

INTELLECTUAL ABILITY. One of our most important questions regarding cognitive ability correlates of the PONS test has been the degree to which scores on the PONS are correlated with scores on standard IQ tests. In the past, most researchers have found a positive but low and nonsignificant corre-

234

lation between the ability correctly to judge nonverbal cues and various measures of intelligence. Gates (1923) found that the ability to identify emotions in pictures increased with mental age (as well as chronological age), and Guilford (1929) found that the correlation between ability to identify pictures of emotional expression and intelligence was not high. Kanner (1931) found a .21 correlation in a sample of 198 subjects between ability to judge emotions from pictures and scores on the Thorndike intelligence test. Adams (1927) reported a correlation of .12 between ratings of intellectual functioning and the ability accurately to rate others on various traits and characteristics. Weisgerber (1956) correlated college entrance test scores of 100 college students with measures of accuracy in understanding facial and hand expressions of emotion. The correlations were small, ranging from .08 to .20. Linguistic ability was the best predictor of affective sensitivity. Davitz (1964) reported a .37 correlation between verbal intelligence and sensitivity to emotion in vocal communication and a .34 correlation between such accuracy and Raven's Progressive Matrices, a test of nonverbal intelligence.

If the correlations between the PONS and IQ were very high, the argument might be made that the PONS test measures not nonverbal sensitivity but rather general intelligence and/or "test-taking ability." If there were, on the other hand, only very low correlations between PONS and standard IQ test scores, the notion that nonverbal sensitivity and intelligence were separate abilities would be supported.

We have considered data from six samples in attempting to answer this question. In table 10.1, we report median correlations of PONS and intelligence variables from two separate samples of high school students from different parts of the United States, a sample of nurses from Belfast, a sample of men and women at an alcoholism treatment center in Kansas, a sample of psychiatric patients from Australia, and a sample of clinical psychology faculty from Australia.

Since table 10.1 is the first of a number of discriminant validity summaries, we should say a word about its interpretation. On the left, one will note the label "median IQ r." This refers to the Pearson product-moment correlation between the measures of intelligence used in the analysis (the median r if more than two measures are employed). The "median PONS r" refers to the median correlation in that sample between the PONS measures used (i.e. four quadrants; tone 40 and video 60; face 60, body 60, and figure 60; and RS 80 and CF 80). The "median PONS-IQ r" refers to the median of the set of correlations between all the available intelligence measures and the PONS variables. The medians of the four IQ, PONS, and IQ-PONS clusters appear at the bottom of each column.

In the two samples of high school students, the intelligence test intercorrelations and the PONS intercorrelations tended, for the most part, to be positive and fairly high. The medians of the median intercorrelations for the intelli-

TABLE 10.1. Convergent and Discriminant Validity Matrix of PONS and IQ for Six Samples

	Midwest High School (N=130)[a]	East Coast High School (N=44)[b]	Irish Nurses (N=56)[c]	Alcoholics (N=44)[d]	Australian Psychiatric Patients (N=82)[e]	Australian Clinical Faculty (N=83)[e]	Median r
Quadrants							
Median IQ r	.48	.66	.04	.53	.50	.34	.48
Median PONS r	.36	.40	.38	.54	.24	.13	.39
Median PONS-IQ r	.21	.08	.13				.17
Tone 40, video 60							
Median IQ r	.48	.66	.04	.63	.50	.20	.48
PONS r	.40	.17	.21	.51	.22	.24	.30
Median PONS-IQ r	.20	.23	.18				.22
Face 60, body 60, figure 60							
Median IQ r	.48	.66	.04	.66	.76	.44	.48
Median PONS r	.65	.53	.45	.50	.27	.12	.59
Median PONS-IQ r	.21	.10	.15				.18
RS 80, CF 80							
Median IQ r	.48	.66	.04	.84	.74	.50	.48
PONS r	.58	.62	.53	.65	.31	.13	.60
Median PONS-IQ r	.18	.16	.13				.17
Medians							
Median IQ r	.48	.66	.04	.64	.62	.39	.48
Median PONS r	.49	.46	.42	.52	.26	.13	.48
Median PONS-IQ r	.20	.13	.14				.17

[a] IQ includes verbal and nonverbal (Metropolitan Test)
[b] IQ includes Otis Beta or Otis Gamma and Verbal and Math SAT scores
[c] IQ includes Mill Hill vocabulary test and Raven's Progressive Matrices
[d] IQ is single variable (Shipley-Hartford)
[e] IQ is single variable (Simpson)

gence tests were .48 and .66, and for the PONS they were .49 and .46. The median correlations between PONS and intelligence were rather low in comparison, ranging from .23 to .08 with median correlations of .20 and .13.

Among the Irish nurses the median of the PONS intercorrelations was .42, while the correlation between the Mill Hill vocabulary test and Raven's Progressive Matrices test was only .04. The PONS-IQ intercluster r's were weakly positive, with a median of .14. Also, among the clinical faculty the PONS-IQ intercorrelations were small, with a median of only .13.

In the sample of alcoholic patients, the pattern was rather different. The PONS intercorrelations were higher than those in the high school samples. The most striking difference was in the magnitude of the PONS-IQ median intercorrelations. These four median intercorrelations were all at least .50 with a median of .52. The strength of this correlation indicates that among these alcoholic patients, there was a substantial positive correlation between intelligence and nonverbal sensitivity as measured by the PONS test. Among the psychiatric patients, the PONS-IQ correlations ranged from .22 to .31, higher than those in the "normal" samples but certainly not as striking as those in the sample of alcoholics.

For all six samples considered together, the intercorrelations among the parts of the PONS test are just as high as the intercorrelations among the parts of the IQ tests (grand median $r = .48$), and the grand median r of parts of the PONS with various measures of IQ was only .17.

In attempting to account for the substantial positive correlation between IQ and PONS in the alcoholic sample, we observed that many of these alcoholic subjects possessed below average IQ scores. Subjects whose IQ scores approached the lower end of the IQ distribution might have been expected to experience difficulty in any testing situation. As IQ increased, so would PONS score. Thus, if this were true we would expect that at the upper end of the IQ distribution, where subjects' IQ scores were average or above average, IQ and PONS scores would be relatively uncorrelated. We divided the sample into thirds based on IQ score. The three groups consisted of (1) fifteen subjects with IQ score less than or equal to 96 (low IQ), (2) fourteen subjects with IQ score between 96 and 112 (intermediate IQ) and (3) fifteen subjects with IQ score greater than or equal to 112 (high IQ). We recomputed the PONS-IQ correlations within each group.

The three median PONS-IQ correlations of .34, .34, and .33 showed that our hypothesis was, to a large extent, unsupported. In all three groups, IQ accounted for about 11.5 percent (r^2) of the total variance in PONS scores. Although these correlations were by no means large, it is clear that the PONS-IQ relationship did not disappear when subjects' IQ's were high enough that their intellectual ability to take the PONS was not likely to be impaired.

Apparently, among subjects with relatively severe psychological, toxicological, or encephalopathological problems, the PONS does, to a limited extent, measure general ability or intelligence. We should note, however, that although the IQ range of the high IQ group of alcoholics exceeded the average IQ of the normative sample, the PONS total scores of these alcoholics (75 percent) were lower than those of the norm group (77 percent). For further discussion of the PONS performance of alcoholic patients, see chapter 12.

We decided to validate further the independence of PONS scores and measures of intelligence for one of our samples with a method suggested by Donald Rubin. Using the data from the east coast high school sample (part of the norm group), we performed a principal components analysis using four PONS measures and three measures of intelligence. These seven measures were scores on the four PONS quadrants, Otis IQ, verbal SAT, and math SAT. Under the hypothesis that PONS and intelligence are relatively independent, we specified that the analysis should yield two principal components. We expected that, after orthogonal rotation (Varimax), the four PONS variables would be located on one axis in the factor space and the three intelligence measures would be located on the other axis.

Our expectations were strongly supported. The four PONS variables were located on the positive end of factor 1 (the PONS factor) and the two SAT variables were located on the positive end of factor 2 (the intellectual ability factor). This indicates that, for this sample, PONS performance and scholastic aptitude performance were orthogonal to one another. The IQ variable, located between the two axes, was related to both abilities, although IQ loaded much more highly on factor 2 than it did on factor 1. Table 10.2 presents the rotated factor loadings for the seven variables on the two factors.

Analyses of the relationship between PONS and self-reported scores on the Scholastic Aptitude Test told a story similar to that told by analyses of the PONS-IQ relationship. We computed the median PONS-SAT correlations and intercorrelations for five samples of college students and one sample of high

TABLE 10.2. Principal Components of PONS and Intelligence Variables (Rotated Factor Loadings) (N=110 High School Students)

Variable	Factor 1 (PONS)	Factor 2 (Intellectual Ability)
IQ	+.19	+.64
SAT Verbal	−.02	+.89
SAT Math	−.07	+.84
Positive-Submissive	+.66	+.02
Positive-Dominant	+.82	−.00
Negative-Submissive	+.77	+.06
Negative-Dominant	+.78	+.06

school students (median N = 38). In general, the median correlations between PONS and SAT scores tended to be low. Across all samples and all PONS measures reported, the median PONS-SAT correlation was .15, the median PONS r was .39, and the median verbal-math SAT r was .54. This finding provides further evidence that nonverbal sensitivity as measured by the PONS and general scholastic aptitude are relatively independent.

Further evidence for this independence came from an analysis of high school achievement among three samples of college students and one sample of high school students (median N = 47). There was only a minimal relationship between PONS and high school achievement, with a PONS-achievement correlation of .03. A subsequent study by Claire Schmais found a correlation of .03 between PONS total and college grades in a sample of students of dance therapy.

Among third graders, however, the PONS bore a moderately strong positive relationship to achievement (measured by the Metropolitan Test) in reading and mathematics, where high achievers scored higher on the PONS (median PONS-achievement r = .36, N = 41). Among subjects this young, however, it might be expected that reading and math achievement would be correlated with PONS score because of the positive relationship all three variables would be expected to bear to proficiency at reading answers and performing well in a testing situation. Children whose verbal and analytical abilities were low were probably at a loss in taking the PONS test, while good readers suffered no handicap in reading and understanding the meanings of the alternatives. Within the group of relatively good readers and those with higher mathematical ability, we would expect all children to have roughly equal ability to take the PONS. Among these subjects, we would expect that PONS does indeed measure nonverbal skill and that achievement and PONS scores are uncorrelated. We would expect that the children at the lower end of the achievement distribution would experience some difficulty in taking the PONS, and that the task would become easier as achievement increased.

To test this hypothesis, we divided the sample of third graders into three groups: (1) those in the lower third of the theoretical percentile distribution (i.e., those with percentile scores of less than or equal to thirty-three) on the measure of reading achievement; (2) those in the middle third (percentile scores in the inclusive range of thirty-four to sixty-six); and (3) those in the upper third of the distribution (percentile scores equal to or above sixty-seven). Three groups of subjects were formed in the same manner as above using mathematics achievement percentile scores. Correlations between PONS scores and achievement scores were computed within each of the three groups for each test.

An examination of these correlations revealed support for our hypothesis that as achievement level increases, the correlation between PONS and achievement decreases. The high correlations of PONS with achievement evidenced in the entire sample occurred only in the low reading achievement and low math achievement groups (median PONS-reading $r = .32$, median PONS-math $r = .48$). Where ability was at an intermediate or high level, PONS and achievement were relatively independent. For reading, the analogous r's for intermediate and high achievement were .04 and .06, and for math they were .11 and .16. Dimitrovsky (1964) reported a similar finding in which verbal mental ability and vocal expression recognition were correlated significantly only among five year olds where verbal ability played an important role in understanding the instructions.

An additional sample of children was tested by Robert Clark in New York City, who administered the full PONS and the Lorge-Thorndike test of intelligence to twenty eight-to-nine year olds, twenty ten-to-eleven year olds, and twenty twelve-to-thirteen year olds. The correlations he obtained were $-.18, .52$, and .10, respectively. The median r of .10 was consistent with the generally low correlations obtained between the PONS and intellectual ability.

Since PONS score seems only weakly related to general intellectual ability, we wondered whether it might instead be related specifically to verbal ability. The question we considered, then, was whether verbal and nonverbal skills were correlated. We computed the correlation of PONS with two measures of verbal ability: the vocabulary score of the Wechsler Adult Intelligence Scale (WAIS) and a vocabulary test modeled on the Graduate Record Examination. For eighty male and female college students, the median PONS-verbal ability correlation was only .18, a positive but weak relationship.

As part of a study done by Debra D. Kimes, thirty male and female undergraduate artists (painters, writers, dancers, actors, and musicians) took the PONS and the Quick Word Test of IQ. This is a 100-item synonym test that correlates .80 with the WAIS. The correlation between PONS and this test of verbal IQ was $-.02$.

Among sixty-nine teachers of English in Singapore, we found a substantial positive correlation between PONS and three tests of English proficiency (median PONS-proficiency $r = .60$). However, when the sample was separated into male and female subsamples, the correlations became slightly stronger for males ($r = .62$) and nearly disappeared among the females ($r = .14$). Since the females in this sample scored significantly higher ($p < .001$) than did males on all three tests of English ability, we suggest that among individuals whose English proficiency is sufficiently high to eliminate problems in understanding directions or choosing alternatives on the test, verbal ability and nonverbal sensitivity as measured by PONS are relatively independent.

Before we can accept this interpretation, however, it is necessary to demonstrate that the existence of a positive correlation between English proficiency and PONS among males and an absence of this correlation among females is due to subjects' levels of proficiency in English and not merely due to a sex difference. We divided our sample into thirds on the basis of a composite score of English proficiency (the sum of the scores on the three tests). Correlations between PONS and English proficiency were then computed within these three groups. As the level of English proficiency of our subjects increased, the relationship of this variable to nonverbal skill diminished considerably. The median PONS-proficiency r's for the low, intermediate, and high proficiency groups were .60, .27, and .14.

FIELD INDEPENDENCE. The Group Embedded Figures Test was developed by Witkin and his colleagues as a form of the Embedded Figures Test suitable for administration to large groups of subjects at once. Like the Embedded Figures Test, the GEFT measures "field independence" by testing subjects' ability visually to disembed hidden figures. According to Witkin et al. (1971), high scores on the GEFT indicate cognitive clarity, an analytical versus global perceptual mode, and a general disposition to structure experience. Subjects who score high have the ability to analyze a complex configuration and to respond to some parts of it, ignoring others.

The field independent person might thus be expected to excel at identifying certain nonverbal cues in the behavior of a stimulus person, ignoring other irrelevant behavioral cues in the visual field. Because of this, we might expect the field independent person to score higher on the PONS test. On the other hand, the individual who is field dependent responds in a global perceptual manner and has a more or less "gut" response to the nonverbal behavioral cues of a stimulus person. Thus, the field dependent person may be the high scorer on the PONS test. Some evidence in favor of the former hypothesis comes from a study by Wolitzky (1973). In this study, thirty-six subjects (twelve male, twenty-four female) took the EFT and the Rod and Frame test, as well as two tests of sensitivity to affective vocal expressions. More field independent subjects were found to be more sensitive to affective expressions.

When we undertook to investigate this relationship, a clear prediction of the direction of the correlation was not made. The PONS and the GEFT were administered to 111 U.S. high school students, 80 U.S. college students, and 288 Canadian college students. The median PONS-GEFT correlations for these three samples were .07, .02, and .24 ($p < .001$), respectively. For the Canadian sample, our results parallel those of Wolitzky.

A sample of sixty children tested in New York City by Robert Clark were given the full PONS and the Children's Embedded Figures Test. The correlations with total PONS were: age eight to nine, $r = .10$; age ten to eleven, $r = .36$; age twelve to thirteen, $r = .19$. Thus, for children, skill at embedded figures is positively and modestly correlated with nonverbal decoding ability.

ASSESSING PROGRAMMED CASES. The Dailey Programmed Case method of life history assessment (Dailey 1971) measures an individual's skill at understanding the interrelationships among and significance of others' behaviors. It defines as its primary criterion accuracy in intuitive prediction, which results from a judge's recognition of intelligible interconnections among episodes in a life. This method of assessment presents behavioral events to a judge and measures his or her ability to predict other behavioral events in the same history.

The programmed case is a written life history structured in such a way that the judge learns to make increasingly valid predictions in the case and the experimenter obtains measures of the validity of the judge's predictions. The basic unit of information to the judge is the event, and the judge receives the case in increments of one event after which he or she predicts the next event. Prediction is made by discriminating among alternative events. The event is a behavioral episode that occurs at a particular time and place in the verbal account of an individual's life. It is in response to a particular situation, and the account of the person's behavior includes reports of his overt behavior, words, and gestures that indicate his feelings and probable motives.

We might expect that those individuals who tend to be more sensitive to cues emitted nonverbally may have, throughout their lives, developed greater experience tracing the events of others' lives and have developed skill at understanding the interrelationships among and significance of others' behaviors. Since such people may, in effect, be more "interpersonally sensitive," we might expect a positive correlation between subjects' scores on the programmed cases and scores on the PONS.

We computed median correlations of the PONS variables with accuracy scores on the Dailey Programmed Cases for fourteen college students. Consistent with our prediction, moderately positive correlations were evidenced. Those individuals with high scores on the programmed cases tended also to have high accuracy on the PONS (median PONS-Dailey Programmed Cases r = .26).

OTHER TESTS OF NONVERBAL DECODING. Several researchers have recently developed measures of decoding accuracy that we correlated with the PONS. Miron Zuckerman's audio-video judging task consisted of color slides of college students portraying six emotions (anger, fear, happiness, surprise, disgust, and sadness), all in the face channel. An audio tape presented the voices of these same students reciting standard content sentences using the six different affects. Subjects (some of whom were the "senders" in the test) judged both the audio and video segments of this test and received audio and video scores (as well as scores on the different affects) based on their ability accurately to identify the emotion being conveyed.

The correlations of the audio-video total, video, and audio scores with

PONS total, video 60, and tone 40 were .31 ($p < .01$), .37 ($p < .01$), and .09. With the exception of the correlation for voice tone, these correlations are encouraging, since the two tests do differ in a number of ways. The PONS has one sender, displays motion, shows body and face + body, and has masked voice; the audio-video judging test has more than one sender, presents still photographs of face only, has a standard content voice channel, and the voice never occurs simultaneously with the video.

In another study, reported in more detail in Zuckerman, Hall, DeFrank, and Rosenthal (1976), the PONS was correlated with a task of decoding videotaped facial expressions of sixty male and female senders. Each sender was surreptitiously videotaped while watching an emotionally suggestive videotaped episode. Then each sender was surreptitiously videotaped while talking about his or her feelings while watching these episodes. Finally, each sender was videotaped while posing (re-creating) his or her feelings in front of the video camera. Each sender later participated as judge, judging all the facial expressions besides his or her own. The correlation between PONS total and total decoding on this task was .31 ($p < .05$). The correlations between PONS total and decoding scores on spontaneous, talking, and posed expressions were .15, .34, and .24, respectively.

The Communication of Affect Receiving Ability Test, version 1 (CARAT 1) (described in Buck et al. 1972) measures the subject's ability to decode facial and gestural responses of college student "senders" to emotionally laden color slides. The correlation of total PONS accuracy and total CARAT 1 accuracy was $-.01$ in a sample of forty-seven U.S. college students. The correlation of total PONS with the subjects' ability to predict the senders' ratings of the pleasantness of the color slides just from viewing the senders' faces was .13. One possible reason for these low correlations may be that the stimuli were spontaneous facial expressions, whereas the PONS scenes were portrayed more self-consciously. Recently, however, Zuckerman, Hall, De-Frank, and Rosenthal (1976) obtained a correlation of .58 ($p < .001$) between accuracy at decoding spontaneously sent facial expressions (using Buck et al.'s paradigm) and accuracy at decoding posed expressions sent by the same senders a few minutes after the spontaneous expressions were recorded. Though this larger correlation may be due in part to the short time interval between sendings and between judgments, and by having the same senders do both kinds of sending, nevertheless, it does suggest that the low correlations between PONS and CARAT 1 may not be due to the posed-spontaneous difference between the tasks.

The Social Interpretations Task (SIT) (Archer and Akert, 1977) measures an individual's ability to interpret correctly the meaning in a social situation. It is a video tape test in which a subject attempts, among other things, to decide what is happening in an interpersonal scenario based on the interactants' nonverbal cues as well as verbal cues and situational (contextual) cues.

In a sample of thirty artist undergraduates (actors, painters, musicians, writers, and dancers), PONS total was correlated positively with the total score on a pilot version of the SIT ($r(28) = .25$, $p < .10$, one-tailed). In addition, among a sample of summer school students at the University of California at Santa Cruz who took the pilot SIT and the forty-item original sender audio PONS, the correlations were .39 ($p < .05$) for RS and .33 ($p < .05$) for CF.

In summary, the median correlation of the PONS total with the four other measures of nonverbal decoding for adults was .28 (combined $p = .00017$; Rosenthal 1978). If we consider the results based on the audio PONS as well, the result is still more significant and that median correlation becomes .31.

In a recent study employing sixty children in New York City, Robert Clark administered the full PONS along with a facial affect judging task consisting of thirty slides of adult faces, which he selected from the prepared slides of Paul Ekman and Wallace Friesen. For the three age groups of eight to nine, ten to eleven, and twelve to thirteen years old, the correlations of total PONS with scores on this instrument were .31, .22, and .23, respectively (combined $p = .025$).

COGNITIVE STYLE

COGNITIVE COMPLEXITY. "Cognitive complexity" (measured by the Bieri procedure; Bieri 1955) is described as an aspect of an individual's personality that might be expected to influence his or her ability to discriminate behavioral information. It is an information processing skill that helps predict how an individual transforms specified behavioral information into social judgments and may be thought of as the capacity to construe social behavior in a multidimensional way. Cognitively complex persons have a more differentiated system of dimensions for perceiving others' behavior than do cognitively simple persons. We might expect, then, that the more complex individuals would be better able to integrate a number of nonverbal cues to arrive at an accurate perception of the affect conveyed by the stimulus person. We computed the median PONS-Bieri correlations for two samples of college students ($N = 14$ and 45). There was an overall tendency for the more cognitively complex students to score higher on the PONS (median PONS-Bieri $r = -.28$; high scores indicate low complexity). A third study (this one conducted by Barbara Domangue) relating PONS performance to scores on cognitive complexity (Rep test) also showed better PONS performance by more complex persons ($\eta = .17$). But because there are only three studies so far, considerably more data are needed before we can be confident about the relationship between PONS performance and cognitive complexity.

DIFFERENTIAL ATTENTION TO CHANNELS. A variable that may help to explain differential channel accuracy on the PONS is the extent to which subjects choose to attend differentially to channels. In this section we report a study in which scores on the face, body, and CF channels of the PONS test were correlated with scores on an instrument that was developed to measure differential *attention* to face, body, and voice tone (DiMatteo and Hall in press).

Seventeen students enrolled in a college course on nonverbal communication took part in the two-part study. In part one, subjects took the PONS test. About twelve weeks later they were administered the twenty-minute audiovisual channel preference task. Subjects were presented with ninety-six nonverbal stimuli, each of which consisted of information conveyed in *two channels simultaneously* (face and body, face and CF voice, and body and CF voice), sent by a young woman (not the PONS test sender). The two channels did not always transmit the same affect. For each item, the subjects were instructed to select one of two response alternatives. A representative pair of alternatives would be: (A) voice expresses elation, (B) face expresses sadness. Four affects were employed: affection, elation, sadness, and anger. Simultaneity of stimulus presentation was achieved by using a split-screen video monitor and electronically content-filtered soundtrack. For face + body items, both sides of the screen contained an image; for face + voice and body + voice items, one side of the screen contained an image, while the sound emerged from the speaker.

Both response alternatives on the answer sheet for each item correctly described the affects being portrayed in the two channels, though subjects were not told this because the task was presented as an accuracy of judgment task. Thus, a subject's choice had to indicate which of the two channels he or she chose to pay more attention to.

Location of video stimuli on the two sides of the screen and occurrence of response alternatives in the A or B position were counterbalanced, as were the pairings of the four affects with the three channels. These twelve pairings occurred with equal frequency. Items 1 to 48 were repeated as items 49 to 96 in order to allow for a determination of the internal reliability of the instrument.

Test-retest reliability was computed by correlating the number of times each channel was chosen in the first half of the test (item 1–48) with the number of times it was chosen in the second half, and then applying the Spearman-Brown formula (Guilford 1954, p. 354). Channel scores were very reliable:$r_{face} = .89$; $r_{body} = .78$; $r_{voice} = .62$.

We also examined the extent to which subjects tended to choose the same alternative both times a particular item appeared in the test. A count was made for each subject of the number of items in which he or she chose the same alternative both times. A comparison of the number of consistent choices with the number of inconsistent choices gave an indication of the consistency of each subject in his or her choice of alternatives. Chi-square was computed for each of the seventeen subjects. The standard normal deviate equivalent of the average of the χ^2 values was 12.87 ($p < .001$), indicating that subjects' actual choices of channels were significantly consistent throughout the test.

The correlation between face-only PONS accuracy and face preference was .48 ($df = 15$, $p < .06$) and between body-only PONS accuracy and body preference was .72 ($df = 15$, $p < .001$). The correlation between CF-only PONS accuracy and content-filtered voice preference was only .07 ($df = 15$, n.s.). Thus, accuracy and preference (attention) were highly correlated for the video channels but not for the audio channel.

The findings of our research do not allow us to assess the causal relationship between channel accuracy and attention, but they do indicate that accuracy and attention were highly positively correlated in the video channels of face and body. Whether a subject's perception of his accuracy determines attention or attention determines accuracy cannot be decided from these correlational results. That attention determines accuracy is more plausible than its converse. Individuals who concentrate their attention on reading nonverbal cues in face and/or body during their day-to-day lives probably develop greater receiving skills as a result of the experience. It is less likely that self-perceived accuracy on the PONS test determined attention on the preference task. In chapter 11, we report that, for the most part, subjects' predictions of their ability to decode face, body, and voice cues are generally not very accurate.

That the relationship of attention and accuracy for the voice channel was weak may be due to lower reliability for voice on both tasks. As we report, however, some impressive validity coefficients have been found for the content-filtered voice channel of the PONS, suggesting that its low internal consistency may not be responsible for the lowered correlation on the audio channel evidenced in this study. A more plausible explanation of this result may be that while receiving skill on the video channels can be improved by the experience gained from increased attention to those channels, ability to decode the voice channel correctly cannot be as easily improved by the practice and experience resulting from increased attention.

The reason for this is not readily apparent, however, and in attempting to account for such an effect, we hypothesize that more information is available in video cues than in audio cues. A ceiling on accuracy at reading communication in the audio channel is reached early so that significant improvement from learning or attention is not possible. More and more of the information available from the video channels is processed as experience or attention increase, resulting in substantial improvement. Of course, future research is needed to examine the validity of this hypothesis.

LISTENING WITH THE LEFT EAR. James Dwyer's doctoral dissertation at the University of California at Santa Cruz investigated whether nonverbal communication was more efficiently processed by the right or left cerebral hemisphere (Dwyer 1975). For some years, evidence had been accumulating that the left hemisphere might ordinarily be more involved in the processing of verbal material while working in a relatively analytical, sequential manner, while the right hemisphere might ordinarily be more involved in the processing of spatial and emotional material while working in a relatively intuitive, holistic, and patterned manner (Bever and Chiarello 1974; Gordon 1975; Languis 1976; Ornstein 1972; Schwartz, Davidson, and Maer 1975). It seemed to Dwyer, therefore, that the type of decoding of nonverbal cues required by the PONS might require relatively more of the hypothesized right brain processing than would be required by more ordinary verbal materials.

To address his question, Dwyer employed dichotic listening tasks in which different material was presented to each ear simultaneously. If the material presented to the right ear dominated or "drowned out" the material presented to the left ear, the left hemisphere would be implicated, and if the left ear dominated the right ear, the right hemisphere would be implicated.

The two tasks in which we are most interested here were the Kresge Consonant Vowel Dichotic Listening Task (CV-DLT) and a portion of the content-filtered channel of the PONS. The CV-DLT requires the subject to indicate which of the following syllables he or she has just heard: ba, da, ga, ka, pa, and ta. On each trial one of these syllables is presented to the right ear while another of these syllables is presented to the left ear at just the same time. Syllables presented to the right ear are normally reported correctly more often, thereby implicating the left hemisphere. The second task was constructed from the twelve items of the PONS CF channel showing the highest mean accuracy rates (all above 50 percent). The items were randomly paired with one another and the pairs were presented simultaneously, one to each ear.

TABLE 10.3. Percentages of Subjects Showing Right or Left Ear Advantage in Two Dichotic Listening Tasks

	Task	
Advantage	Verbal (CV-DLT) (N=89)	Nonverbal (PONS-DLT)[a] (N=84)
Right ear[b]	67%	30%
None	4	15
Left ear[c]	28	55

[a]differs from distribution of verbal tasks at $p < .001$, $\chi^2 = 61$, $df = 2$
[b]left hemisphere
[c]right hemisphere

TABLE 10.4. Correlations of Degree of Left Ear
(Right Hemisphere) Advantage in Processing CF
Cues with Accuracy in Nonverbal Decoding

Decoding Task	Males	Females	Mean
CF	−.13	−.17	−.15
RS	−.44[a]	−.09	−.27[b]
SIT[c]	−.43[a]	−.02	−.22[b]
Median	−.43[a]	−.09	−.22[b]

[a] $p \leq .01$
[b] $p \leq .05$
[c] Archer's test of ability to interpret social situations, pilot
version

Subjects were eighty-nine University of California summer students; half
were male and half were female.

Table 10.3 displays the results of the comparison of the two tasks in terms
of the percentages of subjects showing a right ear, left ear, or neither ear
advantage. For the verbal task, most subjects showed a right ear advantage,
while for the nonverbal PONS task most subjects showed a left ear advantage.
At least for the twelve items of the CF channel of the PONS employed by
Dwyer, then, processing of nonverbal cues appears to involve greater right
hemisphere activity by more people than is the case for more standard verbal
material. This result is consistent with researchers' thinking about the relative
superiority of the right hemisphere in processing nonverbal stimuli and it aids
in further filling in the network of relationships of variables with the PONS,
thereby increasing its construct validity.

As a provocative hypothesis, Dwyer also reported that, although decoding
CF channel stimuli more often involved the right hemisphere, those subjects
who showed greater accuracy at decoding nonverbal cues tended to show
smaller right hemisphere advantages. Table 10.4 shows the results of these
analyses. Thus, the right hemisphere may be more involved in processing
nonverbal cues but it may not be involved quite so much in processing them
accurately.

LOOKING WITH THE LEFT EYE. Barbara Domangue's doctoral dissertation
at the University of Delaware investigated whether nonverbal communication
was more accurately processed by subjects who showed a relative dominance
of the right or left cerebral hemisphere (Domangue 1979). There were two
important differences between Domangue's study and Dwyer's study. First,
Domangue defined hemispheric dominance in terms of eye dominance rather
than ear dominance. Second, Domangue's investigation was a between-
subjects type study while Dwyer's was a within-subjects type study. Domangue found that those subjects who were left-eye dominant (right hemisphere)

performed significantly better on the CF channel than did subjects who were right-eye dominant ($p < .03$, effect size $= 0.50\sigma$). Interestingly, Domangue also found that another sample of subjects, one that showed familial left-handedness, was significantly superior to the sample mentioned above, which was right-handed, at decoding the CF channel ($p < .02$, effect size $= 0.47\sigma$). It remains for future research to clarify the differences between the results of the studies by Dwyer and Domangue. The former had found greater nonverbal accuracy in the CF channel to be weakly associated with left hemisphere dominance, while the latter found the opposite.

11 | Psychosocial Correlates

In this chapter we will examine the manner in which various psychosocial variables are related to nonverbal sensitivity as measured by the PONS test. In the first section we will consider the relationship between PONS scores and scores on various standardized personality tests. The second section deals with the relationship of PONS scores to an individual's ratings of his or her own interpersonal success and nonverbal skill in everyday life. In the third section we will examine correlations of the PONS with an important validity criterion—ratings of the individual's sensitivity by persons to whom he or she is well known.

OBJECTIVE PERSONALITY TESTS

We have examined the correlation of PONS scores with the subscales of the California Psychological Inventory (Gough 1957), the Personality Research Form (Jackson 1967), Fiedler's Least Preferred Coworker Test (Fiedler 1967), the Machiavelli Scale (Christie and Geis 1970), the Minnesota Teacher Attitude Inventory (Cook, Leeds, and Callis 1951), the A-B therapist scale (Whitehorn and Betz 1954), the Dogmatism Scale (Rokeach 1960), the Marlowe-Crowne Social Desirability Scale (Crowne and Marlowe 1964), the Study of Values (Allport, Vernon, and Lindzey 1960), and the Self-Monitoring Scale (Snyder 1974). We will describe each of these tests, their functions, and their relationship to nonverbal sensitivity as measured by the PONS test.

CALIFORNIA PSYCHOLOGICAL INVENTORY. The California Psychological Inventory (CPI) was developed by Gough (1957) to make possible a comprehensive multidimensional assessment of "normal" persons in a variety of settings. It is concerned with characteristics of personality that have wide applicability to human behavior and that relate to the favorable and positive aspects of personality. The scales of the CPI are addressed principally to personality characteristics important for social living and social interaction. There are eighteen scales in all, grouped into four broad categories that bring together scales having similar implications. The logic of grouping is interpretational, not statistical. We list these categories below, along with the scales contained in them.

1. Measures of poise, ascendancy, self-assurance, and interpersonal adequacy (Dominance, Capacity for Status, Sociability, Social Presence, Self-Acceptance, Sense of Well-Being).
2. Measures of socialization, maturity, responsibility, and interpersonal structuring of values (Responsibility, Socialization, Self-Control, Tolerance, Good Impression, Communality).
3. Measures of achievement potential and intellectual efficiency (Achievement via Conformance, Achievement via Independence, Intellectual Efficacy).
4. Measures of intellectual and interest modes (Psychological-mindedness, Flexibility, Femininity).

Information about the reliability of these scales and a more thorough explanation of them can be found in the CPI manual by Gough (1957).

Because the PONS test may tap a factor of social competence—the ability to understand another's emotions—we undertook an examination of its relationship to the CPI, which is in part a measure of successful social functioning. We developed our hypotheses about the relationship between PONS and CPI both intuitively and on the basis of a study reported by Fields (1950). Fields examined the relationship between social and emotional adjustment (as measured by the Bell Adjustment Inventory) and the ability to discriminate facial expressions (in still photographs of males and females). He found a positive correspondence between discrimination and social adjustment ($r(205) = .24$, $p < .01$).

In the manual for the CPI, Gough suggests that the higher an individual scores on the CPI scales, the more effectively he is functioning both socially and intellectually. Low scorers tend to experience significant difficulties in interpersonal adjustment. Under the assumption that some degree of reasonably normal social experience is necessary for the development of nonverbal sensitivity, we might expect PONS scores to be positively related to the CPI. In particular, we would hypothesize that scales in class 2, especially Socialization, would correlate positively with the PONS. Since Psychological-mindedness attempts to measure interpersonal responsiveness to others' needs, we might expect it to be positively related to the ability to understand nonverbally communicated affect. Finally, since female subjects tend to perform better on the PONS test than do males (see chapter 7), we might expect male subjects with more feminine interests (as measured by the Femininity scale) to score higher on the PONS than male subjects with masculine interests.

In order to examine the relationship between PONS and the CPI, both tests were administered to forty-six male and thirty-four female U.S. college students, to ten male architecture students from Sydney, Australia, and to fifteen male and sixty-seven female U.S. student teachers. The correlations of PONS scores with the CPI variables were, for the most part (88 percent) positive, as we had predicted, although few were very strong (6 percent reached an $r \geq +.50$). Table 11.1 presents the correlations of PONS total with the four classes of CPI variables.

Three of the eighteen CPI variables were found to correlate significantly and consistently with the PONS total score in at least two of the five samples. These variables were Sense of Well-Being (median $r = .24$, combined $p < .001$), Socialization (median $r = .30$, combined $p = .0011$), and Communality (median $r = .50$, combined $p < .001$). Thus, those who scored higher on the PONS scored on the CPI as significantly more confident, more socially mature, and more typical in terms of CPI responding. Of these three replicated correlations, we had predicted only one: Socialiazation, an index of social maturity. We had also predicted a significant positive correlation between PONS performance and Psychological-mindedness, and while the median r of .23 was in the predicted direction, the results from the five studies wer too heterogeneous to warrant any conclusion. Our final prediction was that males scoring higher on the PONS would score higher on Femininity. Once again the results were inconsistent but, if anything, they were in the direction opposite to those we had predicted (median $r = -.38$).

PERSONALITY RESEARCH FORM. A second personality inventory whose relationship to the PONS we have investigated is the Personality Research Form (PRF) developed by Jackson (1967). Like the CPI, this test is designed to yield a set of scores for personality traits broadly related to the functioning of individuals in a wide variety of situations. It, too, is primarily focused upon areas of normal functioning rather than on psychopathology. The test contains 440 items that form twenty-two scales measuring various traits on bipolar dimensions. Each scale is named for the end of the dimension corresponding to high scores on the scale.

The twenty-two scales can be organized into a number of superordinate categories based in part on theory and in part upon the results of a number of factor analytic studies:

1. Measures of impulse expression and control (Impulsivity, Change, Harm Avoidance, Order, Cognitive Structure).
2. Measures of orientation toward work and play (Achievement, Endurance, Play).
3. Measures of orientation toward direction from other people (Succorance, Autonomy).
4. Measures of intellectual and esthetic orientations (Understanding, Sentience).

TABLE 11.1. Correlations of PONS with California Psychological Inventory for Five Samples

CPI Scale	Male Student Teachers (N=15)	Male College Students (N=46)	Male Architecture Students (N=10)	Female Student Teachers (N=67)	Female College Students (N=34)	Median
Class 1						
Dominance	.15	.28	.51	.00	.30	.28
Capacity for Status	.14	.20	.35	-.15	.24	.20
Sociability	.10	.06	.40	.06	.26	.10
Social Presence	.36	.09	.61	-.11	.26	.26
Self-Acceptance	.33	.25	.31	.04	.34	.31
Sense of Well-Being	.05	.50[a]	.73[b]	.01	.24	.24
Class 2						
Responsibility	-.10	.18	.37	-.06	.33	.18
Socialization	-.26	.44[c]	.68[b]	.14	.30	.30
Self-Control	-.12	.21	.21	-.17	.01	.01
Tolerance	.26	.20	.48	-.24[b]	.34[b]	.26
Good Impression	-.26	-.06	.10	-.26[b]	-.07	-.07
Communality	-.19	.58[a]	.58	.29	.50[b]	.50
Class 3						
Achievement via Conformance	-.01	.27	.36	-.01	.30	.27
Achievement via Independence	.18	.31[b]	.55	-.32[c]	.34	.31
Intellectual Efficiency	.10	.46[c]	.59	-.06	.32	.32
Class 4						
Psychological-Mindedness	.23	-.04	.46	-.38[c]	.25	.23
Flexibility	.37	.34[b]	.31	-.15	.05	.31
Femininity	-.38	.13	-.46	.14	.14	.13
Median	.10	.23	.46	-.06	.28	.23[d]

[a] $p < .001$
[b] $p < .05$
[c] $p < .01$
[d] combined $p < .035$, one-tailed, $z = 1.82$

5. Measures of degree of ascendancy (Dominance, Abasement).
6. Measures of degree and quality of interpersonal orientation (Affiliation, Nurturance, Exhibition, Social Recognition, Aggression, Defendence).
7. Measures of test-taking attitudes and validity (Desirability, Infrequency).

More detailed definitions of these scales are available in Jackson (1967).

In considering the correlations obtained between PONS and CPI scores, we can make some tentative predictions about the relationship between PONS and the scales of the PRF. We might expect that individuals high in Succorance (seeking frequent sympathy or advice) would be nonverbally sensitive, since their relationships with other people depend upon their ability to recognize indications of sympathy, love, reassurance, and acceptance. We might also expect persons exhibiting a high degree of interpersonal orientation to be more nonverbally sensitive. Those high in Nurturance, who are accustomed to recognizing and responding to persons (especially children) in need of help and comfort, have probably developed sharp nonverbal skills; and persons high in Social Recognition (desiring to be held in high esteem) may be more nonverbally sensitive because of a need to feel approval and recognition by others.

The PONS test and the PRF were administered to fourteen male and female graduate students in clinical psychology, thirty-nine teachers from the United States, and thirty-eight interns and residents in internal medicine. The correlations of the PRF scales (excluding Infrequency, which indicates careless or random responding) with PONS total for these samples appear in table 11.2. It is clear that the hypotheses delineated above were not supported. For the most part, few systematic trends appeared in the data from these three samples, although among physicians the Nurturance scale correlated significantly positively with PONS total.

LEAST PREFERRED COWORKER SCALE. Fiedler (1967) has found that a leader's style of interacting with members of his group and the favorableness of the group situation are important determinants of the leader's effectiveness. He has developed a test, called the Least Preferred Coworker (LPC) Scale, to measure a person's "leadership style." This test requires the person to describe the individual he has found it most difficult to work with. Descriptions are made on simple bipolar adjective scales similar to the semantic differential. Persons who describe their least preferred coworkers in very unfavorable terms (i.e., persons who score low on LPC) tend to reject those with whom they cannot work well. Low LPC people tend to be "task oriented" in their leadership style and seek need gratification from working and accomplishing the task. Persons who describe their least preferred coworker in relatively favorable terms (high LPC) tend to be relationship oriented (or "socioemotionally" inclined). High LPC persons seek need gratification in interpersonal

TABLE 11.2. Correlations of PONS with Personality
Research Form for Three Samples

Scale	Clinical Graduate Students (N=14)	Teachers (N=39)	Interns and Residents[a] (N=38)
Impulsivity	−.24	−.18	.20
Change	−.11	−.06	
Harm avoidance	−.14	−.07	−.05
Order	.40	.08	.03
Cognitive structure	.38	.02	
Achievement	.14	.13	−.01
Endurance	.06	.02	.07
Play	.01	−.01	.22
Succorance	.00	−.07	
Autonomy	.12	−.18	−.11
Understanding	−.07	.05	−.07
Sentience	−.27	−.16	
Dominance	−.03	.02	−.12
Abasement	−.40	−.08	
Affiliation	−.16	−.00	.24
Nurturance	.02	−.00	.42[b]
Exhibition	.12	−.23	.03
Social recognition	.00	.04	.06
Aggression	.47	−.24	−.11
Defendence	.13	−.24	
Desirability	−.20	.06	

[a]form A of the PRF contains fourteen scales (plus one
indicating invalid reponses)
[b]$p < .05$

relationships and, as leaders, use their task situation as a means of achieving
satisfying interpersonal relationships.

Under the hypothesis that nonverbal sensitivity is an element of leadership
style, we undertook an investigation of the relationship between the LPC and
the PONS. Our predictions were not precise, however, because nonverbal
sensitivity may be an element of both task-oriented leadership and socioemo-
tional orientation. The task-oriented leader may have developed his or her
nonverbal skill in working with others in order to better understand their
behavior and thinking. Such an understanding could serve task-oriented leaders well as they direct their group toward completing the task. The socioemo-
tional, high LPC individual may have developed this nonverbal skill and
understanding of others in order to form closer and more lasting relationships
with them.

Ron Johnson administered the PONS and the LPC Scale to seventy-six
male and female college students from Nova Scotia. Correlations of LPC with

nearly every PONS measure were moderately negative, indicating that task-oriented subjects received higher scores on the PONS. The correlations of PONS total with the LPC was $-.21$ ($p < .07$), and CF 80 correlated $-.25$ ($p < .05$) with the LPC. Thus, those subjects whose leadership style was task oriented tended to possess the higher degree of sensitivity to nonverbal cues. Perhaps low LPC individuals develop greater sensitivity from experiencing a greater number of human interactions, for Steiner (1959) has found that low LPC individuals tended to have a larger number of friends than high LPC individuals.

MINNESOTA TEACHER ATTITUDE INVENTORY. The Minnesota Teacher Attitude Inventory (MTAI) was designed by Cook, Leeds, and Callis (1951) to measure a specific teacher attribute. This attribute involves, at the one extreme, a belief in and preference for "democratic" values and a tendency to use democratic teaching methods versus, at the other extreme, a belief in and preference for "autocratic" values and a tendency to use autocratic teaching methods. Democratic MTAI scores tend to be correlated with warmth and permissiveness in the classroom. Although no previous examinations of the relationship between the MTAI and nonverbal sensitivity of teachers had been undertaken, we hypothesized a positive correlation between MTAI and PONS based on our knowledge of what both tests purport to measure. We expected that teachers with more democratic attitudes would be more sensitive and responsive to the feelings of others, especially children. They may have developed their democratic attitudes because they could plainly perceive children's needs or, on the other hand, developed nonverbal sensitivity because their democratic attitudes allowed them to have closer and warmer relationships with their students.

We collected data on both tests from two samples of student teachers in a U.S. teachers college. The correlation of total MTAI score with PONS total in a sample of fifty-three student teachers was .25. In this sample, the correlation of MTAI with the audio channels tended to be higher than the correlation with the video channels (.26 for tone 40, and .34 ($p < .05$) for CF 80 as opposed to .11 for video 60). In a sample of thirty-nine teachers, the MTAI-PONS correlations were .24 for total, .40 ($p < .05$) for tone 40, and .23 for video 60. Thus, democratic attitudes toward children in the classroom were positively related to total nonverbal sensitivity (median $r = .25$, combined $p < .013$), and particularly to sensitivity to tone of voice (median $r = .33$, combined $p = .0013$).

As reported in chapter 13, in two samples of student teachers, the correlations between PONS total and scores on "encouragingness toward pupils" based on direct observations of classroom behavior were .78 and .74 (both $p < .001$). This would support the MTAI-PONS correlations. In these two samples, however, the correlations with tone of voice accuracy were not higher than correlations with video accuracy.

THE A-B THERAPIST VARIABLE. Whitehorn and Betz (1954) first distinguished A and B therapists; research evidence collected since then has strongly suggested that the A-B variable may be related to therapist characteristics, styles of therapeutic interaction, and therapy outcomes (see Razin 1971). Whitehorn and Betz (1960) provide descriptions of A and B therapists: "A" therapists tend to be problem solvers, are not regulative nor coercive, and seem to be more acceptable to the schizophrenic, while "B" therapists tend to see things in black and white and to see patients as wayward, in need of correction.

"B" therapists value conformity and rigidity, and they tend to do better with neurotic patients. "A" therapists tend to help the schizophrenic patient guide his life, and they become very personally involved with patients. Bergin (1967) noted that "A" therapists offer patients warm acceptance, while "B" therapists force rational approaches to patients' problems. Campbell et al. (1968), using in their research a revised form of the A-B scale, described "A" therapists as verbally oriented and more intellectual, while "B" therapists were more practical, straightforward, and nonintellectual.

James O'Neil at Illinois State University administered the A-B scale to sixteen clinical psychology students enrolled in a practicum course on counseling. The correlation between the A-B scale (higher score indicates that therapist is more "A" type, lower score that therapist is more "B" type) and total PONS score was .05. "A" therapists were significantly better at reading positive-submissive affect ($r(14) = .61$, $p < .05$) and "B" therapists were significantly better at reading negative-dominant affect ($r(14) = -.55$, $p < .05$). These were the only two significant correlations of PONS scores with the A-B scale, and they occurred despite a very small relationship between positive-submissive and negative-dominant scores ($r(14) = .13$). "A" therapists were better at reading all submissive affect ($r(14) = .44$) and "B" therapists at reading all dominant affect ($r(14) = -.43$).

Chantal Fisch from the University of Ottawa administered the A-B scale to two groups of first-year clinical psychology graduate students (both $N = 16$). Group 1 took the PONS before they received a program in systematic training of empathy; group 2 took the PONS after this training. In group 1, "B" therapists performed somewhat better on the PONS measures than "A" therapists (many of these differences were significant). In group 2, the results were mixed. "A" therapists performed higher on some PONS scores, "B" therapists on others. A summary of correlations of PONS scores with the A-B scale in all three samples is presented in table 11.3. In all three samples, "B" therapists were superior in decoding dominant affects (median $r = -.35$, combined $p = .012$), while there was a tendency for "A" therapists to be superior in decoding submissive affects (median $r = +.32$).

DOGMATISM. Related to our investigation of nonverbal skill and teacher attitudes is our examination of the relationship between PONS scores and

TABLE 11.3. Correlations of PONS with Whitehorn-Betz A-B Therapist Scale for Three Samples

Scale	Clinical Psychology Graduate Students (Illinois) (N=16)	Clinical Psychology Graduate Students (Preempathy Training PONS) (N=16)	Clinical Psychology Graduate Students (Postempathy Training PONS) (N=16)	Median
Total	.05	-.42	.03	.03
Tone 40	.09	.09	.18	.09
RS 80	-.01	-.34	.11	-.01
CF 80	-.06	-.19	.05	-.06
Face 60	-.16	-.42	.37	-.16
Body 60	.08	-.39	-.25	-.25
Figure 60	.12	-.34	-.11	-.11
Video 60	.22	-.55[a]	-.13	-.13
Positive-submissive	.61[a]	-.55[a]	-.26	-.26
Positive-dominant	.21	-.29	-.26	-.26
Negative-submissive	.11	-.08	.65[b]	.11
Negative-dominant	-.55[a]	-.32	-.16	-.32
All positive	.22	-.50[a]	-.33	-.33
All negative	-.24	-.18	.46	-.18
All submissive	.44	-.40	.32	.32
All dominant	-.43	-.35	-.32	-.35

[a] $p < .05$
[b] $p < .01$

scores on the Dogmatism Scale (Rokeach 1960). This scale is intended to identify ideological dogmatism in a person, a closed way of thinking that could be associated with any ideology, an intolerance toward those with opposing beliefs, and an acceptance of only those with similar beliefs. The scale focuses on the structure of the person's beliefs, not on their content.

A clear prediction for the direction of the relationship between nonverbal skill and dogmatism is somewhat difficult to put forth. It is possible that the highly dogmatic person, who is intolerant of those persons with beliefs opposing his own, will learn to "tune out" the nonverbal cues of others in order to prevent his being exposed to or influenced by others whose beliefs are different from his own. On the other hand, as Rokeach has suggested, the dogmatic person tends to be authoritarian and is therefore very sensitive to the presence of authority in his or her social environment. The highly dogmatic person is likely, in such a situation, to adopt a respectful, acquiescent façade. Thus, in order to determine accurately the needs and desires of the authority figure so that they may be catered to, the dogmatic person may develop a keen nonverbal skill. In support of this hypothesis, Scodel and Mussen (1953) found a positive correlation between the California F scale of authoritarianism and the ability analytically to judge people.

The Dogmatism Scale and the PONS test were administered to forty-five U.S. college students and to thirty-eight interns and residents in internal medicine. In both samples, those scoring higher on the PONS tended to be less dogmatic ($r(43) = -.12$; $r(36) = -.29$; combined $p = .035$, one-tailed).

SOCIAL DESIRABILITY. The Marlowe-Crowne Social Desirability Scale (MCSDS) was developed by Crowne and Marlowe (1964) to identify individuals with a high need for social approval. These researchers concentrated on differences among people in their tendencies to answer questions in a socially desirable way. The test is composed of thirty-three "true or false" items, each having one answer that is more socially desirable than the other. The person who answers questions, regardless of content, in a socially acceptable way is one who has a chronic need for social approval.

In an interesting validational study of the MCSDS, Crowne and Strickland (1961) found that subjects with a high need for approval were more easily conditioned by nonverbal reinforcement (both negative and positive) than were subjects with a low need for approval. This suggests that perhaps individuals with a higher need for approval may be more aware of the nonverbal behavior of others, and more accurate in perceiving it. Since they receive satisfaction from social approval, they may learn to recognize and fulfill the expectations of others as well as to perceive nonverbally communicated approval or disapproval. Thus, we would expect a positive correlation between need for social approval and nonverbal skill, such that those with a high need for social approval would obtain high scores on the PONS test.

Our prediction is qualified because other researchers have found either the opposite or a zero relationship between need for social approval (MCSDS) and sensitivity to nonverbal communication. Buck (1974, 1976) found that subjects with a high need for social approval tended to evidence less ability to decode nonverbal cues (nonsignificant) than did subjects with a low need for social approval. Mehrabian (1972) found that ability to decode nonverbal communication in face and voice was not related to need for social approval.

We administered the MCSDS to the same forty-five college students who took the Dogmatism Scale as well as to forty-four institutionalized alcoholic patients from the United States. We, too, found no consistent relationship between MCSDS and PONS total. For the students, $r(43) = .06$, while for the patients, $r(42) = -.35$, $p < .02$. More studies are needed before we can begin to assert something of the true relationship of MCSDS to accuracy of decoding nonverbal cues.

The Good Impression Scale of the California Psychological Inventory (Gough 1957) and the Desirability Scale of the Personality Research Form (Jackson 1967, 1974) both appear also to measure the need for social approval. The median correlation between Good Impression scores and PONS total for the five samples named in table 11.1 was $-.07$. The median correlation between the PRF Desirability Scale and PONS total for the first two samples named in table 11.2 was also $-.07$. Considering all three measures of need for approval, it would seem that our prediction for a positive relationship was not supported. Indeed, the bulk of our findings suggest that the correlation may be negative though small.

MACHIAVELLI SCALE. Another personality scale whose relationship to the PONS we have investigated is the Machiavelli Scale (Mach) (Christie and Geis 1970). This scale was developed in an effort to identify individuals who are effective in manipulating others. The perfect manipulator was assumed to be unconcerned with conventional morality and to be basically cool and detached from other people. A validational study of the Mach Scale employed a coalition formation task in which three subjects were given $10 to divide between any two of them. The researchers found that the high Mach was in the winning combination in every group and that high Machs won significantly more money than would be expected by chance. In another study, subjects were induced to cheat and then accused of doing so during a postexperimental interview. In this stressful confrontation with the experimenter, high Machs resisted confessing and looked the experimenter in the eye longer while denying that they had cheated than did low Mach subjects. Thus, the Mach Scale does seem to identify the good manipulators.

Christie and Geis reported other studies that show that high Machs are unaroused emotionally by stimuli and tend to be uninvolved with other people. They are extremely resistant to social influence and are effective manipulators not because they read other persons' feelings and take advantage of their weaknesses but rather because they remain insensitive to other persons, permitting the pursuit of coolly rational goals. Geis and Leventhal (1966) reported that high Machs were significantly less able than low Machs to determine whether a stimulus person was lying or telling the truth (67 percent versus 50 percent accuracy). Therefore, we might expect that PONS scores and scores on the Mach Scale would be correlated negatively.

The data bearing on this issue came from four samples (94 U.S. high school students, 45 U.S. college students, 154 U.S. college students, and 30 U.S. adults). In all four studies the correlations between the PONS total and Mach scores were negative, although the median r of $-.08$ was small and not very highly significant (combined $p < .037$, one-tailed).

THE STUDY OF VALUES. Another personality scale whose relationship to the PONS we have investigated is the Study of Values (Allport, Vernon, and Lindzey 1960). This instrument measures a large region of generic evaluative tendencies and measures the degree to which people subscribe to six slightly covarying values. They are: Theoretical, Economic, Esthetic, Social, Political, and Religious.

The Study of Values was administered to a sample of thirty-nine U.S. teachers along with the PONS test. The correlations of PONS total, tone 40, and video 60 appear in table 11.4. High scores on the scales of Religious and Social values were associated with high PONS scores, while high Theoretical values were associated with lower PONS scores.

EXTRAVERSION-INTROVERSION. In two samples of students of dance therapy, the extraversion-introversion factor of the Myers-Briggs Type Indicator (Myers 1962) was correlated with the PONS such that, except for RS, more extraverted subjects scored higher on the PONS. Table 11.5 shows these

TABLE 11.4. Correlations of PONS with Study of Values for Thirty-Nine Teachers

	PONS Score		
Study of Values	Total	Tone 40	Video 60
Theoretical	$-.29$	$-.36$[a]	$-.22$
Economic	$-.20$	$-.08$	$-.22$
Esthetic	$-.02$	$.20$	$.02$
Social	$.22$	$.04$	$.18$
Political	$-.17$	$-.06$	$-.14$
Religious	$.35$[a]	$.16$	$.30$

[a]$p < .05$

TABLE 11.5. Correlations of PONS with Introversion Scores for Three Samples

| | Dance Therapists | | Personnel Managers | |
| | Sample 1 (N=14) | Sample 2 (N=15) | Sample 3 (N=24) | |
Channel	Full PONS	Full PONS	Full PONS	Photo PONS
RS 20	.26	.15	.23	
CF 20	−.40	−.10	.27	
Body 60	−.05	−.22	−.07	−.12
Face 120	−.30	−.17	.35	−.39
Total	−.22	−.19	.29	−.39

results as well as the results from a sample of industrial personnel managers who had rated themselves on a nine-point scale of introversion and who took both the full PONS and the booklet form of the PONS. Results from the booklet form of the PONS were consistent with those of the dance therapy students but results from the full PONS were in the opposite direction. The only consistent result of even moderate size was that more introverted subjects scored higher on RS (median $r = .23$, combined $p = .074$, one-tailed). There was a still smaller (and even less significant) but consistent tendency for more extraverted subjects to score higher on body 60 (median $r = −.10$). A good deal of research is needed before we can say much about the nature of the relationship between introversion and sensitivity to nonverbal cues.

SELF-MONITORING SCALE. The Self-Monitoring Scale (SM) (Snyder 1974) was designed to measure differences in the extent to which individuals can and do monitor (observe and control) their self-presentation, expressive behavior, and nonverbal affective displays. This scale consists of twenty-five true/false self-descriptive statements that describe (1) concern with social appropriateness for self-presentation, (2) attention to social comparison information as cues to appropriate self-expression, (3) ability to control and modify self-presentation and expressive behavior, (4) use of these traits in particular situations, and (5) the extent to which the respondent's expressive behavior and self-presentation are cross-situationally consistent or variable. The SM scale has a KR-20 internal consistency reliability of .70 and a test-retest reliability of .83 (based on 192 undergraduate subjects). Cross-validation KR-20 reliability in an independent sample of 146 was .63.

Table 11.6 presents the correlations of the SM scale with the PONS total in six samples. The results were inconsistent and none of the correlations was large.

TABLE 11.6. Correlations of PONS with Self-Monitoring Scale for Six Samples

Sample	N	r
U.S. college	154	.01
U.S. college	60	−.14
Nursing faculty	58	−.16
M.D.'s (internal medicine)	39	−.03
Business executives	24	.16
M.D.'s (surgery)	16	−.20
Median		−.08 [a]

[a] combined $p = .172$, one-tailed

SELF-RATINGS

SELF-RATINGS OF INTERPERSONAL SUCCESS. In examining the relationship of psychosocial factors to the PONS, we explored self-reported "success" in interpersonal relationships. Specifically, we asked many samples of subjects to complete a questionnaire on which they rated, on nine-point scales, the "quality" of their same-sex and opposite-sex relationships. Although the self-report of such information can never be truly "objective," we believe that these variables may give us some measure of the kind of interpersonal climate the subject himself is experiencing. This self-reported measure may even be a better gauge than a more "objective" measure of the subject's interpersonal environment, for it may provide some insight into what the subject is perceiving and the forces that are, to a large extent, directing his or her interpersonal development. In figure 11.1 are listed the sixteen questions and the variable names we will use to refer to them.

In order to determine whether these sixteen questions should be treated as sixteen distinct variables or whether some were sufficiently highly correlated as to be considered together, we subjected the questionnaire to a principal components analysis. The data for this analysis came from 369 high school students (from two of the high schools comprising the norm group). With this principal components analysis, five factors were extracted that accounted for 66.4 percent of the total variance (the factor extraction being halted because the sixth factor added too little to the percentage of variance accounted for by the factor structure). These five factors were then rotated (using Kaiser's varimax method) and five well-defined factors emerged. By "well-defined" we mean that the factor loadings on the variables defining a factor were substantially higher than the loadings of variables not defining that factor. Table 11.7 shows the rotated factor loadings, sum of squares of factor load-

FIGURE. 11.1. The sixteen interpersonal variables and their variable labels.

Please rate your current relationships with *people of the same sex as yourself,* on the following scales, as follows: you would circle a 1 or 2 if you felt the adjective on the left-hand side of the scale is very correct, and 8 or 9 if the adjective on the right-hand side of the scale is very correct, or some number in between that seems appropriate.

Cold	1 2 3 4 5 6 7 8 9	Warm	*SS warm*
Dishonest	1 2 3 4 5 6 7 8 9	Honest	*SS honest*
Short-lived	1 2 3 4 5 6 7 8 9	Enduring	*SS enduring*
Generally unsatisfying	1 2 3 4 5 6 7 8 9	Generally satisfying	*SS satisfying*
I have trouble in understanding my friends' feelings	1 2 3 4 5 6 7 8 9	I understand my friends' feelings completely	*SS I understand*
My friends don't understand my feelings	1 2 3 4 5 6 7 8 9	My friends understand my feelings completely	*SS am understood*

Now rate your current relationships with *people of the opposite sex,* on the same scales.

Cold	1 2 3 4 5 6 7 8 9	Warm	*OP warm*
Dishonest	1 2 3 4 5 6 7 8 9	Honest	*OP honest*
Short-lived	1 2 3 4 5 6 7 8 9	Enduring	*OP enduring*
Generally unsatisfying	1 2 3 4 5 6 7 8 9	Generally satisfying	*OP satisfying*
I have trouble in understanding my friends' feelings	1 2 3 4 5 6 7 8 9	I understand my friends' feelings completely	*OP I understand*
My friends don't understand my feelings	1 2 3 4 5 6 7 8 9	My friends understand my feelings completely	*OP am understood*

When you meet someone of the *same sex,* how quickly are you likely to make friends with that person?

Very slowly	1 2 3 4 5 6 7 8 9	Very quickly	*SS makes friends quickly*

When you meet someone of the *opposite sex,* how quickly are you likely to make friends with that person?

Very slowly	1 2 3 4 5 6 7 8 9	Very quickly	*OP make friends quickly*

If you were to describe the kind of friendships you have currently with people of the *same sex* as yourself, which of the following labels would you choose?

Many very intimate friends	Some very intimate friends	No very intimate friends	*SS number of friends*

If you were to describe the kind of friendships you have currently with people of the *opposite sex,* which of the following labels would you choose?

Many very intimate friends	Some very intimate friends	No very intimate friends	*OP number of friends*

TABLE 11.7. Summary of Factor Analysis of Sixteen Interpersonal Variables
(N=369 High School Students)

Variable[a]	Factor 1	Factor 2	Factor 3	Factor 4	Factor 5
SS warm	+.095	−.722[b]	−.091	+.221	+.209
OP warm	+.736[b]	−.069	+.022	+.345	−.022
SS honest	+.174	−.715[b]	−.127	−.021	+.014
OP honest	+.746[b]	−.248	−.052	−.103	+.014
SS enduring	+.135	−.716[b]	+.107	−.085	+.153
OP enduring	+.809[b]	−.067	+.024	+.084	+.068
SS satisfying	+.058	−.658[b]	+.113	+.288	+.256
OP satisfying	+.750[b]	−.192	+.125	+.221	+.023
SS I understand	+.115	−.248	−.027	+.045	+.736[b]
OP I understand	+.694	−.094	+.034	+.008	+.268[b]
SS am understood	+.111	−.251	−.022	+.179	+.797[b]
OP am understood	+.606	+.049	+.109	+.049	+.476[b]
SS make friends quickly	+.021	−.256	−.037	+.789[b]	+.073
OP make friends quickly	+.355	+.080	+.104	+.762[b]	+.174
SS number of friends	−.042	−.021	+.913[b]	−.013	+.002
OP number of friends	+.171	+.042	+.883[b]	+.061	−.016
Total of Squared Loadings	3.408	2.296	1.708	1.568	1.650
Variance accounted for by factor	21.30%	14.35%	10.67%	9.80%	10.31%
Median factor loadings of variables defining factor	+.748	−.716	+.898	+.776	+.606
Median factor loadings of variables not defining factor	+.125	−.082	+.023	+.055	+.045

[a]SS = same sex; OP = opposite sex
[b]variable defining factor

ings, percentage of variance accounted for by each factor, the median loadings for variables defining each factor, and the median loadings for variables
not defining that factor. Based on the variables that comprise the five factors,
we suggested the following names for them:

Factor 1: quality of opposite-sex relationships

Factor 2: quality of same-sex relationships

Factor 3: number of friends

Factor 4: speed in making friends

Factor 5: understanding in relationships

The factor analysis allowed us to reduce the sixteen variables to five well-
defined clusters, which we were able to use to examine the relationship
between PONS scores and "interpersonal success" in ten large samples. To
do this, we again employed the technique of the "convergent and discriminant
validity matrix" (see chapter 10 on cognitive correlates). In these validity
matrices, we record the median intercorrelations of interrelated PONS variables, interpersonal success variables (as defined by our five factors), and the
intercorrelations of these clusters.

Our samples, all from the United States, fell naturally into three groups according to age: adults (two samples), college students (seven samples), and high school students (one sample). In table 11.8 we report the median intra-cluster and intercluster correlations of the PONS and interpersonal success variables (median of the samples within each age group). Many of the median intercorrelations are near zero. We should remember, however, that these are median correlations of clusters of variables and as such are very stable estimates of the extent of the relationship among these many variables. Thus, even some correlations of only modest size may still be worth our attention.

Among the adult samples, a trend indicating that the more nonverbally sensitive have "better" relationships with persons of the same sex was apparent. Among college students, only two intercluster correlations are worth noting. In the sample of twenty-eight college students, higher nonverbal sensitivity was associated with more understanding in friendships. Among samples 5 and 6 of college students, higher PONS scorers tended to report making friends more quickly than lower PONS scorers.

In the high school student sample of 369, there was a tendency for higher PONS scorers to have significantly "better" same-sex friendships ($p < .02$) and to make friends more quickly ($p < .01$) than lower PONS scorers, but a tendency for the more nonverbally sensitive to report having significantly fewer friends ($p < .02$). Perhaps among high school students, where superficial relationships may often take the place of true friendships, the more nonverbally sensitive enjoy fewer but deeper, and more lasting, associations.

Considering all samples, the grand medians of the PONS-interpersonal cluster correlations were consistently and significantly positive but they were quite small in magnitude.

In a sample of twenty-eight male and female college students who took the PONS test twice (with a six-week interval between testings), we examined the relationship between interpersonal success and improvement in PONS scores. Table 11.9 presents a summary of the correlations between the interpersonal variables from our questionnaire and improvement scores (posttest score minus pretest score). Although the relationship between improvement in PONS and both the quality of same-sex relationships and number of friends was not far from zero, the correlations for the other three interpersonal clusters were moderately positive. A low median correlation between improvement and understanding in relationships was evidenced but those subjects who improved most on PONS tended to have better opposite-sex relationships as well as greater ability to make friends quickly. These relationships, however, were not significant. More on interpersonal correlates of improvements in PONS scores is given in chapter 14.

SELF-RATINGS OF NONVERBAL SENSITIVITY. We wondered about the extent to which an individual could predict his or her general nonverbal/interpersonal

TABLE 11.8. Convergent and Discriminant Validity Matrix of PONS and Interpersonal Success

Subjects	Quality of Same-Sex Relationships	Quality of Opposite-Sex Relationships	Number of Friends	Speed in Making Friends	Understanding in Relationships	Median
Adults (N=26)						
Median interpersonal r[a]	.34	.36	.44	.36	.26	.36
Median PONS r[b]	.22	.22	.22	.22	.22	.22
Median PONS-interpersonal r[c]	.20	-.02	.10	.08	.06	.08
College students (N=378)						
Median interpersonal r	.49	.54	.23	.40	.39	.40
Median PONS r	.34	.34	.34	.34	.34	.34
Median PONS-interpersonal r	.06	.05	.04	.08	-.02	.05
High school students (N=369)						
Median interpersonal r	.42	.55	.66	.44	.34	.44
Median PONS r	.55	.55	.55	.55	.55	.55
Median PONS-interpersonal r	.08	.02	-.12	.12	.07	.07
Grand medians						
Median interpersonal r	.42	.54	.44	.40	.34	.42
Median PONS r	.34	.34	.34	.34	.34	.34
Median PONS-interpersonal r	.08	.02	.04	.08	.06	.06
Percentage of all ten samples showing positive median correlations between PONS and interpersonal ratings	90%	80%	60%	90%	50%	89%
Binomial p	.011	.055	.38	.011	.62	.055

[a] median intercorrelation of variables comprising interpersonal success factor
[b] median intercorrelation of four quadrants, tone 40, video 40, face 60, body 60, and figure 60, and RS 80, CF 80 (i.e., all marginals)
[c] median intercorrelation of interpersonal success variables and quadrants plus all marginals

TABLE 11.9. Correlations between Improvement in PONS Scores (First to Second Testing) and Interpersonal Variables for Twenty-Eight College Students

Variable	Quality of Same-Sex Relationships	Quality of Opposite-Sex Relationships	Number of Friends	Speed in Making Friends	Understanding in Relationships	Median
Change in quadrants						
Median interpersonal r	.49	.64	.63	.34	.40	.49
Median PONS r	.13	.13	.13	.13	.13	.13
Median PONS-interpersonal r	-.06	.26	.04	.25	.09	.09
Change in tone 40, video 60						
Median interpersonal r	.49	.64	.63	.34	.40	.49
Median PONs r	-.04	-.04	-.04	-.04	-.04	-.04
Median PONS-interpersonal r	-.04	.42	.12	.18	.17	.17
Change in face 60, body 60, figure 60						
Median interpersonal r	.49	.64	.63	.34	.40	.49
Median PONS r	.40	.40	.40	.40	.40	.40
Median PONS-interpersonal r	-.17	.25	-.08	.27	-.06	-.06
Change in RS 80, CF 80						
Median interpersonal r	.49	.64	.63	.34	.40	.49
Median PONs r	-.03	-.03	-.03	-.03	-.03	-.03
Median PONS-interpersonal r	-.09	.34	.11	.32	.17	.17
Median						
Median interpersonal r	.49	.64	.63	.34	.40	.49
Median PONS r	.05	.05	.05	.05	.05	.05
Median PONS-interpersonal r	-.08	.30[a]	.08	.26	.13	.13

[a] A recent replication by Tony Castelnovo found a rank correlation of +.78 ($df = 6$, $p < .03$) between PONS improvement scores and quality of relationship with the opposite sex as judged by a group leader.

sensitivity as well as his or her accuracy in reading nonverbal cues in specific channels, using the PONS test as a criterion.

Subjects from twenty-six of our samples filled out a six-item questionnaire on which they were asked to rate their own warmth and their ability to understand other people, social situations, tones of voice, body movements, and facial expressions, on nine-point scales. Although these are self-ratings, we might expect their validity and reliability to be slightly higher than the self-ratings of interpersonal success discussed above. It may seem to subjects more socially desirable to rate themselves as "warm" rather than "cold" persons, but the other five questions appear to present fewer demand characteristics. The inability to understand social situations or people or nonverbally communicated affect may not seem so socially undesirable to subjects and they may be more likely to rate themselves honestly. Whether or not they can or do rate themselves accurately on their PONS performance is another question, however. Beldoch (1964) has found that subjects were able to predict at better than chance level their emotional sensitivity to speech and graphic art.

We correlated subjects' responses to the six questions with their PONS scores. The first three questions (concerning warmth, understanding of people, and understanding of social situations) were correlated with PONS total score, and the questions regarding sensitivity to specific nonverbal channels (face, body, and tone of voice) were correlated with their corresponding marginal scores on the PONS test (face 60, body 60, and tone 40). We grouped the twenty-six samples into eight categories based on age, occupation, or country of origin (whichever was the most salient defining characteristic of the sample). Table 11.10 contains the median correlation of the samples within each category on each of the six variables.

Of the twenty-four correlations between PONS total and the self-rated variables of warmth, understanding of people, and understanding of social situations, about half were very weak or near zero. For Sydney, Australia, college students, U.S. adults, and professionals in the arts, these correlations were especially low. Worthy of note are the moderately positive correlations for the New Guineans and the psychiatric patients, whose self-ratings of warmth and personal and social understanding predicted their total PONS scores reasonably well.

The correlations more closely associated with prediction of nonverbal sensitivity are those appearing in the last three columns. These three correlations were highest for the psychiatric patients and the U.S. college students, who were fairly accurate in assessing their nonverbal skills. The clinical psychologists tended to be reasonably accurate in predicting their skills on tones of voice and body, but tended to be wrong in their assessment of their ability to understand facial expressions. The New Guinea persons were relatively accurate at predicting their sensitivity to face and body channels.

Although self-ratings of accuracy did not correlate consistently with PONS

TABLE 11.10. Correlations of PONS with Self-Ratings of Interpersonal Sensitivity and Nonverbal Skill

Sample Group	"I Am Warm" with PONS Total	"I Understand People" with PONS Total	"I Understand Social Situations" with PONS Total
U.S. college students			
2 samples; total N=53	−.14	−.21	.21
Sydney, Australia, college students			
3 samples; total N=207	−.12	−.03	−.08
U.S. adults			
4 samples; total N=74	.17	.00	−.03
Non-U.S. teachers			
6 samples; total N=71	.12	.13	−.22
Professionals in arts, design, theater			
5 samples; total N=67	−.15	−.02	−.08
Natives of New Guinea			
4 samples; total N=102	.16	.26	.13
Clinical psychologists			
1 sample; N=28	.10	−.10	−.20
Neuropsychiatric patients			
1 sample; N=25	.09	.38	.42
Median of 8 groups	.10	−.01	−.06
Median of 28 samples	−.02	.02	−.06

NOTE: Each entry is the median for samples listed at left.

[a]based on only one sample; data unavailable from other three samples considered separately

scores, they did tend to correlate with *gains* in PONS performance from pretesting to posttesting. This finding is described in chapter 14.

RATINGS BY OTHERS

An important criterion measure for establishing the validity of the PONS is the rating of subjects' nonverbal skills or sensitivity by others who know them. We have conducted a number of studies in which we have examined the relationship between subjects' PONS scores and ratings of "interpersonal sensitivity" or "sensitivity to nonverbal communication" made by other persons.

One of our studies involved the administration of the PONS and the six-item self-rating questionnaire (described in preceding section) to twenty-two married couples. These couples ranged from those married as few as two years to those with teenage children. Each member of the couple was asked to fill out the questionnaire twice: once rating himself (or herself) and once rating his (or her) spouse. Thus, each subject received PONS scores, self-ratings of his or her nonverbal sensitivity, and ratings by his or her spouse.

"I Understand Voice Tone" with Tone 40	"I Understand Body" with Body 60	"I Understand Face" with Face 60	Median of Last Three Columns
.26	.30	.32	.30
.12	.05	.03	.05
.00[a]	.00	.02	.00
.05	−.02	.13	.05
−.10	−.06	.23	−.06
.00	.28	.15	.15
.20	.15	−.18	.15
.21	.32	.53	.32
.08	.10	.14	.10
.08	.06	.08	.08

These scores were correlated, and the pattern of results was quite provocative. The correlations of the ratings of sensitivity to nonverbal cues in tones of voice, face, and body with PONS scores appear in table 11.11. For this sample, the correlations between predicted nonverbal skill and obtained PONS score were near zero or negative when the ratings were made by the subjects themselves. When the ratings were made by the subjects' spouses, however, these correlations were moderately high, positive, and, in four cases, significant. Thus, their spouses' assessments of their nonverbal skills were more accurate than the subjects' own estimates. We might also consider this finding as some evidence for the validity of the PONS. If we consider as the criterion of a person's nonverbal sensitivity the assessment of that skill by someone who knows the person intimately, then we find that PONS correlates substantially with this criterion.

In an attempt to replicate this finding, we administered the PONS and the rating scales, as above, to eleven somewhat older couples of varying ages. The findings were less clear in this study. As in the earlier sample, correlations of PONS with self-ratings were nearly all zero or negative. As seen in table 11.11, spouses' ratings correlated positively in a few cases with PONS scores and negatively in others. None of these correlations was significant.

TABLE 11.11. Correlations of PONS with Self-Ratings and Spouse Ratings of Nonverbal Skill for Two Samples

PONS Variable	Correlation of PONS with Self-Rating		Correlation of PONS with Spouse Rating	
	Family Study (N = 44)	Temple Club Couples (N = 22)	Family Study (N = 44)	Temple Club Couples (N = 22)
"I understand tone"				
RS 20	-.28	-.04	.14	-.03
CF 20	-.13	.04	.43[a]	-.17
Tone 40	-.27	-.00	.34[b]	-.11
RS 80	-.09	.07	.10	.12
CF 80	.07	.02	.19	.27
"I understand body"				
Body 20	-.05	-.15	.25	.24
Body 60	-.04	.09	.32[b]	.08
"I understand face"				
Face 20	-.04	-.06	.24	.11
Figure 20	-.02	.38[b]	.11	-.36
Face 60	.00	-.04	.31[b]	.24
Figure 60	-.08	.01	.15	-.01

[a] $p < .01$
[b] $p < .05$

It is possible that sampling error, resulting from a diminished sample size, could account for this result. An additional difference between this second sample and the first is the age of the couples. In this second sample, all subjects were about the same age as the older ones in the first sample. Since nonverbal sensitivity seems to decline slightly after the twenties (see chapter 8), perhaps sensitivity to someone else's sensitivity (in this case, the spouse's) declines as well. Further research on this question is important both for the further validation of the PONS and also for the understanding of the development of spouses' sensitivity to each other.

The correlation of subjects' PONS scores with ratings by other persons is, as we have mentioned, an important area of research in establishing the

TABLE 11.12. Correlations of PONS Total with Judged Interpersonal or Nonverbal Sensitivity

Subjects	Raters	N	r	Z
counselors	supervisors	7	.55	+1.02
undergraduate students	instructor	9	.49	+1.15
high school students	teachers	40	.46	+2.92
student teachers	supervisors	24	.45	+2.11
dance therapists	supervisors	15	.34	+1.24
dance therapists	supervisors	14	.33	+1.06
teachers	supervisors	39	.32	+1.91
therapists	peers and supervisors (median)	46	.31	+2.10
student teachers	supervisors	24	.29	+1.31
student helper role players[a]	helpees	23	.26	+1.14
clinical psychology graduate students	supervisors	14	.22	+0.69
clinical psychology graduate students	supervisors	16	.22	+0.76
Ph.D. candidates in clinical psychology	instructor	6	.20	+0.27
M.A. candidates in clinical psychology	instructor	11	.15	+0.39
nursing school faculty	peers	58	.11	+0.81
surgeons in training	peers and supervisors (median)	16	.10	+0.34
internists in training	peers, supervisors, patients (median)	39	.06	+0.35
student teachers	supervisors	86	.01	+0.09
kindergarten teachers	supervisors	46	.00	+0.00
graduate students	instructor	8	−.04	−0.08
counselor trainees	clients	33	−.19	−1.03
various ages	acquaintance or relative	13	−.35	−1.07
	Σ	587	+4.29	+17.48
	Median		.22	
	Unweighted mean		.20	
	Weighted mean		.16	

$$\text{Combined } Z = \frac{\Sigma Z}{\sqrt{22}} = 3.73$$

Combined $p < .0001$

[a]employed forty-item face + body PONS, not full PONS

validity of the PONS. In twenty-two studies we have administered the PONS to subjects and asked persons acquainted with these subjects to rate their "sensitivity" (nonverbal and/or interpersonal). These ratings were then correlated with the PONS. In table 11.12 are listed some details of these twenty-two studies as well as the obtained correlation between PONS total and the criterion measure.

The PONS-sensitivity rating correlations were overwhelmingly positive (median $r = .22$, $p < .0001$) and many were quite substantial, indicating that the validity of the PONS is reasonably high if we use another's ratings of sensitivity as a criterion measure of a subject's nonverbal skill. Eight of the twenty-two correlations (36 percent) exceeded .30, and validity coefficients of this magnitude are, on the average, about as high as we can realistically hope to obtain with personality-relevant measures of this type (Cohen 1969, p. 78). These correlations tell us that PONS scores, in effect, have some "real world" meaning and that we are indeed measuring a subject's sensitivity to and ability to understand social stimuli.

POPULARITY

In order to investigate further the correlation between PONS and interpersonal success, we collected others' ratings of students' "popularity" for three samples that took the PONS test. The first sample consisted of 92 male and female high school students who took the full PONS test. Each student was rated by five teachers (who were teaching classes in which they were enrolled at the time of the study) on the degree of popularity he or she possessed among peers. Each subject's "popularity score" consisted of the mean of the five teachers' ratings. The second sample consisted of 275 male and female fourth and fifth graders who took the forty-item face and body PONS and the forty-item child sender audio PONS (see chapter 8). "Popularity" in this case was a dichotomous variable (popular versus not popular). A subject was described as popular if the peer sociometric ratings he or she received fell above the median on "acceptance" and above the median on "attraction." Thus, the "popular" subjects were those who were highly accepted by their peers and also those to whom their peers were highly attracted. The third sample consisted of 106 male and female high school students who took the forty-item face and body PONS and the forty-item original sender audio PONS. Several teachers (mean = 2.4, range = 1–5) rated the students whom they knew on their popularity with the same and opposite sex.

Correlations between PONS performance and popularity ratings were relatively homogeneous: for sample 1, $r(90) = .15$; for sample 2, $r(273) = .18$; for sample 3, $r(104) = .25$; combined $p = .00003$. Thus, children and teenagers who scored higher on the PONS were judged to be more popular.

12 | Impaired Groups

PSYCHOPATHOLOGY

Our purpose here is to examine the relationship between sensitivity to nonverbal communication and psychopathology, broadly defined. Initially, five samples of psychiatric patients were available for testing with the PONS, all of them hospitalized at the time of testing: two samples came from different psychiatric hospitals in the Belfast area of Northern Ireland ($N = 11$ and 15), two samples came from a single private psychiatric hospital in the Boston area of the United States ($N = 11$ and 9), and one sample came from a psychiatric hospital in the Sydney area of Australia ($N = 22$). A preliminary analysis of variance showed no significant differences among the five samples in total PONS score, in differential performance on the eleven channels, or in differential performance on the four quadrants. All five samples were, therefore, combined to form a single sample of psychiatric patients ($N = 68$).

Two samples of alcoholic patients were also available for testing with the PONS; all of the patients were enrolled in residential treatment programs of a "halfway house" nature. One of the samples was from an urban setting in the Boston area ($N = 17$), the other from a rural setting in Kansas ($N = 44$). A preliminary analysis of variance showed no significant differences between these two samples in total PONS score, in differential performance on the eleven channels, or in differential performance on the four quadrants. These two samples were, therefore, combined to form a single sample of alcoholic patients ($N = 61$).

The PONS performance of the psychiatric patients and alcoholics was then compared with the PONS performance of 482 members of our norm group (high school students from the east and west coasts and the midwestern part of the United States). Table 12.1 shows the results of this comparison. For each of the eleven channels of the PONS, the mean accuracy is given in percentage form for each of the three samples. The performance of the 482 normal subjects conformed very closely to that of the smaller, more preliminary norm

TABLE 12.1. Accuracy in All Channels for Alcoholic Patients, Psychiatric Patients, and Normal Subjects

Subjects	Channel				
	None	Body	Face	Figure	Mean
Alcoholic patients (N=61)					
None	50.0%[a]	72.2%	75.8%	74.2%	68.0%
Content-filtered	57.9	65.8	74.2	78.6	69.2
Randomized spliced	56.9	70.3	82.8	79.7	72.4
Mean	54.9	69.4	77.6	77.5	69.9
Psychiatric patients (N=68)					
None	50.0[a]	71.7	74.8	72.4	67.2
Content-filtered	58.6	64.9	75.7	75.8	68.7
Randomized spliced	57.4	71.3	80.5	79.7	72.2
Mean	55.3	69.3	77.0	76.0	69.4
Normal subjects (N=482)					
None	50.0[a]	77.6	81.0	80.6	72.3
Content-filtered	60.9	72.0	82.5	85.4	75.2
Randomized spliced	63.0	76.6	88.8	84.0	78.1
Mean	57.9	75.4	84.1	83.3	75.2

[a]theoretical accuracy

group (N = 359) that was the basis for the construction of the standard scoring sheet and that was a subset of the total sample. The performances of the psychiatric patients and the alcoholics were quite similar to each other channel for channel but were consistently lower than the performance of the normal subjects. These results are consistent with those of Turner (1964), who found psychiatric patients to perform significantly more poorly at decoding affect from tone of voice than normal controls.

EFFECTS OF ADDING INFORMATION. Using analysis of variance, the patient groups were compared with the normal subjects to see the effects on accuracy of adding the information from tone of voice, body, and face channels of nonverbal communication. Because the alcoholic and psychiatric patients performed so similarly, they were combined into a "patient" group for these analyses. We computed the mean level of accuracy obtained by patients and normals with or without the presence of tone of voice cues. For this analysis, the row means of table 12.1, listed in the right-hand column, were the basic data, with presence of tone of voice defined by the mean of the accuracy obtained in the content-filtered and randomized spliced channels.

Normals were significantly more accurate overall than patients ($F(1,608)$ = 58.65; $p < .001$, effect size = .62σ), and adding tone of voice cues led to improved performance ($F(1,608) = 151.19$, $p < .001$, effect size = 1.00σ). The significant interaction, though small in magnitude, showed that normals were able to make significantly better use of the addition of the audio channels than were the patients ($F(1,608) = 5.17$, $p = .025$, effect size = .18σ).

We computed the mean level of accuracy obtained by patients and normals with or without the presence of body cues. Adding body cues led to very greatly improved performance overall ($F(1,608) = 589.55$, $p < .001$, effect size $= 1.97\sigma$). The significant interaction effect, though small in magnitude, showed that normals were able to make significantly better use of the addition of the channels carrying body cues than were the patients ($F(1,608) = 5.52$, $p = .02$, effect size $= .19\sigma$).

We also computed the mean level of accuracy obtained by patients and normals with or without the presence of face cues. Adding face cues led to enormously improved performance overall ($F(1,608) = 2,412.87$, $p < .001$, effect size $= 3.98\sigma$). The significant interaction effect, though modest in magnitude, showed that normals were able to make significantly better use of the addition of the channels carrying face cues than were the patients ($F(1,608) = 11.18$, $p < .001$, effect size $= .27\sigma$).

To summarize, overall, normal subjects were more accurate than patient groups in reading nonverbal communications. The three analyses also tell us that the addition of tone of voice, body, and face cues, each considered independently of the others, increased the levels of accuracy obtained and to increasing degrees: 1.00σ for audio cues, 1.97σ for body cues, and 3.98σ for face cues. For the PONS test, then, adding body cues adds about twice the information, in σ units, as adding tone of voice cues, and adding face cues adds about twice the information as adding body cues. (These ratios of information added in adding channels were nearly identical when just the norm group was considered; see chapter 3.) Finally, the three analyses tell us that the addition of tone of voice cues, body cues, and face cues was differentially more advantageous to normal subjects than to patient groups. While all of these effects are modest in magnitude (about one-fifth of a standard deviation for each channel), they are remarkable in their consistency. Taken together, they suggest strongly that psychiatric patients and alcoholic patients are less able than normal subjects to profit from the addition of further channels of nonverbal information considered independently of one another.

The finding that patients were less able than normal subjects to profit from the addition of channels of nonverbal communication is consistent with a number of findings reported in the literature of psychopathology. Maher (1966) has summarized the general attentional problems often found in schizophrenic patients and Meiselman (1973) has noted that chronic schizophrenics may be especially impaired when required to process information from two sense modalities simultaneously. There are also specific theoretical and empirical formulations that suggest that psychiatric patients may differ from normals in the efficiency with which they can deal with stimuli carried in the auditory and visual channels. McGhie (1973), for example, has suggested that schizophrenics perform relatively more effectively in the auditory than in the visual channel and, in addition, that adding visual information to auditory information may have relatively disruptive effects. Although the authors cited were writing specifically of schizophrenia, or even of restricted subtypes of schizophrenia, their formulations could be tested on our more heterogeneous group of hospitalized psychiatric patients.

We computed the mean accuracy obtained by the psychiatric patients (N = 68) and the normal subjects (N = 482) for the pure audio channels (CF and RS) and the pure video channels (face, body, figure). Despite the diagnostically and nationally heterogeneous nature of our patient sample, their performance was what McGhie would have predicted for schizophrenic patients— relatively better on the audio than on the video channels ($F(1,608)$ = 6.70, p < .01, effect size = $.21\sigma$).

The work of both McGhie and Meiselman would suggest further that psychiatric patients should be more impaired when confronted with channels combining audio with video information than on pure channels. We examined this suggestion by obtaining for each of our patients and normals a "pure channel" accuracy score based on single-mode channels (CF, RS, face, body, figure) as well as a "mixed channel" accuracy score based on the remaining six channels having both audio and video components. The psychiatric patients were more impaired in their performance relative to normal subjects when confronted with mixed channel information than when confronted with pure channel information, though the effect was small in magnitude ($F(1,608)$ = 3.04, p < .09, effect size = $.14\sigma$).

Alcoholic patients were also compared to normal subjects both for their relative performance in audio versus video channels and for their relative performance in pure versus mixed channels. In both comparisons, alcoholic patients' performance was in the direction of psychiatric patients' performance (i.e., better performance on audio than video, better performance on pure than on mixed channels), but not significantly so.

It seemed likely in view of the results presented thus far that psychiatric patients might be relatively impaired in handling greater amounts of information regardless of the specific sense modality involved. For the eleven channels of the PONS, the definition of information transmitted is the mean accuracy score obtained by a large norm group (N = 482). The channels in which accuracy was greatest are assumed to be those in which the most information was transmitted. If psychiatric patients were to be most impaired in channels conveying the most information, there should be a sizeable correlation between a channel's information level (that is, its accuracy when judged by normals) and the degree to which psychiatric patients would be disadvantaged in performing in that channel relative to the normal subjects (that is, the difference between psychiatric and normal samples). The correlation obtained was quite substantial (r = .65), suggesting that the more information available in a channel, the less efficiently would psychiatric patients utilize that information. The analogous correlation employing alcoholic rather than psychiatric patients was in the same direction, but smaller in magnitude (r

= .43). An alternative definition of channel information level was also employed to avoid the problem that accuracy-as-judged-by-normals entered into both the definition of information level and the degree of disadvantage of the patient groups. In the alternative analysis, a weight of 1 was given to a channel if tone occurred (RS or CF), a weight of 2 was given if body was shown, and a weight of 4 was given if face was shown. Channel weights varied, then, from 1 for RS and CF to 7 for figure RS and figure CF. These weights were based on the earlier analyses weighting patients and normals equally so that they contributed equally to the results. The correlation between channel information level defined by these weights and degree of disadvantage was .57 for psychiatric patients and .33 for alcoholic patients. By this different definition of amount of channel information, too, the more information that is carried in a channel, the less efficiently the patient groups, especially the psychiatric patients, utilize that information.

EFFECTS OF QUADRANTS. The performances of the psychiatric patients and the alcoholics were also compared with the performance of the normal subjects on each of the four affect quadrants. Table 12.2 shows the results. For all three samples, higher accuracy was obtained on negative than on positive affect scenes and higher accuracy was obtained on dominant than on submissive orientation scenes. This advantage of the dominant over submissive scenes was greatest for the normal subjects and smallest for the psychiatric patients ($F(1,608)$ linear contrast $= 7.69$, $p < .01$, effect size $= .22 \sigma$). Perhaps the patient groups, especially the psychiatric patients, found the dominant orientations of the female sender sufficiently unpleasant that they

TABLE 12.2. Accuracy in Four Quadrants for Alcoholic Patients, Psychiatric Patients, and Normal Subjects

Subjects	Quadrant		
	Negative	Positive	Mean
Alcoholic patients (N = 61)			
Submissive	70.3%	66.4%	68.4%
Dominant	77.0	65.8	71.4
Mean	73.6	66.1	69.9
Psychiatric patients (N = 68)			
Submissive	69.5	67.3	68.4
Dominant	76.7	64.2	70.4
Mean	73.1	65.8	69.4
Normal subjects (N = 482)			
Submissive	74.5	71.8	73.2
Dominant	82.9	71.6	77.2
Mean	78.7	71.7	75.2

reduced their attention to these scenes with a corresponding drop in relative accuracy. Such a speculation stems more from a psychodynamic framework than from a framework of information processing.

A thorough understanding of the effects of the quadrants on the accuracy of our patient groups required that we also analyze the effects of the quadrant location of the incorrect alternatives paired with the correct alternatives of each of the four quadrants. For all three samples, accuracy was lowest when the incorrect alternative was from the same quadrant as the correct alternative and highest when the incorrect alternative was from the quadrant diagonally opposite to the quadrant of the correct alternative (i.e., the quadrant that differed on both dimensions of positiveness and dominance). This result, that greater confusion occurs when the correct and incorrect alternatives are from the same quadrant, adds to our understanding of the reliability of the quadrants of the PONS and is summarized in table 12.3. The effects are very large in size for all three samples, attesting to the within-quadrant reliability of all three samples. The right side of table 12.3 shows the residuals when the effects of quadrant similarity and of sample have been removed. These residuals show that normals obtained the greatest benefit from having incorrect alternatives that were very dissimilar to the correct alternatives, while psychiatric patients obtained the least benefit. This appears to be yet another instance, then, when adding information to the test situation was relatively least useful to the psychiatric patient, more useful to the alcoholic patient, and most useful to the normal subject.

EFFECTS OF PRACTICE. There is one more result suggesting that psychiatric patients are less able than normal subjects to profit from the addition of information—prior exposure to PONS scenes. Psychiatric patients showed essentially no improvement whatever in going from the first half to the last half of the PONS, while normal subjects showed gains of a full standard deviation. Alcoholic patients showed gains as large as those of the normal control samples.

TABLE 12.3. Accuracy at Three Levels of Similarity of Incorrect to Correct Alternative

Subjects	Quadrant Similarity			Residuals		
	Most	Intermediate	Least	Most	Intermediate	Least
Alcoholic patients (N=61)	60.6%	71.8%	78.8%	−0.1	0.0	0.1
Psychiatric patients (N=68)	59.3	69.4	75.5	0.9	−0.1	−0.9
Normal subjects (N=482)	64.8	76.9	84.4	−0.9	0.1	0.7

ANALYSIS OF OMITTED ITEMS. In most samples, items are rarely omitted by subjects. However, alcoholic patients, and especially psychiatric patients, left a fairly large number of items unanswered. Psychiatric patients omitted many more items (11.7 percent) than did alcoholic patients (1.5 percent) ($F(1,138) = 20.35$, $p < .001$, effect size $= .77\sigma$). It is interesting to note that the overall accuracy rates of alcoholic and psychiatric patients were very similar despite the very much greater rate of omissions by the psychiatric patients. In part, this similarity is fostered by the scoring procedure, which gives a credit of .5 units for each omitted item.

Although the alcoholic and psychiatric patients differed in several ways in their patterns of omitted items, there were a great many points of similarity. Generally, if one group omitted many items in a given channel, the other group was also likely to omit many items in that channel ($r = .67$, $p < .015$). Table 12.4 shows the percentage of items omitted in all channels by the two groups combined as well as the resulting analysis of variance. The three significant main effects each tell a very clear story. Adding audio, body, or face cues served to reduce significantly the rate of omission of items. Thus, as we might expect, when more information was added to make the task a bit easier, fewer items were omitted. (We recall that, though items containing more information were relatively harder for psychiatric/alcoholic patients than for normals, such items were still judged more accurately in absolute terms

TABLE 12.4. Items Omitted in All Channels by Both Alcoholic Patients and Psychiatric Patients and Table of Variance ($N = 140$)

Audio Channel	Video Channel				
	None	Body	Face	Figure	Mean
None	10.5%[a]	8.1%	6.8%	6.6%	8.0%
Content-filtered	8.8	6.2	4.7	4.5	6.0
Randomized spliced	7.9	5.1	5.2	4.6	5.7
Mean	9.1	6.5	5.6	5.2	6.6

Source	Variance			
	df	MS	F	p
Audio	2	6.145	21.15	.001
Body	1	6.457	22.23	.001
Face	1	16.807	57.85	.001
Audio × body	2	0.042		
Audio × face	2	0.462	1.59	
Body × face	1	3.849	13.25	.001
Audio × body × face	2	0.006		
Error	1380	0.290		

[a] estimated value (Snedecor and Cochran 1967, p. 318)

than items containing less information.) The significant interaction between the body and face channels appears to be due primarily to the fact that giving both body and face cues did not reduce omissions much beyond the level achieved by giving either body or face cues. These results suggested that, in general, omissions were positively related to the overall difficulty of a channel; harder items may have been omitted more. This formulation could be checked by computing the correlation between the rate of item omissions of a channel and the difficulty of a channel defined by the performance of the norm group. This correlation was .77, $p < .01$.

We also analyzed the percentage of items omitted in the four affect quadrants by the two patient groups combined. There were significantly fewer omissions when affects were negative rather than positive ($F(1,414) = 18.15$, $p < .001$), and there was a tendency for fewer omissions to occur on dominant rather than submissive scenes ($F(1,414) = 1.71$, $p < .20$). Both of these results are consistent with the finding that omissions increase as the difficulty level of items increases. Omissions, then, appear to reflect uncertainty.

SCHIZOPHRENIC/NEUROTIC PATIENTS VERSUS CHARACTER DISORDERS. For our Australian sample of psychiatric patients, we had available a subsample of ten patients who had been diagnosed by the hospital staff as having character disorders and a subsample of eleven patients who had been diagnosed as schizophrenic or severely neurotic. All these patients had made self-ratings of the degree to which they felt they understood (a) other people, (b) social situations, (c) tones of voice, (d) body movements, and (e) facial expressions. These self-ratings, made on a nine-point scale, were correlated with PONS performance. Table 12.5 shows the correlations between total PONS performance and the five self-ratings for the schizophrenics/neurotics, those with character disorders, and all patients combined. The combined

TABLE 12.5. Correlations between PONS and Self-Ratings for Australian Psychiatric Patients

Self-Ratings of Understanding of:	Schizophrenic/ Neurotic Patients (N = 11)	Character Disorder Patients (N = 10)	All Patients (N = 25)
Other people	.33	.33	.38
Social situations	.62[a,b]	−.06[b]	.42[a]
Tone of voice	.46	.21	.35
Body movements	.54	.04	.17
Facial expressions	.64[a]	.68[a]	.62[c]
Median	.54	.21	.38

[a] $p < .05$
[b] z of difference = 1.51
[c] $p < .001$

group of patients included four that could not be diagnosed as either character disorders or schizophrenics/neurotics. Examination of the correlations suggests that schizophrenic/neurotics tended to be more accurate, on the whole, in their self-ratings of interpersonal sensitivity than the character disorder patients. In addition, of all the self-ratings made, ratings of how well patients felt they understood facial expressions correlated most strongly with total PONS.

The five self-ratings of understanding shown in table 12.5 were highly intercorrelated, the correlations ranging from .37 to .65 with a median of .48. Therefore, a new composite variable of self-ratings of understanding was generated by summing over the five self-ratings. The correlations between this composite variable and PONS channel scores showed, as we would expect on the basis of table 12.5, that the schizophrenic/neurotic patients tended to show higher correlations between PONS scores and self-ratings of understanding (r for PONS total $= .61$, $p < .05$) than did the ones with character disorders ($r = .33$). Before leaving this section we should note that, in general, our Australian psychiatric patients were much better able to tell us, through their self-ratings, how well they would perform on the PONS than were our American samples of normal students and adults. It will be recalled that for these American samples, subjects' self-ratings of interpersonal sensitivity showed very small positive correlations with PONS scores, although subjects' spouses' ratings of subjects' interpersonal sensitivity did correlate more positively with subjects' PONS performance.

THE LYLE RESEARCH. Jack Lyle of the University of Sydney in Australia has conducted an extensive study of psychiatric patients drawn from several psychiatric hospitals in the greater Sydney area. Complete PONS scores were available for eighty-two of these patients, and the mean accuracy obtained in all channels is shown in table 12.6. Compared to the earlier sample of sixty-eight psychiatric patients (table 12.1), the present sample performed slightly lower (68.4 percent versus 69.4 percent). The profiles of the two samples of

TABLE 12.6. Accuracy in All Channels for Eighty-Two Psychiatric Patients (after Lyle)

	Video Channel				
Audio Channel	None	Body	Face	Figure	Mean
None	50.0%[a]	68.7%	73.4%	71.9%	66.0%
Content-filtered	56.0	63.8	75.4	74.9	67.5
Randomized spliced	58.2	70.1	80.8	78.1	71.8
Mean	54.8	67.5	76.5	75.0	68.4

[a]theoretical accuracy

psychiatric patients were quite similar, however. For each of the eleven channels the performance of each sample of patients was subtracted from the performance of the norm group subjects (N = 482, table 12.1), and the resulting differences were correlated for the two samples. The correlation between these difference scores for the two samples was .83. Subtracting the performance of the patients from the performance of the normal subjects serves to reduce the effect of the very strong channel differences in difficulty that would otherwise inflate the correlation between the two psychiatric samples. When the eleven channel scores of the two samples were correlated directly, without correcting for the performance of the norm group, the correlation of .83 increased to .99.

Earlier, we saw that the addition of information was of significantly less benefit to the patient groups than to the normal group. Table 12.7 shows the results of the analogous analysis for the patients studied by Lyle. The first column shows the benefits in percentage points that accrued to Lyle's patients when tone of voice, body, and face cues were added. The last column shows the analogous benefits of added information that accrued to the normal subjects. The second column shows the extent (in σ units) to which Lyle's patients benefited less than did the normals from the addition of tone, body, and face cues. The third and fourth columns review the analogous results obtained from the patients discussed earlier in this chapter.

In general, the results based on Lyle's patients are quite similar to those obtained from the earlier samples of patients. For both sets of patients the addition of facial, body, or tone of voice cues was less helpful than it was to normals, and the magnitude of this effect was about one-fifth of a standard deviation for each channel of information. It should be emphasized that Lyle's psychiatric patients, although they profited less than the normal subjects from the addition of further nonverbal cues, nevertheless did benefit substantially from the addition of such cues. With these benefits expressed in σ units, the addition of tone of voice, body, and face cues improved performance by

TABLE 12.7. Improvement in Accuracy Due to the Addition of Tone of Voice, Body, and Face Cues for Three Samples

| Cue Type | Lyle's Patients (N=82) | | Prior Patients (N=140) | | Normals (N=482) |
	Percentage	Effect Size[a]	Percentage	Effect Size[a]	Percentage
Tone of voice	3.7%	.08	3.0%	.18	4.3%
Body	5.6	.33	6.8	.19	8.4
Face	14.6	.29	14.8	.27	17.0
Mean	8.0	.23	8.2	.21	9.9

[a]effect size (σ) comparing percentage improvement of patients with percentage improvement of normals

0.95σ, 1.87σ, and 4.72σ, respectively. The analogous benefits for the patients described earlier combined with the normals were 1.00σ, 1.97σ, and 3.98σ. The agreement between these two sets of effective sizes was excellent: an r of .996 reflected the great similarity in the patterns of the two sets of three scores and a t of 0.14 reflected the small degree of mean difference between the two sets of scores.

Earlier, we saw that psychiatric patients were relatively more accurate in the pure audio than in the pure video channels in comparison to the normal subjects. We were able to make the analogous comparison for Lyle's patients, and the results were quite consistent with those of the earlier analysis. Whereas the magnitude of the effect had been $.21\sigma$ for the earlier group of patients, the magnitude of the effect for Lyle's patients was $.27\sigma$. We also saw that psychiatric patients were relatively more accurate in either the pure audio or pure video channels than in the mixed channels (having both audio and video information) in comparison to the normal subjects. This effect was small, however (effect size $= .14\sigma$), and though the trend was in the same direction for Lyle's patients, the effect was smaller still in magnitude ($.08\sigma$).

All indications were that psychiatric patients might be most impaired in those channels conveying the most information. If that were the case, we suggested earlier, we might expect a sizeable correlation between the amount of information carried in each of the eleven channels and the degree to which psychiatric patients might be disadvantaged in performing on each of the channels *relative to normal subjects*. The correlation obtained for our earlier group of patients was substantial ($r = .65$), suggesting that the more information carried in a channel, the less efficiently would psychiatric patients be able to utilize that information. The analogous correlation could be computed for the patients tested by Lyle and the results were remarkably consistent: this time the correlation was equally substantial ($r = .64$).

Table 12.8 shows the mean accuracy obtained in each of the four affect quadrants by Lyle's patients. These results were quite consistent with those obtained by the earlier group of psychiatric patients (table 12.2). The earlier analysis had suggested that the psychiatric patients benefited significantly less from scenes showing dominant affects than did the normal controls. That result was also obtained when the analogous comparison was made for the

TABLE 12.8. Percent Accuracy in Four Quadrants
for Eighty-Two Psychiatric Patients (after Lyle)

	Negative	Positive	Mean
Submissive	68.4%	66.0%	67.2%
Dominant	75.3	64.1	69.7
Mean	71.8	65.0	68.4

later group of patients. This time, the effect size was slightly smaller than in the original analysis (.16 σ instead of .22 σ).

Of the eighty-two patients tested by Lyle, twenty-seven had been clearly diagnosed as neurotic, twenty-eight had been clearly diagnosed as psychotic, and ten had been clearly diagnosed as having personality disorders. The neurotic patients performed significantly better (73.4 percent) than did the psychotic or personality disorder patients (67.7 percent), who did not differ from each other (point biserial $r = .31$, $p < .05$).

Less severely disturbed patients often show a higher level of intellectual functioning, and that was the case for the present sample as well. The neurotic patients showed a significantly higher score on the Simpson Vocabulary Scale (point biserial $r = .29$). In addition, scores on the IQ scale were positively correlated with scores on PONS total ($r = .30$), raising the question of whether the superior PONS performance of the neurotic patients might not be due to their higher IQ. The correlation of .31 between status as a neurotic and PONS total was recalculated, partialing out the effect of IQ. The results showed only some shrinkage due to the "removal" of the effects of IQ, from $r = .31$ to $r = .24$.

The greatest advantage of the neurotic patients over the remaining patients had been found in the scores on the forty tone-only items ($r = .37$). This subtest of the PONS was also significantly correlated with IQ ($r = .27$), and once again we partialed out the effect of IQ from the relationship between neurotic status and PONS performance. There was some shrinkage due to partialing, but the partial correlation of .32 was still substantial. The superior performance of the neurotic patients could not simply be attributed to their superior intellectual functioning. Perhaps their superior PONS performance was related to their presumably superior social adjustment when compared to the psychotic or more characterologically involved personality disorders.

In his research Lyle had administered two scales of psychoticism to his patients: one described by Overall, Hunter, and Butcher (1973) and one described by Eysenck and Eysenck (1968; see also Claridge and Chappa 1973). The correlation between these scales was .45, each correlated $-.20$ with patients' having been classified as neurotic, and the Overall, Hunter, and Butcher and Eysenck measures correlated .16 and .10, respectively, with patients having been psychiatrically classified as psychotic. The less psychotic or the better adjusted patients were found to be on these two scales, the better was their total PONS performance. The correlations were found to be $-.30$ and $-.29$, respectively, both correlations reaching significance at the .01 level. Both measures of psychoticism were found to be negatively related to IQ, and so partial correlations were again computed to "remove" the effects of IQ from the relationships between psychoticism scale performance and PONS performance. The resulting partial correlations did not show much shrinkage, with the original correlations of $-.30$ and $-.29$ reduced only to $-.24$ and $-.25$, respectively.

Thus, whether defined by psychiatric diagnosis or by scores on two different scales of psychoticism, more severely disturbed patients appear to perform less well on the PONS even after the effects of differences in IQ have been removed through partialing.

SENSORY IMPAIRMENT

THE BLIND. Twenty male and female blind students at a school for the blind near Boston, Massachusetts, ages twelve to nineteen, were tested in three testing sessions. IQ scores and grade levels were available for nineteen of the twenty students. The students took the forty-item original sender audio test. Subjects used Braille answer sheets on which item numbers 1–40 were listed; following each item number were Braille symbols for the letters A–E. The subjects had used identical answer sheets before and they had no difficulty understanding that only response alternatives A and B were to be used in the present test.

A member of the school's psychology department, whom the students knew, administered the test by reading each item number and the two response alternatives, clearly identifying them as A and B, and then playing the test item. Subjects made a pencil mark on A or B for each item after they heard it.

Table 12.9 shows the performance of the blind subjects, broken down by sex. Males performed significantly better than females on the CF channel $(t(18) = 2.59, p < .05$; effect size $= 1.22\,\sigma)$. IQ was moderately correlated

TABLE 12.9. Audio Accuracy for Blind Students, Sexes Pooled and Separately (N=20)

Audio Channel	Sex	Accuracy		
		Item	Percentage	SD[a]
Randomized spliced	males (N=13)[b]	12.92	64.6%	2.06
	females (N=7)[c]	12.29	61.4	2.25
	all (N=20)[d]	12.70	63.5	2.15
Content-filtered	males	13.31	66.6	1.54
	females	11.29	56.4	1.67
	all	12.60	63.0	1.86
Total	males	26.23	65.6	2.26
	females	23.57	58.9	3.11
	all	25.30	63.2	2.88

[a] standard deviation based on item accuracy
[b] mean IQ = 107.23
[c] mean IQ = 101.33
[d] mean IQ = 105.37

with PONS skill (*r* between IQ and RS, CF, and total = .25, .23, and .33, *df* = 17).

Figure 12.1 compares the PONS performance of these blind students with sighted comparison groups selected from among other PONS samples. These comparison samples were chosen to match on age, to have large sample size, and to be as representative as possible; they were chosen without reference to their PONS scores. As the comparisons show, the blind students performed somewhat worse in the older ages and somewhat better in the younger ages, even though the blind students' grade levels were slightly behind those of their sighted counterparts. This finding offers some suggestion that blindness may be associated with some degree of auditory compensation.

Figure 12.1 also shows a comparison between blind students and the same comparison samples with the blind plotted according to mental age rather than chronological age. For the blind, mental age was computed on the basis of chronological age and IQ (MA = (IQ × CA)/100). For the sighted, in the absence of IQ data, mental age was considered equivalent to chronological

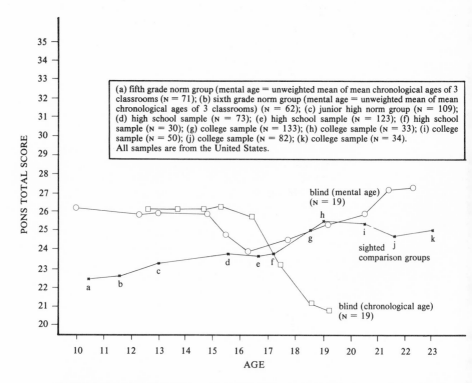

FIGURE 12.1. PONS audio performance: Smoothed blind/sighted comparison on chronological and mental ages

age. Figure 12.1 shows that the blind students performed at least as well as the sighted groups.

Blau (1964), in a study comparing the nonverbal decoding accuracy of fifty-seven blind and sixty-six sighted adolescents, found that blind students' ability to judge the affects in standard content speech was significantly worse than that of the sighted students (effect size = $.72\,\sigma$). He found, however, that the blind were significantly more alert to the presence of affect than to content in dialogue than the sighted (effect size = $.48\sigma$). However, this was a task of differential attention to affect, not a task of accuracy. On the basis of Lowenfeld's (1971) summary suggesting that the blind are not generally superior to the sighted in hearing and that their overall adjustment is comparable, we might have expected to find no clear difference in PONS performance between the blind and the sighted.

THE DEAF. Thirty male and female students, ages ten to fifteen, were tested in three testing sessions at a school for the deaf near Boston, Massachusetts. WISC IQ and Stanford Achievement Test scores were obtained for many of the children, as well as ratings of degree of hearing loss and lip reading ability. Lip reading ability was rated for nineteen children by six teachers; since not all six teachers rated all nineteen children, our liaison person at the school "scaled them" (*sic*) before sending a composite that yielded one rating per child (probably by averaging).

The students were administered a sixty-item video-only test consisting of twenty face-only, twenty body-only, and twenty figure-only items from the full PONS test. Subjects used the large print, simplified-vocabulary answer sheet that has been used in other samples of children (chapter 8). The sixty items were shown on a screen at the front of the classroom. An instructor who was familiar to the children went over the instructions and the response alternatives to be sure all words were understood by the students. Sufficient time was allowed between items for all subjects to record their responses. Table 12.10 shows the PONS performance of this sample, broken down according to sex.

In order to assess the possible effect of degree of hearing loss, four analyses of variance were performed in which deaf subjects were nested in a 2 × 2 classification of age level (10–12 versus 14–15) and hearing loss (less deaf versus more deaf, defined by a split at the median value of hearing loss). The first analysis used face, body, and figure scores as levels of a repeated measures factor; the other three analyses used one channel at a time as the dependent variable.

The repeated measures analysis revealed a significant main effect for hearing loss ($F(1,26) = 4.45$, $p < .05$; effect size = $.83\,\sigma$), in which less impaired subjects performed better than more impaired subjects. To fully understand this effect, it would be necessary to have better information on etiology

TABLE 12.10. Video Accuracy for Young Deaf Students, Sexes Pooled and Separately (N=30)

Video Channel	Sex	Accuracy		
		Item	Percentage	SD[a]
Face	males (N=14)[b]	11.04	55.2%	1.56
	females (N=16)[c]	11.00	55.0	1.66
	all (N=30)[d]	11.02	55.1	1.64
Body	males	10.32	51.6	1.63
	females	9.72	48.6	1.89
	all	10.00	50.0	1.83
Figure	males	10.82	54.1	2.60
	females	11.31	56.6	1.45
	all	11.08	55.4	2.12
Total	males	32.18	53.6	3.70
	females	32.03	53.4	2.54
	all	32.10	53.5	3.19

[a] standard deviation based on item accuracy
[b] mean IQ = 94.86
[c] mean IQ = 97.33
[d] mean IQ = 96.14

than was available in this study. The age main effect and the age–hearing loss interaction, though not significant, were of comparable magnitudes to the F reported above ($F(1,26) = 2.65$, effect size = $.64\sigma$); $F(1,26) = 3.87$, effect size = $.77\sigma$). Younger subjects tended to perform better than older subjects.

The three individual-channel analyses showed that the pattern of interaction between age and hearing loss was not consistent across the three channels; for body and face, the less deaf younger subjects and the more deaf older subjects performed relatively worse than more deaf younger subjects and less deaf older subjects (for face this interaction was significant, $F(1,26) = 6.83$, $p < .02$, effect size = 1.02σ). For figure, the interaction pattern was reversed and nonsignificant.

Rated skill at lip reading was nonsignificantly correlated with face, body, figure, and total accuracy ($r(17) = .02$, $-.03$, $.07$, and $.02$). IQ was correlated nonsignificantly with PONS skill ($r(27)$ [with face, body, figure and total] = $-.27$, $-.22$, $.16$, and $-.16$).

Figure 12.2 presents a comparison of deaf students with hearing samples, similar to the comparison for blind students presented in figure 12.1. As in figure 12.1, the hearing comparison samples were selected for similar mean ages, large sample sizes, and representativeness, and without reference to their PONS scores. It is clear that, unlike the blind children, deaf children appear to perform considerably worse than their hearing counterparts. Figure 12.2 also shows the curve for the deaf students plotted according to mental

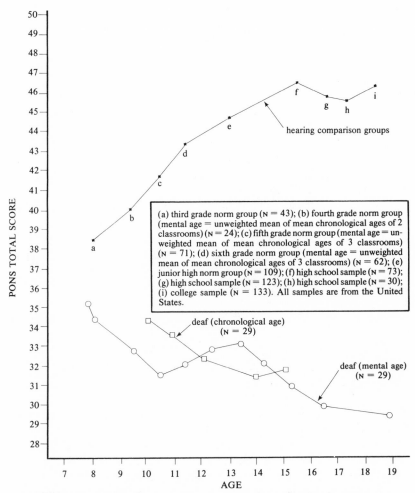

FIGURE 12.2. PONS video performance: Smoothed deaf/hearing comparison on chronological and mental ages

age rather than chronological age (mental age = (IQ × CA)/100). For the hearing samples, chronological age and mental age were considered to be equivalent. The figure suggests that deafness may be associated with a marked disadvantage in ability to judge visual nonverbal stimuli.

One possible explanation for this apparent discrepancy between the adequacy of blind and deaf sensory compensation is artifactual. Blind children responded to orally presented choices, whereas deaf children had to read response alternatives before they could respond. If the reading level of these deaf children were below that of the hearing comparison groups, then their scores could have suffered because the children could not process the words well enough to be able to display whatever degree of nonverbal skill they possessed. However, the correlations between the three visual channels and Stanford Achievement Test scores on word meaning and paragraph meaning (N = 23) do not support this explanation: the median of six correlations among the PONS scores and achievement scores was −.13. Deaf children who could read better did not perform better on the PONS than deaf children who could read less well.

Another possible explanation is also artifactual. The unimpaired samples took the entire PONS test; thus they stood to benefit from many opportunities to judge auditory and visual cues together in the mixed channels. It may be that a score on video-only items is more improved by having judged the mixed channels than a score on audio-only items. If this is the case, then the normal groups used for comparison with deaf students may have had more of an advantage over deaf students than the normal groups had over the blind students. The proper comparison samples would therefore be unimpaired groups who took exactly the same tests as did the impaired groups. This possible artifact was controlled for in the deaf college sample described below.

If, in fact, sensory impairment is no disadvantage for the blind but a real disadvantage for the deaf, at least in these age groups, we must ask why this is so. It has been proposed (Gesell and Amatruda 1947; Baker 1953; Wiley 1971) that deaf children are more socially handicapped than blind children. Reasons might include greater sensory deprivation in deafness than in blindness or more negative or withheld social response to deaf people. Klinghammer (1964) reports that judges found deaf students' voices to be more irritating and less likeable than blind students' voices. People may therefore avoid interacting with deaf people, which could result in slow development of social skills, including nonverbal skill, among deaf people.

We were also able to obtain data from deaf college students. Forty-four deaf and eighty-one hearing students attending the Rochester Institute of Technology took the full PONS test with the soundtrack turned off. Hence, they answered 180 video-only items (3 channels × 20 items × 3 occurrences). The students were enrolled in social science courses and represented all four college years. Among the deaf students, half were tested with the usual rating pause of five seconds per item, and half were tested with ten seconds per item. Data analysis revealed essentially no correlation between accuracy and length of rating pause (r between rating time and total = .05). In all subsequent analyses the two deaf subsamples were pooled.

Analysis of variance revealed no appreciable effect for deaf status ($F(1,118) = 1.36, p < .25$, effect size = $.26\sigma$) and no two-way interaction of deaf status and channel accuracy. Significant effects not involving deaf status showed females to perform better than males and face cues to be very important in improving accuracy.

This analysis suggests that highly selected college-age deaf students show no disadvantage at judging visual nonverbal cues. We do not know if this is the case among deaf people in the general population. We also do not know if the marked disadvantage found among deaf children is real or is an artifact of the testing procedure employed for them versus the hearing comparison groups. If the disadvantage is real, we cannot say on the basis of our research whether the disadvantage disappears over time, since the college-age deaf sample was highly selected and may not accurately represent the nonverbal ability of deaf people in general. Clearly, much more research is needed on nonverbal abilities among sensorily impaired populations.

13 | Roles and Relationships

OCCUPATIONS AND INTERESTS

For several decades, researchers have looked for occupational and interest correlates of nonverbal judging accuracy. One of the earliest and most complete studies was done by Estes (1938). He asked his subjects to match short films of persons performing various tasks with written personality sketches. Table 13.1 shows the accuracy rates Estes obtained from six vocational and avocational groups. Although the sample sizes were too small for useful significance testing, it was interesting to note that both the personnel workers and the three artistic groups were more accurate than the psychologists and the teachers. One might have expected people in the last two groups to have a special vocational need to be accurate in making interpersonal judgments. Other researchers have also found that psychologists were not particularly good judges of others (Taft 1955), that psychotherapists were not particularly better judges than nontherapists (Dittmann, Parloff, and Boomer 1965), that counselors were not much better than noncounselors (Sweeney and Cottle 1976), and that any differences between clinical and experimental psycholo-

TABLE 13.1. Accuracy of Matching Filmed
Behavior with Personality Sketches by Occupational
and Interest Groups (after Estes)

Group	N	Accuracy[a]
Personnel workers	4	76.8%
Painters[b]	14	73.3
Actors[b]	11	68.2
Musicians[b]	11	50.5
Psychologists	9	42.1
Teachers (college)	13	40.1

[a]chance accuracy = 33%
[b]avocation rather than vocation

gists in accuracy of judging others tended to be in favor of the experimentalists (Taft 1955; and more indirectly, Fancher 1966, 1967). Cline (1964), however, reported that clinicians were more accurate than nurses in training, who, in turn, were more accurate than college students or church members.

Other researchers have also reported tendencies for artists or those with artistic interests to be superior judges of others (Buck 1974, 1976; Taft 1955; Walton 1936), along with dancers (Dittmann, Parloff, and Boomer 1965; Ekman 1964), those interested in speech and drama (Dusenbury and Knower 1938; Pfaff 1954; Taft 1955), and students majoring in business (Buck 1974).

UNITED STATES SAMPLES. None of the studies cited above employed as its criterion of accuracy sensitivity to nonverbal communication defined by both motion picture cues and tone of voice cues such as are involved in the PONS. We did not know, therefore, whether to expect occupational and interest correlates of PONS performance to be similar to the correlates we have summarized. Table 13.2 shows total PONS accuracy for samples from the United States that might be expected to show above average performance either on a priori grounds or on the basis of the earlier research. By way of comparison groups, the bottom section of table 13.2 lists the performance of high school and college students.

The best performance was obtained from two small groups of actors: four who were associated with Harvard University's Loeb Drama Center (83.4 percent accuracy) and seven who were members of the Proposition, a professional troupe in Boston specializing in improvisation (84.7 percent accuracy).

The second best performance was obtained from three groups of students of nonverbal communication. There was a group of twenty-one undergraduate

TABLE 13.2. Accuracy of Various U.S. Occupational and Interest Groups

Group	Weighted Mean	Number of Subjects	Number of Samples
Actors	84.3%	11	2
Students of nonverbal communication	83.7	40	3
Students of visual arts	82.1	11	3
Clinicians	80.8[a]	125	8
Teachers	77.8	452	10
Business executives	77.4	60	3
Comparison Group			
College students	80.2%	737	19
High school students	77.5	482	10

NOTE: mean square within groups = 32.2831

[a]The mean accuracy for a sample of thirty-one Canadian graduate students in clinical psychology tested by Professor E. F. Casas was nearly identical: 80.6 percent; an additional sample of fifty-eight U.S. nursing school faculty members tested by Gloria Shoemaker obtained a mean accuracy of 79.5 percent.

and graduate students in an advanced undergraduate seminar in nonverbal communication taught by Professor Laurence Wylie in the department of anthropology (82.8 percent accuracy), a group of five advanced students in a seminar on nonverbal communication taught by Professor Klaus Scherer (84.2 percent accuracy), and a group of fourteen graduate students of social psychology enrolled in a unit on nonverbal communication that was part of a proseminar in social psychology (84.9 percent accuracy). This unit was taught by one of us (Rosenthal) with the assistance of two others (Hall and Rogers). All three of these courses were taught at Harvard University, and the performance of these three samples was higher than the performance of the six other samples of Harvard students enrolled in advanced courses in psychology ($t(7)$ = 5.10, $p < .0007$, one-tailed, effect size = 3.86σ).[1]

The third best performance of table 13.2 was obtained from a mixed group of students of visual arts studying photography, animation, and history of film. The top three groups did not differ significantly from one another, but together they were significantly superior to the clinicians listed in table 13.2 ($t(185) = 3.08$, $p < .003$, effect size = $.45\sigma$). The eight groups of clinicians did not differ significantly from each other ($F < 1$); indeed they were remarkably homogeneous considering the range of ages, experience levels, disciplinary affiliations, and geography (from Honolulu to Boston).

Returning to table 13.2, we note that the business executives and teachers were quite similar to each other in performance ($t < 1$), but significantly lower in accuracy than the clinicians ($t(635) = 5.29$, $p < .0001$, effect size = $.42\sigma$).[2] The three samples of business executives were from national industrial corporations. The ten groups of teachers were appreciably more variable among themselves than were the eight groups of clinicians ($F(9,7) = 4.04$, $p < .08$, $\eta = .92$), but only the best two groups of teachers out of ten were as accurate as even the worst of the eight samples of clinicians ($\chi^2(2) = 11.38$, $p < .004$).

Of the ten samples of teachers, six were currently in the role of student and four samples were made up primarily of experienced teachers. It was interesting to find that the student samples performed better than the more seasoned samples ($t(8) = 2.48$, $p < .04$, effect size = 1.75σ). Later, in our discussion of clinicians, we shall note once again that students appear to perform better than those who are professionally further advanced.

---

1. Another finding suggesting that students in courses on nonverbal communication tend to decode nonverbal cues especially well was reported in chapter 5: students enrolled in a seminar on nonverbal communication at Harvard University scored significantly higher on the brief exposure PONS than did three other samples of graduate and undergraduate students ($t(2) = 2.62$, $p = .06$, one-tailed, effect size = 3.70σ).

2. Most of the thirty-six businessmen of the first two samples were supervisory personnel, and it is of interest to note that these supervisors scored as significantly more sensitive to nonverbal cues than the nonsupervisors. The correlation between supervisory status and total PONS accuracy was .34, $p < .05$, $df = 34$.

Although teachers did not score very high on the PONS in general, it was of interest to note that those who scored higher on the PONS were generally evaluated as better teachers in two samples tested by Frankie Phillips. The correlations between total PONS and supervisors' ratings of teaching ability were .38 and .43 ($p = .03$ and $p < .02$, one-tailed). In addition, direct observations of these teachers were made and the extent to which their interactions with students were rated as encouraging in manner was recorded. For both samples, teachers scoring higher on the PONS were observed to behave in a more encouraging manner toward their pupils ($r = .78$, and $r = .74$ for the two samples, both $p < .001$). A subsequent study by Charles Reavis, however, found no relationship between PONS total and supervisors' ratings of teaching ability ($r = .00$). Finally, in a study of twenty-eight elementary school principals, William Person found that principals scoring higher on PONS total were judged as providing more satisfactory leadership by the teachers working in their schools , $r(26) = .21$, $p = .14$, one-tailed.

The groups listed in table 13.2 fell into three quite different levels in terms of overall sensitivity to nonverbal cues. The actors and the students of nonverbal communication and of visual arts were in the top level, superior to American college students in general and to Harvard students in particular (weighted mean of nine Harvard undergraduate samples including summer school = 80.5 percent, N = 265). Next came the clinicians, who were essentially no better than college students in general but better than teachers or business executives. Last were the teachers and business executives, with overall accuracy at a level comparable to that of our high school groups.

Does acting, studying nonverbal communication, or studying visual arts make people more sensitive to nonverbal cues, or are the people attracted to these fields already more sensitive? We do not know, but we might guess that the selection factor may be more important than the training factor. For example, the best group ever tested with the PONS film was the group of graduate students enrolled in a unit dealing with nonverbal communication. Testing was done on the first day of class, however, before any formal training was undertaken, suggesting that selection (i.e., into a program of graduate study in social psychology) must have been more important than training in accounting for their very high performance.

Discussions with Clay Hall, a former professional actor, suggest that actors too may bring their high level of sensitivity to nonverbal cues with them rather than developing them as part of their craft. He felt that many actors were characterized by very high need for social approval and a resultant motive to ''read'' what others expect of them so that they might accommodate their behavior to the expectations of others to ensure continued approval.

CANADIAN CLINICAL SAMPLES. Professor E. F. Casas tested four groups of Canadian clinicians at various stages of their professional careers: eleven candidates for a master's degree in clinical psychology, fourteen applicants for a Ph.D. program in clinical psychology who were participating in a summer tryout program, six Ph.D. candidates in clinical psychology, and seven members of the faculty who were teaching the students in the first three groups. The weighted mean performance of these groups (80.2 percent) was quite similar to the weighted mean performance of the U.S. samples of clinicians (80.8 percent).

The four samples could be arranged in increasing order of academic status from M.A. students to aspiring Ph.D. candidates, to Ph.D. candidates, and to clinical faculty members. Interestingly, as this academic status increased, mean PONS performance decreased ($r = -.96$, $p < .04$, two-tailed); the mean accuracies of these four groups were 82.4, 80.1, 78.6, and 78.1 percent. In order to assess the generality of this interesting result, we examined more closely the relationship of academic progress to PONS performance for the American clinical samples. Only for clinical psychologists and for psychiatrists did we have samples at both the student and professional levels, and in both cases the students (clinical graduate students and psychiatric residents) performed better than the professionals (psychologists and staff psychiatrists). For the five samples involved, the correlation between professional level (coded as 0 or 1) and PONS performance was $-.93$ ($p = .01$, one-tailed). One additional assessment of the generality of this negative relationship was possible. For a sample of twenty-seven clinical psychologists from Sydney, Australia, we could code the degree status of each (Ph.D., M.A., and A.B. degrees coded as 2, 1, and 0). The correlation was $-.31$ ($p < .06$, one-tailed), showing once again that more professionally advanced clinicians performed more poorly on the PONS. Although not in a study of psychologists or psychiatrists, Gloria Shoemaker also found that her nursing school faculty members scored lower on the PONS when they had earned higher academic degrees ($r = -.22$, $p < .05$, one-tailed).

There appear, then, to be indications from Australia, Canada, and the United States either that clinicians "lose" some of their sensitivity to nonverbal cues as they advance academically and professionally and/or that those who achieve greater advancement are those who are less sensitive to begin with. In the absence of longitudinal data we are in no position to judge which of these alternatives is more likely, although there might be plausible explanations for either one. The sensitivity "loss" alternative might be explained by the decreased need of the clinician to read accurately the nonverbal cues of others as he or she gains in status. As these gains in status occur, the clinician may have less time for direct patient contacts and may spend more time in teaching and administrative functions in which nonverbal sensitivity may be less valued and less necessary for effective task performance. The selection for sensitivity alternative might be explained by the operation of a selection mechanism that discriminated against the academic advancement of nonverbally more sensitive clinicians. The explanations offered are, of course, nothing more than speculations, since we could not control for the general confounding of age with professional status. For the Sydney clinicians, however, a sample for whom ages were readily available, we found essentially no relationship between age and PONS performance ($r = .05$), despite the fact that age and degree status were substantially correlated ($r = .44$). The correlation between PONS performance and degree status with age partialed out was $-.37$ ($p < .03$, one-tailed).

AUSTRALIAN SAMPLES. Table 13.3 shows PONS total for samples from Australia that might be expected to show above average performance either on a priori grounds or on the basis of earlier research. To provide relevant comparison groups, the bottom section of table 13.3 lists the performance of Australian high school and college groups.

None of the samples performed any better than a general Australian college sample, though several performed more poorly. Overall, the samples of table 13.3 fell into three groups. The top group was comprised of the general college students and the students of architecture and of art teaching. The next group, performing significantly less well ($t = 4.00$, $p < .001$, effect size $= .33\sigma$), was comprised of high school students, clinicians, teachers, and students of industrial and interior design, four groups that did not differ appreciably among themselves. The third group, performing significantly less well than the second ($t = 2.45$, $p < .02$, effect size $= .29\sigma$), was comprised of students of painting and sculpture.

For the Australian samples, then, the artistically interested groups were not better than other college level groups; clinicians and teachers, who did not differ from each other, performed no better than Australian high school students.

TABLE 13.3. Accuracy of Various Australian Occupational and Interest Groups

Group	Weighted Mean	Number of Subjects	Number of Samples
Students of architecture	80.0%	24	1
Students of art teaching	79.7	31	1
Clinicians	78.2[a]	90	2
Teachers	77.9	44	3
Students of industrial and interior design	77.6	64	2
Students of painting and sculpture	75.7	43	4
Comparison Group			
College students	79.9%	282	4
High school students	78.2	55	1

[a]The mean accuracy for an additional sample of eighty-three Australian clinicians tested by Jack Lyle was nearly identical: 78.6 percent.

CLINICAL SKILL. What are the implications for the validity of the PONS of the finding that neither American nor Australian clinicians scored higher than college students in general? Since clinicians "ought" to be better decoders of nonverbal cues, does it suggest a deficiency of the PONS that clinicians do not excel? Probably not. As we saw earlier, other investigators have also found psychologists and therapists to be not especially sensitive to nonverbal cues (Estes 1938; Taft 1955; Dittmann, Parloff, and Boomer 1965; Sweeney and Cottle 1976).

But though the superiority of clinicians in decoding nonverbal cues is not required in the nomological network validating the PONS, it would nevertheless be helpful to the validation if those clinicians who were judged by their supervisors to be more effective interpersonally were the ones to score higher on the PONS. Lewin (1965) theorized about the importance of the therapist's interpersonal sensitivity and ability to understand his patients' nonverbal communications. Gladstein (1974) has pointed out, however, that an extensive review of the literature reveals little empirically based knowledge to link the ability to understand nonverbally communicated affect with effectiveness as a clinician. One study by Campbell, Kagan, and Krathwohl (1971) found a .26 correlation between counseling effectiveness and a scale measuring affective sensitivity.

Table 13.4 shows the correlations between PONS factor scores, quadrant scores, and total with the judged clinical effectiveness of the first four samples of clinicians we obtained. The samples shown in the first three columns were

TABLE 13.4. Correlations of Clinical Ability with PONS Performance

| | Graduate Students | | | Alcoholism Counselors (United States) | |
| | United States | | Canada | | |
Scale	(N=16)	(N=14)	(N=11)	(N=7)	Median
CF 20	.38	−.39	−.00	.22	.11
RS 20	.21	−.25	−.16	−.48	−.20
Body 60	.05	.36	.23	.18	.20
Face 120	.14	.18	.15	.77[a]	.16
Positive-submissive	−.05	−.34	.45	−.50	−.20
Positive-dominant	.20	.19	−.23	.70	.20
Negative-submissive	.53[a]	.00	.15	.57	.34
Negative-dominant	−.27	.70[b]	−.10	.42	.16
Total	.22	.22	.15	.55	.22[c]

[a] $p \leq .05$
[b] $p \leq .01$
[c] The median correlation between PONS total and rated clinical ability in nine additional samples was .20.

of graduate students, while the fourth sample was counselors of alcoholic patients. Analysis of the 9×4 matrix of correlations of table 13.4 showed no appreciable correlations among either rows or columns, and the F test on the grand mean correlation coefficient of .14 yielded $F(1,35) = 6.70$, $p = .014$. The weighted mean correlation of just the four correlations of the total PONS scores with ratings of clinical ability was .25, $p = .055$, one-tailed. Such average correlations (i.e., .14 or .25) ranged between what Cohen (1969) would regard as small and what he would regard as medium in size.

Examining the row marginals of table 13.4 suggests as hypotheses for further investigation that clinical ability as rated by clinical supervisors is better predicted by clinicians' sensitivity to visual cues than by sensitivity to audio cues. In addition, it may be that clinical ability is better predicted by clinicians' sensitivity to negative cues and to positive-dominant cues rather than by their sensitivity to positive-submissive cues. Perhaps the more effective clinicians are more attuned to negative affect subtly communicated by their patients, since the clinician's recognition of these negative affects is a necessary precondition of the patients' learning of the nature of these frequently unacknowledged affects in themselves. In addition, clinicians who are more effective may also be the ones more attuned to positive affect as it develops in combination with appropriate assertiveness.[3] Table 11.12 shows additional results to suggest that more effective clinicians perform better on the PONS. Of the eleven studies summarized there, ten show positive correlations, with a median r of .20, combined $p < .025$.

The sample of counselors of alcoholic patients had also been asked to make a number of ratings of themselves. Of these ratings, those most relevant to clinical sensitivity were ratings of the extent to which the counselors understood the feelings of their same-sex and opposite-sex friends. Each of these two variables was then correlated with PONS performance factor scores, quadrant scores, and total. The results, shown in table 13.5, suggest substantial correlations between the self-ratings of interpersonal understanding and the total PONS performance. In addition, these self-ratings show substantial correlations with three of the four factor scores and three of the four quadrant scores. Only the correlations with RS 20 and with positive-submissive affect are either low or negative; both these scores had been negatively correlated with ratings of counselors' effectiveness made by their clinical supervisors.

THE APA SAMPLE. In the summer of 1973, the PONS was administered to a volunteer sample of eighty-five attendees at a session on nonverbal communi-

---

3. A recent large-scale study conducted by J. A. Burruss (1977) of therapists working with alcoholics found that therapists' performance on the PONS, especially on the positive-dominant items, was more predictive of client change than were peer, self, or supervisor ratings of therapist characteristics, including ratings of therapist effectiveness.

TABLE 13.5. Correlations of PONS Accuracy with Counselors' Ratings of Their Own Level of Understanding of Their Same-Sex and Opposite-Sex Friends (N=7)

Scale	Understanding Same-Sex Friends[a]	Understanding Opposite-Sex Friends[a]	Combined: Weighted Mean
CF 20	.67	.56	.62
RS 20	−.34	.08	−.13
Body 60	.66	.68	.67
Face 120	.80[b]	.23	.52
Positive-submissive	−.02	.42	.20
Positive-dominant	.80[b]	.41	.61
Negative-submissive	.61	.30	.46
Negative-dominant	.71	.37	.54
Total	.92[c]	.62	.77[b]
Counselor effectiveness	.71	.12	.42

[a]Correlated with each other at .71
[b]$p \leq .05$
[c]$p \leq .01$

cation at the Montreal meetings of the American Psychological Association. The vast majority of the APA sample members were advanced students or professional psychologists. Subdivision by field of interest showed no major differences in profiles, so the results are summarized for the entire group. The overall performance was slightly better than that of the high school norm group (79 percent versus 77.5 percent). In addition, there was a notable tendency for the APA group to be relatively poor at decoding the CF channel. Further analysis suggested in addition that the psychologists were no better than the high school norm group in decoding positive affect (73 percent) but that they were substantially better (about .5σ) at decoding negative affect (85 percent). Similar results were obtained when we examined the profiles of the U.S. and Australian clinicians combined. Both pure tone channels tended to be the least accurate of the eleven channel scores relative to the high school norm group, and the negative affects were more accurately decoded than the positive affects, though the difference was only about .3σ, compared to the .5σ obtained with the APA sample.

SEX DIFFERENCES IN PONS INTERCORRELATIONS. In examining the intercorrelations among the various PONS quadrant and marginal scores for various samples of clinicians, it became apparent that the patterns for males and females were substantially different. For the female clinicians, as for the males and females of the norm group, correlations among subtests were substantial. For the male clinicians, however, these intercorrelations were very much lower and from time to time substantially negative. To check this observation in a more systematic manner, a standard set of eleven intercorrela-

TABLE 13.6. Median PONS Intercorrelations for Males and Females for Three Types of Samples

Scale	Norm Group[a] Males (N=185)	Norm Group[a] Females (N=319)	U.S. Adults[b] Males (N=33)	U.S. Adults[b] Females (N=39)	Clinicians[c] Males (N=79)	Clinicians[c] Females (N=99)
Positive-submissive–positive-dominant	.47	.46	.20	.40[d]	.04	.44[e]
Positive-submissive–negative-submissive	.36	.35	.01	-.11	-.08	.35[e]
Positive-submissive–negative-dominant	.51	.38	.22	.21	-.17	.18
Positive-dominant–negative-submissive	.57	.53	.10	.23	.28[d]	.22[d]
Positive-dominant–negative-dominant	.54	.46	-.10	.41[d]	.10	.28[f]
Negative-submissive–negative-dominant	.53	.45	.16	.35[d]	.04	.48[e]
Face 60–body 60	.64	.60	.38[d]	.22	-.04	.62[e]
Face 60–figure 60	.77	.67	.48[f]	.82[e]	.46[e]	.54[e]
Body 60–figure 60	.68	.58	.46[d]	.28	.29[f]	.62[e]
RS 80–CF 80	.70	.62	.37[d]	.57[e]	.02	.57[e]
Tone 40–video 60	.34	.41	-.34	.23	-.31[f]	.22[d]
Median	.54	.46	.20	.28	.04	.44[e]

[a]all $p \leq .001$
[b]median of three samples
[c]median of six samples
[d]$p \leq .05$
[e]$p \leq .001$
[f]$p \leq .01$

tions was computed for six samples of clinicians from the United States and Australia, for the norm group of high school subjects, and for three samples of U.S. adults who were to serve as a rough control for age differences between the clinicians and the norm group. Table 13.6 shows the results of these comparisons and table 13.7 shows the results of tests of significance of the differences among the median correlations obtained. The three groupings of female subjects did not differ from one another in magnitude of median intercorrelation, and the median intercorrelation for males did not differ from that for females for either the norm group or the U.S. adult groups. However, male clinicians showed a significantly lower median intercorrelation than did the female clinicians. Apparently for male clinicians sensitivity to nonverbal cues is more a matter of multiple, relatively unrelated skills than it is for female clinicians. In at least one case, furthermore, male clinicians' skills were negatively correlated. Thus, in five of the six samples, male clinicians who were more accurate at the pure tone channels (tone 40) were less accurate at the pure video channels (video 60). The same result was obtained in two of the three samples of U.S. adults as well, so that this negative relationship between accuracy in pure audio and pure video may be as much a function of being an older male as of being a male clinician specifically. These results lead to the speculation that as men age they may focus on either pure tone or pure video cues as a preferred mode of reading nonverbal cues at the expense of the other mode. The longitudinal data to test this hypothesis are, unfortunately, not available.

FOREIGN SERVICE OFFICERS. An extensive study of performance on the original sender audio PONS among U.S. Information Agency officers was conducted by David McClelland and Charles Dailey, who kindly made their data available to us. As we might have expected for clinicians on a priori grounds, we might have expected foreign service officers to be more accurate

TABLE 13.7. Median PONS Subtest Correlations by Type of Sample and Subject Sex

Item	Females		Males		Test of Difference	
	r	N	r[a]	N	Z	p
Norm group	.46	319	.54	185	1.15	NS
Adult samples	.28	39	.20	33	0.34	NS
Clinician samples	.44	99	.04	79	2.81	$p < .005$
χ^2 of difference ($df = 2$)	1.41		18.54			
p	NS		.001			

[a]The correlation of .54 differs from that of .20 at $p < .05$ and from that of .04 at $p < .00005$ while the latter two correlations do not differ significantly from each other.

at decoding nonverbal cues than some representative norm group. But just as was the case for clinicians, foreign service officers as a group did not perform better than a comparison group, in this case an audio PONS norm group of 119 east coast high school students ($t < 1$). However, as with the clinicians, among the foreign service officers, those who were judged as more effective did score significantly higher on the audio PONS. Table 13.8 shows these results employing two different criteria of foreign service officer effectiveness. The correlation between these two criteria was .81. The first column of table 13.8 lists the various measures of the audio PONS followed by a new measure, the Spanish CF 20, developed by McClelland and Dailey for this research. This test consists of the content-filtered speech of a Spanish man who portrayed the twenty PONS scenes. Better foreign service officers performed better on the Spanish CF 20 version and on both the CF and RS channels of the standard audio PONS with its female sender. As we might expect on the basis of considerations of reliability alone, the best predictor of foreign service officer performance was the total score on the standard audio PONS combined with the Spanish CF 20 form ($r = .32$, $p < .004$).

Although the correlation between the criterion and the RS channel was not appreciably different from the correlation between the criterion and the CF channel, there was an indication that the CF channel may be a somewhat better predictor of foreign service success. This indication comes from a small additional study of twenty-eight foreign service officers in which only the CF channel showed the expected correlation with the criterion ($\phi = .28$).

TABLE 13.8. Correlations of Audio PONS with Ratings of Quality of Foreign Service Information Officers (after McClelland and Dailey)

	Criterion Rating	
Scale	More Precise[a] (N=74)	Less Precise[b] (N=82)
CF 20	.25[c]	.21[d]
RS 20	.22[d]	.21[d]
Total	.30[e]	.27[c]
Positive-submissive	.29[c]	.21[d]
Positive-dominant	.31[e]	.26[c]
Negative-submissive	.06	.08
Negative-dominant	−.06	−.01
Spanish CF 20	.20[d]	.21[d]
Spanish CF 20 + total	.32[e]	.32[e]
Median	.25[c]	.21[d]

[a]eight-point scale
[b]three-point scale
[c]$p \leq .05$
[d]$p \leq .10$
[e]$p \leq .01$

Since skill in interpersonal relations seems obviously required by foreign service officers and since the PONS measures such skill at least to some degree, we would expect to find the obtained correlations between PONS score and officer effectiveness. An interpretation of this relationship that is more specific to the audio PONS has been advanced by Beverly Crane. She suggested that in most foreign assignments the foreign service officer will not be totally fluent in the language of the host country. To some extent, then, the officer will be operating in a linguistic audio environment that sounds phenomenologically as though content-filtered and randomized spliced speech were being produced. Officers more adept at extracting meaning from this audio environment may have the same type of advantage as that of a more fluent speaker and comprehender of the host country's language.

Table 13.8 also shows the interesting result that officer effectiveness is not especially related to skill at decoding negative affects but is substantially related to skill at decoding positive affects. Perhaps it represents an advantage to the foreign service officer if he or she is able to seek and find the positive affects in the tones being emitted in their interactions with representatives of their host country. Such favoring of the positive affects might increase the likelihood of smooth, cordial relationships.

Although the foreign service officers did not perform better overall than the audio PONS norm group, they did perform differentially well in the four affect quadrants. Table 13.9 shows that foreign service officers were significantly superior to the norm group on positive-dominant and negative-submissive affects but significantly inferior on positive-submissive affect. Unfortunately, we cannot say whether these differences are best attributed to the occupational differences between the two groups or simply to the age differences between high school and adult samples. The table does show clearly, however, that the foreign service officers as a group did not perform better overall than the high school students of the norm group.

HUMAN SERVICE WORKERS. McClelland and Dailey and their colleagues have also studied a sample of eighty-five human service workers, paraprofessionals for whom sensitivity to nonverbal cues should be an asset. For the total

TABLE 13.9. Audio PONS Accuracy in Four Quadrants for Two Groups

Quadrant	Norm Group (N = 119)	Foreign Service Group (N = 131)	t	p
Positive-submissive	58.7%	52.1%	−3.81	≤ .001
Positive-dominant	60.3	64.9	2.53	≤ .02
Negative-submissive	73.7	78.9	3.44	≤ .001
Negative-dominant	75.6	74.8	−0.62	
Mean	67.1	67.7	0.72	

audio PONS, the accuracy (67.2 percent) of these workers was essentially the same as the accuracy of the audio norm group (67.1 percent). However, those human service workers who had been judged to be more effective did tend to perform better at the audio PONS, but the relationships were small (for CF 20, $r = .05$; for RS 20, $r = .20$; for tone 40, $r = .10$) and not significant ($df = 51$). The largest of these correlations, that for RS 20, was similar in size to that obtained in the sample of foreign service officers, lending further support to the validity of the RS 20 channel. The correlation for CF 20 was very small and slightly weakens the validity of that channel. However, we should recall the independent study of additional foreign service workers that supported the validity of CF 20 but not that of RS 20. Both channels considered separately appear to show promise despite the fact that they show internal consistency reliabilities that are quite low. It should be noted, however, that it is possible psychometrically to have good criterion validity coefficients despite low internal consistency, so long as the retest reliabilities are respectable (see chapter 3).

CREATIVE UNDERGRADUATES. Debra Kimes of the University of California at Santa Cruz employed the first eighty items of the PONS in testing creative undergraduates (dancers, actors, painters, musicians, writers, and a group of nonartist controls). All were recruited from university classes. Table 13.10 shows the mean accuracy for all these groups and for a comparison group of 482 norm group subjects for whom the mean scores on just the first eighty items of the PONS are given. The six groups of subjects tested by Kimes differed significantly among themselves ($F(5,38) = 2.56$, $p < .05$, $\eta = .50$). The best performance was shown by the dancers, who scored 1.67 standard deviations higher than the mean of Kimes's six samples.

TABLE 13.10. Accuracy of Artistic and Control Groups (after Kimes)

Group	N	Accuracy	Pure Video[a]	Pure Audio[a]
Dancers	7	81.9%[b]	1.78	−0.41
Actors	7	78.6	0.51	−1.13
Painters	10	77.9	−0.58	−0.04
Musicians	10	77.8	−0.41	1.52
Writers	9	76.6	−0.36	0.83
Controls	7	74.7	−0.94	−0.78
Norm group	482	75.6[c]		

[a]in standard score form
[b]The mean accuracy for a sample of fourteen dance therapy students tested by Claire Schmais was 80.8 percent for the full PONS, which, after correction for the trend to improve in performance from the first 80 items to the last 140 items, corresponds approximately to a score of 78.9 percent for the first 80 items.
[c]based on the first 80 items of the full PONS

From among the eighty items administered to her subjects, Kimes selected those that contributed to the pure video marginal score (face, body, figure) and those that contributed to the pure audio marginal (RS, CF). The mean scores of Kimes's six groups were then converted to standard scores separately for pure video and pure audio. The last two columns of table 13.10 show that dancers and actors were substantially superior to all other groups on the pure video channels, while the musicians and writers were substantially superior to all other groups on the pure audio channels. This result is very suggestive, because dancers and actors are presumably experts at visual cues while musicians and writers are presumably experts at auditory cues. We might have expected the painters to be superior at visual cues also by virtue of their concern with visual matters, but painters deal more with stationary than with moving visual stimuli.

PARENTS OF PRELINGUISTIC CHILDREN

The earliest efforts of children to communicate are entirely nonverbal. For most of the first two years of life, the child is unable to use language to express feelings, needs, or desires. During this period, an adult is able to understand the expressions and emotions of the child only to the degree that the adult is able to decode a wide variety of nonverbal behaviors.

During the first two years of life, the child moves away from a world that is entirely nonverbal to one that is progressively more filled with syllables, words, pairs of words, and sentences. One researcher (McCarthy 1930) estimated that only 26 percent of the verbal responses of children aged eighteen months were comprehensible. Even at this age, however, children may understand many nonlinguistic aspects of conversation. For example, fifteen- to eighteen-month-old children sometimes hold "babbling conversations" with each other, complete with gesturing, but without recognizable words (Bridges 1932, 1933).

During the next six months of the child's life, a dramatic increase in language skill occurs, and McCarthy (1930) found that 67 percent of the child's verbal responses were intelligible by the age of two. This period from the age of eighteen to twenty-four months, therefore, constitutes the child's transition to understandable speech. Development continues more gradually after twenty-four months: McCarthy found that 89 percent of the child's verbal responses were comprehensible at thirty months, 93 percent at thirty-six months, and 99 percent at forty-two months (1930, 1946).

In addition to the increasing comprehensibility of the child's efforts at individual words, development also occurs in the child's ability to construct two-word phrases and to approach actual sentences. Brown (1965, p. 286) reported that children begin to use two or more words in combination in the second year of life and that some children can produce single sentences ten or eleven words in length by the age of thirty-six months.

Since the prelinguistic child is limited exclusively to various channels of nonverbal communication, adults who are exposed to prelinguistic children are faced with the opportunity or the need to decode the child's nonverbal messages. The child's prelinguistic vocalization (i.e., sounds that are not recognizable as words or sentences) differs from adult paralanguage (tone of voice, emphasis, pitch, etc.) in that the child's prelanguage occurs in place of words, while adult paralanguage occurs in company with words. It could be, however, that the child's prelanguage and the adult's paralanguage might have enough in common that an ability to decode the first might be an asset in the understanding of the second.

The adults with the most extensive opportunities to learn to understand the child's prelanguage are, of course, the child's parents. Since the preverbal child exposes his parents to an animated barrage of nonverbal messages, it is possible that the child "teaches" the parents the meaning of some elements or sequences of his or her prelanguage. The possibility that children could educate their parents has been largely neglected. The traditional focus of research in developmental psychology, of course, has been the ways in which parents influence or socialize their children. The possibility that parent-child interactions might produce reciprocal changes has only been recognized fairly recently (e.g., Lewis and Rosenblum 1974).

To investigate the possibility that the prelanguage child cultivates in the parents an increased sensitivity to vocal paralanguage, and perhaps to other channels of nonverbal communication as well, we administered the PONS to two groups: (1) parents of prelanguage children, and (2) a matched control group of couples who did not have children. Advertisements in Boston area newspapers requested "1. Mothers 20–35 years old, married 2–4 years, with a toddler 14–19 months old, and 2. Women 20–35 years old, married 2–4 years, with no children." These advertisements recruited fourteen women, and the women who responded were asked to bring their husbands with them to the testing session. The twenty-eight people included sixteen (eight couples) who were parents of a prelinguistic child and twelve (six couples) who were married but had no children.

The mothers of the toddlers appeared to have a distinct advantage on the PONS. The eight toddler mothers had a mean total PONS score of 81.9 percent compared to 77.7 percent for the six nonmothers. This difference between the mothers and the nonmothers on the PONS is particularly interesting, since it appears to reflect a generalized ability to interpret nonverbal expressions. The difference would be somewhat less impressive if the task had involved decoding video tapes of infant behaviors. Presumably, the mothers would do better on such a task simply out of familiarity with infants. But the PONS film measures a person's ability to decode adult nonverbal behavior. The toddler mothers may, therefore, have acquired a sensitivity to their infants' prelanguage that generalized to a sensitivity to adult nonverbal behavior. Since this was not a randomized experiment, we cannot be sure, of course, that experience with the baby was responsible for the effect. More sensitive women might be the ones who decide to have babies.

A longitudinal design would help somewhat by providing "pretest" PONS data: giving the PONS to a group of young women without children, and then administering the PONS again several years later when some (but not all) of the original group had prelinguistic toddlers. Presumably, the toddler mothers would show greater PONS gains between the first and second testing than the nonmothers. A longitudinal design of this nature, however, would probably require a very large sample in view of the unlikelihood that a large proportion of the sample would have children at about the same time. Furthermore, since the women would decide for themselves whether to have babies, we still would not know for sure that the increase in nonverbal skill was caused by experience with the baby.

The fathers of the toddlers also had higher PONS scores than the nonfather males, although the magnitude of the difference was not as large as the difference between mothers and nonmothers. The toddler fathers had a mean PONS total of 79.3 percent and the nonfathers had a mean PONS total of 78.6 percent. The finding that toddler fatherhood appeared to have less effect on PONS scores than toddler motherhood may be due to the greater involvement, in most families, of the mother in child rearing. If fathers begin to spend more time in child care, one might expect the PONS gains for the men to be more like those we have obtained for women. Since some American men are taking more responsibility for childcare, particularly in families with working women, an interesting comparison of this nature is becoming possible. It would be interesting to compare the PONS scores of a sample of fathers actively involved in the care of their prelanguage toddlers with a sample of fathers who spend less time with their toddlers.

Because of the small sample size in this first study, we attempted to replicate our findings with a second study. Six months after the first study, we recruited seven more mothers and thirteen more nonmothers. Men were not tested here. This study replicated our original finding: toddler mothers had higher PONS scores than the comparison group of nonmothers. Although the magnitude of the differences was not as great as in the first study, the toddler mothers still did consistently better than the nonmothers. In this replication study, the mean PONS total of the toddler mothers was 80.3 percent, and the mean PONS total of the nonmothers was 78.7 percent.

The scores of all twenty-three toddler parents (fathers and mothers) from the two studies were pooled for an overall comparison with the scores of all twenty-five nonparents (male and female). The two groups did differ significantly ($t = 1.71$, $p < .05$, one-tailed, effect size $= .50\sigma$). Most of this

PROFILE OF NONVERBAL SENSITIVITY: STANDARD SCORING SHEET
Channel Scores and Total

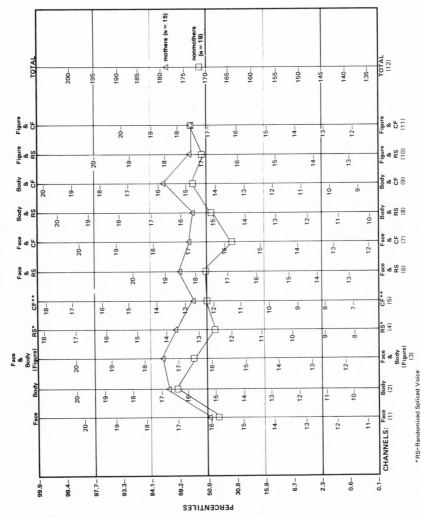

* RS=Randomized Spliced Voice
** CF=Electronically Content-Filtered Voice

FIGURE 13.1. PONS channel scores for toddler mothers and for a matched group of nonmothers

difference, as noted above, was due to the difference between mothers and nonmothers. The channel scores of these two groups of women can be compared to see whether the advantage of the toddler mothers was relatively greater in some channels than in others. The unweighted mean channel scores of the two samples of mothers ($N = 15$) are compared to the unweighted mean scores of the two samples of nonmothers ($N = 19$) in figure 13.1.

As indicated in figure 13.1, the nonmothers did not do a great deal better than the PONS norm group (the fifty-percentile line). The pooled samples of toddler mothers, however, did much better than the norm group. The mothers' PONS advantage was relatively greater in some PONS channels than in others. For example, the two groups were closely matched on the pure channels of face and body and on the mixed channel of figure + CF. On the other eight channels, however, the mothers of the toddlers enjoyed a clear advantage over the nonmothers. This suggests that although the mothers did consistently better than the nonmothers, this advantage was greatest on PONS items containing either RS or CF.

Toddler parents, then, did significantly better on the PONS than a matched group of nonparents. This difference is particularly striking for women, and this may be due to the fact that in our society at this time women are (more than men) the principal caregivers for infants. As a result of this finding about the ways in which infants appear to ''educate'' their parents nonverbally, we decided to see whether the role of nonverbal sensitivity in parenting was generally recognized. We asked eight adults how important they thought it was for each of four groups to be able to understand nonverbal communication. The four groups were: the average U.S. family, language experts, parents of toddlers, and professional actors. They were asked to rate the four groups using a ten-point scale, with 1 indicating that nonverbal communication was unimportant for a given group and 10 indicating that this communication was very important. The results of this small rating study were: the average U.S. family, 4.38; language experts, 5.75; parents of toddlers, 7.88; and professional actors, 7.38. This small group of raters saw the ability to understand nonverbal communication as more important for toddler parents than for the other three groups.

MARRIED AND DATING COUPLES

We investigated the question of whether members of a romantic dyad tend to have more similar or more complementary nonverbal skills compared to randomly paired individuals. We also examined how their similarity or complementarity is related to various characteristics of the couple's relationship. Some research has suggested that personality similarities between husbands and wives increase marital happiness. Dymond (1954) and Cattell and Nessel-roade (1967) published findings indicating that happily married couples had more similar personality test scores than did unhappily married couples. Banta and Hetherington (1963) found a general preference in mate and friendship selections of college students for a person with similar needs, and Schellen-berg and Bee (1960) found tendencies toward similarity in the need patterns of recently married and courting couples.

Winch (1952) has proposed that certain patterns of personality dissimilarity can enhance the happiness of a couple. His "theory of complementary needs in mate selection" states that each individual chooses as a mate a person who is more likely to provide him or her with maximum need gratification. Winch's theory includes attraction between same- and opposite-sex friends as well as engaged and married couples. Some support for this theory comes from studies by Winch, Ktsanes, and Ktsanes (1954) and by Kerckhoff and Davis (1962). Evidence supporting neither the similarity nor need com-plementarity hypothesis was presented by Murstein (1961) and Becker (1964).

Extending the theories of similarity and complementarity of needs and personality to the area of nonverbal sensitivity, we examined the differential sensitivity to channels of nonverbal communication of members of married and courting couples. First, we attempted to determine whether these couple members were "more similar" or "more different" in their PONS profiles than were randomly paired "couples." In order to do this, we recorded the eleven channel scores for each subject in the following samples.

1. Twenty-five dating couples recruited from a study of college student dating couples, conducted at Harvard University by Zick Rubin and his colleagues (mean age: males = 21.0, females = 20.1 years; recruited from the greater Boston area).

2. Eight married couples with at least one teenage child (mean age: males = 45.5, females = 42.2 years; recruited from the greater Boston area).

3. Eight married couples (married two to five years) with a toddler child (mean age: males = 26.6, females = 25.4 years; recruited from the greater Boston area).

4. Six married couples (married two to five years) with no children (mean age: males = 26.2, females = 24.5 years; recruited from the greater Boston area).

For each subject, we computed the z-score of each of the eleven channel scores (using the mean and standard deviation of each channel computed across all the subjects in the sample to which the subject belonged). Between the eleven channel z-scores of the male and female of each couple we com-puted the Pearson product-moment correlation (r) as well as the sum of the squared differences (d^2). The higher the r value, the more similar in shape are the profiles; the lower the d^2 value, the closer together the two profiles are in scores on the eleven channels. The mean and standard deviation of r and d^2 for each sample appear in table 13.11.

In order to provide a comparison for the r and d^2 values for the couples, we computed r and d^2 for randomly paired couples within each sample. The mean and standard deviation of these values in each sample are presented in table 13.11 as well.

The mean r for the real and random couples in all four samples was usually close to zero. None was significantly different from zero and no mean profile r for real couples differed significantly from its corresponding mean profile r for random couples. The profile scores of dating or married couples were, overall, neither significantly similar to each other nor significantly dissimilar. As indicated by the large standard deviations, the range of the correlations was rather large. For the most part, these values ranged from high negative for some couples to high positive for others, so that some couple members were significantly similar to each other while some were significantly dissimilar.

The means and standard deviations of the d^2 values for the real and random couples tell a similar story. The profile distance means for the real couples did not differ significantly from the profile distance means for corresponding random couples. All four samples, however, showed real couples to be slightly to moderately less similar than the random couples.

Though as a group romantic dyads did not show more similarity or complementarity (dissimilarity) than randomly paired couples, there remains the possibility that similarity and/or complementarity may be related to various characteristics of the relationship, especially considering the variability of the scores. Our most comprehensive set of data dealing with the relationship of similarity (or complementarity) of couples' PONS profiles and characteristics of their relationship comes from the sample of twenty-five dating couples. As part of Zick Rubin's study, each member of these couples independently answered a large number of questions dealing with many aspects of their own lives and of their relationship with each other. The questions ranged from estimates of facts such as the length of time they had known each other to subjective evaluations of their feelings about each other. We correlated their answers to these questions with their profile shape similarity scores (r) and their profile distance scores (d^2). A number of very interesting correlates of similarity and complementarity on the channels, affective quadrants, and four factors (RS, CF, face 120, and body 60; see chapter 3) were evidenced in this analysis.

The results of the analysis indicated that the apparent degree of stability of the relationship was consistently correlated with one or more of the measures of profile similarity. Couples who indicated that they were engaged to be married, for example, had more discrepant profiles as measured by d^2 (median correlation between d^2 and engaged status for factors, channels, and

TABLE 13.11. Means and Standard Deviations of Similarity (r) and Distance (d^2) for Real and Random Couples (over Eleven Channels)

	r[a]				d^2[b]				Median Effect Size of Difference[c]
	Real		Random		Real		Random		
Sample	Mean	SD	Mean	SD	Mean	SD	Mean	SD	
Dating couples (N=25)	−.038	.361	−.010	.374	23.76	12.30	23.43	14.06	−.05σ
Married couples with teenager (N=8)	.000	.456	−.116	.250	27.89	16.57	27.84	17.17	.16σ
Married couples with toddler (N=8)	−.235	.234	−.065	.391	24.42	4.94	20.50	7.01	−.59σ
Married couples without children (N=6)	−.104	.266	.057	.143	20.74	12.35	17.85	8.08	−.52σ
Median	−.071		−.038		24.09		21.96		−.28σ

[a]high value indicates more similarity
[b]high value indicates less similarity
[c]effect size in σ units averaged over both r and d^2

quadrants = .42, p = .05) and less similar profiles as measured by r (median correlation between r and engaged status for factors, channels, and quadrants = −.28) than did nonengaged couples.

To investigate systematically the effects of (1) defining profiles by channels, quadrants, or factors, (2) employing d^2 or r as the index of similarity, and (3) employing the male or female couple member's judgment of the quality or stability of the relationship, an analysis of variance was undertaken with correlations between d^2 or r and various self-reports of the couple's relationship serving as the dependent variable. This analysis showed that d^2 was a more productive index than r for the present study, and that profiles based on the four factors were productive of larger correlations than were profiles based on the eleven channels or the four quadrants.

The dating status of these twenty-five couples was recorded at two later points, at about four months and at one year after they took the PONS test. Couples whose profiles were farther apart (greater d^2) were more likely still to be together (correlation for factors = .25 at time 1, .33 at time 2). Those with more similar scores (in terms of d^2) were more likely to have broken up.

Examining the larger correlations of profile similarity and discrepancy with variables reflecting the couple members' subjective evaluations of aspects of their relationship, we found that couples in which the male reported that his girlfriend knew him very well had greater distance (in terms of d^2) between their PONS profiles (correlation for factors = .44, p < .05). The better the male reported his couple member liking his friends, the farther apart were their profiles in terms of d^2 (correlation for factors = .49, p < .05) and the more satisfied with the relationship the female member was, the farther apart were their profiles (correlation for factors = .33).

On the questionnaire, each couple member indicated the degree to which he or she had disclosed various kinds of information about himself or herself to the other member. Each also indicated the amount of disclosure of various kinds of information he or she had received from the other member. Indices of the total amount of disclosure given and received were computed. The correlations with profile similarity and distance appear in table 13.12.

Table 13.12 reveals that the correlation between couple members' eleven-channel profiles was weakly negatively related to the amount of disclosure they reported giving to and receiving from one another. Couples who disclosed more tended to be less similar to each other in their channel profiles. Consistently substantial correlations were found between disclosure and the total distance between couple members' profiles (in terms of d^2). Couples who disclosed more were less similar to each other in absolute levels of nonverbal decoding skill. All of the correlations of table 13.12 reaching $|.20|$ or greater were in the direction supporting this result.

It appears, then, that the less similar in shape and the farther apart were couple members' profiles, the more "successful" (in a sense) was their rela-

TABLE 13.12. Correlations of Similarity (r) and Distance (d^2) of Profiles with Measures of Disclosure Given and Received (N = 25 dating couples)

Variable	Total Disclosure Given			Total Disclosure Received			
	Male Report	Female Report	Mean	Male Report	Female Report	Mean	Grand Median
r channels	-.18	-.14	-.16	-.29	-.11	-.20	-.18
r quadrants	.15	.08	.12	-.04	.14	.05	.08
r factors	-.12	.09	-.02	-.08	-.12	-.10	-.06
Median	-.12	.08	-.02	-.08	-.11	-.10	
d^2 channels	.29	.45[a]	.37[b]	.42[a]	.27	.35[b]	.36[b]
d^2 quadrants	.01	.17	.09	.33	.08	.21	.15
d^2 factors	.41[a]	.43[a]	.42[a]	.31	.33	.32	.37[b]
Median	.29	.43[b]	.37[b]	.33	.27	.32	

[a] $p \leq .05$
[b] $p \leq .10$

tionship. Those with more dissimilar nonverbal decoding skills tended to be more likely to be engaged, to get along better with each other's friends, and to disclose more about themselves to each other. Thus, some support for Winch's theory of complementary needs appears to be provided by these results, at least for this realm of nonverbal decoding sensitivity.

KNOWING THE SENDER

Frijda (1953), in a study using films and photos of facial expressions, found no difference in judging accuracy between observers who knew the senders and observers who did not. Similarly, Wolf, Gorski, and Peters (1972), using alphabet recitation as a content standard technique for conveying various emotions via tone of voice, found no correlation between degree of prior acquaintanceship with the senders and judges' auditory decoding skill. Zuckerman and Przewuzman (in press), however, found that adults decoded facial expressions of their own children better than facial expressions of other children. Perhaps very intimate knowledge of the sender is required before a judge has any advantage in decoding that sender.

We did one study to examine how performance might be affected by subjects' having prior acquaintance with the PONS sender. The thirteen subjects who knew the sender were her parents, her sister, her sister's husband, and nine friends of one to twelve years' standing (mean number of years of acquaintanceship for the nine friends was 4.9). Thirteen "strangers" (people unacquainted with the sender) were also tested; these people were recruited by invitation of the members of the acquaintances group, each acquaintance inviting one person who was unacquainted with the sender and who was as much like the inviting acquaintance as possible on age, sex, and socioeconomic status.

Analysis of variance of these two groups' PONS scores revealed no overall effect of group ($F(1,21) = 0.12$, $p > .50$), but a nearly significant interaction of group and channel ($F(10,210) = 1.68$, $p < .09$). Inspection of the means associated with this interaction showed that this effect was largely due to the interaction of group and mode (audio versus video). Further analysis showed that the interaction of group and mode was significant (with mode defined as pure audio versus pure video), $F(1,210) = 9.64$, $p < .002$, effect size $= .43\sigma$, with acquaintances performing "too well" on audio and the strangers performing "too well" on video.

One might attribute the relatively greater audio skill of the acquaintances to their long-term prior practice on audio cues sent by the sender. Audio cues, at least in the PONS test, are more difficult to judge than video cues (chapter 3); audio skill does not seem amenable to short-term practice effects, presumably because of its difficulty, whereas video skill does (chapter 14); and there is evidence that audio accuracy is not improved by paying more attention to audio cues, whereas video skill is positively related to the amount of attention paid to video cues (chapter 10). These findings together lead us to hypothesize that the acquainted group may have profited from *long-term* exposure to cues sent in the audio channel by this particular sender.

Although we would like to attribute the acquaintances' relative advantage on tone of voice in this study to effects of prior acquaintanceship with the sender, we cannot rule out the possibility that some other factor or combination of factors may be responsible. For example, the sender's own family may have been unusually good at tone of voice regardless of who the sender was. Because of this or for independent reasons, the sender may have had a propensity for selecting friends who were relatively skilled at reading voice tone. Therefore, we cannot be certain that a practice effect rather than a selection factor is working here. One way to control for selection and other factors would be to manipulate acquaintanceship experimentally, using subjects who are all initially unacquainted and varying the amount and channels of exposure.

14 | Practice and Training

For over fifty years there have been serious efforts to increase sensitivity to nonverbal cues. In 1924, F. H. Allport investigated the effects of didactic training on such sensitivity. First he administered to twelve young women a test requiring the accurate identification of facial expressions. Then he asked them to study a chart of facial expressions for fifteen minutes, after which they were retested with the same test. Accuracy before the fifteen-minute training period was 48.8 percent and accuracy after the training was 54.7 percent, a gain of 5.9 percent, which, in terms of the variance of the pretest scores, was equivalent to a gain of .55 σ units. Because there was no control group, we cannot conclude that the study of the chart of facial expressions was responsible for the significant gain in accuracy ($t(11) = 1.83$, $p < .05$, one-tailed); but regardless of whether the training or simple practice was responsible, Allport did show that it was possible to improve accuracy in judging nonverbal cues.

In a follow-up of Allport's study, Guilford (1929) tested and trained a group of fifteen students of social psychology over a period of ten days. The students were tested five times on various tests of facial expression. After the first test, subjects studied the anatomy of facial expressions. After the second test, the stimuli of that test were shown again, but with the correct answers given along with the distinguishing features of each facial expression. Further analytic training was given, and this procedure was followed again after the administration of the next two tests. The fifth test was a "posttest" to show how much benefit had accrued from all the interposed teaching. While tests 2, 3, and 4 were all different from each other and from the pretest, the posttest was identical to the pretest. Over the course of the five testings, subjects showed a generally monotonic increase in performance ($\rho \cong .95$). The overall gain from pretest to posttest was substantial: from 27.2 percent to 41.0 percent. From the data presented it was not possible to compute the exact effect size, but it was probably between 1.28 σ (σ estimated from Allport's pretest data) and 2.08 σ (σ estimated from Guilford's table 1). Once again, we cannot be sure whether this substantial gain was due to the ten-day training program or simply to the practice in test taking offered the students. In either case, however, we have seen that performance at judging facial affect can be improved, though we cannot say with confidence how it was accomplished.

Jenness (1932b), a student of Allport's, replicated Allport's study and found an effect size almost as large as Allport's (.52 σ versus .55 σ). In a subsequent study, Jenness lengthened the training program from fifteen minutes to forty-five minutes and found a larger effect (.98 σ). An increase in training time may lead to an increase in sensitivity to nonverbal stimuli, but we cannot be sure because subjects were not assigned at random to these two conditions. Subject sampling differences, therefore, rather than length of training period, might have been the critical variable.

Two further studies were conducted by Jenness, examining the effects on performance of prior testing. In the first study the interval before retesting was fifteen minutes; in the second study the interval was three months. In both studies there was no appreciable benefit from pretesting alone; effect sizes were $-.08\sigma$ and .02 σ, respectively.

Kline and Johannsen (1935) investigated the relative amount of information carried in photographs of the face alone as compared to the face and body combined. The sophisticated design of their experiment permitted an analysis of the effects of practice on the accuracy of decoding both types of stimuli under a variety of test conditions. The median effect size associated with practice or retesting was .34 σ. Shortly after Kline and Johannsen's study was published, Walton (1936) also investigated the effects of retesting on accuracy of decoding facial expressions in still photos. The size of the effect he obtained was only slightly smaller (.22 σ).

Several studies were not available for direct examination but were summarized helpfully by other workers. Izard (1971) described a study by Mittenecker (1960) in which significantly greater improvement in sensitivity to nonverbal cues was achieved by telling subjects whether they were correct or not in their judgments, compared to the improvement achieved in a control group that was not offered such feedback. Hoffman (1964) described several studies by Ekman and Hoffman (1963) in which the basic element of training was feedback on the correctness of the subject's judgment of whether a still photo had been taken during a stressful or cathartic phase of an interview. In the first study, training on specific stimulus persons led to significantly greater improvement on those same stimulus persons when compared to the improvement of a control group. In the second study, training was on a stimulus person other than the one on whom posttesting was to be done. In that case the benefits of training, while positive in direction, were not significant. In the third study, four groups were employed, two of which were trained on either of two stimulus persons, while the other two groups served as controls. Pretest scores showed the groups to be noncomparable, so that results of the study were difficult to interpret. However, all four groups showed substantial improvement in performance, suggesting that possibly the pretesting itself might have been of benefit in improving performance.

So far, all the studies we have examined have dealt with still photos as the stimulus materials. Marvin Hoffman (1964) employed five-second silent motion picture clips in his study of the effects of training on sensitivity to nonverbal cues. He had worked with Ekman and employed Ekman's procedure of requiring judgments of whether a given stimulus was drawn from a stressful or cathartic portion of an interview. Hoffman employed eight groups, all receiving the same amount of feedback training but differing as to which stimulus person or how many stimulus persons were shown in the training. Differences among these groups were equivocal, but for all groups combined it was clear that substantial improvements were possible in judging nonverbal stimuli in motion picture form (effect size $= 1.78\,\sigma$).

Table 14.1 presents a brief summary of these studies as well as the results

TABLE 14.1. Studies of Increasing Sensitivity to Nonverbal Stimuli (Visual)

Study		Effect Size (σ)	Training Method
Allport (1924)		+0.55[a]	didactic
Ekman and Hoffman (1963)	I	+ [a,b]	feedback
	II	+ [b]	feedback
	III	+ [b]	various methods
Guilford (1929)		+1.68[a,c]	didactic + feedback
Hoffman (1964)[d]		+1.78[a]	feedback
Jecker, Maccoby, and Breitrose (1965)[d]		+1.00[a]	didactic + feedback
Jenness (1932)	I	+0.52[a]	didactic
	II	+0.98[a]	didactic (more taught)
	III	−0.08	no training (retest)
	IV	+0.02	no training (retest)
Kline and Johannsen (1935)		+0.34[a]	no training (retest)
Kohnle (1971)[d]		+1.14[a]	didactic
Lanzetta and Kleck (1970)[d]		0.00[c]	feedback and punishment
Miller, Giannini, and Levine (1975)[d]		0.00[c]	no training (retest)
Mittenecker (1960)		+ [a,b]	feedback
Mohamed (1974)[d]		+1.26[a,c]	encounter group
Walton (1936)		+0.22	no training (retest)
Median		+0.54	(omitting entries marked[b])
Mean		+0.67[e]	(omitting entries marked[b])

NOTE: For an experiment involving tone of voice rather than visual cues, Davitz (1964) reported a significant effect of training. The pretest-only control group showed a gain of .45 σ, while the pretest + practice + feedback experimental group showed a gain of .78 σ.

[a] $p < .05$
[b] not reported and not estimable
[c] estimated
[d] motion picture, video, or live stimulus; others were still photos
[e] confidence interval (95 percent) extends from +0.31 to +1.04 ($t = 3.95$, $df = 13$, $p < .001$)

of several more recent studies. Overall, we can conclude with some confidence that training of several kinds can lead to improved sensitivity to nonverbal cues. We cannot be confident, however, about the specific training methods likely to be most effective with any particular type of stimulus materials. Both didactic procedures and feedback procedures have been employed more or less successfully. There is some evidence, though, that pretesting alone may not be very effective. For the studies listed in table 14.1, the median size of effect of pretesting only was .02 σ, while the median size of effect of all other methods of training was 1.00 σ. We should note that four of the five studies employing pretesting as their only method of "training" were studies using still photos. Thus, we are left with little firm basis for predicting the effect of pretesting alone on PONS performance.

EFFECTS OF PRETESTING ON THE FULL PONS

One kind of training for sensitivity to nonverbal communication consists simply of giving people practice in decoding nonverbal cues. We would not expect such practice to be maximally efficient, of course, since simple practice does not include knowledge of results (feedback). Nevertheless, we wanted to know the effects of pretesting with the PONS on subsequent PONS performance.

Four studies were carried out primarily as part of the standardization procedure in which the estimation of retest reliability was the primary goal. These studies, involving an average of six weeks between testings, included a U.S. state college sample (N = 28), an Australian university sample (N = 74), a U.S. university sample (N = 17), and a U.S. high school sample (N = 37). Analysis of variance showed no significant (or large) differences among the four groups in their relative improvements in the eleven channels ($F < 1$), so the four samples were combined, without weighting, for further analysis. Figure 14.1 shows the results for all groups combined.

A quasireplication study involved retesting after an eight-day interval, and was conducted by Paul Guild as part of an investigation of the effects of meditation on sensitivity to nonverbal communication among Canadian university student meditators and nonmeditators. The design was completely counterbalanced so that half the subjects during each PONS administration were meditators and half were not; within each of these groups, half took the PONS after meditating and half took the PONS after resting. Figure 14.2 shows the results of the first and second testing for each channel and for the total. Comparison of figure 14.2 with figure 14.1 shows remarkable consistency of profiles. While the average subject of the first four retest studies gained 3.6 percent, or about 8 items, on the 220-item PONS (effect size =

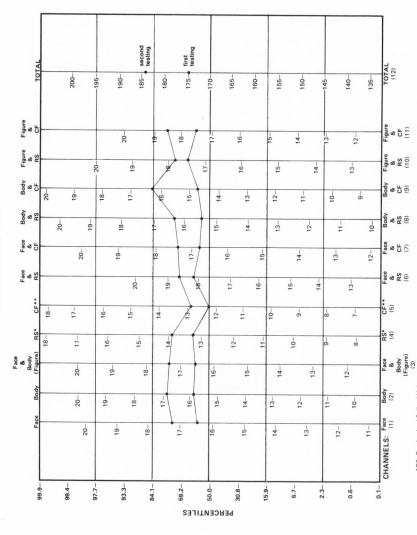

FIGURE 14.1. PONS performance of four samples on two occasions (total N = 156)

PROFILE OF NONVERBAL SENSITIVITY: STANDARD SCORING SHEET
Channel Scores and Total

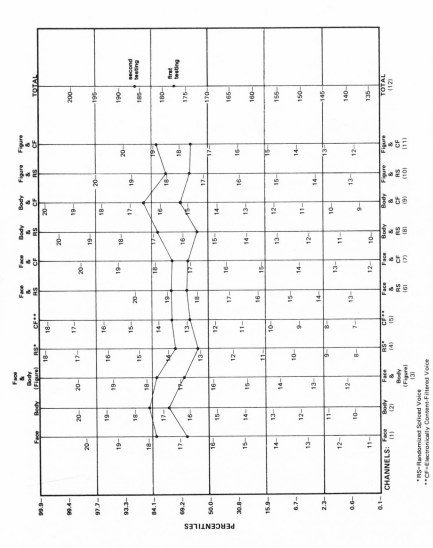

FIGURE 14.2. PONS performance of Canadian university students on two occasions (N = 60)

1.48 σ), the average subject of the Canadian study gained 4.2 percent, or about 9 items (effect size = 2.50 σ). Another way to judge the relative similarity of these two sets of results is to correlate the gains made in each channel by the subjects of the fifth study with those made by the subjects of the earlier set of studies. That r was .75, $p < .004$.

Some time after these five studies were conducted, three additional quasireplication studies became available in which American subjects were tested on two occasions, although the estimation of retest reliabilities had not been the primary goal. One of these studies, by Boyd Purdom, employed eighty-one experienced teachers; a second study, by Robert McCoid, employed fifty-six undergraduate students enrolled in educational psychology; the third study, by Ruth Pinnas, employed fourteen graduate students of counseling. All three of these studies used some form of training that might have been expected to affect sensitivity to nonverbal cues, but two of these studies (Purdom and Pinnas) used control groups that showed substantial gains from retesting alone, gains that were just as great as the gains of the experimental groups. Therefore, we disregarded experimental and control group conditions within each of the three studies and simply examined all subjects' gains in PONS scores over time. The retest intervals were approximately two weeks, three weeks, and ten weeks for the McCoid, Pinnas, and Purdom studies, respectively.

Figure 14.3 shows the results of the first and second testings for each of the eleven channels and the total for all three studies combined without weighting. The average subject gained 4.4 percent (effect size = 1.96 σ). Despite the differences in sampling and in procedure, the effects of retesting displayed in figures 14.1, 14.2, and 14.3 were all remarkably homogeneous. Over the eleven channels, the retesting gains of the last three samples correlated very highly with the gains of the first four samples ($r = .87, p < .00025$) and of the fifth sample ($r = .54, p < .05$). The average (intraclass) correlation among the three sets of gain scores was .72 and the reliability of the unweighted mean of these three sets of gain scores was .89.

We examined the accuracy for the total of the pretest, posttest, and gain scores for all eight samples. Although the conditions of the last four studies were quite different from the simple retest designs of the first four studies, the gain scores of the former did not differ from the gain scores of the latter ($t <$ 1). The overall results were unequivocal, both in terms of statistical significance (p very close to zero) and in terms of effect size (1.79 σ). Even without feedback, accuracy on the PONS is greatly improved by a second testing ($t(356) = 16.89$).

We considered next the question of whether some channels or groups of channels profit more than others from simple retesting. For all three groups of retest studies, stimuli showing the body profited more from retesting than did

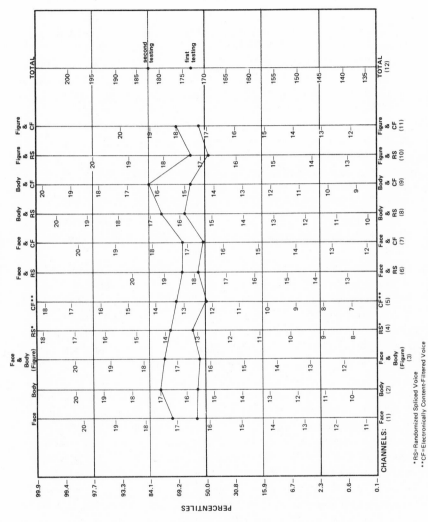

FIGURE 14.3. PONS performance of three samples on two occasions (total N = 151)

the stimuli not showing the body. For the combined first four samples, $F(1,152) = 17.89$, $p < .0001$, effect size $= .69\,\sigma$; for the first quasireplication, $F(1,56) = 12.11$, $p < .001$, effect size $= .93\,\sigma$; for the three subsequent samples, $F(1,148) = 14.51$, $p < .0002$, effect size $= .63\,\sigma$.

Since the body-showing channels are more difficult than the face-showing channels, one might think that they improve more because they start lower and have more room in which to increase. This interpretation is greatly weakened by the result that the two pure tone channels (RS and CF) showed less than average improvement despite the fact that they are the most difficult of all the channels. The RS stimuli, in fact, profit relatively little from the retest experience even when they are combined with facial cues. Only when the RS cues are combined with body cues does performance gain approach or exceed the average performance gain for the full PONS. Comparison of the three row marginals for stimuli carrying no audio versus CF audio versus RS audio shows for all eight samples a modest effect such that channels with RS information gain less from retesting than do the other two levels of audio information ($F(2,712) = 8.53$, $p < .001$, $\eta = .15$).

PRETESTING AS AN EXPERIMENTAL CONDITION. For the samples considered so far, all subjects had been pretested and posttested and the gain scores for all were computed. It would be very desirable to have available a study in which some subjects were assigned to a pretesting condition at random while other subjects were assigned to a no-pretesting control condition, so that the effects of pretesting could be evaluated within the context of a true experiment. Just such a study has been conducted by Ruth Pinnas. The sample described earlier that had been obtained by her had been assigned to their pretest-posttest condition at random. A comparable group of her subjects had been randomly assigned to a posttest-only condition. A comparison of the posttest data of those subjects who had been pretested with those who had not been pretested would give an experimental evaluation of the effects of pretesting. The results were quite consistent with the results of the nonexperimental studies. The mean gain on the total PONS was 6.2 percent, equivalent to an effect size of $r = .52$ or $1.23\,\sigma$ ($t(27) = 3.20$, $p < .002$). And, just as was the case with the nonexperimental studies, the sixty scenes showing only the body profited most from the effects of pretesting. Compared to the mean of the remaining eight channels (4.4), the mean of the three body channels (11.0) was much greater (effect size $= 1.35\,\sigma$) and the difference was significant at $p < .002$ ($F(1,27) = 12.40$). Frankie Phillips has also conducted an experiment in which pretesting was one of the independent variables. He too found a significant advantage on the total PONS of having been pretested ($t(60) = 2.46$, $p < .009$, effect size $= .63\,\sigma$ or $r = .31$). Phillips, however, found greater benefits of pretesting on the two pure tone channels than on the channels showing body (effect sizes of $.83\,\sigma$ versus $.42\,\sigma$).

EFFECTS OF PRETESTING ON THE AUDIO PONS

So far in our consideration of the effects of retesting on nonverbal sensitivity, we have examined only the effects of having been tested with the full PONS on subsequent full PONS performance. We now report the results of a study in which pretesting was with the full PONS but retesting was limited to the pure tone channels (RS and CF). This study offered the additional advantage that we had a control group of subjects who had not been given the full PONS prior to their being tested on the audio channels.

The experiment was conducted in a suburban high school, with the participation of 145 students. All students were tested with the male audio PONS (RS and CF) and with the two audio channels of the full PONS. Some of the students had taken the full PONS some weeks earlier and some had not. Within each of these groups some had served as judges of nonverbal cues in a different study some weeks earlier and some had not. Each group included both male and female students. Finally, within each group some of the subjects were tested first with the male audio PONS and then with the female audio PONS and some were tested in the opposite sequence. In addition to these four between-subject factors there were two within-subject factors, male versus female sender and RS versus CF channel. Considering no effects more complex than a three-way interaction, there were 16 F tests involving the factor of prior exposure to the full PONS. We might expect 1.6 of these to reach the .10 level of significance but actually 7 reached that level.

Although there was no significant overall effect ($F < 1$) on subsequent audio PONS testing of having been given the full PONS, the RS channel did gain significantly more than the CF channel because of prior testing ($F(1,129) = 4.68, p = .04$, effect size $= .38\sigma$). This effect was almost entirely due to the subjects who had some additional prior experience as judges of nonverbal cues in a different study ($F(1,129) = 4.07, p = .05$, effect size $= .36\sigma$). This finding of greater benefit of practice for the RS than the CF channel, especially for a more experienced group, is consistent with the results of a preliminary study of the effects of direct training on sensitivity to nonverbal cues. In that study, to be reported later in this chapter, more experienced clinicians showed greater benefits of training for the RS than the CF channels.

Prior testing benefited audio PONS scores more when the female sender's voice was played first ($F(1,129) = 3.23, p = .08$, effect size $= .32\sigma$). Perhaps when the female's voice was played first subjects were able to benefit from their having heard her voice in the full PONS, while when they heard the male voice first it interfered with their recollection of the female voice. This interaction was significantly stronger for female subjects than for male subjects ($F(1,129) = 4.46, p = .04$, effect size $= .37\sigma$).

Scores on the female audio PONS improved significantly more than did the male audio PONS scores with prior exposure to the full PONS ($F(1,129) =$

4.16, $p = .05$, effect size $= .36\sigma$). That seems readily interpretable, since the female sender's voice was heard throughout the full PONS while the male sender's voice was never heard. The effect of the sex of the sender on the benefits of having taken the full PONS earlier was greater when the male audio PONS was administered first ($F(1,129) = 3.33$, $p = .08$, effect size $= .32\sigma$). This may have been due to the interference generated by interposing the male voice between the two administrations of the female voice.

Finally, the greater benefits of retesting with the female audio PONS were due primarily to the subjects who had had prior experience as judges of nonverbal cues ($F(1,129) = 3.19$, $p = .08$, effect size $= .31\sigma$). This finding of greater benefit of practice for more experienced judges is consistent with the results of a preliminary study of the effects of direct training on sensitivity to nonverbal cues. In that study, to be described more fully later in this chapter, more experienced clinicians showed greater benefits of training than did less experienced clinicians.

PERSONAL CORRELATES OF IMPROVEMENT FROM RETESTING

In one of our studies on the effects of retesting, twenty-eight U.S. college students filled out a questionnaire at the time of the initial testing. This questionnaire, described in chapter 11, inquired about subjects' relationships to others of the same sex and of the opposite sex. In addition, we inquired about the extent to which subjects felt they were accurate in understanding cues from tones of voice, body movements, and facial expressions. We also asked subjects their scores on the verbal and quantitative sections of their SAT examinations. Each of the above variables was then correlated with the gain in scores on the PONS total from pretest to retest.

Table 14.2 shows these correlations. Subjects who gained more in PONS scores from retesting rated their relationships with the opposite sex as substantially better than did subjects who profited less from retesting. We wonder whether having better heterosexual relationships makes it easier to learn more about nonverbal cues or whether the ability to profit from experience in assessing nonverbal cues makes it easier to relate to others of the opposite sex. It may be that being able to learn more about nonverbal stimuli confers an evolutionary advantage in that better learners may stand a better chance of contributing their genes to the gene pool. Correlations between PONS improvement scores and self-ratings of relationships with the same sex were not significant and, unaccountably, tended to be negative in direction.

Table 14.2 also shows that subjects who rated themselves as more accurate in receiving in various channels of nonverbal communication showed greater gains from retesting, especially when self-ratings were of ability to understand body movements. It is interesting to note that subjects' self-ratings of accu-

TABLE 14.2. Correlations of Improvements in PONS Total with Interpersonal Success for Twenty-Eight U.S. College Students

Self-Rating Variable	Relationships with Same Sex	Relationships with Opposite Sex
Warm	−.14	.51[a]
Honest	−.13	.19
Enduring	−.18	.52[a]
Satisfying	−.24	.58[a]
I understand friends	.14	.10
Friends understand me	−.12	.42[b]
Median	−.14	.46[b,c]
Median intercorrelation among variables listed	.42[b]	.59[a]

Other Self-Report Variable	r
Accuracy in understanding	
Tone	.29
Body	.60[d]
Face	.49[a]
Performance on SAT	
Verbal	−.21
Quantitative	.60[a]

[a] $p \leq .01$
[b] $p \leq .05$
[c] A recent replication by Tony Castelnovo found a rank correlation of .78 ($df = 6, p < .03$) between PONS improvement scores and quality of relationship with the opposite sex as judged by a group leader.
[d] $p \leq .001$

racy did not correlate significantly with their pretest total PONS scores, only with their improvement (median pretest $r = .19$). When people judge their own sensitivity to nonverbal stimuli perhaps they really judge their ability to learn to decode someone they have not known before rather than any current accuracy level.

Finally, table 14.2 shows that those who benefited more from practice on the PONS had earned very much higher scores in their quantitative SAT exams. Perhaps the same kinds of analytic skills are required both for high performance on this section of the SAT and for benefit from further exposure to nonverbal cues.

In Robert McCoid's study of the effects of retesting, subjects filled out brief self-rating scales before they took the PONS the first time. They rated their warmth, their ability to understand other people and social situations, and their accuracy in understanding tones of voice, body movements, and facial expressions. All these ratings were then correlated with subjects' gains in PONS performance from the first to second testing.

Self-ratings of warmth and of accuracy in understanding tones of voice were virtually uncorrelated with gains in PONS performance ($r = -.02$ and .01). Gains on the PONS were, however, correlated with self-ratings of the ability to understand people ($r = .32$, $p < .05$), social situations ($r = .38$, $p < .01$), body movements ($r = .20$), and facial expressions ($r = .20$).

EFFECTS OF PRACTICE WITHIN A SINGLE TESTING

We have already learned that added exposure to the PONS, as in retesting, is associated with a substantial improvement in accuracy (1.79σ). Perhaps a similar kind of learning occurs within a single testing; if so, there might be substantial learning between the first half and the last half of the PONS. To examine this possibility we selected eight quite different samples and, for each, calculated the percentage accuracy scores for the first 110 items and the last 110 items of the PONS. Table 14.3 shows the results. All but two of the samples, the young children and the psychiatric patients, showed substantial improvement in going from the first half to the last half of the PONS. The overall effect size for all eight samples was $.89\sigma$—an effect that, though quite substantial, was only about half the size of the effect of pretesting on a subsequent administration of the full PONS.

In considering the interpretation of gains in accuracy during a single testing we must consider the possibility that the last 110 items were easier than the first 110 items. This alternative appears unlikely, however, because items were allotted to their serial position randomly but with sufficient blocking to ensure a fairly balanced representation of the different channels and quadrants among items presented earlier and later.

TABLE 14.3. Improvement in Accuracy from First Half to Last Half of PONS for Eight Samples

Sample	N	First Half	Last Half	Gain
U.S. high school students	482	76.5%	78.5%	2.0%
Nova Scotia college students	156	76.6	78.4	1.8
Mexican university students	106	74.3	77.8	3.5
New Guinea college students	88	68.4	70.7	2.3
APA psychologists	89	78.0	80.8	2.8
Children (U.S., grades 3–6)	200	67.4	66.8	−0.6
Alcoholic patients	61	70.6	72.8	2.2
Psychiatric patients	78	71.1	71.1	0.0
Median	98	72.7	75.3	2.1
Unweighted mean	157.5	72.9	74.6	1.8[a]
Weighted mean		73.8	75.5	1.7

[a] $t = 15.67$, $df = 1252$, effect size of $r = .40$ or $.89\sigma$; an additional study by Robert McCoid found a mean gain of 1.9 percent (pretest = 77.6 percent, posttest = 79.5 percent; N = 56).

Table 14.4 shows the median gains in accuracy for each of the eleven channels and four quadrants. For both channels and quadrants there was some sample-to-sample variation in relative gains in accuracy, but there was substantial reliability of the pattern of gains from sample to sample. The reliability of gains over quadrants from sample to sample was .95 and that for channels was .90 (both reliabilities consisting of average [intraclass] correlations among samples in patterns of gains).

Table 14.4 shows very substantial differences in benefits from within-test practice for different channels ($F(10,12470) = 268.62, \eta = .42$) and for different quadrants ($F(3,3756) = 288.91, \eta = .43$). Greatest improvement occurred on stimuli showing only the body + content-filtered or randomized spliced speech and on stimuli showing only the face + content-filtered speech. Next after this set of three channels, in order of gains from intratest practice, came the two video-only channels showing body; these channels showed only small gains. Two channels showed a small loss in going from the first to the last half of the PONS: face-only and face + RS. Finally, four channels showed substantially worse performance over time: CF, RS, figure + CF, and figure + RS.

The eleven channels fall into four groups on the basis of their gains in performance:

1. face + CF, body + CF, body + RS (median gain = + 12.0)
2. figure, body (median gain = +3.0)
3. face, face + RS (median "gain" = −2.7)
4. figure + RS, RS, figure + CF, CF (median "gain" = −9.4)

The four best channels in terms of gains over time had in common that they offered two and only two channels of information, with face, body, CF, and

TABLE 14.4. Improvement in Accuracy from First Half to Last Half of PONS for Eleven Channels and Four Quadrants (Median Gains of Eight Samples)

Audio Channel	Video Channel				
	None	Body	Face	Figure	Marginals
None		1.0%	− 2.6%	5.0%	1.1%
Content-filtered	−12.0%	12.0	14.9	−10.2	1.2
Randomized spliced	− 8.5	11.6	− 2.8	− 7.8	−1.9
Marginals	−10.2	8.2	3.2	− 4.3	

Quadrants	Negative	Positive	Marginals
Submissive	−5.2%	7.4%	1.1%
Dominant	2.2	9.1	5.6
Marginals	−1.5	8.2	

RS each considered a channel of information (figure has both face and body). The worst four channels in terms of gain over time had in common that they offered either three channels or only one channel, and in all cases either CF or RS was present. Perhaps these two difficult channels are improvable from simple practice only if they are presented along with a single other channel. Presented alone or with two other channels there may be too little or too much additional information to aid in learning.

The lower half of table 14.4 shows that for quadrants, those conveying positive affect manifested much greater improvement within a single adminis- tration of the PONS than did those conveying negative affect. In addition, those conveying dominant affects showed greater improvement than those conveying submissive affects.

We have already mentioned that the overall improvement in going from the first half to the last half of the PONS was about half the size of the improve- ment in going from a pretesting to a retesting with the full PONS. For four samples that had been specifically retested to investigate retest reliability, we computed the accuracies in percentage for the first half and last half of both the pretesting and posttesting. The mean gain from first half to last half of the pretest PONS was 1.9 percent (the median gain was 2.5 percent), a value quite comparable to that obtained for the eight larger samples of table 14.3 (mean = 1.8 percent, median = 2.1 percent). Within the retest there was very little further improvement from the first half to the last half: the gain was only 0.4 percent (mean) or 0.1 percent (median). The results of these four studies are well supported by the results of McCoid's subsequent study. During his first PONS testing he found a gain of 1.9 percent (from 77.6 percent to 79.5 percent) from first half to last half, but during his second PONS testing he found a gain of only 0.4 percent (from 82.7 percent to 83.1 percent) from first half to last half (N = 56). Apparently, learning occurs during the administra- tion of the PONS the first time and during the administration of the PONS the second time, but during this second administration a point of diminishing returns is reached with respect to further learning.

EFFECTS OF DIRECT TRAINING

Through the interest of Dr. William Berkowitz and with the cooperation of the staff of the Solomon Mental Health Center (Lowell, Massachusetts), it was possible to conduct a preliminary study of the effects of specific training on sensitivity to nonverbal cues. A total of forty-one clinical staff members participated in the research by taking the PONS after having been exposed or not exposed to a short-term training program designed to increase sensitivity to nonverbal communication. These staff members included social workers, counselors, nurses, paraprofessionals, and a few psychologists and psychia- trists.

The training program, lasting about ninety minutes, contained the following nonverbal materials, none of them having the original PONS sender's face or voice:

1. A brief lecture on the possible importance of nonverbal communication in clinical settings.
2. A demonstration of content-filtered and randomized spliced speech and a description of how these techniques helped us to focus on tones of voice.
3. Practice in judging the affects or situations represented in the voices of a male adult, a female adult, and a female child (content-filtered, randomized spliced, and standard content speech).
4. Practice in listening for slight differences in the emphasis given various words of instructions read by a psychological experimenter.
5. Practice in judging the affects or situations represented in adult male and adult female faces shown in color slides.
6. Practice in judging the affects or situations represented in an adult female's face and/or body shown in brief video tape clips.

Of the forty-one staff members participating, twenty-five could be assigned at random either to the training program or to a waiting list control group of staff members who could avail themselves of the training program at a later date. This postexperimental training program for the control group staff members was, of course, subsequently conducted. All subjects were tested with the PONS one week after the training program had been administered to those who had been assigned to that condition. Based on the data of the twenty-five who had been assigned to conditions at random, there was a tendency for those who had been given the training ($N = 14$) to perform somewhat better on the PONS than did the waiting list controls ($N = 11$). The mean total scores were 78.7 percent for trained subjects and 76.7 percent for untrained subjects, a difference that was not significant statistically ($p < .09$, one-tailed) but was of promising magnitude ($.58 \sigma$).

Despite the random assignment of staff members to groups, assignment to the training condition was found to be significantly correlated with the clinicians' level of professional experience ($r = -.57$, $p < .01$): more experienced clinicians were assigned too often to the control condition. This confounding of training with years of clinical experience makes the results of this pilot study even more tenuous and more in need of replication.

In an attempt to reduce this confounding of training experience with clinical experience, we used the level of subjects' experience as a blocking variable. Effects of training were examined separately for those with three or fewer years of experience and for those with five or more years of experience. Table 14.5 shows the results of this analysis. Effects of training appeared to be greater for more experienced than for less experienced clinicians. This difference in training effects was not reflected in a significant interaction, however ($F = 1.40$, $p = .25$).

TABLE 14.5. Effects on Training on PONS Performance for More and Less Experienced Clinicians

Experience	No Training	Training	t	One-tailed p	Effect Size (σ)
Three years or less (N=15)	78.3%	78.5%	0.09		.04
Five years or more (N=10)	75.4	79.3	1.77	.05	.77
Mean	76.8	78.9	1.34	.10	.59

To examine whether blocking had reduced the confounding of training with years of experience, we computed the training and years of experience correlation separately within each of our blocking levels. For the less experienced group, r was .24; for the more experienced group, r was $-.56$. Because blocking had not succeeded in eliminating the confounding of training with experience, we computed the correlation of training with PONS total, partialing out the effects of years of experience within each level of experience. Among the less experienced clinicians the partial r was $-.04$, while among the more experienced clinicians the partial r was .42. These results, suggesting greater effects of training for more experienced clinicians, are quite consistent with the results of table 14.5.

The partial correlations between training and PONS performance (with years of experience partialed out) were also computed for each of the eleven PONS channels and the marginal (pooled) channels for just the ten more experienced clinicians (five or more years). The results, shown in table 14.6, suggest that the effects of training may be greater for randomized spliced than for content-filtered stimuli and greater for stimuli involving any body cues than for stimuli employing only facial cues. Because these data are based on

TABLE 14.6. Effects of Training for More Experienced Clinicians in Eleven PONS Channels (Partial Correlation Coefficients)

Audio Channel	Video Channel				
	None	Body	Face	Figure	Marginals
None		.13	.05	.43	.28
Content-filtered	−.12	−.32	.06	−.03	−.21
Randomized spliced	.47	.60	.19	.71	.66
Marginals	.22	.26	.13	.42	
All face	.33				
All body	.42				
Total	.42				

only ten clinicians, all of whom had five or more years of experience, and because of the wide confidence intervals around these correlations, they should be regarded as hypothesis generating rather than as hypothesis testing. Finally, we should note that these partial correlations tend to be lower than the equivalent unpartialed correlations, with medians of .26 and .44, respectively. The relative magnitudes of the partial correlations for all eleven channels and all ten marginals combined, however, are in good agreement with the relative magnitudes of the original correlations (ρ for twenty-one pairs of rs = .78).

EFFECTS OF INDIRECT TRAINING

MEDITATION. An interesting question, alluded to earlier, was raised by Paul Guild, who wondered whether transcendental meditation might improve sensitivity to nonverbal communication. The design employed thirty meditators and thirty nonmeditators, each PONS tested once just after meditating and once just after resting (not meditating). Within each of the two types of people, half were tested first after meditating for twenty minutes and then, eight days later, after resting for twenty minutes. The remaining half were tested first after resting and then, eight days later, just after meditating. All meditators had two or more years of experience and most were teachers of meditation. Within the two groups, the age and sex distributions were comparable.

Our analysis showed that subjects improved dramatically with practice, an effect of great magnitude reflected in a point biserial correlation of .78 or a gain of $2.50\,\sigma$ units. A significant interaction showed that each group performed better when it was "doing its own thing." Meditators gained more when meditating and nonmeditators gained more when not meditating. The size of this effect was moderate ($F(1,56) = 5.70, p = .02$, effect size = $.64\,\sigma$). Subjects using their own type of treatment on the second testing gained 5.0 percent and 5.4 percent, while subjects using the opposite type of treatment gained only 3.9 percent and 2.2 percent.

This significant effect of each group's doing better at its "own thing" did not, itself, interact significantly with the eleven channels of the PONS. There was a tendency, however, for this effect to be greater for those six channels in which the body could be seen than in the five channels in which it could not be seen ($F(1,56) = 2.70, p = .106$, effect size = $.44\,\sigma$ or $r = .21$). There was also a tendency for this effect to be greater for negative than for positive stimuli ($F(1,56) = 3.73, p < .06$, effect size = $.52\,\sigma$ or $r = .25$).

MICROCOUNSELING. Ruth Pinnas found that training in microcounseling did not improve PONS performance of counselors in training beyond the performance of the control group (effect size = $-.03\,\sigma$).

COURSE WORK. Boyd Purdom found that course work in nonverbal communication did not improve PONS performance of college students beyond the performance of the waiting list control group (effect size $= -.04\sigma$).

WORKSHOP. A more recent experiment by Frankie Phillips showed a tendency for teachers undergoing special training in sensitivity to nonverbal communication to gain more on the PONS total than the teachers of the control group ($t(60) = 1.80$, $p < .04$, one-tailed, effect size $= .46\sigma$). Some training programs, apparently, are able to improve sensitivity to nonverbal cues as measured by the PONS total.

PRACTICE AND TRAINING: AN OVERVIEW

The results presented in this chapter show very clearly that it is possible to increase sensitivity to nonverbal stimuli. On the basis of eight samples and a total of 367 subjects that were tested with the PONS on two occasions, we can conclude that retesting alone is sufficient to improve performance very substantially (effect size $= 1.79\sigma$). Even the practice involved in going from the first 110 items to the last 110 items of the PONS results in a very substantial improvement. Based on eight samples and a total of 1,260 subjects, the magnitude of the improvement was $.89\sigma$—a large effect but only about half the size of the effect of pretesting.

A preliminary study of the effect of a training program designed specifically to increase sensitivity to nonverbal cues yielded a result that was far less definitive, based as it was on a randomized experiment of only twenty-five clinicians. Yet even here the results were at least encouraging, with a training effect size of $.58\sigma$. Effect sizes may be seen as a ratio of signal to noise. In the pilot study of training, the effect size was probably decreased somewhat because of the greater noise or variance in that research compared to the noise or variance in the studies of the effects of pretesting or practice within a single testing. In these latter studies, the variance was a within-subject term, since each subject had been measured twice. In the training study, the variance was a between-subject term, variation that is usually appreciably greater than within-subject variation.

From the data available we can make only a very general estimate of the effect size we might expect from a carefully developed program of training to increase sensitivity to nonverbal communication. Estimated from the earlier studies of the effects of training (summarized in table 14.1), the range might be from zero to nearly 2.0σ, with perhaps the most likely value centering at about $.5\sigma$. Some of the effect sizes shown in table 14.1, however, are based on somewhat inflated between-subject sources of variance (e.g., pretest variance) because the within-subject sources of variance (e.g., occasion × subject interaction variance) were not available in some of the older studies. This unavailability should in no sense be regarded as a shortcoming, since some of the concepts under discussion were simply not known at the time of the pioneering work of Allport, Guilford, and Jenness.

Knowing that performance on the PONS can be greatly improved by practice and perhaps by training, we wanted to consider whether some channels or channel combinations and some affect dimensions profit more than others from such practice or training. A useful way to examine channel effects is to consider the four factors known to underlie our eleven channels: body present without face (60 items), face present (120 items), RS-only (20 items), and CF-only (20 items) (see the section on factoring channels in chapter 3). The top half of table 14.7 shows the gains for each of these channel factors for four types of studies.

The first type of study summarizes the gains in going from the first 110 items of the PONS to the last 110 items. The second type of study, not described earlier in this chapter, shows the gains in performance in going from

TABLE 14.7. Summary of Effects of Practice and Training on Channel Factors and Affects

| | Channel Factor | | | |
| | Video | | Audio | |
Study	Body 60	Face 120	RS 20	CF 20
Gain first half to last half (%) (8 samples, N = 1260)	8.2	−0.6	−8.5	−12.0
Gain first fifth to last fifth (%) (3 samples, N = 97)	18.6	6.4	−14.6	−33.3
Gain from retesting (%) (8 samples, N = 367)	5.7	3.3	3.1	3.7
Gain from training (r) (1 sample, N = 25)	.38	.32	.00	−.16

| | Affect Dimension | | | |
| | Positivity | | Dominance | |
	Positive	Negative	Dominant	Submissive
Gain first half to last half (%) (8 samples, N = 1260)	8.2	−1.5	5.6	1.1
Gain first fifth to last fifth (%) (3 samples, N = 97)	13.7	−5.2	8.0	0.4
Gain from retesting (%) (3 samples, N = 197)	4.5	3.1	4.1	3.5
Gain from training (r) (1 sample, N = 25)	.26	.26	.24	.26

the first fifth (44 items) to the last fifth (44 items) of the PONS in three quite different samples for which those data happened to be readily available: (1) a group of thirty-nine U.S. university students who were tested with an early video tape version of the PONS, (2) a group of thirty-three U.S. university students enrolled in a course in small group dynamics, and (3) a group of twenty-five adults of all ages, many of whom were very well acquainted with the young woman sender on the PONS. The third type of study summarizes the gains attributable to pretesting. These first three types of study show percentages of gains under each entry. The fourth row shows our training study, and the entries are not gains in percentages but correlations (point-biserial) between PONS performance and having been assigned at random to the training condition.

For all four kinds of studies (N = 1,749), greater gains from practice or training were made in the visual than in the auditory channels. Within the visual channels, greater gains were made in the body channels (60 scenes) than in the face channels (120 scenes). Within the auditory channels only retesting was beneficial to both channels, while within single-testing sessions both channels showed a drop in performance, a drop that was greater for CF than for RS. Neither of these channels, incidentally, seemed to benefit from our training program, except that among our most experienced clinicians, RS did show some benefits of training.

We do not know why the body factor channels showed the greatest benefits of practice and/or training. One possible explanation is in terms of task novelty. Subjects have everyday experience decoding facial expressions and tones of voice but they rarely have the opportunity to decode nonverbal cues emanating from a faceless body. Practice may, therefore, benefit these channels most because there has been the least prior opportunity to practice in everyday life. Another possible explanation is in terms of level of difficulty. The three body channels are almost exactly midway in difficulty level between the six face channels and the two pure audio channels. Perhaps the face stimuli are too hard to improve upon because of ceiling effects, while the pure audio channels are so difficult that subjects become somewhat demoralized at what they interpret as their own poor performance during the course of a single testing. The difference between the two pure audio channels is consistent with this hypothesis. The CF channel, which shows less benefit than the RS channel during the course of a single testing, is also significantly more difficult than the RS channel (about .3 σ difference).

There is further evidence to suggest that, even in retesting, CF may profit less than RS. In the study of the effects of retesting on the audio PONS described earlier, pretesting on the full PONS brought greater gains to the RS than to the CF channel, especially for more experienced judges of nonverbal cues. Interestingly, our more experienced clinicians also showed greater benefits of training for the RS than for the CF channel (table 14.6). Why RS should profit more than CF, particularly when judges are more experienced, may be because the RS channel may be more manageable by a rational, analytic orientation, while CF may be more manageable by an intuitive, nonanalytic orientation. Some support for this view may be found in the study of personal correlates of gains in PONS retest scores. In that study, described earlier, the correlations between gains in RS and SAT scores were substantial (.34 verbal, .39 quantitative), while the correlations between gains in CF and SAT scores were near zero (.04 verbal, .09 quantitative).

The bottom half of table 14.7 shows the gains from practice or training for both affect dimensions of the PONS. These results are based on almost the same set of studies as those shown in the top of table 14.7 except that in category 3, gain from retesting, the data were available for only three of the eight studies. With the exception of the small study of the effects of training, which showed no differential effects on affect dimensions, the results were very clear. Positive affects benefited substantially more from practice than did negative affects, and dominant affects benefited more from practice than did submissive affects, with the former difference larger than the latter difference.

A natural hypothesis involves ceiling effects. Perhaps positive stimuli are more improvable because they started out lower than the easier negative stimuli. However, this hypothesis cannot explain the greater benefits of practice to the dominant over the submissive affects, since the dominant affects started out at a higher level than the submissive affects.

Perhaps positive scenes showed greater benefits of practice both because there was greater room for improvement and because it was more pleasant for subjects to continue to study the more pleasant, positive affects than the less pleasant, negative affects. No explanation presents itself, however, to account for greater practice effects for dominant compared to submissive scenes.

15 | Interpersonal Expectancy Effects

In this chapter, we examine in a variety of studies the relationship between scores on the PONS test and interpersonal expectancy effects. Sometimes we relate PONS skill to a person's ability to detect biasing behavior on the part of another and to susceptibility to another's expectancies. Sometimes we relate PONS skill to a person's ability to influence others by the person's expectancies for their behavior.

The area of interpersonal expectancy effects, like the whole area of social influence, invites an exploration of the role of nonverbal judging and sending skills in determining the success and nature of interpersonal outcomes. We feel that we have just begun to explore this important area, so many questions remain unanswered in the chapter that follows.

SENSITIVITY TO BIAS IN EXPERIMENTER BEHAVIOR

We wanted to investigate the relationship between sensitivity to nonverbal cues as measured by the PONS and the ability correctly to diagnose the direction and degree of bias in the filmed behavior of experimenters. There were three reasons for our interest. First, a positive relationship might suggest that subjects more sensitive to nonverbal cues might be more susceptible to the biasing effects of experimenters' expectations. Such an outcome might be expected on the basis of the research by Conn et al. (1968), which suggested that children who were more accurate in decoding the tone of voice of an adult female speaker were significantly more affected by their teachers' favorable expectation for gains in intellectual performance. A second reason for our interest was the optimistic hope that, given a sufficiently strong correlation between PONS performance and bias detection, high PONS scorers could be employed as the observers of choice to help screen for biasing behavior by data collectors. A third reason for our interest was simply to obtain additional data relevant to the construct validation and understanding of the PONS test.

Our measure of accuracy in assessing bias in the behavior of experimenters was based on a sound motion picture film that had been made some years earlier for a different purpose (see Rosenthal 1966, 1976, pp. 282–83). The film shows three experimenters interacting with subjects in the course of a person-perception task. In the film, experimenters showed their subjects a series of photographs of faces and asked them to rate the degree of success or failure shown in each face. Subjects were to use a rating scale from −10 (extreme failure) to +10 (extreme success) with intermediate labeled points. Shortly before these three experimenters met their subjects they had been randomly assigned a number between −10 and +10 that represented the mean photo rating that the experimenter was to try subtly to influence his subject to give. When we employed this film as the basis for a measure of accuracy in assessing the bias of experimenters, we explained to subjects that each experimenter was trying to influence his subject to respond with a particular photo rating, and we then asked our subjects to tell us what that particular photo rating was for each experimenter, based upon that experimenter's behavior. As soon as the experimenter had read his instructions to the subject, the projector's sound system was turned off so that the photo rating responses given by the subjects in the film could not be heard. The actual score defining our subjects' accuracy in assessing biased behavior was simply the rank correlation over the three experimenters between their statements of what mean photo rating each experimenter was trying to obtain and the actual mean photo rating the experimenter had been assigned.

Seven samples took both the PONS and the bias-judging task based on the film of biased experimenters. Four of these samples (total N = 163) were students of college age and three (total N = 52) were of older persons (a group of Australian clinical psychologists, a group of adults closely acquainted with the young woman sender of the PONS, and a control group of adults who were strangers to the PONS sender). Table 15.1 shows, for each of these

TABLE 15.1. Correlations between PONS Performance and Accuracy in Assessing Biased Behavior of Experimenters for Seven Samples

| | Factor Score | | | |
| | Video | | Audio | |
Sample	Face 120	Body 60	RS 20	CF 20
U.S. college summer school students (N = 79)	.15	.12	−.16	.14
Australian college students (N = 61)	.16	.21	.10	−.05
U.S. graduate students (N = 14)	.03	.51	.39	.50
U.S. undergraduates (N = 9)	.25	.03	.38	.12
Australian clinicians (N = 27)	−.13	−.04	.19	.00
Friends of sender (N = 12)	−.19	−.52	−.20	.33
Strangers to sender (N = 13)	−.36	−.22	.45	.17

samples, the correlation between the subjects' accuracy in assessing biased experimenter behavior (defined by a rank correlation) and subjects' accuracy on each of the four factor scores of the PONS. Table 15.2 shows the mean correlations for the two types of samples for each of the two types (video and audio) of PONS factor scores.

We performed an analysis of variance of the data of table 15.1. All three contrasts shown in table 15.2 were significant:

a. The contrast for age showed that the correlation between PONS score and bias detection was significantly greater for the students than for the adults (effect size $= 1.20\sigma$).

b. The contrast for modality showed that the correlation between PONS score and bias detection was significantly greater for the audio than for the video modality (effect size $= .92\sigma$).

c. The contrast for age $\times$ modality showed that the correlation between PONS score and bias detection was significantly greater for students when tested on video PONS performance and for adults when tested on audio PONS performance than in the remaining two conditions (effect size $= 1.09\sigma$).

As an alternative to the three contrast analyses of these data, we note that table 15.2 indicates that college students showed a positive correlation between PONS score and bias detection under both PONS modalities, but adults did so only in the audio PONS modality, while actually showing a negative correlation in the video PONS modality.

The overall tendency for at least the younger subjects scoring higher on the PONS to be better detectors of the biasing behavior of experimenters was a predicted result tending to increase further the construct validity of the PONS. The magnitude of the correlations obtained, however, was not high enough to offer much hope that the PONS could be used to select bias detectors who might be employed in the selection and training of behavioral research data collectors. The finding that accuracy in bias detection was more consistently

TABLE 15.2. Summary of Three Contrasts (Based on Correlations in Table 15.1)

Subjects (N)	Samples (k)	Type of Sample	Video	Audio	Mean
163	4	college	.18	.18	.18[a]
52	3	adults	−.24	.16	−.04[b]
	(k-weighted)	mean	.00	.17	.08[c]

[a]median r for 220-item PONS $= .20, p < .01$, one-tailed
[b]median r for 220-item PONS $= −.06$, not significant
[c]median r for 220-item PONS $= .13, p \cong .03$, one-tailed

correlated with accuracy at decoding audio rather than video PONS channels was consistent with the findings of Conn et al. (1968).

These results also provide further indirect evidence of the potential importance of tones of voice in the mediation of interpersonal expectancy effects (Adair and Epstein 1968; Duncan, Rosenberg, and Finkelstein 1969; Duncan and Rosenthal 1968; Rosenthal 1969; Rosenthal and Fode 1963; Troffer and Tart 1964; Zoble and Lehman 1969). The question that remains without adequate answer is why, among the adult samples, those who were more accurate at decoding the video channels of the PONS were less able to detect biased experimenter behavior.

PONS AND BIAS ON THE PERSON-PERCEPTION TASK

In this section we will describe a series of experiments on experimenter effects on subjects' performance on the person-perception task described above. Following the description of the studies, we will examine the relationship between subjects' PONS scores and their susceptibility to experimenter influence.

In several studies, an experimental manipulation of the experimenter's taped voice was used to bias subjects' photo ratings in the person-perception task (Rosenthal 1966, 1976). In this method, which has been used successfully to bias photo ratings (Scherer, Rosenthal, and Koivumaki 1972), the relative emphasis (in terms of volume only) given to key words by the experimenter during instruction reading is manipulated. The two studies reported below used the same taped instruction readings used by Scherer, Rosenthal, and Koivumaki (1972). In preparing these stimulus materials, an unbiased (no expectancy) instruction reading was tape-recorded, and then the words "success," "plus" (positive words), and "failure," "minus" (negative words) were carefully raised or lowered very slightly in volume in subsequent rerecordings of the original tape. Here is the text of the instructions of the person-perception task:

> Now I will show you a series of photographs. For each one I want you to judge whether the person pictured has been experiencing success or failure. To help you make more exact judgments you are to use this rating scale. As you can see, the scale runs from −10 to +10. A rating of −10 means that you judge the person to have experienced extreme failure. A rating of +10 means that you judge the person to have experienced extreme success. A rating of −1 means that you judge the person to have experienced mild failure, while a rating of +1 means that you judge the person to have experienced mild success. You are to rate each photo as accurately as you can.

In some studies of this kind, four experimental tapes have been used (positive words louder and negative words softer; positive words softer and negative words louder; both kinds of words louder; both kinds of words softer). In the present studies, only the first two tapes were used, those in which positive and negative words were manipulated in opposite directions. It should be noted that the volume manipulations are extremely subtle; even a listener who knows the general nature of the manipulation has difficulty identifying the manipulation incorporated into a particular tape.

STUDY 1. Thirty-six male and five female Harvard-Radcliffe College freshmen participated in this expectancy experiment in four groups and then took the full PONS test in one group. Subjects were randomly assigned to experimental treatment conditions. Analysis of variance was performed on subjects' mean photo ratings (each subject's mean across ten photo ratings), with treatment and arrival order (first half of subjects versus second half of subjects) as between-subjects factors. (Subjects were randomly assigned and sent into the experimental room as they arrived; hence groups 1 and 2 contained subjects who arrived earlier than those in groups 3 and 4.)

Treatment produced a significant effect ($F(1,37) = 5.24$, $p < .03$; effect size $= .75\,\sigma$; $\overline{X}$ for positive expectancy condition $= .02$, $\overline{X}$ for negative expectancy condition $= -.76$). Treatment did not interact significantly with order ($p < .22$), but order by itself produced a significant main effect ($F(1,37) = 4.21$, $p < .05$; effect size $= .68\,\sigma$; $\overline{X}$ for early arrivers $= -.72$, $\overline{X}$ for late arrivers $= -.02$). To summarize, the positive and negative expectancy manipulations led to significant differences in photo rating scores in the predicted direction, and early-arriving subjects tended to rate the photos as more negative than late-arriving subjects.

STUDY 2. This study, like study 1, used the taped person-perception task instructions biased positively or negatively by raising or lowering the volume of positive and negative words. It was carried out in Sydney, Australia, employing eleven male and fifty-three female undergraduate education students at the University of Sydney. Each subject participated in the person-perception experiment, then took either the forty-item male audio PONS or the forty-item original sender audio PONS, and then took the full PONS. The expectancy experiment and the audio PONS testing were done in four separate sessions in the university language laboratory, each time with a different group of subjects. In each of these four testing groups, subjects were randomly assigned to four conditions comprising the four cells of a 2 × 2 factorial of expectancy (negative/positive) and audio PONS sender (male/female). Each subject was assigned to a listening booth and a pair of earphones through which first the biased instruction-reading and later the audio PONS test were played. Later in the day, all subjects took the full PONS test in one sitting.

An analysis of variance was carried out to see if the expectancy conditions had differential effects on mean photo ratings. In this analysis, subjects were nested in a 4 × 2 factorial of testing session (four levels) and expectancy condition (negative/positive). No main effects or interactions of session and expectancy were apparent ($F < 1.5$, $p > .24$). Individual t-tests performed between expectancy conditions within each session were all nonsignificant. In testing sessions 1 and 2, subjects tended to rate photos in the directions opposite to the experimental expectancy (difference between positive and negative conditions = $-.11$ and $-.78$). In sessions 3 and 4, bias was in the expected direction but was small (difference between positive and negative conditions = $.52$ and $.23$).

Two additional analyses of variance were carried out in order to assess effects of expectancy, testing session, and version of audio PONS test on PONS performance. Both analyses included expectancy, testing session, and audio PONS sender as between-subjects factors; in the first analysis the levels of the repeated measures factor were the two channels of the audio PONS test and in the second analysis the levels of the repeated measures factor were the eleven channels of the full PONS. In both analyses, the session factor produced nonsignificant effects ($F = .38$ and $.57$). In both, expectancy condition had negligible effects on PONS scores ($F = 1.30$ and $.01$). Which audio test was taken affected scores on the audio tests ($F(1,48) = 24.16$, $p < .001$; effect size = $1.42\,\sigma$; average score = 63.1 percent on male audio PONS, 72.0 percent on original sender audio PONS), showing simply that the audio test using the original sender was easier for this sample. Which audio test was taken had no differential effect on the channel scores of the full PONS, at least not for this F-test, which had ten df for channels ($F = .19$). In neither analysis were the interactions of expectancy condition or session with other factors significant.

That expectancy effects were not apparent overall does not lessen the need to examine the relationship of PONS scores to expectancy advantage scores any more than the absence of a main effect for a factor lessens the need to examine the interaction of that factor with other factors, since main effects and interactions are orthogonal. Hence, studies yielding nonsignificant experimenter effects are included in the analysis of individual differences in susceptibility to bias reported below.

STUDY 3. In this study, 103 girls at a public high school in Marblehead, Massachusetts (mean age = 14.2 years), participated in an expectancy study conducted by Leo Cohen and also took the full PONS. The person-perception task was used to measure effects of the experimenter's expectancy. Unlike studies 1 and 2, the biased stimulus materials were not mechanically manipulated voice tapes, but were the videotaped instruction readings from an earlier expectancy study involving live experimenters (Barker and Adler, unpublished data). The experimenters used in the present study were the two highest biasing experimenters from the earlier study (both male). Their readings of the person-perception task instructions were separated into audiovisual mode (experimenter's face and synchronous voice) and audio mode (voice of experimenter). Each subject was assigned to one of the two experimenters, one mode (audiovisual/audio), and one expectancy condition (negative/positive).

An analysis of variance was performed in which the 103 subjects were nested within the cells of this $2 \times 2 \times 2$ factorial design. The dependent variable was the subject's mean photo rating. Expectancy condition produced only a weak main effect ($F(1,95) = 2.49$, $p < .12$; effect size $= .32\sigma$), though the means indicated that the trend was in the expected direction. The audiovisual condition, regardless of expectancy, produced significantly higher photo ratings than did the audio condition ($F(1,95) = 8.80$, $p = .004$, effect size $.61\sigma$). The only other notable effect was the three-way interaction of experimenter, expectancy, and mode ($F(1,95) = 3.63$, $p = .06$; effect size $= .39\sigma$), in which experimenter 1 tended to generate relatively high photo ratings in his positive-audiovisual and negative-audio conditions and relatively low photo ratings in his negative-audiovisual and positive-audio conditions, and experimenter 2 tended to produce the reverse pattern. No specific interpretation of this effect is possible without knowing more about these two experimenters.

STUDY 4. In this study, eighty-one male and female students attending Harvard summer school participated in an experimenter expectancy experiment using the person-perception task and took both the full PONS test and the forty-item male audio PONS. In this study, as in study 3, the biased instruction reading was videotaped from an earlier (but different) experimenter expectancy study involving live experimenters (Cohen 1974); the video tape was subjected to the kinescope process (transferred onto film) for showing to this large group of subjects. The experimenter who had generated the greatest degree of bias in Cohen (1974) was selected for the present study. This experimenter read the instructions twice, once in the positive expectancy condition and once in the negative expectancy condition. The film of this experimenter included his instruction readings in both conditions, and in each case his face and voice were synchronous.

In the present study, half the subjects were randomly assigned to the positive condition and half to the negative condition. After viewing and hearing the instructions, they performed the person-perception task. Then each subject performed the task a second time, after being exposed to the other instruction reading condition. In other words, each subject was exposed to both expectancy conditions in random order.

The analysis of variance revealed no effects of expectancy. Subjects did tend to rate the photos more positively the second time, regardless of which condition they were in ($F(1,73) = 3.10$, $p = .083$; effect size $= .41\sigma$). In addition, sex and arrival order (early versus late arrival at the experiment) produced no significant main effects or interactions.

STUDY 5. In this study, unlike studies 1 to 4, the experimenter's instruction reading was not recorded, manipulated mechanically, or divided into sending channels. Rather, each subject was individually administered a task by a live experimenter. Hence, we had no way of controlling the nature of the nonverbal cues that might have been sent by the experimenter, nor do we have a video or audio record of the experiment.

Ron Johnson at St. Francis Xavier University in Nova Scotia, Canada, carried out the research. Eight experimenters (four of each sex) tested approximately nineteen undergraduates each (N = 151). Subjects were tested in one of four treatment conditions, which were created by the crossing of two factors: expectancy (negative/positive) and task (person-perception/latency of word association). Thus, each subject was exposed to only one expectancy and performed only one task. For neither task was there a significant effect of expectancy (t for person-perception task = 1.03, $df = 72$, $p > .20$, two-tailed; t for word association = $-.67$, $df = 75$, $p > .50$, two-tailed).

STUDY 6. In this study (Zuckerman, DeFrank, Hall, and Rosenthal 1978), the facial encoding ability of the ten experimenters conducting the person-perception task had been assessed as part of an earlier study in which the ten experimenters had been subjects (Zuckerman, Hall, DeFrank, and Rosenthal 1976). These ten experimenters were the five highest-scoring and the five lowest-scoring encoders out of fifty-nine encoders in the earlier study (where encoding score was the proportion of judges who accurately identified the facial expressions of the sender). In the present study, the experimenters administered the person-perception task to a total of 139 subjects whose ability to decode nonverbal cues was assessed using the PONS test. Each experimenter administered the task in both the success (positive expectancy) and failure (negative expectancy) conditions. In this experiment there was no significant effect of the experimenters' expectancies ($t(17) = -.59$).

SUSCEPTIBILITY TO INFLUENCE AND PONS. We now turn to the individual differences question of relevance to PONS research. Did subjects who were more or less biased by these instruction readings perform systematically differently from each other on the PONS test? A "bias score" was computed for each subject, indicating how much the subject was influenced by the experimental treatment. We computed this score by subtracting the mean of the negative expectancy group from each subject's score if that subject was in the positive expectancy group; for subjects in the negative expectancy group, the bias score was computed by subtracting the subject's own score from the mean of the positive expectancy group. These bias scores are therefore posi-

TABLE 15.3. Correlations between Bias Score on Person-Perception Task and PONS Scores for Seven Samples

Scale	Study 1 (N=41)	Study 2 (N=64)	Study 3a (N=51)	Study 3b (N=52)	Study 4 (N=81)	Study 5 (N=74)	Study 6 (N=139)	Median
RS 20	.06	.11	.14	−.26	−.18	−.12	−.08	−.08
CF 20	.06	−.01	−.03	−.17	−.11	.15	.06	−.01
Body 60	−.24	.10	.16	−.18	−.06	−.05	.18[a]	−.05
Face 120	−.06	.12	.18	−.10	.12	−.26[a]	.09	.09
Total	−.13	.14	.18	−.20	−.00	−.10	.12	−.00
Positive-submissive	−.21	.13	.04	−.17	−.02	−.19	.05	−.02
Positive-dominant	−.06	.12	.25	−.18	−.12	−.06	.10	−.06
Negative-submissive	−.04	.07	.14	−.20	.07	−.20	.03	.03
Negative-dominant	−.04	.02	.07	−.12	.07	−.14	.18[a]	.02
Median of 25 r's with PONS scores	−.06	.10	.14	−.15	.04	−.10	.09	−.01
Channel of E's cue transmission	recorded voice	recorded voice	recorded face + voice	recorded voice	recorded face + voice	live E	live E	

[a] $p < .05$

tive when the subject's photo ratings differ from those obtained in the other group in the expected direction, zero when the subject's ratings do not differ from those obtained in the other group, and negative when the subject's ratings differ from those obtained in the other group in the direction opposite to that predicted. In study 1, bias scores were computed within each level of arrival order; in study 2, bias scores were computed within each of the four testing sessions; in study 3, bias scores were computed within each experimenter × mode block; in study 4, bias scores were computed within each sex; and in study 5, bias scores were computed without blocking.

Table 15.3 shows the correlations between PONS and bias scores in the six studies described. Study 3 is listed twice because independent subsamples were exposed to the experimenter in the audio-only and the audiovisual modes. It is clear that over all six samples of subjects, there was no relationship between subjects' PONS skill and the extent to which they responded in the expected direction to experimenter cues.

In two studies one of the audio PONS tests was administered in addition to the full PONS. The correlations of bias with these scores are given in table 15.4. Study 2 is listed twice because independent subsamples were each administered one of the two audio tests. These correlations are higher than those in table 15.3, including the audio-only channels given in that table. Table 15.4 shows that persons who decoded audio cues better tended to be more biased by experimenter cues. It is not clear why no such relationship seemed to exist for the full PONS.

In study 5 we were able to relate subjects' bias scores to the PONS scores of their experimenters, and we found no relationship. We computed bias scores for the expectancy task involving latency of word association, and found a correlation of $-.09$ with the PONS total and a median correlation for twenty-five PONS scales of $-.05$. For this task, as with the person-perception task, there was no relationship between subjects' bias scores and their experimenters' PONS scores.

TABLE 15.4. Correlations between Bias Score on Person-Perception Task and Audio PONS Scores for Three Samples

Scale	Original Sender (Study 2a) (N=35)	Male Sender (Study 2b) (N=29)	Male Sender (Study 4) (N=81)	Median
RS	.22	$-.28$	.18	.18
CF	.17	.22	.21	.21
Total	.26	$-.03$	.25[a]	.25[b]

[a]$p < .05$
[b]combined $p < .02$

TABLE 15.5. Experimenter Expectancy Effects by Experimenters'
Encoding Ability and Subjects' Decoding Ability (after Zuckerman,
DeFrank, Hall, and Rosenthal)

	Subjects' Decoding Ability		
Experimenters' Encoding Ability	Low	High	Mean
High (N=5)	−0.34	0.79	0.23
Low (N=5)	−0.88	−0.21	−0.55
Mean	−0.61	0.29	−0.16[a]

[a]t for expectancy effect overall $= -0.59$

JOINT EFFECTS OF EXPERIMENTERS'
ENCODING SKILL AND SUBJECTS' DECODING SKILL

In study 6 above, it was possible to examine the combined effects of
subjects' decoding skill and experimenters' encoding skill. The magnitude of
the expectancy effect for each experimenter was computed by subtracting the
mean photo rating obtained from subjects of whom low photo ratings were
expected from the mean photo rating obtained from subjects of whom high
photo ratings were expected. For each experimenter, these expectancy effect
scores were computed separately for subjects who scored above and below the
median on the PONS total. In the analysis of variance, experimenters' encoding ability (low or high) was a between-experimenters factor and subjects'
decoding ability (low or high) was a within-experimenters factor.

Table 15.5 shows the mean magnitude of experimenter expectancy effect
from this analysis. Greater expectancy effects were obtained when experimenters were better encoders and also when subjects were better decoders. Thus,
while there was no overall significant effect of experimenter's expectancy
($t(17) = -0.59$), expectancy effects were significantly larger in dyads com-

TABLE 15.6. Analysis of Variance of Experimenter Expectancy
Effects for Combined and Individual Effects of Encoding and
Decoding (after Zuckerman, DeFrank, Hall, and Rosenthal)

Source	df	MS	F	η	Effect Size (σ)
Experimenter encoding	1	3.00	2.07	.33	0.70
Subject decoding	1	4.04	2.79	.38	0.81
Combined effect contrast	1	7.01	4.83[a]	.47	1.07
Pooled error	17	1.45			

[a]$p = .021$, one-tailed

posed of better encoding experimenters and better decoding subjects than in dyads composed of poorer encoding experimenters and poor decoding subjects (combined effect contrast $t(17) = 2.20$, $p = .021$; effect size $= 1.07\sigma$) or in all three remaining types of dyads combined ($t(17) = 2.04$, $p = .029$; effect size $= .99\sigma$).

Table 15.6 shows the analysis of variance of the data of table 15.5. The between-experimenters and within-experimenters error terms and the encoding × decoding interaction were all homogeneous, and were pooled to increase the stability of the final error term. For each effect, η and the size of the effect in σ units are presented to give some feel for the magnitude of the effects involved. All three effects were substantial as defined by Cohen (1969).

Though high encoding experimenters tended to bias their subjects more in the direction of their hypothesis and high decoding subjects tended to be more susceptible to bias, the combined effect of these two types of experimenters and subjects greatly enhanced the probability that the communication of expectancy would take place. The equivocal picture of the relation between subjects' decoding ability and susceptibility to bias emerging from studies 1 through 5 reviewed in this chapter would perhaps be clearer if the encoding abilities of the experimenters in those studies were known.

EXPECTANCY EFFECTS IN PSYCHOPHYSIOLOGICAL RESEARCH

An experiment was conducted to investigate the effects of experimenters' expectancies on two physiological variables: (1) the gross electrical activity of the cortex as recorded in the electroencephalogram (EEG), and (2) the state of the spinal segmental mechanisms as reflected in the amplitude of the phasic stretch reflex ("Achilles heel" response) as measured by the electromyogram (EMG). The details of the experimental procedure are reported elsewhere (Clarke et al. 1976), so we will give only an overview here.

Twenty-four Australian first-year undergraduate students served as subjects and six third-year undergraduate students served as experimenters. Subjects and experimenters were tested on the full PONS and on Rotter's I-E Scale. During each experimenter-subject interaction, twenty taps were delivered to the subject's heel tendon. Experimenters were led to believe that half of these taps were delivered with lighter force and half with heavier force; actually, all taps were automatically delivered with equivalent force. The overall hypothesis was that, during taps believed by the experimenter to be heavy, subjects would respond with an increase in their EMG response and a decrease in EEG alpha activity. Results showed the predicted effect for EEG alpha activity, particularly in the one-second intervals preceding and following the stimulus. An additional EEG result was that experimenter-subject dyads with more similar I-E Scale scores showed greater predicted biasing effects than did dyads with less similar I-E Scale scores. For EMG response there was only a significant interaction between experimenters' expectations and subjects' I-E Scale scores; subjects scoring as more internal showed predicted expectancy effects, while subjects scoring as more external showed reversed expectancy effects.

Table 15.7 shows the correlations between subjects' selected PONS scores (total, factor scores, quadrant scores) and their physiological responses. The first three rows of table 15.7 show the correlations for total EEG frequency, total EEG amplitude, and total EMG response. The next three rows show the correlations for the expectancy effects occurring for each of these three physiological variables, with expectancy effects defined as the physiological response under experimenter's expectancy for heavy taps minus the response under experimenter's expectancy for light taps. The final three rows show the correlations for the increase in expectancy effect from the first half to the last half of the experimenter-subject interaction.

The clearest result of table 15.7 appears to be the positive and significant relationship between EEG alpha frequency during the course of the experiment and PONS performance. Subjects producing more alpha performed better at the PONS overall but especially on body cues, tone of voice cues, and cues characterized by negative-dominant affects. Results for EEG alpha amplitude were in general support of the results for EEG alpha frequency but somewhat smaller in magnitude. Results for the EMG generally showed no relationship to PONS performance. Why subjects showing greater EEG alpha activity should be superior at decoding nonverbal cues is an intriguing mystery.

Table 15.7 shows no significant correlations between magnitude of expectancy effect as defined by any of our three physiological variables and PONS performance. (In interpreting expectancy effect variables, we must keep in mind that a positive correlation with PONS variables means that PONS performance is associated with greater biasing in the predicted direction for EMG but greater biasing in the *unpredicted* direction for the EEG variables.) When we consider the correlations between PONS performance and increases in expectancy effects during the course of the experimenter-subject interaction, we find only two significant and large correlations. Subjects scoring higher on the RS factor and on the negative-dominant quadrant showed a greater increase in the reversal of the expectancy effect for EEG frequency during the course of the experiment. Perhaps those more accurate at decoding these nonverbal cues were also the ones more inclined not to comply with the experimenters' expectations, expectations mediated by cues that subjects learned to decode only as the experimenter-subject interaction progressed.

Table 15.8 shows the correlations between subjects' physiological responses and the PONS performance not of the subjects themselves but of their

TABLE 15.7. Correlations between Subjects' PONS and Physiological Responses

	PONS Score								
	Factor Score					Quadrant Score			
Physiological Variable	Total	Face 120	Body 60	RS 20	CF 20	Positive-Submissive	Positive-Dominant	Negative-Submissive	Negative-Dominant
Total Score									
1. EEG frequency[a]	.42[b]	.06	.46[b]	.55[c]	.36	−.03	.36	.10	.65[d]
2. EEG amplitude[e]	.24	−.12	.29	.47[b]	.39	−.11	.40	−.02	.42[b]
3. Electromyogram[f]	.16	.29	.12	−.08	−.10	.16	.14	.20	−.11
Expectancy Effect									
4. EEG frequency[g]		.16	.00	−.05	.11	.11	.05	.05	.00
5. EEG amplitude[h]		.21	.26	.13	.10	.30	.26	.11	−.02
6. Electromyogram[i]		−.13	−.01	.27	.29	−.06	−.25	.06	.28
Increase in Expectancy Effect									
7. EEG frequency[j]	.22	−.07	.37	.41[b]	.07	.08	.03	−.04	.47[b]
8. EEG amplitude[k]	.06	−.10	.05	.30	.15	−.18	.09	.06	.21
9. Electromyogram[l]	.14	.18	.25	.01	−.34	.27	.26	−.08	−.09

[a] correlation with 2 = .81; with 3 = −.26
[b] $p \leq .05$, two-tailed
[c] $p \leq .01$, two-tailed
[d] $p \leq .001$, two-tailed
[e] correlation with 3 = −.27

[g] correlation with 5 = .63; with 6 = −.12
[h] correlation with 6 = −.29
[j] correlation with 8 = .53; with 9 = .15
[k] correlation with 9 = .12

TABLE 15.8. Correlations between Experimenters' PONS and Their Subjects' Physiological Responses

| | PONS Score | | | | | | | | |
| | Factor Score | | | | | Quadrant Score | | | |
Physiological Variable	Total	Face 120	Body 60	RS 20	CF 20	Positive-Submissive	Positive-Dominant	Negative-Submissive	Negative-Dominant
Total Score									
EEG frequency	.23	.07	.28	.22	.26	.24	.16	.16	-.14
EEG amplitude	.03	-.02	.04	.12	.00	.29	.01	-.12	-.14
Electromyogram	.17	.03	.14	.32	.11	.18	-.30	.10	.30
Expectancy Effect									
EEG frequency	-.10	-.03	-.10	-.17	-.04	-.15	.07	-.03	-.07
EEG amplitude	.04	-.06	.04	.18	.08	.03	-.33	.04	.29
Electromyogram	-.15	.02	-.18	-.28	-.21	-.10	.25	-.15	-.26
Increase in Expectancy Effect									
EEG frequency	.62[a]	.54[a]	.38	.53[a]	.17	.53[a]	-.00	.44[b]	.18
EEG amplitude	.28	.38	-.02	.27	-.16	.13	-.44[b]	.23	.58[a]
Electromyogram	.35	.11	.31	.52[a]	.26	.28	-.38	.27	.45[b]

[a]$p \leq .01$, two-tailed
[b]$p \leq .05$, two-tailed

experimenters. Thus, significant correlations would suggest the operation of experimenter effects such that experimenter attributes were exerting an unintended influence on subjects' responses (Rosenthal 1966, 1976). Table 15.8 shows a very significant but very anomalous set of results in the lowest third of the table. These results demonstrate that experimenters who were more sensitive to nonverbal cues showed a decrease over time in the predicted effects of their expectancy on their subjects' EEG responses but an increase over time in the predicted effects of their expectancy on their subjects' EMG responses. Such complex results, so heavily dependent on the particular physiological response in question, defy ready interpretation.

VOLUNTEERS FOR BEHAVIORAL RESEARCH

There is a large and expanding literature detailing the characteristics of people who are likely to volunteer to participate in behavioral research (Rosenthal and Rosnow 1975). Some of this literature suggests that volunteers may be more susceptible to the effects of the experimenter's expectations, so that experiments conducted with volunteers might more often support the experimenter's hypothesis than would be the case if nature were operating without the benefit of the experimenter's expectations. Personality characteristics of volunteers suggest that they may be inclined to cooperate more with the experimenter and that if they can accurately determine what it is the experimenter expects of them, they may be more likely to respond in the desired direction. There is also considerable evidence to suggest that much of the communication of experimenters' expectations to their research subjects occurs in nonverbal channels (Rosenthal 1966, 1969, 1973, 1976). If volunteers turned out to be more sensitive to nonverbal cues in general, the hypothesis that volunteers might be especially sensitive to experimenter expectations would gain considerably in plausibility. Volunteers might then be suggested to be better able to understand experimenters' nonverbal cues as well as more willing to respond in accordance with those cues once they have been accurately received. The following research was conducted to address the specific question of the relationship between volunteering and sensitivity to nonverbal cues.

A sample of thirty-six east coast high school students took the full-length PONS and the sixty-item photo PONS on two occasions about two months apart. At the time of the second testing the students also took a forty-item brief exposure form of the PONS and were asked to volunteer for unspecified research to be conducted by psychologists from Harvard University. Students were asked to list the number of hours they would be willing to volunteer, from a low of zero hours to a high of ten hours. Volunteering, coded as 0 for not volunteering and 1 for volunteering, was then correlated with the pretest and posttest full-length PONS, the pretest and posttest photo PONS, and the posttest-only brief exposure PONS.

All five measures of sensitivity to nonverbal cues were positively, substantially, and significantly related to volunteering, with a median point biserial correlation of .39, $p < .01$ and a range of .34 to .59. The degree of homogeneity of these five correlations is especially remarkable in view of the fact that the intercorrelations among several of the five measures of sensitivity were not particularly high (range from .28 to .71, median $r = .51$). It is also of interest to note that the various component scores of the five measures showed little variation among themselves and that when the index of volunteering was changed from volunteering versus not volunteering to the actual number of hours volunteered, the correlations between volunteering and sensitivity to nonverbal cues fell dramatically. From the point of view of variations in nonverbal sensitivity, the important differences appear to be between those who volunteer at all versus those that do not volunteer at all rather than between those who volunteer more rather than fewer hours.

The very clear finding that volunteers were substantially more sensitive to nonverbal cues increases the plausibility of the hypothesis that volunteers may be more sensitive to nonverbal cues indicating their experimenters' expectations. This greater sensitivity, coupled with volunteers' greater likelihood of wanting to please their experimenters, suggests that experiments conducted with volunteers may too often provide data consistent with experimenters' expectations.

PSEUDOVOLUNTEERS. There are indications to suggest that volunteers who fail to keep their appointments for research may be more like nonvolunteers than volunteers in terms of personal characteristics. In a summary of twenty studies of pseudovolunteering, Rosenthal and Rosnow (1975, p. 25) found a median rate of pseudovolunteering of 31.5 percent. In a recent study by Frankie Phillips, 30 percent of the twenty teachers scheduled for special training in nonverbal communication failed to keep one or more of their appointments. One teacher missed one session, another missed two sessions, and four teachers missed all three sessions that had been scheduled. Fourteen of the teachers were tested before and after the scheduled training sessions with the full PONS. The correlation between pretest PONS total and keeping one's experimental appointment was .46 ($p = .05$, one-tailed), suggesting again that those subjects more likely to contribute their responses to the data pool may be more sensitive to nonverbal cues.

Interestingly, however, those subjects who were more faithful about keeping their research appointments showed smaller gains in PONS score from pretest to posttest than did the less faithful subjects ($r(12) = -.66, p = .017$). This correlation showed little shrinkage when the pretest PONS score was partialed out; the correlation changed only from $-.66$ to $-.62$ ($p < .024$).

The greater gain over time by the pseudovolunteers may be due to their taking the pretest less seriously than the more faithful subjects. If the more responsible subjects tried their best the first time, they might be expected to show smaller gains on retesting. If the less responsible subjects did less than their best the first time, it would have been easier to improve and they may have tried harder the second time, partly to show the data collectors that they had no need for the intervening training program they had not attended faithfully.

TEACHER EXPECTATIONS

Robert McCoid designed a study to investigate (a) the effects of teachers' expectations on pupils' improvement in reading ability, (b) the relationship between teachers' PONS performance and the magnitude of the effect of teachers' expectations, and (c) the relationship between other teacher characteristics and the magnitude of teachers' expectancy effects.

The sample consisted of thirty-eight teachers in West Virginia, most of whom had been born and educated in that state. Approximately half the teachers were certified in special education, about half were married, half were black, and most were women. Each teacher was responsible for one group of children and half the teachers were led to believe that their group of children had unusual potential for gains in reading ability. The remaining half of the teachers were given no special expectation for their children's performance. Our analysis of the data of this study was made possible by Robert McCoid's generosity.

We computed the pretest, posttest, and gain scores in reading for the experimental and control group children at each of three levels of pretest reading scores (Wide Range Achievement Test). Although all children gained substantially in reading scores ($t(32) = 9.49$, effect size $= 3.35\sigma$), the children of the experimental group gained more than the children of the control group at each of the three levels of pretest reading score, with effect sizes ranging from 0.56σ to 2.59σ. The average effect size was 1.51σ, and it was associated with $p < .0001$. Although larger effects of teachers' expectations were obtained among children who had scored lower on the pretest, this tendency was not significant.

The question of greatest interest in the present context was the extent to which magnitude of expectancy effect might be correlated with teachers' sensitivity to nonverbal cues as measured by the PONS. In order to compute an index of magnitude of expectancy advantage, each teacher of the experimental group was paired with that teacher of the control group whose pupils' pretest reading scores most closely matched the pretest reading scores of the pupils of the experimental group teacher. The gain in pretest to posttest reading score was then computed for each teacher, and expectancy advantage was defined by the gain score of the control group teacher subtracted from the gain score of the experimental group teacher. This procedure yielded nineteen matched pairs of teachers and, therefore, nineteen expectancy advantage scores that could be correlated with the PONS scores of the experimental group teachers. There was only a trend for more sensitive teachers as defined by the PONS test to show a greater expectancy advantage. For face 120, body 60, CF 20, RS 20, and total, the correlations were: .19, .17, .28, −.02, and .15, respectively. None of these correlations approached statistical significance.

All of the teachers had been rated by their supervisor on their efficiency as teachers and on their interpersonal sensitivity. For the nineteen teachers of the experimental group, these scores were correlated with their expectancy advantage scores, and the correlations were found to be .38 for efficiency (not significant) and .53 for sensitivity ($p < .02$). This tendency for better teachers to show greater effects of their expectancies is consistent with the trend obtained in an earlier study of the effects of teachers' expectations (Rosenthal and Jacobson 1968, p. 84). It is of interest to note also that supervisors' ratings of teachers' efficiency and sensitivity were significantly related to teachers' performances on the PONS total; correlations were .44, $p < .01$, and .32, $p < .05$, respectively. This result not only adds to the general validation of the PONS test but also suggests that the positive correlations between PONS performance and teacher expectancy advantage may have been more than sampling fluctuations.

Jackson's Personality Research Form (Jackson 1974) had also been administered to all the teachers of McCoid's study, and although none of the twenty-two scales was found to be significantly correlated with magnitude of expectancy advantage, seven scales showed correlations of .3 or greater. These suggested some hypotheses to be investigated in the future: teachers showing greater expectancy effects might be higher in dominance, exhibition, order, play, and sentience and lower in aggression and nurturance.

16 | Summary and Prospectus

The PONS test has been given to over 200 samples of subjects in the United States and other countries. In addition to these samples' PONS scores and national origins, we were often able to gather data on other theoretically important variables such as age, gender, sensory and psychiatric impairment, cognitive ability, psychosocial attributes, and occupation. The preceding chapters of this book detail the results of our analyses of these studies. In this chapter we will offer a summary of what we consider to be some of the important results of these studies as well as some suggestions for future research.

At various times, short versions of the full PONS were developed to address specific theoretical questions (e.g., regarding the sex or age of sender). These have also proved useful for investigators with less testing time available than is required by the full PONS. Table 16.1 lists four short form tests in the video channels and three in the audio channels.

Although several important validational results were obtained using the short forms of the PONS, the summary that follows is based only on the results of studies in which the full PONS test was administered. There are only two exceptions to this: (1) results for deaf and blind samples are re-

TABLE 16.1. Short Forms of the PONS Test

Video Form	Audio Form
Still photo PONS[a]	Original sender Audio PONS
Slides (35 mm)	Male sender audio PONS
Photos	Child sender audio PONS
Photo booklet PONS	
Face and body PONS	
Brief exposure PONS	

[a]The still photo PONS has sixty items; all other short form PONS tests have forty items.

ported, since they had no option but to judge only certain channels of the PONS; and (2) results using the brief exposure PONS are reported, since this form addresses the question of length of communication exposure and is thus more than just a short or alternate form of the PONS. The decision to report only full PONS test results in our summary is based on considerations of brevity, simplicity, and robustness.

SUMMARY

NORMATIVE DATA. Table 16.2 shows the basic reliability of the full PONS with respect to both internal consistency and stability over time. These reliabilities were quite adequate, reaching the level obtained by standardized group-administered tests of intelligence.

Table 16.3 shows the reliability of the classification of the twenty scenes of the PONS into the quadrants formed by the crossing of the two dimensions of positive-negative and dominant-submissive. When only the physical characteristics of the audio channels were considered, the dominant-submissive dimension was very much more clearly differentiated (by frequency and amplitude) than the positive-negative dimension. When methods of establishing the reliability of scene classification other than the physical characteristics of the audio channels were employed, the median reliabilities tended to be .80 or higher for both the positive-negative and dominant-submissive dimensions.

Table 16.4 shows the effects on PONS accuracy of adding information from tone of voice, body, and face channels and of providing information from dominant and negative scenes rather than from submissive and positive

TABLE 16.2. Basic Reliability of the PONS

Type of Reliability	r
Internal consistency[a]	
Armor's θ	.92
KR-20[b]	.86
Retest Reliability[c]	.69

[a]based on norm group of N=492

[b]For a group of 200 elementary school children, KR-20 was also .86.

[c]median of six samples. The median retest reliability of the eleven-channel profile based on four samples was .41. In general, channels with higher retest reliabilities showed greater internal consistency ($r = .43$).

TABLE 16.3. Reliability of Classification of Scenes within Quadrants

Item	Positive-Negative	Dominant-Submissive	Four Quadrants
Analysis of alternatives			
(medians of four samples)	.70	.91	.92
U.S. judges' ratings	.97	.92	
English judges' ratings	.79	.67	
Agreement of U.S. judges with English judges	.88	.63	
Agreement among ratings of three channels			
(face, body, figure)	.80	.85	
Median	.80	.85	
Audio analyzer			
Frequency[a]	.00	.91	.77
Amplitude[a]	.00	.90	.77

[a]median of RS, CF, and original unfiltered voice

scenes. For the PONS test, tone, body, and face cues contribute to accuracy in judging the scenes in the approximate ratios of 1:2:4, respectively.

Table 16.5 presents the results of the factor analysis of the eleven channels of the PONS. The four factors corresponded to the randomized spliced and content-filtered channels taken alone, the three channels showing only the body, and the six channels showing the face.

GROUPING SAMPLES. In several analyses we attempted to group samples according to the shapes of their eleven-channel and four-"factor" profiles. This was done by performing a principal components analysis using samples as "variables" and PONS channels or "factors" as "units" (Q-type factor analysis). These analyses, using 142 samples, yielded several factors that we found fairly easy to interpret. The interpretations, highly tentative, were made by comparing the characteristics of high and low loading samples on each

TABLE 16.4. Effects on Accuracy of Adding Information from Channels and Quadrants

Source	Effect on Accuracy in σ Units
Channels	
Tone	1.85
Body	3.57
Face	6.81
Quadrants	
Dominant scenes	1.73
Negative scenes	2.48

TABLE 16.5. Factor Analysis of Eleven Channels

Factor	Median Loading	Number of Channels	Number of Items
Face present	.68	6	120
Randomized spliced	.95	1	20
Content-filtered	.96	1	20
Body without face	.59	3	60

factor. Following the interpretation, the profile shapes of the high and low loading samples were compared to see if any interpretation of the profiles could be made that made sense in light of the factor interpretations. Interpretations of factors and their associated profile shapes must be seen as tentative and subject to validation.

The strongest factor of the eleven-channel analysis, accounting for 20.3 percent of the variance after rotation, was named the ''sophisticated-unsophisticated'' factor because one pole was characterized by a relatively large number of college and professional groups while the other pole was characterized more by young samples, mental patients, and ''exotic'' non-Western samples. The ''sophisticated'' samples' profiles showed relatively good performance on video and poorer performance on audio channels, while the ''unsophisticated'' samples' profiles showed the reverse pattern. We suggested that reading tones of voice may be an ''unsocialized'' skill compared to reading visual cues.

The analysis of the four-''factor'' profile also revealed a factor that we called ''sophisticated-unsophisticated,'' accounting for 41.6 percent of the variance after rotation. The samples loading on the two poles of this factor were similar to those described above, and their profiles showed even more clearly their contrasting performances on tone and visual cues.

From this four-''factor'' analysis there emerged another relatively easily interpreted factor (42.7 percent of variance after rotation). This factor was called the ''American–non-American'' factor, in accordance with the identities of the high and low loading samples. The ''American'' samples showed higher scores on CF speech than on RS, and the ''non-American'' samples showed the reverse pattern. We suggested that intonation contours in American-spoken English, which are retained in CF speech, may be more powerful cues to affective meaning for American listeners than for foreigners, and that the reliance placed on such cues by Americans may have hurt their performance on RS speech. Foreigners, on the other hand, may have been misled in their interpretations of CF speech insofar as the American intonation contours differed from those that would be used in their own languages.

In an analysis of variance of 126 samples, in which samples were clustered into fourteen a priori categories, it was found that the categories comprising mental patients, alcoholics, children, and ''exotic'' non-Western samples (the "unsophisticated") scored relatively better on pure tone channels and relatively worse when video cues were present, compared to the remaining samples (effect size $= .65\,\sigma$). In addition, the "unsophisticated" performed relatively "too well" on scenes showing positive-submissive affect (effect size $= .88\,\sigma$).

LENGTH OF COMMUNICATION EXPOSURE. A forty-item brief exposure form of the PONS was developed to permit us to study the effects of length of exposure on accuracy in decoding nonverbal cues from the face and body. The twenty face-only and the twenty body-only scenes from the full PONS were each subdivided into four groups of scenes varying in length of exposure. These four lengths were $^1/_{24}$th, $^3/_{24}$ths, $^9/_{24}$ths, and $^{27}/_{24}$ths of a second, corresponding to one, three, nine, and twenty-seven frames, where twenty-four frames are shown in one second.

The results of nine studies of high school and college students and U.S. adults (N = 506) were quite consistent in showing accuracy very much greater than chance (and large in magnitude) at even the one-frame length of exposure. Accuracy showed a dramatic increase in going from one to three frames, but no further increase in going from three frames to nine frames or to twenty-seven frames. Accuracy rates in going from one to three to nine to twenty-seven frames were 56, 74, 73, and 74 percent, respectively. The very dramatic gain in accuracy in going from one to three frames may have been due to the introduction of motion in the longer exposure or simply to the longer visual access to the stimulus materials or to both.

Decreasing exposure length to nine or fewer frames from twenty-seven frames actually increased accuracy for body but greatly decreased accuracy for face. Perhaps body cues are rapidly processed in high-speed exposures in an intuitive, global, nonanalytic manner, with additional small increases in exposure length serving more to confuse than to assist decoding.

Subjects' self-ratings of their relationships with others tended to be negatively correlated with accuracy at high-speed exposures. Perhaps those most accurate at the fastest speeds have less satisfactory interpersonal relationships because they are able to decode cues they are not intended to decode. The hypothesis is put forward that people who are especially accurate at high-speed exposures may "know too much" about others to be socially acceptable.

GENDER. Main effects of gender were examined for several age levels. Females were almost always more accurate at the PONS task, and table 16.6 shows effect sizes (in σ units) for grade school, junior high school, high school, and college samples. These effects are of moderate and fairly consistent magnitude across all four age levels and for a large pool of 133 samples. Consistent with the results of table 16.6, several analyses of variance on

TABLE 16.6. Gender Effects at Various Age Levels

Age Level	N	Effect Size (σ) [a]
Grade school norm group	200	.62
Junior high school norm group	109	.49
12 High school samples (weighted mean)	581	.57
34 College samples (weighted mean)	1725	.44
Median		.53 [b]

[a] positive values indicate better performance by females
[b] The median effect size for all 133 samples available at the time of the analysis was .42 σ.

subsets of samples revealed only small interactions of age and sex, indicating that the gender effect is relatively stable over time, at least cross-sectionally.

Two interactions of PONS subscales with gender were found for both the grade school and high school norm groups and for a college sample. Females were relatively better than males at judging stimuli in which body cues were present (effect sizes = .46 σ for grade school, .26 σ for high school, and .14 σ for college). Females were also relatively better than males at judging negative affect cues (effect sizes = .45 σ for grade school, .26 σ for high school, and .46 σ for college).

In four samples, the median correlation of PONS total with Math SAT was .30 for males and .02 for females. The failure of the Math SAT to correlate with PONS for females raises the intriguing possibility that different strategies of judgment may work best for males and females. Perhaps an analytic approach profits males on the PONS but for females a more global, intuitive process is more profitable.

AGE. The full-length PONS test was administered to a grade school norm group of 200 children in grades three to six. The children used an answer sheet that had large type and simplified vocabulary. Internal consistency reliability (KR-20) for this group was .86. Accuracy improved linearly with grade level in this sample (effect size = .87 σ). In addition, an analysis of age and dimensions of affect showed that the third graders were "too good" at judging negative cues, compared to grades four to six (η = .21).

In an analysis of variance of the performance of four age levels (grade school, junior high school, high school, and adults), a large linear trend was found (effect size = 3.59 σ). The simple correlation between PONS total and mean age in 124 nonpsychiatric samples was .34, whereas a more powerful analysis in which samples were blocked into five age levels showed a somewhat larger linear effect (η = .49) and also a quadratic trend (η = .47), indicating that performance starts to level off somewhere between twenty and thirty years of age.

It was found that younger samples showed a *relative* advantage at judging tone as opposed to video cues (p between age level and pure video minus pure audio $= .86$). This finding, which fits with some of our other findings as well as with some published results by other researchers, leads to the suggestion that the ability to read vocal cues may be developmentally prior to the ability to read visual cues, and perhaps may even be "unlearned" to some degree during socialization.

CULTURAL VARIATION. Extensive cross-cultural testing was undertaken with the PONS; over 2,000 subjects from nearly 60 samples from 20 nations took the PONS. The cultures best able to decode the PONS were those that were rated as most similar to American culture (r for 30 samples $= .70$), although every culture tested performed very substantially better than chance. Those cultures best able to decode the PONS were also most similar linguistically to American language ($r = .62$), suggesting the possibility that linguistic similarity may be paralleled by paralinguistic similarity.

Cultures that were more modernized (as defined by per capita steel consumption, automobiles in use, and physician availability) showed greater accuracy on the PONS (median $r = .52$), and cultures that were more developed in the communications area in particular (as defined by per capita energy consumption, newsprint consumption, telephones in use, television sets, and radios) were especially likely to be better decoders on the PONS (median $r = .79$). Interestingly, indices of contact with the United States (trade with the United States, tourists from the United States, and foreign mail received) showed a lower median correlation with PONS accuracy ($r = .15$). Cultures more developed in the communications area may have greater experience with, and practice in, decoding nonverbal cues in the variety of channels tested by the PONS, and they may also be more motivated to understand communications conveyed through various channels.

Within the United States, ethnic and social class correlates of full PONS performance have not been studied extensively. What evidence there is so far suggests no overall difference in PONS performance between whites and nonwhites. For two samples of high school students, we found that girls from higher social class backgrounds scored higher on the PONS (mean $r = .26$), while boys from higher social class backgrounds scored lower on the PONS (mean $r = -.15$, differing from the girls' mean r of .26 at $p < .001$).

COGNITIVE CORRELATES. Two kinds of cognitive correlates were examined: performance measures and cognitive style measures. Within the performance category, we can further distinguish general intellectual abilities, for which we would predict a low relationship with PONS, and specific judging abilities in person perception, for which we would predict more substantial correlations with PONS.

TABLE 16.7. Intellectual Performance Correlates of
PONS (High School and College Groups)

Variable	N of Samples	r^a
IQ	4	.14
SAT	6	.15
School achievement	4	.03
Vocabulary	1	.18
Median		.14

[a]entry is median r across N samples of median r's of PONS
subscales with cognitive variable or its subscales

Table 16.7 shows that the relationships between PONS and general intellectual abilities (IQ, SAT, School Achievement, and Vocabulary) were
small, indicating that the PONS test does not measure merely general intellectual ability.

For several special groups the overall correlations between PONS and
intellectual ability were considerably higher. For third graders, Reading and
Math Achievement were correlated .36 with PONS; for teachers in Singapore,
the correlation between English Proficiency and PONS was .60; and for
psychiatric patients and alcoholics, the correlations of IQ with PONS were .26
and .52. All of these groups, we would expect, might have difficulty with
language. As table 16.8 shows, when the groups are subdivided according to
their levels of intellectual functioning, it is apparent that the substantial correlations occur mainly in the low category. For persons in the high category, the
median correlation with PONS is the same as it was for unimpaired samples (r
= .14).

To explore further the relationship of PONS to intellectual abilities, we
performed a principal components analysis on data from a high school sample

TABLE 16.8. Intellectual Performance Correlates of PONS
(Linguistically Impaired Groups)

Variable	Sample	r^a Low	r^a Medium	r^a High
Reading and math	3rd grade	.40	.08	.11
English proficiency	Singapore teachers	.60	.27	.14
IQ	alcoholics	.34	.34	.33
IQ	psychiatric patients		.26[b]	
Median		.40	.26	.14

[a]entry is median r of PONS subscales with cognitive variable or its subscales
[b]sample not divided into low, medium, and high performance groups

for which we had PONS, SAT, and IQ scores. Two factors were derived, one representing PONS and the other representing intellectual ability. The loadings of IQ, Verbal SAT, and Math SAT on the PONS factor were .19, −.02, and −.07, respectively. This finding supports our general conclusion that PONS decoding skill is not related in any important way to general intelligence.

Table 16.9 shows correlations for person-perception skill and cognitive styles. The Programmed Cases task measures the ability to postdict personality from verbal information. The four nonverbal decoding tasks involved judging emotions from visual or auditory cues, postdicting the pleasantness of the sender's mood, or postdicting personality or other personal facts from minimal verbal and nonverbal cues. As the table shows, both of these kinds of judging tasks were correlated positively with PONS total (r = .26 and .28).

Cognitive complexity showed a positive relationship with PONS (r = .28). Differential attention, defined as the degree of attention paid to each of three channels when faced with a choice between that channel and one of the two others, was positively associated with PONS video accuracy but not with tone. This and several other of our findings relating to difficulty and learning suggest that accuracy on tone is not as responsive to effort, attention, and practice as is accuracy in the video channels.

PSYCHOSOCIAL CORRELATES. Many studies have been conducted in which PONS performance was correlated with standard tests of personality, ratings by self, and ratings by others. Table 16.10 summarizes the results of these studies and shows that PONS performance is somewhat better predicted by standard tests of personality and by judges' ratings than by measures involving self-report.

Subjects scoring higher on the PONS total also scored as better adjusted,

TABLE 16.9. Other Cognitive Correlates of PONS Total

Variable	N of Samples	r^{a}
Person perception		
Assessing programmed cases	1	.26
Other nonverbal decoding tests	4	.28
Cognitive style		
Cognitive complexity	2	.28
Differential attention	1	
Face		.48
Body		.72
Tone		.07

[a] entry is median r across N samples

TABLE 16.10. Median Correlations of PONS Performance with Psychosocial Measures

Variable (and Scale)	Number of Studies	Median r
Interpersonal adequacy (median of 6 CPI scales)	5	.25
Maturity (median of 6 CPI scales)	5	.22
Achievement potential (median of 3 CPI scales)	5	.31
Intellectual and interest modes (median of 3 CPI scales)	5	.23
Task orientation (LPC)	1	.21
Democratic orientation (MTAI)	2	.24
Encouraging toward pupils (observational)	2	.76
Masculine therapeutic style (A-B)	3	.03[a]
Nondogmatic (Dogmatism)	2	.20
Low in need for approval (MCSD, CPI, PRF)	9	.07
Low in Machiavellianism (Mach)	4	.08
Social-religious values (Study of Values)	1	.28
Extraversion (Myers-Briggs, self-ratings)	3	.19[b]
Low in self-monitoring (SMS)	6	.08
Self-reports of interpersonal success	10	.06
Opposite-sex relationships and gains in PONS (self-ratings and judge's ratings)	2	.62
Self-report of nonverbal sensitivity	28	.08
Spouses' report of nonverbal sensitivity	2	.20
Interpersonal sensitivity (judges' ratings)	22	.22
Popularity (judges' ratings)	1	.15
Volunteering and appearing for research (behavior)	2	.40
Low in psychoticism (psychiatric patients) (2 scales)	1	.30
Median		.22

[a]for dominant scenes only, median $r = .35$
[b]for RS 20 only, median $r = -.23$

more interpersonally democratic and encouraging, less dogmatic, more extraverted, more likely to volunteer for and appear for behavioral research, more popular, and more interpersonally sensitive as judged by acquaintances, clients, spouses, or supervisors. This last result, based on twenty-four studies (of which twenty-one showed positive correlations) and yielding a median correlation of .22, provides especially consistent evidence for the validity of the PONS test as a measure of interpersonal sensitivity.

IMPAIRED GROUPS. Several samples of psychiatric patients and alcoholic patients were tested with the PONS, and the results showed that patients consistently scored below the level of the norm group subjects, and by a substantial amount—a full standard deviation.

Nevertheless, the performance of the patient groups was very dramatically better than chance, and patients were able to profit from the addition of audio cues, body cues, and face cues. Just as for the normals, face cues aided accuracy much more than did body cues and body cues aided accuracy much more than did audio cues. However, the addition of audio, body, and face cues improved the accuracy of the patient groups less than it improved the accuracy of the normal subjects. In addition, normals benefited more than psychiatric patients in going from pure audio to pure video channels and in going from pure to mixed channels of nonverbal cues. All of these effects, though not large in magnitude, showed patients to be consistently less able than normals to profit from the addition of more nonverbal information.

Further evidence for this relative handicap in benefiting from the addition of channels of nonverbal cues comes from the correlations showing that as the information level of a channel increases, so does the relative disadvantage to the patient groups (median $r = .64$). The advantage that accrues from the correct response alternative being paired with an incorrect response alternative from a different quadrant is similarly smaller for the patients than for the normals. Finally, psychiatric patients profit very substantially less than normals from the practice obtained in going from the first half to the last half of the PONS. The size of this disadvantage is a full standard deviation.

Although, in general, correlations between PONS performance and self-ratings of sensitivity to nonverbal cues tend to be very small, an interesting exception occurred in the case of a sample of Australian psychiatric patients who showed a large positive correlation ($r = .50$) between total PONS performance and a composite self-rating of interpersonal sensitivity.

For some of the psychiatric patients, scores on two measures of psychoticism were available, and these were correlated with scores on the total PONS. Patients scoring as less psychotic on the two scales scored higher on the PONS (median $r = -.30$). This relationship was only slightly decreased by partialing out the effects of intellectual ability (median $r = -.24$).

A group of blind students took the forty-item original sender audio test, and there was no clear evidence of any overall difference in the performance of the blind group and the sighted comparison groups. However, the blind students age seventeen or less performed better than the sighted students of the same ages. Among students older than seventeen, the performance of the sighted was better than the performance of the blind unless mental age was partialed out.

A group of deaf students (aged ten to fifteen) took the video-only portion (sixty items) of the PONS. Among these students, those whose hearing was more impaired performed substantially less well than did the students whose hearing was less impaired. Interestingly, PONS performance was not related appreciably to skill at reading ($r = -.13$) or at lipreading ($r = .02$), or to IQ ($r = -.16$). The performance of the deaf students as a group was substantially lower than the performance of the comparison groups of students at all age levels. For a sample of deaf college students, however, we found no significant difference between their PONS performance and that of hearing comparison groups.

ROLES AND RELATIONSHIPS. When various U.S. occupational groups were ranked on PONS total, the top three ranks were held by actors (two samples), students of nonverbal communication (three samples), and students of visual arts (three samples). These three groups did not differ significantly among themselves, but together they were significantly higher scoring (effect size = .45 σ) than the fourth-ranked group, eight samples of clinicians, whose scores were comparable to those of U.S. college students. The groups of clinicians did not differ from each other significantly, but together scored better than the fifth- and sixth-ranked groups, teachers (ten samples) and business executives (three samples) (effect size = .42 σ). These two groups scored similarly to U.S. high school students.

Supervisors' ratings of professional skill were obtained for teachers and clinicians. For teachers, the median correlation between PONS total and teaching skill in three samples was .38. For clinicians, the median correlation between PONS total and clinical skill in thirteen samples was .20. Hence, rated excellence in these two occupations requiring interpersonal skills was related to PONS decoding, even though on the average these two groups did not perform outstandingly on the PONS.

For both teachers and clinicians, greater professional advancement was associated with *lower* PONS scores (for teachers in one sample, $r = -.66$; for clinicians, median of four samples, $r = -.62$). In the absence of longitudinal data, we cannot say whether these persons "lose" some of their nonverbal sensitivity as they advance, or whether those who achieve greater advancement are less sensitive to begin with.

It was hypothesized that experience with preverbal children might enhance one's sensitivity to nonverbal cues. When two samples of parents of toddlers were compared with two matched samples of nonparents, the parents were shown to be more accurate on the PONS (effect size = .50 σ). This effect was due mainly to differences between the women who were mothers and those who were not.

Several analyses were undertaken to begin to explore the effects of similarity/dissimilarity of the PONS profiles of romantic couples. Comparison of real couples with randomly paired opposite-sex persons showed a tendency for the real couple members to be more *dissimilar* to each other than the members of the artificial couples, on both profile shape and overall level of PONS accuracy (median effect size for four samples = .28 σ). For dating couples, longevity as defined by whether they were still together one year after taking the PONS test was associated with more dissimilarity in overall accuracy of the couple members ($r = .33$). Among the same couples, more reciprocal self-disclosure was also associated with more dissimilarity in overall accuracy (median r over three indices of PONS dissimilarity, male/female report, and disclosure received/disclosure given = .34). Hence, it would appear that it is adaptive for couple members' nonverbal decoding skills *not to* be too similar. Perhaps dissimilarity in nonverbal decoding skills makes the couple members talk more, which leads to more complete mutual knowledge and better problem-solving.

In a study comparing the PONS performance of friends and family of our PONS sender with the performance of a group of matched "strangers," there was no main effect of group but there was an interaction of mode with group: friends and family performed "too well" on audio and strangers performed "too well" on video (effect size = .43 σ). Long-term effects of knowing the sender may have been especially beneficial for the decoding of tone because the tone channels are so difficult and so resistant to short-term effects of practice, training, and attention.

PRACTICE AND TRAINING. There is considerable evidence to suggest that prior experience in taking the PONS test serves to improve subsequent performance. For eight samples that were tested twice, the average increase in performance from first to second testing was very large (1.79 σ). The gains in performance due to retesting were especially large in the sixty scenes in which only the body was shown. Practice may be more useful to decoding body cues because there is less opportunity in everyday life to decode body cues apart from face cues. An experiment in which subjects were randomly assigned to a pretest or a no-pretest condition yielded essentially the same result as did the earlier cited eight studies. Pretesting yielded a great PONS performance advantage, and this advantage was greatest for the sixty scenes showing only the body.

For two samples we correlated the gains in total PONS scores with self-reported interpersonal success with people of the opposite sex. In both studies, those showing greater gains in PONS accuracy reported better relationships with persons of the opposite sex (median $r = .62$). Perhaps the ability to profit from experience in assessing nonverbal cues makes it easier to relate to people of the opposite sex.

For one of the samples just referred to, subjects rated their accuracy in receiving in various channels of nonverbal communication. Just as we have usually found, these self-ratings did not correlate very highly with actual PONS performance on the pretest (median r for 3 self-ratings = .19). However, they correlated substantially with *gains* in PONS accuracy (median r = .49). Perhaps when people rate their sensitivity to nonverbal cues they are actually evaluating their ability to learn to decode someone they have not met before. A subsequent study obtained results in the same direction, but not as large in size of effect ($r = .17$).

For an additional set of eight samples we examined the gains in accuracy in going from the first half to the last half of the PONS test. The overall size of the gain was substantial (.89 σ), but smaller than the size of the gain from an initial to a subsequent administration of the PONS (1.79 σ). That result seems understandable, however, in view of there being fewer items to practice on in going from the first to last half compared to going from an initial to a subsequent full PONS testing (110 versus 220 items). As was the case for studies of the effects of pretesting, these studies of the single testing situation also showed that the greatest practice effects accrued to the sixty items showing only the body.

A pilot training program was developed to show whether PONS performance could be improved in a single training session lasting about ninety minutes. The program was administered to a randomly selected subset of mental health professionals, while the remaining professionals served as waiting list controls. The results were promising; those receiving the brief training performed better on the PONS than did the controls (.58 σ). Somewhat surprisingly, the more experienced clinicians showed the greater benefits of training.

Finally, a study was conducted in which meditators and nonmeditators were PONS tested once just after meditating and once just after not meditating. The results were very clear; each group performed better on the PONS when it was doing its characteristic thing. Meditators gained more when meditating and nonmeditators gained more when not meditating.

INTERPERSONAL EXPECTANCY EFFECTS. To study the role of nonverbal communication skills as a moderator of interpersonal influence was one important motivating force behind the development of the PONS. We have begun to assess the relationship of PONS skill to the communication of interpersonal expectancies, one kind of interpersonal influence.

Table 16.11 shows that for four dependent measures, there was no overall tendency for persons more sensitive to nonverbal cues in the PONS to be more susceptible to experimenter expectancy effects. Perhaps nonverbally sensitive people can detect subtle biasing attempts and behave so as to counteract or reduce the effectiveness of such attempts. Some slight support for this hypothesis came from our analysis of subjects' ability to detect the direction of the experimenters' expectancies in silent films of experimenters interacting

TABLE 16.11. Correlations of PONS Total with Measures of Susceptibility to Experimenters' Expectancies

Variable	N of Samples	r[a]
Judgments of success and failure in faces	7	−.00
Achilles heel response	1	.04
EEG alpha frequency	1	.09
EEG alpha amplitude	1	.26
Median		.06

[a]each entry is median r across N samples

with subjects in a role-played experiment. For seven samples, the median correlation of PONS total with subjects' ability to detect bias was .13 (median for four college samples = .20, median for three adult samples = −.06). Audio scores were more highly related to this ability than were video scores (effect size = .92 σ).

We would expect that nonverbal decoding skills of the *sending* member of a dyad might also influence the communication of expectancies. In a study of teacher expectancies, the correlation between teacher's PONS total and teacher's ability to bias pupils' intellectual performance in the direction of the teacher's expectancy was .15, which, though small, does suggest that a teacher's decoding skills may play a part in such outcomes.

We would also expect that in a dyad the nonverbal *sending* skills of the sending member and the nonverbal *judging* skills of the receiving member should jointly influence the success of interpersonal influence attempts. In one study, the combined effect of experimenter's sending skill and subject's PONS decoding skill on bias was substantial (effect size = 1.07σ).

CONSTRUCT VALIDITY

The defining feature of construct validation is that there is no single criterion that will validate the instrument. This makes proper construct validation a long and difficult process. The general problem of construct validation is especially acute when the construct has not been extensively researched or measured in the past. That was the situation for the PONS test.

All of the relationships reported in this book between PONS scores and other variables help establish the construct validity of the PONS. In evaluating these relationships one should keep in mind that the magnitudes to be expected are not very large. Along these lines, Cohen (1969) notes that the near-maximum criterion validity coefficients for personality measures fall around .30. The criterion validity coefficients obtained in the PONS research (e.g., table 11.14) fall close to that upper limit on the average, and the correlations of PONS scores with variables that should be less highly correlated (e.g., IQ) are suitably low. All in all, then, the PONS test has fared well in terms of criterion validity and discriminant validity, and hence, in terms of construct validity.

After establishing the network of relationships between scores on one's instrument and other measures, there remains the question of whether the name given to the attribute measured by one's instrument is appropriate. The only test of this is whether any alternative construct fits the observed pattern of relationships better than the construct originally proposed. In the case of the PONS test, we feel that "nonverbal sensitivity" best describes the construct we have been investigating.

PROSPECTUS

ORIGINS OF INDIVIDUAL DIFFERENCES IN NONVERBAL SENSITIVITY. Despite the large amount of research we have done, we know little about factors that directly affect nonverbal sensitivity. Why do people differ in their abilities to "read" various channels and kinds of affect? Some possible determinants and some avenues of research are suggested here.

To the extent that nonverbal sensitivity is a stable ability, developmental, especially longitudinal, research is called for. This would mean developing good decoding tasks for use with younger age groups than we have so far tested, and searching systematically for correlates and determinants of individual differences in children's nonverbal sensitivity. Such determinants could be genetic, physiological, or psychological. Psychological factors might involve a child's response to family characteristics if, for example, children's profiles of skills grew to resemble those of their same-sex or caretaking parent, or if children's skills developed to compensate for nonverbal decoding or encoding "weaknesses" on the part of the parent. Other aspects of early development, such as the quality and quantity of parent-child interaction, could affect the development of nonverbal skills. Research among young children would also enable us to explore one of our most intriguing unanswered questions: What accounts for the fact that females at all ages tested so far score higher than males on the PONS?

To the extent that nonverbal sensitivity can be deliberately changed, research involving various interventions is called for. Research of this type would help us find out whether, for example, experience or training in certain occupations, in certain social situations, or with particular others (such as one's spouse) affects one's ability to decode nonverbal cues. One might also study what kinds of experiences are conducive to the further development of nonverbal sensitivity in one's thirties and later, when our cross-sectional analyses suggest that PONS skill typically levels off.

To the extent that individual differences in nonverbal sensitivity are caused by transient cognitive, motivational, and situational factors, new ways of measuring nonverbal sensitivity that take such factors into account could be developed. For example, judging strategies (e.g., analytic, intuitive, imagistic) may differ among people (or perhaps between the sexes) and might account for some variation in level of skill. Situational and motivational factors affecting decoding ability would include the judge's perception of the consequences of good or bad judging in the particular situation; the judge's willingness to pay attention, which could vary with the judge's liking of the sender or the judge's mood; and the salience of different dimensions of affect for different judges. Other situational factors, involving sender characteristics, could relate to the sender's sending skill or motivation, interactions of sender-judge characteristics (for example, subculture or gender), and the history of the particular sender-judge dyad. In other words, the traitlike skill measured by the PONS is only one component of a person's "true" nonverbal sensitivity—a sensitivity that may vary with shifts in judging strategies, with motivation, with situations, and with stimulus persons.

IMPLICATIONS OF INDIVIDUAL DIFFERENCES IN NONVERBAL SENSITIVITY. There are important general theoretical as well as practical implications of the research on individual differences in sensitivity to nonverbal communication. Perhaps the most general implication is that the outcome of interpersonal interactions may be affected in important ways by the interactants' sensitivity to nonverbal cues. Thus, in such relatively formal relationships as therapist-patient, physician-patient, counselor-client, attorney-client, teacher-student, experimenter-subject, and employer-employee, the extent to which the goals of the dyad or of the dyad members are met may depend to an important degree on the members' sensitivity to nonverbal cues. Similarly, in the more informal relationships found in everyday life, such as the relationships among couples, friends, roommates, acquaintances, and fresh encounters, the outcomes may depend heavily on the members' sensitivity to one another's nonverbal cues.

It seems reasonable to propose as well that the level of ability to *send* nonverbal cues in various channels will also contribute importantly to the outcomes of the formal and informal relationships noted above. If for any formal or informal dyad we could specify the accuracy of sending in each nonverbal channel as well as the accuracy of receiving of each of the dyad members, we might advance our understanding of interpersonal interaction in a very significant way. We would not only learn more about how to build an adequate theory of interpersonal relations, but we would also learn more that would help us to improve the ability to help others, by improving the quality of help-giving dyads such as physician-patient, therapist-patient, and teacher-student. Learning more about the optimal "fit" or "match" between helper's and help receiver's profiles of sending and receiving abilities may improve considerably our capacity to provide culturally important interpersonal services. With optimal "match" between helper and help receiver, patients may be better served by their physicians or therapists, and students may be better served by their teachers.

"Matching" therapists or physicians or teachers implies selecting them for certain characteristics relative to known characteristics of their patients or students. However, selection can be employed even without a specific knowledge of patient or student characteristics. It may be, for example, that selecting therapists, physicians, or teachers on the variable of sensitivity to nonverbal communication could appreciably improve the level of care or education provided. Even a small correlation between helpers' sensitivity to nonverbal cues and helpers' ability actually to be helpful to others would be of great practical utility in terms of the thousands of help receivers who would be better served over the years. Sensitivity to nonverbal cues appears also to be a very useful basis on which to develop selection instruments for professions and occupations other than the helping professions per se.

To the extent that sensitivity to nonverbal cues can be improved (and the evidence suggests that it can be), it may be useful to develop a variety of programs designed to improve sensitivity to nonverbal cues. The benefits to the helping professions of such training programs are obvious, but people in general may be benefited as well by participation in such programs of training. Perhaps improved sensitivity to nonverbal cues could contribute to an improvement in the relationships between the sexes, among ethnic groups and races, and among people in general.

References

Abelson, R. P., and Sermat, V. 1962. Multidimensional scaling of facial expressions. *Journal of Experimental Psychology* 63: 546–54.

Adair, J. G., and Epstein, J. S. 1968. Verbal cues in the mediation of experimenter bias. *Psychological Reports* 22: 1045–53.

Adams, H. F. 1927. The good judge of personality. *Journal of Abnormal and Social Psychology* 22: 172–81.

Algeo, J., and Pyles, T. 1966. *Problems in the origins and development of the English language*. New York: Harcourt, Brace and World.

Allport, F. H. 1924. *Social psychology*. Boston: Houghton-Mifflin.

Allport, G. W.; Vernon, P. E.; and Lindzey, G. 1960. *A study of values*. 3rd ed. Boston: Houghton-Mifflin.

Alpert, M.; Kurtzberg, R. L.; and Friedhoff, A. J. 1963. Transient voice changes associated with emotional stimuli. *Archives of General Psychiatry* 8: 362–65.

Anderson, N. H. 1968. A simple model for information integration. In *Theories of cognitive consistency: A sourcebook*, ed. R. Abelson, E. Aronson, W. McGuire, T. Newcomb, M. Rosenberg, and P. Tannenbaum. Chicago: Rand-McNally.

Anderson, S., and Messick, S. 1974. Social competence in young children. *Developmental Psychology* 10: 282–93.

Archer, D., and Akert, R. M. 1977. Words and everything else: Verbal and nonverbal cues in social interpretation. *Journal of Personality and Social Psychology* 35: 443–49.

Argyle, M. 1969. *Social interaction*. Chicago: Aldine.

————. 1972. Nonverbal communication in human social interaction. In *Non-verbal communication*, ed. R. A. Hinde. Cambridge: Cambridge University Press.

————. 1975. *Bodily communication*. New York: International Universities Press.

Armor, D. J. 1974. Theta reliability and factor scaling. In *Sociological methodology, 1973–1974*, ed. H. L. Costner. San Francisco: Jossey-Bass.

Armor, D. J., and Couch, A. S. 1972. *The Data-Text primer: An introduction to computerized social data analysis using the Data-Text system*. New York: Free Press.

Bain, A. 1875. *The emotions and the will*. 3rd ed. New York: Appleton.

Baker, H. J. 1953. *Introduction to exceptional children*. Rev. ed. N.Y.: Macmillan.

Bales, R. F. 1970. *Personality and interpersonal behavior*. New York: Holt, Rinehart and Winston.

Banta, T. J., and Hetherington, M. 1963. Relationships between needs of friends and fiancées. *Journal of Abnormal and Social Psychology* 66: 401–4.

Barker, P., and Adler, N. Unpublished data (1969), Harvard University.

Becker, G. 1964. The complementary-need hypothesis: Authoritarianism, dominance, and other Edwards Personality Preference Schedule scores. *Journal of Personality* 32: 45–56.

Beier, E. G., and Zautra, A. J. 1972. Identification of vocal communication of emotions across cultures. *Journal of Consulting and Clinical Psychology* 39: 166.

Beldoch, M. 1964. Sensitivity to expression of emotional meaning in three modes of communication. In *The communication of emotional meaning*, ed. J. R. Davitz. New York: McGraw-Hill.

Bergin, A. 1967. An empirical analysis of therapeutic issues. In *Counseling and psychotherapy: An overview*, ed. D. Arbuckle. New York: McGraw-Hill.

Bever, T. G., and Chiarello, R. J. 1974. Cerebral dominance in musicians and non-musicians. *Science* 185: 537–39.

Bieri, J. 1955. Cognitive complexity-simplicity and predictive behavior. *Journal of Abnormal and Social Psychology* 51: 263–68.

Birch, H. G., and Belmont, L. 1965. Auditory-visual integration, intelligence, and reading ability. *Perceptual and Motor Skills* 20: 295–305.

Birdwhistell, R. L. 1970. *Kinesics and context*. Philadelphia: University of Pennsylvania Press.

Black, J. W. 1961. Relationships among fundamental frequency, vocal sound pressure and rate of speaking. *Language and Speech* 4: 196–99.

Blau, S. 1964. An ear for an eye: Sensory compensation and judgments of affect by the blind. In *The communication of emotional meaning*, ed. J. R. Davitz. New York: McGraw-Hill.

Borke, H. 1971. Interpersonal perception of young children: Egocentrism or empathy? *Developmental Psychology* 5: 263–69.

———. 1972. Chandler and Greenspan's "ersatz egocentrism": A rejoinder. *Developmental Psychology* 7: 107–9.

———. 1973. The development of empathy in Chinese and American children between three and six years of age: A cross-culture study. *Developmental Psychology* 9: 102–8.

Bridges, K.M.B. 1932. Emotional development in early infancy. *Child Development* 3: 324–41.

———. 1933. A study of social development in early infancy. *Child Development* 4: 36–49.

Brown, R. 1965. *Social psychology*. New York: Free Press.

Brunswik, E. 1956. *Perception and the representative design of psychological experiments*. Berkeley: University of California Press.

Bryan, T. H. 1974. Social factors in reading disability. Paper read at meeting of the American Educational Research Association, Chicago.

———. 1975. Studies of the verbal interactions of learning disabled children in various classroom settings. Paper read at meeting of the American Speech and Hearing Association, Washington, D.C.

———. 1977. Learning disabled children's comprehension of nonverbal communication. *Journal of Learning Disabilities* 10: 501–6.

Bryan, T. H., and Wheeler, R. 1972. Perception of learning disabled children: The eye of the observer. *Journal of Learning Disabilities* 5: 485–88.

Buck, R. A test of nonverbal receiving ability: Preliminary studies. Unpublished manuscript (1974), Carnegie-Mellon University.

_____. 1975. Nonverbal communication of affect in children. *Journal of Personality and Social Psychology* 31: 644–53.

_____. 1976. A test of nonverbal receiving ability: Preliminary studies. *Human Communication Research* 2: 162–71.

Buck, R. W.; Savin, V. J.; Miller, R. E.; and Caul, W. F. 1972. Communication of affect through facial expressions in humans. *Journal of Personality and Social Psychology* 23: 362–71.

Bugental, D. E.; Kaswan, J. W.; and Love, L. R. 1970. Perception of contradictory meanings conveyed by verbal and nonverbal channels. *Journal of Personality and Social Psychology* 16: 647–55.

Bugental, D. E.; Kaswan, J. W.; Love, L. R.; and Fox, M. N. 1970. Child versus adult perception of evaluative messages in verbal, vocal, and visual channels. *Developmental Psychology* 2: 367–75.

Bugental, D. E.; Love, L. R.; and Gianetto, R. M. 1971. Perfidious feminine faces. *Journal of Personality and Social Psychology* 17: 314–18.

Burruss, J. A. 1977. Evaluating therapists' effectiveness. Ph.D. thesis, Harvard University.

Campbell, D. P.; Stevens, J. H.; Uhlenhuth, E.; and Johansson, C. G. 1968. An extension of the Whitehorn-Betz A-B Scale. *Journal of Nervous and Mental Disease* 146: 417–21.

Campbell, D. T., and Fiske, D. 1959. Convergent and discriminant validation by the multitrait-multimethod matrix. *Psychological Bulletin* 56: 81–105.

Campbell, R. J.; Kagan, N.; and Krathwohl, D. R. 1971. The development and validation of a scale to measure affective sensitivity (empathy). *Journal of Counseling Psychology* 18: 407–12.

Cattell, R. B., and Nesselroade, J. R. 1967. Likeness and completeness theories examined by 16 personality factor measures on stably and unstably married couples. *Journal of Personality and Social Psychology* 7: 351–61.

Chandler, M. J., and Greenspan, S. 1972. Ersatz egocentrism: A reply to H. Borke. *Developmental Psychology* 7: 104–6.

Charlesworth, W. R., and Kreutzer, M. A. 1973. Facial expressions in infants and children. In *Darwin and facial expression: A century of research in review*, ed. P. Ekman. New York: Academic Press.

Christie, R., and Geis, F. 1970. *Studies in Machiavellianism*. New York: Academic Press.

Claridge, G. S., and Chappa, H. J. 1973. Psychoticism: A study of its biological basis in normal subjects. *British Journal of Social and Clinical Psychology* 12: 175–87.

Clarke, A. M.; Michie, P. T.; Andreasen, A. G.; Viney, L. L.; and Rosenthal, R. 1976. Expectancy effects in a psychophysiological experiment. *Physiological Psychology* 4: 137–44.

Cline, V. B. 1955. Ability to judge personality assessed with a stress interview and sound-film technique. *Journal of Abnormal and Social Psychology* 50: 183–87.

———. 1964. Interpersonal perception. In *Progress in experimental personality research,* ed. B. A. Maher. Vol. 1. New York: Academic Press.

Cohen, J. 1969. *Statistical power analysis for the behavioral sciences.* New York: Academic Press.

Cohen, L. 1974. Body regions and communication channels in the mediation of the experimenter expectancy effect. Ph.D. thesis, Harvard University.

Coie, J. D., and Dorval, B. 1973. Sex differences in the intellectual structure of social interaction skills. *Developmental Psychology* 8: 261-67.

Conn, L. K.; Edwards, C. N.; Rosenthal, R.; and Crowne, D. 1968. Perception of emotion and response to teachers' expectancy by elementary school children. *Psychological Reports* 22: 27-34.

Cook, M. 1971. *Interpersonal perception.* Baltimore: Penguin Books.

Cook, W. W.; Leeds, C. H.; and Callis, R. 1951. *Minnesota Teacher Attitude Inventory.* New York: The Psychological Corporation.

Crowne, D. P., and Marlowe, D. 1964. *The approval motive.* New York: Wiley.

Crowne, D. P., and Strickland, B. R. 1961. The conditioning of verbal behavior as a function of the need for social approval. *Journal of Abnormal and Social Psychology* 63: 395-401.

Cüceloglu, D. 1970. Perception of facial expressions in three different cultures. *Ergonomics* 13: 93-100.

———. 1972. Facial code in affective communication. *Comparative Group Studies* 3: 395-408.

Dailey, C. 1971. *Assessment of lives.* San Francisco: Jossey-Bass.

Darwin, C. 1872. *The expression of the emotions in man and animals.* London: John Murray. Reprint ed. Chicago: University of Chicago Press, 1965.

Dashiell, J. F. 1927. A new method of measuring reactions to facial expression of emotion. *Psychological Bulletin* 24: 174-75.

Davitz, J. R. 1964. *The communication of emotional meaning.* New York: McGraw-Hill.

———. 1969. *The language of emotion.* New York: Academic Press.

Davitz, J. R., and Davitz, L. 1959. Correlates of accuracy in the communication of feelings. *Journal of Communication* 9: 110-17.

Dawes, R. M., and Kramer, E. 1966. A proximity analysis of vocally expressed emotion. *Perceptual and Motor Skills* 22: 571-74.

Dickey, E. C., and Knower, F. H. 1941. A note on some ethnological differences in recognition of simulated expressions of the emotions. *American Journal of Sociology* 47: 190-93.

DiMatteo, M. R., and Hall, J. A. Nonverbal decoding skill and attention to nonverbal cues: A research note. *Environmental Psychology and Nonverbal Behavior,* in press.

Dimitrovsky, L. 1964. The ability to identify the emotional meaning of vocal expressions at successive age levels. In *The communication of emotional meaning,* ed. J. R. Davitz. New York: McGraw-Hill.

Dittmann, A. T.; Parloff, M. B.; and Boomer, D. S. 1965. Facial and bodily expression: A study of receptivity of emotional cues. *Psychiatry* 28: 239-44.

Domangue, B. B. 1979. Hemisphere dominance, cognitive complexity, and nonverbal sensitivity. Ph.D. thesis, University of Delaware.

Duchenne, B. 1862. *Mécanisme de la physionomie humaine ou analyse électrophysiologique de l'expression des passions.* Paris: Baillière.

Duncan, S., Jr. 1969. Nonverbal communication. *Psychological Bulletin* 72: 118–37.

Duncan, S.; Rosenberg, M. J.; and Finkelstein, J. 1969. The paralanguage of experimenter bias. *Sociometry* 32: 207–19.

Duncan, S., and Rosenthal, R. 1968. Vocal emphasis in experimenters' instruction reading as unintended determinant of subjects' responses. *Language and Speech* 11, pt. 1, pp. 20–26.

Dunlap, K. 1927. The role of eye-muscles and mouth muscles in the expression of the emotions. *Genetic Psychology Monographs* 2: 199–233.

Dusenbury, D., and Knower, F. H. 1938. Experimental studies of the symbolism of action and voice: 1. A study of the specificity of meaning in facial expression. *Quarterly Journal of Speech* 24: 424–36.

_____. 1939. Experimental studies of the symbolism of action and voice: 2. A study of the specificity of meaning in abstract tonal symbols. *Quarterly Journal of Speech* 25: 67–75.

Dwyer, J. H., 3d. 1975. Contextual inferences and the right cerebral hemisphere: Listening with the left ear. Ph.D. thesis, University of California, Santa Cruz.

Dymond, R. 1954. Interpersonal perception and marital happiness. *Canadian Journal of Psychology* 8: 164–71.

Dymond, R.; Hughes, R.; and Raabe, V. 1952. Measurable changes in empathy with age. *Journal of Consulting Psychology* 16: 202–6.

Efron, D. 1941. *Gesture and environment.* New York: King's Crown. Reprint ed. *Gesture, race, and culture.* The Hague: Mouton, 1972.

Eibl-Eibesfeldt, I. 1972. Similarities and differences between cultures in expressive movements. In *Non-verbal communication,* ed. R. A. Hinde. Cambridge: Cambridge University Press.

Ekman, P. 1964. Body position, facial expression, and verbal behavior during interviews. *Journal of Abnormal and Social Psychology* 68: 295–301.

_____. 1965. Communication through nonverbal behavior: A source of information about an interpersonal relationship. In *Affect, cognition and personality,* ed. S. S. Tomkins and C. Izard. New York: Springer Publishing Co.

_____. 1972. Universals and cultural differences in facial expressions of emotion. In *Nebraska symposium on motivation, 1971,* ed. J. K. Cole. Lincoln: University of Nebraska Press.

_____. 1973. Cross-cultural studies of facial expression. In *Darwin and facial expression: A century of research in review,* ed. P. Ekman. New York: Academic Press.

Ekman, P., and Friesen, W. V. 1969a. Nonverbal leakage and clues to deception. *Psychiatry* 32: 88–106.

_____. 1969b. The repertoire of nonverbal behavior: Categories, origins, usage, and coding. *Semiotica* 1: 49–98.

_____. 1971. Constants across cultures in the face and emotion. *Journal of Personality and Social Psychology* 17: 124–29.

_____. 1972. Hand movements. *Journal of Communication* 22: 353–74.

_____. 1974. Detecting deception from the body or face. *Journal of Personality and Social Psychology* 29: 288–98.

————. 1975. *Unmasking the face: A guide to recognizing emotions from facial clues.* Englewood Cliffs, N. J.: Prentice-Hall.

Ekman, P.; Friesen, W. V.; and Ellsworth, P. 1972. *Emotion in the human face: Guidelines for research and an integration of findings.* New York: Pergamon.

Ekman, P.; Friesen, W. V.; and Tomkins, S. S. 1971. Facial affect scoring technique (FAST): A first validity study. *Semiotica* 3: 37–58.

Ekman, P.; Heider, E.; Friesen, W. V.; and Heider, K. Facial expression in a preliterate culture. Undated manuscript.

Ekman, P., and Hoffman, M. Research notes on training in nonverbal behavior. Unpublished manuscript (1963).

Ekman, P.; Sorenson, E. R.; and Friesen, W. V. 1969. Pan-cultural elements in facial displays of emotions. *Science* 164: 86–88.

English, P. W. Behavioral concomitants of dependent and subservient roles. Unpublished paper (1972), Harvard University.

Estes, S. G. 1938. Judging personality from expressive behavior. *Journal of Abnormal and Social Psychology* 33: 217–36.

Exline, R. V. 1972. Visual interaction: The glances of power and preference. In *Nebraska symposium on motivation, 1971,* ed. J. K. Cole. Lincoln: University of Nebraska Press.

Eysenck, S. B. G., and Eysenck, H. J. 1968. The measurement of psychoticism: A study of factor stability and reliability. *British Journal of Social and Clinical Psychology* 7: 286–94.

Fancher, R. E., Jr. 1966. Explicit personality theories and accuracy in person perception. *Journal of Personality* 34: 252–61.

————. 1967. Accuracy versus validity in person perception. *Journal of Consulting Psychology* 31: 264–69.

Feffer, M. H., and Gourevitch, V. 1960. Cognitive aspects of role-taking in children. *Journal of Personality* 28: 383–96.

Feleky, A. 1914. The expression of the emotions. *Psychological Review* 21: 33–41.

Feshbach, N. D., and Roe, K. 1968. Empathy in six- and seven-year-olds. *Child Development* 39: 133–45.

Fiedler, F. E. 1967. *A theory of leadership effectiveness.* New York: McGraw-Hill.

Fields, S. J. 1950. Discrimination of facial expressions and its relationship to personal adjustment. *American Psychologist* 5: 309.

————. 1953. Discrimination of facial expression and its relation to personal adjustment. *Journal of Social Psychology* 38: 63–71.

Fiske, D. W. 1971. *Measuring the concepts of personality.* Chicago: Aldine.

Friedman, H. 1968. Magnitude of experimental effect and a table for its rapid estimation. *Psychological Bulletin* 70: 245–51.

Frijda, N. H. 1953. The understanding of facial expression of emotion. *Acta Psychologica* 9: 294–362.

————. 1969. Recognition of emotion. In *Advances in experimental social psychology,* ed. L. Berkowitz. Vol. 4. New York: Academic Press.

Frijda, N. H., and Philipszoon, E. 1963. Dimensions of recognition of expression. *Journal of Abnormal and Social Psychology* 66: 45–51.

Gates, G. S. 1923. An experimental study of the growth of social perception. *Journal of Educational Psychology* 14: 449–61.

_____. 1925. A test for ability to interpret facial expressions. *Psychological Bulletin* 22: 120.

_____. 1927. The role of the auditory element in the interpretation of emotion. *Psychological Bulletin* 24: 175.

Geis, F. L., and Leventhal, E. Attempting to deceive and detecting deception. Unpublished manuscript (1966), New York University.

Gesell, A., and Amatruda, C. S. 1947. *Developmental diagnosis: Normal and abnormal child development.* New York: Paul B. Hoeber (Harper & Bros.).

Gilbert, D. 1969. The young child's awareness of affect. *Child Development* 40: 629–40.

Gitter, A. G., and Black, H. 1968a. Expression and perception of emotion: Race and sex. Communication Research Center, report no. 19. Boston: Boston University.

_____. 1968b. Perception of emotion: Differences in race and sex of perceiver and expressor. Communication Research Center, report no. 17. Boston: Boston University.

Gitter, A. G.; Black, H.; and Mostofsky, D. 1972a. Race and sex in the communication of emotion. *Journal of Social Psychology* 88: 273–76.

_____. 1972b. Race and sex in the perception of emotion. *Journal of Social Issues* 28: 63–78.

Gitter, A. G.; Kozel, N. J.; and Mostofsky, D. 1972. Perception of emotion: The role of race, sex, and presentation mode. *Journal of Social Psychology* 88: 213–22.

Gitter, A. G.; Mostofsky, D. I.; and Quincy, A. J., Jr. 1971. Race and sex differences in the child's perception of emotion. *Child Development* 42: 2071–75.

Gitter, A. G., and Quincy, A. J., Jr. 1968. Race and sex differences among children in perception of emotion. Communication Research Center, report no. 27. Boston: Boston University.

Gladstein, G. A. 1974. Nonverbal communication and counseling/psychotherapy: A review. *Counseling Psychologist* 4: 34–57.

Goffman, E. 1956. *The presentation of self in everyday life.* Edinburgh: University of Edinburgh Social Sciences Research Centre.

Goodenough, F. L. 1932. Expression of the emotions in a blind-deaf child. *Journal of Abnormal and Social Psychology* 27: 328–33.

Gordon, H. W. 1975. Hemispheric asymmetry and musical performance. *Science* 189: 68–69.

Gough, H. G. 1957. *Manual for the California Psychological Inventory.* Palo Alto: Consulting Psychologists Press.

Greenberger, E., and Sørenson, A. 1974. Toward a concept of psychosocial maturity. *Journal of Youth and Adolescence* 4: 329–57.

Guilford, J. P. 1929. An experiment in learning to read facial expression. *Journal of Abnormal and Social Psychology* 24: 191–202.

_____. 1954. *Psychometric methods.* 2nd ed. New York: McGraw-Hill.

Hall, E. T. 1959. *The silent language.* Garden City: Doubleday.

_____. 1969. *The hidden dimension.* Garden City: Doubleday.

Hall, J. A. 1978a. Gender effects in decoding nonverbal cues. *Psychological Bulletin* 85: 845–57.

_____. Gender effects in encoding nonverbal cues. Unpublished manuscript (1978b), The Johns Hopkins University.

Harman, H. H. 1967. *Modern factor analysis.* Rev. ed. Chicago: University of Chicago Press.

Harrison, R. P. 1974. *Beyond words: An introduction to nonverbal communication.* Englewood Cliffs, N. J.: Prentice-Hall.

Harrison, R. P.; Cohen, A. A.; Crouch, W. W.; Genova, B. K. L.; and Steinberg, M. 1972. The nonverbal communication literature. *Journal of Communication* 22: 460-76.

Hastorf, A. H.; Schneider, D. J.; and Polefka, J. 1970. *Person perception.* Reading, Mass.: Addison-Wesley.

Heller, K.; Myers, R. A.; and Vikan Kline, L. 1963. Interviewer behavior as a function of standardized client roles. *Journal of Consulting Psychology* 27: 117-22.

Hinde, R. A., ed. 1972. *Non-verbal communication.* Cambridge: Cambridge University Press.

Hoffman, M. 1964. The effects of training on the judgment of nonverbal behavior: An experimental study. Ph.D. thesis, Harvard University.

Honkavaara, S. 1961. The psychology of expression: Dimensions in human perception. *British Journal of Psychology* 32 (monograph supplement, 96 pp.).

Hunt, W. A. 1941. Recent developments in the field of emotion. *Psychological Bulletin* 38: 249-76.

Izard, C. E. 1969. The emotions and emotion constructs in personality and culture research. In *Handbook of modern personality theory,* ed. R. B. Cattell. Chicago: Aldine.

———. 1971. *The face of emotion.* New York: Appleton-Century-Crofts.

Jackson, D. N. 1967. Manual for the Personality Research Form. *Research Bulletin* 43. University of Western Ontario: London, Canada.

———. 1974. *Personality Research Form manual.* Goshen, N. Y.: Research Psychologists Press.

Jecker, J. D.; Maccoby, N.; and Breitrose, H. S. 1965. Improving accuracy in interpreting non-verbal cues of comprehension. *Psychology in the Schools* 2: 239-44.

Jenness, A. 1932. The effects of coaching subjects in the recognition of facial expressions. *Journal of General Psychology* 7: 163-78.

Kagan, J. 1971. *Understanding children: Behavior, motives, and thought.* New York: Harcourt, Brace, Jovanovich.

Kaiser, H. F. 1958. The varimax criterion for analytic rotation in factor analysis. *Psychometrika* 23: 187-200.

Kanner, L. 1931. Judging emotions from facial expressions. *Psychological Monographs* 41 (No. 3, Whole No. 186).

Kellogg, W. N., and Eagleson, B. M. 1931. The growth of social perception in different racial groups. *Journal of Educational Psychology* 22: 367-75.

Kerckhoff, A. C., and Davis, K. E. 1962. Value consensus and need complementarity in mate selection. *American Sociological Review* 27: 295-303.

Kimes, D. D. 1975. Creativity, expression, and perception in nonverbal communication. B.A. thesis, University of California, Santa Cruz.

Kleck, R. E., and Nuessle, W. 1968. Congruence between the indicative and communicative functions of eye contact in interpersonal relations. *British Journal of Social and Clinical Psychology* 7: 241-46.

Kline, L. W., and Johannsen, D. E. 1935. Comparative role of the face and of the face-body-hands as aids in identifying emotions. *Journal of Abnormal and Social Psychology* 29: 415-26.

Klineberg, O. 1938. Emotional expression in Chinese literature. *Journal of Abnormal and Social Psychology* 33: 517-20.

_____. 1940. *Social psychology*. New York: Holt.

Klinghammer, H. 1964. Social perception of the deaf and of the blind by their voices and their speech. *Report of the Proceedings of the International Congress on the Education of the Deaf*. Washington, D.C.: Gallaudet College.

Knapp, M. 1972. *Nonverbal communication in human interaction*. New York: Holt, Rinehart and Winston.

Knapp, P. H., ed. 1963. *Expression of the emotions in man*. New York: International Universities Press.

Kohnle, S. R. 1971. Conflicting verbal/nonverbal communication in therapy. Ph.D. thesis, University of Washington.

Konstadt, N., and Forman, E. 1965. Field dependence and external directedness. *Journal of Personality and Social Psychology* 1: 490-93.

Kozel, N. J. 1969. Perception of emotion: Race of expressor, sex of perceiver and mode of presentation. *Proceedings of the 77th Annual Convention of the American Psychological Association*, pp. 39-40. Washington, D.C.: American Psychological Association.

Kozel, N. J., and Gitter, A. G. 1968. Perception of emotion: Differences in mode of presentation, sex of perceiver, and race of expressor. Communication Research Center, report no. 18. Boston: Boston University.

Kramer, E. 1963. Judgment of personal characteristics and emotions from nonverbal properties. *Psychological Bulletin* 60: 408-20.

_____. 1964. Elimination of verbal cues in judgments of emotion from voice. *Journal of Abnormal and Social Psychology* 68: 390-96.

LaBarre, W. 1947. The cultural basis of emotions and gestures. *Journal of Personality* 16: 49-68.

_____. 1964. Paralinguistics, kinesics, and cultural anthropology. In *Approaches to semiotics*, ed. T. A. Sebeok. The Hague: Mouton.

Landis, C. 1924. Studies of emotional reactions: 2. General behavior and facial expression. *Journal of Comparative Psychology* 4: 447-509.

Languis, M. 1976. Psychobiological dimensions of learning and learning problems in early and middle childhood education. Paper, Ohio State University.

Lanzetta, J. T., and Kleck, R. E. 1970. Encoding and decoding of nonverbal affect in humans. *Journal of Personality and Social Psychology* 16: 12-19.

Leach, E. 1972. The influence of cultural context on non-verbal communication in man. In *Non-verbal communication*, ed. R. A. Hinde. Cambridge: Cambridge University Press.

Leary, T. 1957. *Interpersonal diagnosis of personality*. New York: Ronald.

Lerner, D. 1958. *The passing of traditional society*. Glencoe: Free Press.

Lewin, K. K. 1965. Nonverbal cues and transference. *Archives of General Psychiatry* 12: 391-94.

Lewis, M., and Rosenblum, L. A., eds. 1974. *The effect of the infant on its caregiver*. New York: Wiley.

Liberman, P., and Michaels, S. B. 1962. Some aspects of fundamental frequency amplitudes as related to the emotional content of speech. *Journal of the Acoustical Society of America* 34: 922-27.

Little, K. B. 1968. Cultural variations in social schemata. *Journal of Personality and Social Psychology* 10: 1-7.

Lowenfeld, B. 1971. Psychological problems of children with impaired vision. In *Psychology of exceptional children and youth,* ed. W. M. Cruickshank. 3rd ed. Englewood Cliffs, N. J.: Prentice-Hall.

McCarthy, D. 1930. The language development of the preschool child. *Institute for Child Welfare Monograph Series,* No. 4. Minneapolis: University of Minnesota Press.

————. 1946. Language development in children. In *Manual of child psychology,* ed. L. Carmichael. New York: Wiley.

McClelland, D. C. 1961. *The achieving society.* Princeton: Van Nostrand.

————. 1963. National character and economic growth in Turkey and Iran. In *Communications and political development,* ed. L. W. Pye. Princeton: Princeton University Press.

McCluskey, K. W.; Albas, D. C.; Niemi, R. R.; Cuevas, C.; and Ferrer, C. A. 1975. Cross-cultural differences in the perception of the emotional content of speech: A study of the development of sensitivity in Canadian and Mexican children. *Developmental Psychology* 11: 551-55.

Maccoby, E. E., and Jacklin, C. N. 1974. *The psychology of sex differences.* Stanford: Stanford University Press.

McGhie, A. 1973. Psychological studies of schizophrenia. In *Contemporary abnormal psychology,* ed. B. A. Maher. Harmondsworth, England: Penguin.

Maher, B. A. 1966. *Principles of psychopathology: An experimental approach.* New York: McGraw-Hill.

Mehrabian, A. 1970. A semantic space for nonverbal behavior. *Journal of Consulting and Clinical Psychology* 35: 248-57.

————. 1972. *Nonverbal communication.* Chicago: Aldine-Atherton.

Meiselman, K. C. 1973. Broadening dual modality cue utilization in chronic nonparanoid schizophrenics. *Journal of Consulting and Clinical Psychology* 41: 447-53.

Messick, S., and Damarin, F. 1964. Cognitive styles and memory for faces. *Journal of Abnormal and Social Psychology* 69: 313-18.

Miller, G. 1951. *Language and communication.* New York: McGraw-Hill.

Miller, R. E.; Giannini, A. J.; and Levine, J. M. 1975. Nonverbal communication in man with a cooperative conditioning task. Paper, Western Psychiatric Institute.

Milmoe, S.; Novey, M. S.; Kagan, J.; and Rosenthal, R. 1968. The mother's voice: Postdictor of aspects of her baby's behavior. *Proceedings of the 76th Annual Convention of the American Psychological Association,* pp. 463-64.

Milmoe, S.; Rosenthal, R.; Blane, H. T.; Chafetz, M. E.; and Wolf, E. 1967. The doctor's voice: Postdictor of successful referral of alcoholic patients. *Journal of Abnormal Psychology* 72: 78-84.

Mittenecker, E. 1960. Die Variation von Lern- und Verstärkungsbedingungen bei der eindrucksmässigen Beurteilung von Persönlichkeitsmerkmalen. *Bericht über den 22. Kongress der Deutschen Gesellschaft für Psychologie,* Göttingen.

Mohamed, R. A. 1974. Encounter group experience can help you see the truth in the language of the body. Paper, Lincoln University (Pennsylvania).

Munn, N. L. 1940. The effect of knowledge of situation upon judgment of emotion from facial expressions. *Journal of Abnormal and Social Psychology* 35: 324–38.

Murstein, B. I. 1961. A complementary need hypothesis in newlyweds and middle aged married couples. *Journal of Abnormal and Social Psychology* 63: 194–97.

Myers, I. B. 1962. *Myers-Briggs Type Indicator.* Princeton, N. J.: Educational Testing Service.

Newmeyer, J. A. 1970. Creativity and non-verbal communication in preadolescent white and black children. Ph.D. thesis, Harvard University.

Ochai, Y., and Fukumura, T. 1957. On the fundamental qualities of speech in communication. *Journal of the Acoustical Society of America* 29: 392–93.

Odom, R. D., and Lemond, C. M. 1972. Developmental differences in the perception and production of facial expressions. *Child Development* 43: 359–69.

Olson, H. F.; Belar, H.; and DeSobrino, R. 1962. Demonstration of a speech processing system consisting of a speech analyzer, translator, typer, and synthesizer. *Journal of the Acoustical Society of America* 34: 1535–38.

Ornstein, R. E. 1972. *The psychology of consciousness.* San Francisco: Freeman.

Osgood, C. E. 1966. Dimensionality of the semantic space for communication via facial expressions. *Scandinavian Journal of Psychology* 7: 1–30.

Osgood, C. E.; Suci, G. J.; and Tannenbaum, P. H. 1957. *The measurement of meaning.* Urbana: University of Illinois Press.

Overall, J. E.; Hunter, S.; and Butcher, J. N. 1973. Factor structure of the MMPI-168 in a psychiatric population. *Journal of Consulting and Clinical Psychology* 41: 284–86.

Parsons, T., and Bales, R. F. 1955. *Family, socialization, and interaction process.* Glencoe: Free Press.

Paxton, J., ed. 1972. *Statesman's yearbook, 1972–1973.* London: Macmillan.

Pfaff, P. L. 1954. An experimental study of the communication of feeling without contextual material. *Speech Monographs* 21: 155–56.

Polanyi, M. 1962. Tacit knowing: Its bearing on some problems of philosophy. *Reviews of Modern Physics* 34: 601–16.

Potter, R. K.; Kopp, G. A.; and Green, H. C. 1947. *Visible speech.* New York: Van Nostrand.

Pye, L. W., ed. 1963. *Communications and political development.* Princeton: Princeton University Press.

Razin, A. M. 1971. A-B variable in psychotherapy: A critical review. *Psychological Bulletin* 75: 1–21.

Rogers, P. L.; Scherer, K. R.; and Rosenthal, R. 1971. Content-filtering human speech: A simple electronic system. *Behavior Research Methods and Instrumentation,* 3: 16–18.

Rokeach, M. 1960. *The open and closed mind.* New York: Basic Books.

Rosenberg, S., and Sedlak, A. 1972. Structural representations of implicit personality theory. In *Advances in experimental social psychology,* ed. L. Berkowitz. Vol. 6. New York: Academic Press.

Rosenthal, R. 1967. Covert communication in the psychological experiment. *Psychological Bulletin* 67: 356–67.

———. 1969. Interpersonal expectations: Effects of the experimenter's hypothesis. In *Artifact in behavioral research,* ed. R. Rosenthal and R. L. Rosnow. New York: Academic Press.

———. 1971. Teacher expectations and their effects upon children. In *Psychology and educational practice,* ed. G. S. Lesser. Glenview, Ill.: Scott, Foresman.

———. 1973. Estimating effective reliabilities in studies that employ judges' ratings. *Journal of Clinical Psychology* 29: 342–45.

———. 1974. *On the social psychology of the self-fulfilling prophecy: Further evidence for Pygmalion effects and their mediating mechanisms.* Module 53. New York: MSS Modular Publications.

———. 1976. *Experimenter effects in behavioral research.* New York: Appleton-Century-Crofts, 1966. Enlarged ed. New York: Irvington (Halsted), 1976.

———. 1978. Combining results of independent studies. *Psychological Bulletin* 85: 185–93.

Rosenthal, R., and Fode, K. L. 1963. Three experiments in experimenter bias. *Psychological Reports* 12: 491–511.

Rosenthal, R., and Jacobson, L. 1968. *Pygmalion in the classroom: Teacher expectation and pupils' intellectual development.* New York: Holt, Rinehart and Winston.

Rosenthal, R., and Rosnow, R. L. 1975. *The volunteer subject.* New York: Wiley-Interscience.

Rothenberg, B. B. 1970. Children's social sensitivity and the relationship to interpersonal competence, intrapersonal comfort, and intellectual level. *Developmental Psychology* 2: 335–50.

Rudmose, H. W.; Clark, K. C.; Carlson, F. D.; Eisenstein, J. C.; and Walker, R. A. 1948. Voice measurements with an audio spectrometer. *Journal of the Acoustical Society of America* 20: 503–12.

Ruesch, J., and Kees, W. 1972. *Nonverbal communication.* Berkeley and Los Angeles: University of California Press.

Sagi, A., and Hoffman, M. L. 1976. Empathic distress in the newborn. *Developmental Psychology* 12: 175–76.

Sapir, E. A. 1949. Communication. In *Selected writings of Edward Sapir in language, culture, and personality,* ed. D. G. Mandelbaum. Berkeley and Los Angeles: University of California Press.

Savitsky, J. C., and Izard, C. E. 1970. Developmental changes in the use of emotion cues in a concept-formation task. *Developmental Psychology* 3: 350–57.

Schachtel, E. G. 1949. On memory and childhood amnesia. In *A study of interpersonal relations,* ed. P. Mullahy. New York: Grove.

Scheflen, A. E. 1974. *How behavior means.* New York: Anchor Books.

Scheflen, A. E., with A. Scheflen. 1972. *Body language and the social order: Communication as behavioral control.* Englewood Cliffs, N. J.: Prentice-Hall.

Schellenberg, J. A., and Bee, L. S. 1960. A re-examination of the theory of complementary needs in mate selection. *Marriage and Family Living* 22: 227–32.

Scherer, K. R. 1971. Randomized-splicing: A note on a simple technique for masking speech content. *Journal of Experimental Research in Personality* 5: 155–59.

———. 1974. Acoustic concomitants of emotional dimensions: Judging affect from synthesized tone sequences. In *Nonverbal communication: Readings with commentary,* ed. S. Weitz. New York: Oxford University Press.

Scherer, K. R.; Koivumaki, J.; and Rosenthal, R. 1972. Minimal cues in the vocal communication of affect: Judging emotions from content-masked speech. *Journal of Psycholinguistic Research* 1: 269–85.

Scherer, K. R.; Rosenthal, R.; and Koivumaki, J. 1972. Mediating interpersonal expectancies via vocal cues: Differential speech intensity as a means of social influence. *European Journal of Social Psychology* 2: 163–75.

Schlosberg, H. 1954. Three dimensions of emotion. *Psychological Review* 61: 81–88.

Schutz, W. C. 1958. *FIRO: A three-dimensional theory of interpersonal behavior.* New York: Holt, Rinehart and Winston.

Schwartz, G. E.; Davidson, R. J.; and Maer, F. 1975. Right hemisphere lateralization for emotion in the human brain: Interactions with cognition. *Science* 190: 286–88.

Scodel, A., and Mussen, P. 1953. Social perception of authoritarians and nonauthoritarians. *Journal of Abnormal and Social Psychology* 43: 181–84.

Shanley, L. A.; Walker, R. E.; and Foley, J. M. 1971. Social intelligence: A concept in search of data. *Psychological Reports* 29: 1123–32.

Simner, M. L. 1971. Newborn's response to the cry of another infant. *Developmental Psychology* 5: 136–50.

Sivian, L. J. 1926. Speech power and its measurement. *Bell System Technical Journal* 646.

Snedecor, G. W., and Cochran, W. G. 1967. *Statistical methods.* 6th ed. Ames, Iowa: Iowa State University Press.

Snyder, M. 1974. Self-monitoring of expressive behavior. *Journal of Personality and Social Psychology* 30: 526–37.

Soskin, W., and Kauffman, P. 1961. Judgment of emotion in word-free voice samples. *Journal of Communication* 11: 73–80.

Spence, J. T.; Helmreich, R.; and Stapp, J. 1974. The Personal Attributes Questionnaire: A measure of sex role stereotypes and masculinity-femininity. Abstract, in *Catalogue of Selected Documents in Psychology* 4: 43–44.

Sperling, G. 1969. A model for visual memory tasks. In *Information-processing approaches to visual perception,* ed. R. N. Haber. New York: Holt, Rinehart and Winston.

Staffieri, R., and Bassett, J. 1970. Birth order and perception of facial expressions. *Perceptual and Motor Skills* 30: 606.

Starkweather, J. A. 1956. The communication-value of content free speech. *American Journal of Psychology* 69: 121–23.

Steiner, I. 1959. *Interpersonal orientation and assumed similarity between opposites.* Urbana, Ill.: Group Effectiveness Research Laboratory, University of Illinois.

Stevens, S. S.; Egan, J. P.; and Miller, G. a. 1947. Methods of measuring speech spectra. *Journal of the Acoustical Society of America* 19: 771–80.

Stratton, G. M. 1928. Excitement as an undifferentiated emotion. In *Feelings and emotions,* ed. M. L. Reymert. Worcester: Clark University Press.

Sweeney, D. R.; Tinling, D. C.; and Schmale, A. H., Jr. 1970. Dimensions of affective expression in four expressive modes. *Behavioral Science* 15: 393–407.

Sweeney, M. A., and Cottle, W. C. 1976. Nonverbal acuity: A comparison of counselors and noncounselors. *Journal of Counseling Psychology* 23: 394–97.

Taft, R. 1955. The ability to judge people. *Psychological Bulletin* 52: 1–23.

Tagiuri, R. 1969. Person perception. In *The handbook of social psychology,* ed. G. Lindzey and E. Aronson. Vol 3. 2nd ed. Reading, Mass.: Addison-Wesley.

Thompson, D. F., and Meltzer, L. 1964. Communication of emotional intent by facial expression. *Journal of Abnormal and Social Psychology* 68: 129-35.

Tomkins, S. S. 1962. *Affect, imagery, consciousness.* New York: Springer.

Triandis, H. C., and Lambert, W. W. 1958. A restatement and test of Schlosberg's theory of emotion with two kinds of subjects from Greece. *Journal of Abnormal and Social Psychology* 56: 321-28.

Troffer, S. A., and Tart, C. T. 1964. Experimenter bias in hypnotist performance. *Science* 145: 1330-31.

Tukey, J. W. 1970. *Exploratory data analysis: Limited preliminary edition.* Reading, Mass.: Addison-Wesley.

Turner, J. le B. 1964. Schizophrenics as judges of vocal expressions of emotional meaning. In *The communication of emotional meaning,* ed. J. R. Davitz. New York: McGraw-Hill.

United Nations. 1971. *United Nations Statistical Yearbook.* New York.

United Nations. 1972. *United Nations Statistical Yearbook.* New York.

U.S. Department of Commerce. 1972. *Statistical abstract of the United States.* Washington, D.C.: Government Printing Office.

Vinacke, W. E. 1949. The judgment of facial expressions by three national-racial groups in Hawaii: 1. Caucasian faces. *Journal of Personality* 17: 407-29.

Vinacke, W. E., and Fong, R. W. 1955. The judgment of facial expressions by three national-racial groups in Hawaii: 2. Oriental faces. *Journal of Social Psychology* 41: 185-95.

Walker, H. M., and Lev, J. 1953. *Statistical inference.* New York: Holt, Rinehart and Winston.

Walker, R. E., and Foley, J. M. 1973. Social intelligence: Its history and measurement. *Psychological Reports* 33: 839-64 (monograph supplement 1-V33).

Walton, W. E. 1936. Empathic responses in children. *Psychological Monographs* 48 (No. 1, Whole No. 213): 40-67.

Watson, O. M. 1970. *Proxemic behavior: A cross-cultural study.* The Hague: Mouton.

————. 1972. Conflicts and directions in proxemic research. *Journal of communication* 22: 443-59.

Wechsler, D. 1958. *The measurement and appraisal of adult intelligence.* 4th ed. Baltimore: Williams and Wilkins.

Weisgerber, C. A. 1956. Accuracy in judging emotional expressions as related to college entrance test scores. *Journal of Social Psychology* 44: 233-39.

Weitz, S., ed. 1974. *Nonverbal communication: Readings with commentary.* New York: Oxford University Press.

Whitehorn, J. C., and Betz, B. 1954. A study of psychotherapeutic relationships between physicians and schizophrenic patients. *American Journal of Psychiatry* 111: 321-31.

————. 1960. Further studies of the doctor as a crucial variable in the outcome of treatment of schizophrenic patients. *American Journal of Psychiatry* 117: 215-23.

Wicklund, J. B., Jr. 1974. Noise and interference filter for shortwave receiver. *Popular Electronics* 5: 56-57.

Wiley, J. 1971. A psychology of auditory impairment. In *Psychology of exceptional children and youth*, ed. W. M. Cruickshank. 3rd ed. Englewood Cliffs, N. J.: Prentice-Hall.

Williams, F., and Tolch, J. 1965. Communication by facial expression. *Journal of Communication* 15: 17–27.

Winch, R. F. 1952. *The modern family*. New York: Holt.

Winch, R. F.; Ktsanes, T.; and Ktsanes, V. 1954. The theory of complementary needs in mate selection: An analytic and descriptive study. *American Sociological Review* 19: 241–49.

Winkelmayer, R.; Exline, R. V.; Gottheil, E.; and Paredes, A. Cross-cultural differences in judging emotions. Unpublished manuscript (1971).

Wish, M.; Deutsch, M.; and Kaplan, S. J. 1976. Perceived dimensions of interpersonal relations. *Journal of Personality and Social Psychology* 33: 409–20.

Witkin, H. A.; Oltman, P. K.; Raskin, E.; and Karp, S. A. 1971. *Manual: Embedded Figures Test, Children's Embedded Figures Test, Group Embedded Figures Test*. Palo Alto: Consulting Psychologists Press.

Wolf, G.; Gorski, R.; and Peters, S. 1972. Acquaintance and accuracy of vocal communication of emotions. *Journal of Communication* 22: 300–305.

Wolitzky, D. L. 1973. Cognitive controls and person-perception. *Perceptual and Motor Skills* 36: 619–23.

Woodworth, R. S. 1938. *Experimental psychology*. New York: Holt.

Wundt, W. 1912. *An introduction to psychology*. Translated by R. Pintner. New York: Macmillan.

Zoble, E. J., and Lehman, R. S. 1969. Interaction of subject and experimenter expectancy effects in a tone length discrimination task. *Behavioral Science* 14: 357–63.

Zuckerman, M.; DeFrank, R. S.; Hall, J. A.; and Rosenthal, R. 1978. Accuracy of nonverbal communication as determinant of interpersonal expectancy effects. *Environmental Psychology and Nonverbal Behavior* 2: 206–14.

Zuckerman, M.; Hall, J. A.; DeFrank, R. S.; and Rosenthal, R. 1976. Encoding and decoding of spontaneous and posed facial expressions. *Journal of Personality and Social Psychology* 34: 966–77.

Zuckerman, M.; Lipets, M. S.; Koivumaki, J. H.; and Rosenthal, R. 1975. Encoding and decoding nonverbal cues of emotion. *Journal of Personality and Social Psychology* 32: 1068–76.

Zuckerman, M., and Przewuzman, S. Decoding and encoding facial expressions in preschool age children. *Environmental Psychology and Nonverbal Behavior*, in press.

Name Index

This index was prepared by Robert Rosenthal, in collaboration with Mary Lu C. Rosenthal.

Subject Index

This index was prepared by Robert Rosenthal, in collaboration with Mary Lu C. Rosenthal. Users should also consult the extended table of contents on pages vii–xvii.

Library of Congress Cataloging in Publication Data
Main entry under title:

Sensitivity to nonverbal communication.

    Bibliography: p. 379
    Includes index.
    1. Nonverbal communication (Psychology)—Testing.
I. Rosenthal, Robert, 1933–   [DNLM: 1. Non-
verbal communication.   2. Psychological tests.
BF637.C47 S478]
BF637.C45S43   153.9'4'00156   78–17322
ISBN 0–8018–2159–2

BF637.c45 .s43   CU-Main
c.1
Rosenthal, Robert, /Sensitivity to nonverbal commu

3 9371 00029 7028

DATE DUE

DEC 6 '83			
DEC 1 '88			
FEB 15 '90			
MAY 16 '94			
SEP 2 4 2007			

BF
637
.C45
S43

Sensitivity to non-
verbal communica-
tion

51429

CONCORDIA COLLEGE LIBRARY
2811 N. E. HOLMAN ST.
PORTLAND, OREGON 97211